CLASS IN AMERICAN SOCIETY

CLASS IN AMERICAN SOCIETY

BY LEONARD REISSMAN

THE FREE PRESS OF GLENCOE ILLINOIS

Printed in the United States of America

Library of Congress Catalog Card No.: 59-6825

Second Printing February 1961

DESIGNED BY SIDNEY SOLOMON

For ETHEL, ALISON and CARLA

my favorite middle class people

Preface

THIS BOOK IS ABOUT THE PLACE OF CLASS and its synonyms, status, prestige, and power, in the structure of American society. A dominant theme of the book is that classes do exist even though individuals are not chained to these social positions with unequivocal finality. This point of view, however, does not imply that everyone—or even a majority—reaches the level of economic comfort, social recognition, or authority that he wants or perhaps even deserves. American society at the present time appears to be at a stage that is somewhat short of either extreme, even though we would like to believe in the notion of an open class society that is fair and impartial.

Significantly enough, Americans have become *status* conscious in the last decade or so, to judge by the literature they read and the vocabulary they use. While popular recognition of *class* was prevented for decades by the barrier erected by our professed values of equality and the equal accessibility of opportunities, the idea of *status* has been much more warmly accepted as somehow sounding less harsh, less final, and less materialistic than *class*. This is a semantic delusion.

Both terms convey essentially the same sense of social differences with attached invidious comparisons.

Social science is to be credited in large measure with making many facets of class known, not only to the profession but to the public, even though, as is pointed out in this book, social scientists in the United States were generally slow in performing this service. However, even in the relatively short time that class has been a legitimate and popular subject for social research, it has become clear that it is a dimension of prime importance for understanding why people behave as they do in a wide range of activities and for understanding some of the dynamics behind the wondrously complex human invention that is society.

This book was written to present the reader with a systematic view of class, including the major conclusions that have been reached about the effects of class and also the logic and the methods that have been used to obtain these conclusions. An additional aim was to point out some of the aspects of this subject that need concerted research attention.

At many points the reader will become aware of the particular point of view from which this book was planned and written. This is as it must be. No claim is made of complete impartiality, nor is any excuse offered for bias. Books must be written with at least this minimal commitment by their authors.

There are a number of acknowledgments that I am most pleased to make, for without certain individuals I am sure this book would have taken longer to write and perhaps might not have been completed.

To Paul K. Hatt I owe a debt that I can never repay. He was the first to interest me in the subject of social stratification more than ten years ago and to pass on some of that unbounded enthusiasm for scholarship and research that he possessed in such abundance. As a friend and teacher, he will be remembered.

To my colleagues I am indebted for many discussions that clarified some of my own thinking. But more than that, I must acknowledge that subtle yet most necessary ingredient that they supplied—the intellectual environment within which my ideas have had the room to develop. My thanks then to Munro S. Edmonson, Carl H. Hamburg, William L. Kolb, Thomas Ktsanes, Forrest E. LaViolette, and K. H. Silvert.

A summer grant by the Tulane University Council on Research kept me at my desk to finish the final editing of the manuscript, thereby avoiding the competition between yet another semester of regular teaching duties and the preparation of the manuscript.

The manuscript, in its several stages of preparation, occasioned by the fact that ideas do change and that sentences fight the author for existence, was conscientiously typed by Harriet C. Steele and Irene Vines. I remain grateful for their efforts in this respect.

L.R.

New Orleans, La.

CONTENTS

CHAPTER I

Perspectives

IN 1848, MARX AND ENGELS PUBLISHED the *Manifesto of the Communist Party,* setting forth what they considered to be a "complete theoretical and practical party programme." In language that was bold and unequivocal, they developed the thesis that every aspect of society—its social relations, values and beliefs, and indeed the whole institutional fabric—was conditioned and determined by the existing mode of economic production. The pivotal concept was "class," which, Marx and Engels argued, set the conditions for human existence and cast the destiny of the individual. Whether aware of it or not, the individual was bound to his class. In time, and with full class consciousness, he would come to know that he was committed to a mortal struggle with those not of his class. Indeed, the whole history of mankind, according to Marx and Engels, must be read as a history of class struggles. Each era of human history produced the conquering as well as the vanquished classes in predetermined dialectical stages. The inevitable direction of the unswerving historical forces that guided human civilization was toward the sharpest class antagonism in all of human history—between the bourgeoisie and the proletariat under capitalism. There was no middle ground, no other recourse, and the triumph of the proletariat was assured.

Almost one hundred years later, in 1941, W. Lloyd Warner and a group of social scientists presented the first of four volumes reporting a ten-year study of a small (population: 17,000) New England community, fictitiously called "Yankee City."[1] The guiding theme and the focus here too, as in the *Manifesto,* was on class structure; the history, composition, and relationships between the several classes in Yankee City. Beyond that, however, there was almost no further comparison that could be made. With deliberate care and scientific patience, Warner and his team of research specialists charted the cliques, organizational memberships, house furnishings, motion picture theater attendances, and almost hourly activities of the residents of Yankee City. They interviewed, watched, listened, and participated for a time in a modern American community going about its business. Yankee City emerged in that description as a social structure not with two classes mortally pitted against one another in historically and economically imposed antagonism, as Marx and Engels saw it, but with six classes living together in relative harmony, and oftentimes, in ignorance of one another. In Yankee City, as well as in other American locales, Warner and his associates found that the "simple economic" hypothesis propounded by Marx was ringed with too many exceptions. There was "something more" involved, which turned out to be a matter of *status*—the social position one was judged to hold in a community. Presumably, such judgments depended not upon economic criteria alone, but included as well an appraisal of how the person lived, who his family was, and above all, how people in the community rated these and other biographical items. Even the economic criteria, whatever they were, could not be taken literally but had to be distilled through the community apparatus that judged, interpreted, weighed and compared them.

Warner's study of the class system in an American community was no revolutionary pamphlet; no heated and passionate cry against dehumanizing social forces born of economic necessity. It was meant to be, and more or less was, a documented analysis and detailed catalogue of human behavior as it happened in Yankee City, written in the general spirit and style of a field-working anthropologist. Marx could see only the play of historical necessity that had forged two gigantically powerful classes into two warring camps. Warner, trained in the social universalism of the anthropologist, saw instead the evidence of a human tendency to categorize and to rank individuals in a social scale. Status, not class, was the fact of life in modern America as it was in human societies throughout the world.

The *Manifesto* can be taken as the point of origin for the modern study of social class, and Yankee City can be considered as the study that triggered a major interest in the subject by American social scientists. What is more, Warner established the predominant stance that was taken toward the study of social stratification. There were, of course, important American writings that predated Yankee City, notably, Veblen's *Theory of the Leisure Class* (1899), the Lynds' *Middletown* (1929) and *Middletown in Transition* (1937), Sorokin's *Social Mobility* (1927), and Corey's *The Crisis of the Middle Class* (1935). Yet, surveyed from the present, these were sporadic, isolated pieces when compared with the steady and voluminous deluge of articles and books that has followed the publication of Warner's study. Something of the spirit of Marx's analysis could be found in the earlier writings; in such themes as Veblen's lashing of the exploiting and unproductive leisure class, or the Lynds' sharp contrasts between the life styles of the classes in Middletown. However, the hint of status factors rather than class factors was also felt, giving those pre-Warner books a cast that anticipated the current emphasis. Veblen, after all, was castigating the upper class as much for its shameful efforts to symbolize its status as he was for its economically unproductive behavior. Warner, in his turn, modeled these hints and amplified them into the dominant tone that was to be struck on the subject: an emphasis upon the status rather than the class character of American society. The subsequent bulk of the writing followed the tone he had sounded and studiously avoided that of Marx.

This might be easily explained perhaps if the *Manifesto* and the companion writings of Marx and Engels were nothing more than revolutionary exegeses. However, the central importance given to class and the heavy emphasis upon economic forces in shaping human events lent the *Manifesto* a meaning that has remained continuously relevant for social science. If Marx's writing is shorn of its obviously political polemics and of its doubtful historiography, then his analysis emerges in many places as a cogent commentary on the social mechanics of industrial society. It is not odd, therefore, to discover that most of the literature on class in the last half century can be traced back to Marx, whether the scholarly kinship is made explicit or not.

This commentary upon the scientific relevance of the Marxian class formulation is not meant as a plea for its wholesale and uncritical adoption. In spite of his lightning insights, Marx seriously underplayed many of the effects of social class as they have developed, at least on the American scene. The desire by the proletariat to identify with the life styles of the middle class, for example, was not foreseen by Marx. A similar oversight was committed by Marx in his unconcern with social mobility that, both Corey and Mills noted, has resulted in the explosive expansion of "new" white-collar positions.[2] Still, the evasions from what are relevant Marxian observations are noticeable in much of the sociological literature; are evident in the backhanded way that many have adopted of explicitly rejecting those observations of Marx that clearly are not applicable, or of interpreting narrowly and then rejecting ideas that Marx did not seem to intend. Warner's translation of Marx into the terms of a "simple economic hypothesis" illustrates one of the latter techniques.

In spite of these implied criticisms of Warner, however, there is little doubt that he tapped a responsive American chord. His observations made sense to the majority of those who read him as valid characterizations of social stratification in American communities, even at the same time that his logic and method have been severely criticized, and with some justification. The argument at this point is simply this: the emphasis upon status that Warner established has overshadowed the need for a concern with class along the lines set by Marx. Not that status is totally invalid as a characteristic of American stratification, but rather that comparatively little thought seems to have been given to testing the validity of class dimensions.[3]

Almost parallel with, but a little behind the scientific interest, the subject of social class has become popular with a sizeable segment of the public at large. More and more, references to class are encountered in the mass media, in daily conversation, and it can even be expected, in the daydreams of many, to explain and describe human behavior. It is no longer unique to encounter articles in popular magazines that mention "upward mobility" or "status striving" or any other of the battery of class terms. "Upper middle class" and "lower middle class" have entered the vocabulary of daily usage—a form of specious accuracy because such differences are hard to distinguish, but signifying a sensitivity to class by the very willingness to distinguish such nuances. It has become the vogue to point out class tastes in the music we hear, the books we read, the furniture we buy, and the wines we drink. The class facts behind marriage and family life, known for some time to social scientists, have found public acceptance. It is no longer news to learn that class makes a difference concerning whom and how you marry, how many children you have, how you raise them, and the probability of divorce. Even in the more private world of the individual, class has broken through to make a difference. We have shown an amazing calmness in accepting the fact that sexual patterns as well as neurotic failures can be explained as class-conditioned differences. The class factors behind occupational choice, political choices and leisure activity are almost pedestrian knowledge, and if they keep up that way, are bound to become encrusted in folk wisdom.

What is striking about this popular concern with class is its respectability; that class terms are viewed as necessary categories to convey the greater awareness of social differentiation. After all, this increased dependence upon class labels is somewhat anachronistic in a society that for so long has formally subscribed to the belief in social equality. To be sure, all societies engender and maintain discrepancies between the ideal and the socially real. Social divisions in America were present from the beginning in one form or another despite statements to the contrary in our sacred documents. Nevertheless, the increased dependence upon highly specific class designations in the mass media and elsewhere implies that class differences have come sharply to the fore of public consciousness. Social class has come of age. It is spoken of as a fact of life in much the same manner but with greater ease than discussions about sexual mores following the Kinsey report.

The current respectability of class might also appear strange, especially in view of its close kinship with Marxian theory that depends so much upon a revolutionary orientation toward the social world. Class, within the Marxian context, is hardly a dispassionate or polite type of social category. It organizes a political philosophy that is at sharp variance with the American value system. In spite of these obvious differences, however, the idea of class is popularly accepted. The key for understanding this supposed contradiction in values is found in the shift from the Marxian emphasis upon *class* to the current American emphasis upon *status*. Warner's ideas were acceptable to social scientists and public alike in large measure because of the semantic shift he gave to class. "Status" can be translated into American symbols: into personal achievement, into social position in the community, and into a style of life. A "status" orientation and vocabulary can easily avoid the unwanted innuendoes of revolution, class struggle, and historical destinies that Marx attached so firmly to the idea of "class." "Status" stays within the grasp of individual control, where "class" is far outside, controlled only by super-individual forces in the social universe.

The social philosophy of "status" does not jar a democratic value system but instead fits nicely into it at many points. To define "status" on the basis of community consensus is to define it in democratic quantities. To imply, as "status" does, an emphasis upon personal achievement rather than upon birth or historical process is to stress democratic qualities. It is doubtful, of course, whether the invidious social distinctions that do get emphasized by the status order in a community express democratic sentiments, but this is an accepted consequence. Also, the matter gets close to the larger question of how literally social equality is believed in the real and functioning social world. The close, stereotyped association between "class" and "revolution," then, due primarily to Marx's writings, may have been responsible for steering Americans toward the rhetoric of "status" where they could not accept that of "class."

It is suggested here that the dynamics behind the preoccupation of American social science with questions of "status" are similar to those that hold for the public generally. The scientist is not a "free-floating" personality who can always remain aloof from the social milieu in which he lives. He, like other men, suffers the same human frailty of being a creature of his own era; the interests that motivate him, even in his role as scientist, are often the same interests shared by others. His procedures for scientific inquiry are objective in that they can be duplicated by others, in other places and other times, and thereby checked for reliability and consistency. Why he selects one subject of interest, however, rather than another is explained by his membership within a society; his perspective is to be understood from the position he himself fills in that society. Furthermore, his ideas and his conclusions can only find acceptance outside the scientific community when they are ready to be believed by others. He is, perhaps at the beginning of the cycle, a setter of public opinion, but after a time he becomes as much a follower as a leader, as much a respondent as an initiator. The interest in social class today among the larger public is itself a stimulant for further interest among professional social scientists. Their books are bought and presumably read. In a paraphrase of the language of cybernetics, there is a feedback between public and social scientist in the case of class.

There are reasons, of course, to account for this shift in orientation and emphasis that occurred when the study of social class moved from the hands of European intellectuals in 1848 into those of American social scientists a century later; the same reasons indeed that account for the century-long lag between the European and the American interest in the subject. The answer is to be found in the relevant social values and social facts of the American scene that pushed "bourgeoisie" out of our vocabulary and replaced it with the more complex, but apparently more fitting labels of "upper-upper" and "lower-upper" class among others. The current stance that is assumed toward the subject of class is no accident, but is deeply ingrained in American values and beliefs.

It should be especially noted in the subsequent discussion that social values are not always unequivocal. Inevitably, they contain contradictory elements that become even more marked as changes occur over time. A value may mean one thing in one period, but become translated into its opposite at a later period. The change in social circumstances always has a related effect upon the language of values, and each era comes to have its own unique definition of those symbols. "Equality," for example, stood for one set of ideas in 1776, for another during the early 1900's, and for something else again in our own era of insecurity. Similarly, the secularization of the Protestant ethic altered the intent of that ethic just as our earlier views of an aristocracy became modified. It is beside the issue to expect logical consistency within a system of social values because that system conforms only to its own social logic. Each era must interpret its own past and, motivated by its current needs, must dictate the tone and set the quality of the values that are to be honored.

Anti-aristocracy

ONE major value that can account for the lag in recognizing social classes in America is centered in our sentiments of anti-aristocracy. The United States missed the feudal form of social organization, coming into being with the stirrings of early capitalism. The voices of revolt heard in America were flung against the remaining effects of a feudal order and the economic irrationality of colonial domination. The voices spoke of the newer ideas of democracy and constitutional liberalism, which were more closely suited to the needs of the rising merchant and entrepreneurial classes than to those of an hereditary aristocracy. This meant, in effect, that America began the modern era without the hindrances of a long-held tradition of hard social divisions tied into land ownership and into a belief in the nobility. In one stroke, rather than in the slow pace with which social change usually moves, the American Revolution cut the ties of aristocracy and set the stage for a system of social stratification dissociated for the most part from the fixity of landed wealth as the dominant criterion of social position. The hardier survivors of feudalism's peasantry were hardly receptive to the establishment of a similar set of social conditions in the United States, even if it were contemplated. A prime appeal to immigrants, from the very first, was precisely the economic and political freedom from older restrictions based upon inheritance. Add to these sentiments the geographic fact of the availability of good land, and another prop for feudalism was removed. Except for the plantation system of the South, there were no underpinnings to support an aristocracy of the land, and finally, even in the South the support was forcibly removed.

The affirmation of social equality and the rejection of a

nobility were incorporated into the spirit and text of our sacred documents—the Constitution, the Declaration of Independence, and others. Even class, which after all is not exclusively tied to an aristocracy, could not be recognized with such strong antipathies present. This view, or at least a verbalization of it, became a standard part of the cultural baggage handed down from generation to generation. This desire for equality, for being "like everyone else," in part accounted for the overwhelming responses that they were "middle class" given by individuals when asked about class. The immediate reaction as late as the 1940's was that "there were no social classes in the United States." When pressed, however, as they were in a Gallup poll in 1939, 88 per cent of those asked: "To what social class do you feel you belong?" answered "middle class," the remaining 12 per cent divided equally between "upper" and "lower" class.[4] There is really not much contradiction between the initial reaction of "no classes exist" and the answer of "middle class" given by most Americans. Both responses are part of the same configuration of a belief in social equality. The psychological emphasis is upon the word "middle" and not upon the word "class."

These and other types of formal affirmations of equality as a basic American belief, however, say nothing about whether an aristocracy did or did not exist. Social structures, as has been previously mentioned, do not operate by the strict rules of formal logic but rely upon a rationale of their own making. In each era of American history the nucleus of an aristocracy existed, whether based on land, money, or more ephemeral values. The existence of that aristocracy was legitimated by values other than those of noble birth or other inherent rights typical of feudal society. Washington, Jefferson, and Hamilton were members of a landed aristocracy and attached basically aristocratic qualities to land ownership as a criterion of social rank. In later years, the family snobbery of an Eastern urban gentry became a basis for an exclusive aristocracy, as was the case for the rawer aristocrats of the new wealth in the Midwest and the West. In each era, these people were recognized as such and they lived as such. Only the naive would have interpreted the anti-aristocratic sentiments literally. Doubtless, a mixture of feeling developed among the outsiders: part envy, part hatred; the loud proclamation of the values of equality, and the quieter recognition of the facts of social life. Those driven by strong aspirations to reach the elite could have the faith that the climb was possible. Then, from the vantage point of the upper social pinnacle, one could more easily speak of social equality, at the same time as the social distance from the next lower level was maximized in every possible way.

The belief in social equality coupled with the hatred of a social aristocracy were tempered in time by social realities. American aristocrats depended on forms of wealth other than land upon which to base their claim to a superior social position. And in time the basis has shifted to the same irrational criteria used by all aristocracies: noble birth, family lineage, and a record of continuous generations occupying superior social positions. The sentiments of anti-aristocracy were still publicly proclaimed but their force has diminished, their reflection of reality has become more discrepant. The inevitable result was that Americans finally came to evaluate their own class position with greater accuracy. For example, in 1949 Centers asked a national sample of adults to what class they believed they belonged and found that 52 per cent said that they were "working class," 36 per cent said "middle class," and the rest signified "lower" or "upper class."[5] Part of the differences in identification shown between this poll and the one by Gallup ten years earlier—the great shift from "middle" to "working class" identifications—was due to the fact that Centers had included the category of "working class" to overcome the negative connotations of "lower class," with which few persons could identify. However, some of the difference must also have been a reflection of a real shift in attitudes; class differences were more readily recognized and more realistically accepted. The identification by the majority with "working" rather than with "middle class" can be interpreted as a symbol of that recognition, more in line with the facts of stratification in an industrial society.[6]

The confusion and ambivalence in our sentiments toward aristocracy are by no means completely resolved. There are still signs of equivocation. The public values of anti-aristocracy are still there, as they have always been, even at the same time as there are attempts to legitimize status on essentially aristocratic grounds. Status organizations, such as the Daughters of the American Revolution and the United Daughters of the Confederacy, though not especially important for the structure of American society, point the way by their insistence upon irrational criteria for membership. By closing off membership to those who lack the proper family background and by removing status as a direct reward for individual achievement, such organizations push in the direction of a social aristocracy. And in other ways, upper status groups have sought to insure their position and to stabilize the vagaries of a class system too dependent upon personal worth. The newly arrived, eager, upwardly mobile person, sweaty from his climb up the class ladder, wipes his brow and learns that the doors to full recognition and acceptance are still closed to him. His wealth is too new, his tastes are too crude and his family is too recent. It may be getting harder to own a million dollars at one time, but it is impossible to find a Revolutionary, Mayflower, or Confederate ancestor if there was none to begin with. Entry into the upper status group, just as in an aristocracy, becomes reserved for heirs. In this way, the ownership of land that characterized earlier aristocracies is replaced by other criteria, but the substitution achieves the same goal nonetheless.

Class, which signifies a more or less objective position in the economic world, when translated into status depends more upon the acceptance by others of one's position. It is through the status door, then, that the aristocracy, once despised, can legitimately emerge; by requiring a criterion of acceptability that is outside of the sphere of control by the individual. Money is impersonal and does not discriminate between owners. Taste and style of life, however, are educated and require longer maturation before the style-setters are ready to recognize entrants into the upper status positions.

Frontier Psychology

THE frontier, as a geographical fact and as a social psychological orientation, was an American phenomenon that, like the anti-aristocratic sentiments, supported the belief in social equality and at the same time delayed a recognition of social classes. The existence of an open frontier until relatively recently in our history meant that there was no scarcity of land by which an hereditary aristocracy might be stabilized. For that reason, as noted previously, the *form* of a stratification system was not cast into a rigid mold but remained open and variable. The declassed Easterner could move westward with the frontier instead of remaining in the older established communities. Under such circumstances, it was difficult to establish and maintain a closed class system because those at the bottom of the hierarchy could escape. The possibility of sudden and abundant rewards of wealth, land and power for those that chanced the frontier undoubtedly were greatly over-dramatized and over-idealized. A few of the many westward migrants achieved the goal, but many probably ended up not greatly better off than when they started. In addition, the rigor of frontier life probably claimed its victims in one way or another. Yet, it is almost in the nature of a social myth that it can coerce strong beliefs even though the facts themselves say otherwise.[7]

The psychological orientation nurtured by the frontier, however, came to mean more than the fact. Whether true in fact or not, the belief in rugged individualism, the belief in a dramatic social leap from the bottom to the top of the class structure in a single lifetime, and the belief in a kind of grass roots, earthy measure of a man's worth, found sustenance from that orientation. Under such conditions, a class system could not easily develop nor easily become legitimated, because individuals were not prepared to accept their social position as it was at the moment. Those at the bottom believed in the goal of rags-to-riches; those at the top, at best, could only win a temporary grudging respect, principally for having made the successful climb. Further, if mobility was possible and if it was rewarded by social recognition, then class position could not be determined by inherited qualities but instead by personal achievements. The frontier, then, as a social value fitted neatly into the dominant tones of individualism, self-achievement, and social equality that were so characteristic of the American value system. Like the value of anti-aristocracy, the frontier belief served to delay the recognition of class differences.

Protestant Ethic

THE ethic of Protestantism, in both its religious and secular forms, operated in a socially curious way to hinder class recognition in the United States for a long period. Although that ethic conveyed rather clear notions about social differentiation, it made differentiation dependent upon the activities of the individual himself rather than upon hallowed and inaccessible bases. Even in its religious form the Protestant ethic translated God's selection into the observable deeds of the individual. Furthermore, by a process of development described below, the ethic in its secular form came to emphasize status differences rather than class differences.

The complimentary and harmonious relationship between the ethic of Protestantism and the values of capitalism has been systematically explored and only some of the more relevant points need to be set down here.[8] Briefly, that thesis has argued for the harmony that existed between Protestantism and capitalism in terms of the motivations, dominant values, and ideal personality characteristics prized by both—

an emphasis upon a "this-worldly" orientation and upon one's occupation as a "calling"; a prohibition against idleness and against luxury. The believing Protestant could at the same time be the successful entrepreneur. Material success and spiritual peace were simultaneous rewards for his efforts. In a way that must have been highly productive of personal security for those who succeeded and highly frustrating for those who did not, Protestantism and capitalism pulled together. When the Protestant ethic was predominantly religious—for it changed later—the interest in class or status was too crudely of this world to be a justifiable concern of the believer. To be sure, under Calvinism, the recognition of the division of humanity, into those who were chosen and those who were not, was basic, and thereby the seeds for social stratification were already sown. However, the struggle was too consuming and the censures against luxury, idleness, and egotistic contemplation too strict to condone a ready translation of that religious division into an explicit class system.

The qualities that came to be prized by the religious ethic, it was soon evident, were the same that came to be prized by the secular ethic as well. Success in both forms required heavy commitments to the "calling."[9] Industry was the outstanding character trait required of all those who aspired to success. Idleness was condemned by Franklin and by generations after him as injurious to the person as well as a detriment to the well-being of society. Perseverance was another prized quality required for success and was outstandingly evident, it was said, among those who carefully and diligently saved their money until they amassed great wealth. Sobriety was on this list, as was also the stricture against "the pleasures of bad company" that not only caused one to waste money foolishly but also would lead one astray. Additional virtues that were stressed included punctuality and a ready willingness to perform extra services without extra pay or special recognition. It is difficult to say whether these prescriptions were actually followed by the successful men of the past or instead were only romanticized recollections of those who had already achieved success. In any case, the frequent reiteration of those qualities and their general acceptance even today as prerequisites for success implied that they touched upon a responsive set of American values. "Behind all these exhortations to economic virtue lay the idea that the drama of economic salvation paralleled that of spiritual salvation in every particular. The god of the business universe was the employer, who, like the true deity, was just, providing for all a way into salvation."[10] The psychological forces that impelled those who sought the favor and security of success were too consuming to permit the luxury of enjoying the social fruits of that success. With religion to provide the spiritual rationale for success as well as the justification for the existence of the poor (who clearly were damned), becoming wealthy was more psychologically satisfying than it appears to have ever been since then. Today, we are informed, wealth itself charges a high psychic cost in ulcers and other psychosomatic ailments.

Material success, then, was defended since God dominated the social life of man as much as the life after death. Hence, one who labored earnestly, diligently, and successfully in his worldly calling was simply doing God's work on earth. Further, his economic success was a favorable sign that he was among the chosen. Religion, and the dominating American religion at that, thereby sanctified the efforts of the businessman, motivated him to accumulate more wealth, and married the virtues needed for success in business to those of religion. The rich were looked upon as heavenly majordomos since God was the real force behind the successful accumulation of wealth. Money was not to be used for sheerly personal gain nor for the immoral ends of personal vanity, but rather used exclusively for doing God's work. It would have been presumptuous, to say the least, for the individual to exploit his success by demanding social deference from his less fortunate fellow men; and what good is deference from those who have been cast out? Aside from the greater material ease and more pleasant material comforts, the major rewards for success derived from the knowledge that God

pletely with his theory and its politics. In that form, "class" became synonymous with "revolution" and "radicalism."

There have been a variety of social protest movements in American history, and in particular eras there has been rather widespread protest. But since 1776 the closer the ideology of the protest came to an intent for social revolt, the less likely were the movements' chances for success. Americans have been especially predisposed to social, economic, and political conservatism. Even during periods of severe economic crisis, the ideologies of revolt have had but limited adherents because most Americans preferred to believe that conditions would better themselves in quick time. In no other country, especially in those at equal levels of industrial development, has there been such a history of continuous, widespread and consistent acceptance of existing political forms. In the bleakest period of an economic depression, the hope for prosperity still held, supported by catch slogans. The hope defeated any ideology that called for radical alterations in social and political conditions. As in the early thirties, Americans preferred to blame a political party, a man or any other comparable symbol for the low state of the economy rather than locating the cause anywhere near the economic and political system itself. A vote for Roosevelt in 1932 was what the majority of Americans seemed to consider as a positive and constructive step toward solving the problem rather than seeking recourse to a party and a program of revolt.

The history of American trade unionism bears out this conclusion in clear detail. The working man may have been considered as the agent of revolutionary change as Marx portrayed him, but in the United States he seldom fulfilled that image and kept as far away as possible from the prophets of radicalism. Trade union movements that were primarily organized around a radical political philosophy of change—as the I.W.W. or the Socialist labor parties—failed repeatedly in their attempts to unionize the mass of American workers. Even England for a moment in 1926 felt the radical flare of a general strike, as did Holland (1903), Sweden (1909), and

Belgium (1913). Not that this was the only form of radical protest, but the general strike was one of the very few forms of protest that was mass organized, inherently political, radical in philosophy and aimed just short of revolution. It paralyzed a community and was "an attempt to compel, by the exercise of tremendous economic pressure, economic or political concessions."[11] The United States has never had a general strike on a national scale and very few that have even involved all organized labor in a single city. Strike patterns in the United States, whether organized or wildcat, have seldom even carried an intentional political conviction behind them. Even the more violent labor actions that have studded the history of labor unionism have remained almost purely economic in scope, and sometimes, as in the case of the Haymarket affair, have discouraged further union action for some time afterwards by their failure.[12] It was the business unionism of Samuel Gompers that successfully organized labor on a national scale, precisely because Gompers deliberately kept the radical label away from the AF of L and ostensibly kept it out of politics.[13]

In that kind of atmosphere there is a strong inclination to reject class as a definitive and primary social characteristic. Class, as a feature associated with political radicalism, never found mass acceptance in America. During periods of social stress and strain Americans were more likely to look to patent remedies for the immediate alleviation of their problems rather than to drastic surgery upon the body politic. Certainly, most societies of the West have been stable and not easily amenable to revolutionary actions. However, the political tone of those societies, at times, has shown at least a degree of radicalism that has not been evident to the same extent in the United States. The inclination of most Americans during periods of stress seems rather to be one of reiterating and bolstering the belief in existing institutional forms rather than of subjecting them to critical analysis.

This anti-radical spirit and philosophy, then, also worked to keep Americans from becoming conscious of class. Class was an alien social category that most Americans did not want to recognize or use.

Urbanization

Beside these four endemic values of American society that hindered an earlier recognition of class, certain factual aspects of American social development also operated in the same direction. One such fact that held back the recognition of social class was the rapid growth of large cities in the United States, especially in the last half century. As the urban population grew, the social relationships characteristic of the small community had to change. The greater human density of the urban environment required that impersonality be substituted for the intimacy formerly characteristic of small town life. Physical contact between persons increased in the city, but social contacts, and thereby the more personal intimate social knowledge of others, decreased. The effect was to spread out social relations, even as the density of persons within the urban area increased. In addition, the city grew in social and economic importance as well as in size. The small town consequently diminished in both respects, as the basic character of American social structure shifted from a rural to a predominantly urban orientation. The influence of the city reached far beyond its geographical limits to alter attitudes and social perceptions. In short, it has been essentially urban, not rural, attitudes that for the last two decades at least have defined social relations in the United States.

Under urban circumstances it became difficult to define social classes with accuracy. The narrower, more universal consensus about class and who belonged to what stratum that might have been obvious in the smaller community, was no longer as evident in the large city. To be sure, money still talked in the city. Wealth and poverty could be easily contrasted in the city by the houses people lived in and the way they lived. But under conditions of minimal social contact it was difficult to achieve consensus either about the relative importance among several criteria, or indeed, about how to match up the specific person with his property or lack of it. Add to this a central fact that most American cities were populated by large proportions of immigrants coming from a diversity of cultural backgrounds and the confusion became all the greater, for the symbols of class varied from culture to culture.

The growth of suburbs, significantly enough, altered many of these typical urban conditions and in effect created a sensitivity to status that was not as evident in the city. Suburbs acted as social filters, screening out equal elements from the urban population so that individuals from a common social stratum were attracted to the same suburban niche. In this way, the cultural heterogeneity of the city was broken down into more homogeneous social units in the growing suburban pattern. Furthermore, the very fact that suburbs contained smaller population aggregates than the city reintroduced a level of intimacy in social relations that was more characteristic of the small town than it was of the city. Through that channel, the concern with status in the suburban community became a major one. Suburbanites came to know more about each other than they ever did as city dwellers. Not only were there more opportunities for collective action and personal contact in the suburb—through the school, local government, the church, the home and even the hardware store—but the desire for greater social intimacy was also prevalent. This desire for intimacy was only increased by the social similarity of suburban residents.[14] A greater sensitivity to status has become the distinguishing hallmark of suburbia, seen in the greater desire of suburbanites to copy the behavior of each other, especially in the middle class suburbs.

Industrialism

INDUSTRIALIZATION, like the urbanization that it engendered, was a social process of some consequence in delaying the concern with class. Although the growth of industry brought with it many unwanted social effects in the beginning, it also created a social revolution in the manner by which society was stratified. In America, industrialization meant an abundance of opportunities for rapid and dramatic social mobility. Permanent attachment to a given class was discouraged as much as the opportunities for advancement were publicized. The belief in the equality of opportunity was strongly bolstered under such conditions and there was no footing whereby a class consciousness could develop. Only later, as industrialism aged, could such consciousness develop as Marx had reasoned.

The opportunities in an industrializing society during the years of rapid technological advancement and economic growth could not support a philosophy of class based upon fixed social positions. This generalization was even more applicable to the United States where there was no tradition of rigid social divisions, no culture of fixed social positions. The American Dream was spiritedly believed: a society without class distinctions.

It is strange but true that industrialization turned attention away from the recognition of class and at the same time set the basis upon which class distinctions were to be made. The seeming contradiction occurred because there was more than one stage to industrial development. In the earlier phases the shift from an agricultural to an industrial society was a revolutionary one that upset the former aristocratic bases of social divisions and substituted a newer and rawer measure of a man's social worth. In the later phases the social pace of industrialization necessarily slowed down and with it the range of opportunities for advancement narrowed. At first, industrialization destroyed the heritage of the past, but then later tried to establish its own tradition in order to achieve stability. Not only did our history show this, but so too the recent events of underdeveloped countries, as discussed in Chapter Seven, make this transition apparent.

Industrialization, of course, means many more things for social stratification. Not only does it engender and support the belief in the equality of opportunity by the very fact of upsetting the previously existent structure of society, but it provides the basis for newer inequalities. The present

American concern with status, for example, is directly tied to the organization of an industrial society displaying such features as the notion of occupational prestige, the minute prestige weights that they carry, the proliferation of middle-ranking occupations to fill the needs of large bureaucratic structures, and the emphasis upon mobility as a motivation for individuals to move up through those structures.

In short, industrialization kept class awareness at a minimum by the social revolution it introduced in the stratification of society and by the number of new opportunities it presented. Only later did it also begin introducing a concern with status differences based upon the social divisions it had created.

The several factors that have been mentioned were integral aspects of the American social scene that delayed the recognition of social classes. However, social stratification, whether functionally integrated into a formal set of values or not, was a feature of American social structure from the very beginning. The patterns of beliefs, values, and geography for a time kept attention away from those socially divisive characteristics. Where the belief in social equality was dominant, where opportunities for upward social mobility were considered abundant, and where the use of a class vocabulary was so closely associated with a marginal, radical, political philosophy, it was little wonder, then, that a consciousness of class was absent.

Still, the consciousness of status in the present period depends upon a pattern of values that is similar to that required for a consciousness of class. The outstanding difference is only that the first is somewhat more acceptable to a democratic ethos than the other, principally because status carries the connotation of individual worth supported by community judgment, while class emphasizes more a supra-human determinant somewhat removed from the community's sphere of effective control. In other words, if the recognition of social division had to come to America, as indeed it had to, then it was logical to expect it to come in a form that did the least violence to the existing patterns of beliefs. Herein lies the central importance of a status vocabulary for the American scene.

Just as there were reasons that created an insensitivity to class, so too there are reasons behind the recent concern with status. What is more, they are to be found in the same place —in the social values currently held and in the modifications of social structure as a result of various social processes.

Industrialization was the major force behind an open class system, producing as it did a wide range of opportunities for upward mobility by the expansion of the middle ranks of the occupational hierarchy. Yet the process of rapid expansion could not continue indefinitely nor at the same pace. In time, it had to reach a point nearer to saturation, where, if the opportunities for upward mobility were not completely restricted, they were at least considerably reduced. Stabilization of the industrial process meant that the structure of labor skills and the pattern of capital investment became standardized and set. Occupations, especially near the top of the skill hierarchy, were more rigidly defined and became more dependent upon specialized training. The positions of the professional, the manager, and even the white-collar clerk, were no longer to be open simply to those with sincere intentions and perseverance alone, but were to be filled rather by those who could satisfy the necessary prerequisites. It is less likely today, for example, that the manager of a large corporation will be someone whose only qualification is that he came up through the ranks. Increasingly, specialist's requirements are being set for more and more jobs in the industrial labor market.

Similarly, the pattern of capital investment and expansion precludes the entrance of the wildcatter and the privateer capitalist of an earlier era. Patent rights, monopolies, cartels, and interlocking corporate controls make it much more difficult, if not impossible, for a neophyte entrepreneur to get a toe-hold in a major segment of the economy. With so many large corporations devoting so much time and money to research development, even the independent inventor working on his own has less than an even chance of coming up first with a commercially valuable product. If he does, his best hope is to sell the rights to an established concern for as good a settlement as he can get.

Both of these major industrial trends meant that the upward climb has been slowed considerably, especially when compared with earlier eras, and the drama of the climb from rags-to-riches becomes more of a social myth than a social reality. Upward social movement is still possible, of course, but it is a movement that takes place below the highest class level. Under those conditions, individuals come more to accept their present position and to turn their attention to ways by which it can be enhanced. Occupation, naturally enough, becomes one such dimension. It becomes converted into prestige terms and arranged in a status hierarchy. "Naturally enough," because occupations are functionally wedded to the industrial process and because they can form a basis for social divisions. Now it is no longer wealth alone that matters in the judgments of prestige; wealth is scaled down in importance. What comes to matter almost as much are education, training, responsibility, and the social welfare aspects of the occupations that can confer social prestige. On these bases, occupations become status differentiated; a differentiation based on almost minute differences as occupations proliferate to meet the demands of high level industrialization.

Suburbanization, too, tends to emphasize status dimensions. The residential movement of the population to suburban areas has taken on many features of a status movement. Although some of the motivation behind suburbanization understandably enough is the desire for more space, modern housing, and the delights of home ownership, the result has produced remarkably homogeneous social areas. The social heterogeneity of the city has been equalized in the suburb so that social peers come to be attracted to a common area; those whose occupation, income, tastes, and life styles are quite similar. For those reasons, residence has now come to symbolize a person's status in a way that was not so easily possible in the city with its complex variation and juxtaposed settlement of divergent social strata in the same residential area. The homogeneity of the suburb thereby has allowed, and indeed encouraged, an emphasis upon status that was not ecologically possible before. At the same time, the greater social intimacy engendered by suburban life, whether spurious or not, has placed a great premium on individual status, further heightening and emphasizing the struggle for status and allowing it to invade more dimensions of contemporary social structure. Whether the suburb is the cause or simply the effect of a general trend toward this status emphasis is impossible to say. What is clear, however, is that the suburb is strongly implicated in that trend.

Finally, from an analysis of the current political tone,[15] there comes the suggestion that the economic prosperity in our time has encouraged the turn to status awareness. In the case of politics, it has been suggested that "status politics" —"the clash of various projective rationalizations arising from status aspirations and other personal motives"[16]—is a consequence of prosperity. Once their material needs are adequately satisfied, it would appear, people turn their attention toward considerations of status. Clearly, this is not a unique characteristic of prosperity alone, but rather of prosperity in the present period when social mobility has lessened and when status groups attempt to hold and to insure their own position. This is especially true for those, who still clinging to the belief in upward mobility, only encounter failure.

As mentioned earlier, this is part of the process whereby individuals become increasingly aware that their position today is likely to be their social ceiling, beyond which they very likely will not be able to rise. With access to the upper reaches of the structure made more difficult, the person turns to a closer inspection of the position that he holds and tends to enhance it with essentially irrational and nonfunctional criteria that make it seem more prestigeful. Style, taste, family lineage, and occupation, for example, come to be depended upon as status criteria, while the harder features such as wealth and power, which are characteristic of relatively few of the topmost positions, come to be underplayed.

From the denial that classes exist, then, American society

has come to the stage of recognizing the existence of status. It took the hundred years from Marx to Warner for that social process to unfold and to develop. The anti-aristocratic heritage, an anti-radical philosophy, a frontier psychology and a secularized Protestant ethic all were so deeply ingrained in the American value system that the realities of a class system could never come through to public awareness. Added to these beliefs were the facts of a rapidly expanding industrial system, the growth of cities, massive immigration, and the absence of a feudal heritage, all of which hid some of the more obvious class differences and at the same time heightened the opportunities for social advancement.

Yet, the beliefs and the social facts began to produce counter tendencies as well. The pace of industrialization had to slow and with it the rapidity and the channels for social mobility had to change and become more fixed. The growth of cities splintered into a suburban expansion that heightened an awareness of status differences by bringing social peers together into a socially homogeneous environment. The values of equality, although still publicly announced as before, became tempered by the recognition of social realities; by the awareness that one's social position of the moment was likely to be unchanged in the future. In short, Americans appeared to come to the point of reassessing and re-evaluating their positions within society. The inevitable result was the recognition finally that there were social differences and that these were real.

But a society does not simply add on new values and new beliefs without reference to the existing patterns of beliefs that it already holds. For this reason, class as a major social value could not simply be taken into the American value system. Instead, Americans apparently preferred the notion of status which was more amenable to what they already believed. This is not a meaningless terminological difference but a crucial value difference. Class as an idea was antithetical to all of the things that Americans believed about their society. It was radical in tone, revolutionary in connotation, and what was most important, carried with it the implication that social differences were determined by social and economic forces outside of the control of the individual. Status, on the contrary, began by placing social differentiation in the hands of a community judging a person's worth and his achievements. At the same time, status tended to connote social differences of a more ephemeral and vague character than did class which spoke only of harder social characteristics such as wealth, power, and authority rather than of prestige and social standing.

Strangest of all are the trends that the status emphasis has taken, veering sharply away from its earlier harmonious dependence upon American values of democracy and individual worth. The very vagueness of status judgments, and the fact that status depends upon the standards established by the style and taste leaders of the community, has become the means by which status can be controlled. Those who have been recognized as holding high status win thereby the right to set the standards of status, especially for the higher social positions in a community. The right, in turn, becomes a form of social power to establish status on whatever ground the possessors of high social position choose. This latter development on the American stratification scene, however, is not yet fully fixed nor socially congealed. The appeal of status rather than class to most Americans is still the foremost consideration at the present time.

Given these widely different connotations, it is little wonder that American society was more attracted to status than to class as a descriptive social category. Forced as they finally were into the recognition of social differences in spite of past beliefs and values, Americans apparently preferred the somewhat milder connotations of a status vocabulary to those of a class vocabulary. American social scientists for the most part have followed that choice. As is seen throughout the succeeding chapters commenting upon the studies of social stratification, the majority of the writings have shown a concern with what are status rather than class differences. "Prestige" rather than "power" has been the popular focus of studies of social stratification; community status structures rather than a national class system has been the locale for most research in stratification.

The hundred-year lag between Marx and Warner and the emphasis upon status rather than upon class has not been accidental. As this chapter has tried to show, the reasons are to be found in the American value system and in the facts of American social development.

CHAPTER II

Theories of Class

THEORY OCCUPIES A SALIENT PLACE in the study of class as it does in all scientific investigation. It provides the scientific framework of concepts and relationships that organizes and holds reality in a way that can be studied. With it, the scientist can grapple with a slice of the world; without it, he only wanders among unrelated events that seem to be cast up without purpose.

In the study of class, and doubtless with other subjects as well, theory carries additional baggage along with its primary scientific purpose. It serves another more subtle function that perhaps is unintended and often is unnoticed. The theory molds an attitude and sets a stance that predetermines how class is seen; and because of the close relationship, the theory of class comments upon the organization of society itself. The conception and the orientation that a theory invariably creates of the class structure—values supporting class, class dynamics, and modes of class expression—hold direct consequences for the way that the organization and operation of society as a whole is viewed.

Marx, of course, deliberately made the linkage between theory and social orientation clear and unequivocal. Perhaps it is part of the heritage he left, for all of the theorists of stratification who have followed him have continued to tie class structure to social structure and in every instance have implied a marked social philosophy. For Marx, class was pivotal for his conception of social organization. Class struggles were the constant and universal feature of society and they flooded over to color all social institutions and inundate all interpersonal relations. Neither the person nor his society were ever free from class forces. Weber reached similar conclusions although by another path as he sought to break loose from the single-minded determinism of Marx's theory. Even so, class or its counterparts, according to Weber, operated in the market-place, in politics, and in the community: in other words, class was a basic element in social structure. For the functionalists, Parsons, Davis and Moore, stratification by class or by any other dimension depended upon the supporting values of a society. Without it, they implied, organized social existence was impossible. Warner, too, saw class as a basic characteristic of American society, the only locus of his interest. He chose to regard social divisions by rank as basic to the understanding of American society, for it "permeate[s] every aspect of social life of that country."[1]

Although each of the theorists just mentioned has accepted the close relationship between class and social structure, each has treated the nature and content of that relationship differently, and thereby each has fashioned a distinctive orientation toward the relationship of class and society. Such differences are to be expected if only because the subject is so broad that each can pick his own preferred acreage. Yet, whatever the selection, once made it is a commitment and an expression of ideology.

No one theory systematically accounts for all the varied facets and nuances of class. Even though the architectures of the four theories of class considered in this chapter are relatively wide in scope, each has made its particular emphasis, and each has carved out its unique segment from the whole. There is no single recipe for the analysis of class, nor is it possible to combine the available theories into some grand pattern. Necessarily, therefore, each theory develops its own commitment toward class and its own view of what class means for society. One theory has stressed the determinism of economic values and has almost excluded prestige factors from consideration. Another has downgraded the importance of economic values and upgraded those of status. One has emphasized the place of power in establishing class relationships. Another has deliberately excluded the power dimension. One has been limited to community class systems; another to a national class system. It is little wonder then that the concept of "class" has come to mean different things, depending as it must upon the theoretical context from which it is taken.[2] Nor should it be any greater wonder that each theory contains its own built-in views, often only implicit, about the place, the social force, and the consequences of class for society and its organization.

The research on class that is surveyed in succeeding chapters must depend upon the theory from which it proceeds and therefore must be conducted within a commitment that is woven into the fabric of the research design itself. The selection of occupational prestige as a measure of class position, for example, implies not only a method but also a particular theoretical stance and a frame of reference that varies from other alternatives. The dependence upon an index of prestige rather than, say, upon power, economic life-chances, or ethnic origins commits the research to a selected perspective and restricts its conclusions to one segment of the range of possibilities. In much the same way, each theory forces a commitment. It makes a difference whether class is considered as a problem for democracy that should be solved, as a permanent feature of social life that can never be escaped, as an historical phenomenon that must disappear, or as a desirable condition in a competitive society by which the majority gains.

These commitments border hard by the terrain of social ideologies. Perhaps this, too, is the Marxian heritage. Certainly he was crystal clear in tying the analysis of class to a political ideology and a social philosophy. The reason for this nexus between class and ideology is not hard to find. The study of class is perforce a study in social inequality. It must be so and every theory of class must take a stand on the matter, explicitly or not, in trying to explain the character, the form and the necessity of such divisiveness for social existence. The scientific objective becomes somewhat more difficult to reach because social inequality connotes ethical, moral, and ideological biases that can shake the neutrality of the scientist even as he tries to maintain it. It is one of the penalties of class study. Therefore, it would seem the better part of scientific wisdom to face these involvements rather than to hide from them.[3]

The matters of commitment, orientation, and ideology are overtones that a theory sounds and ones that have to be dealt with. Additionally, however, an adequate theory of social stratification is confronted by specific problems with severe methodological consequences.[4]

One such difficulty is phrased by the dilemma of whether to consider class as an objective fact or as a subjective identification. In the first instance, individuals are placed in a class according to certain criteria without special regard for whether or not individuals are indeed aware of their class memberships. Social, economic, and political forces that in a sense function outside of the person's control become the determinants of social position according to this view. The subjective alternative, on the contrary, requires that individuals be conscious of class as the basis for placing them in one class rather than in another.

There is more involved here than simply choosing between one or the other, for each alternative carries additional consequences. On the subjective side, the need quickly arises to clarify the nature of class consciousness more precisely. Rocher has phrased the matter this way: "These are two different problems . . . the former [consciousness of belonging to a class] related to the self-identification of the individual with a social class, the latter [class consciousness] to the class considered as a group."[5] Further, the problem arises of the relationship between an individual's self-judgment and the judgments of others about what his class "really" is. In an extreme form, the class into which an individual might choose to place himself may bear little resemblance to the class in which he is placed by others.

Throughout all of these alternatives of dilemma runs the possibility that the concern with class and class consciousness is part of the social outlook of only some groups. For others, class may have little social reality or meaning. It must be admitted that concern with class does appear at times to be the peculiar property of the middle class alone. Does it not follow then that class consciousness may also be the peculiar mark of membership in the middle class? The aspiring and upwardly mobile perhaps are those more sharply attuned to class differences and class styles than either those at the very top or at the very bottom of the class hierarchy. What happens to class awareness as a criterion if it turns out that large segments of the population are totally unconcerned with class?

The problems are not greatly simplified by using the objective definition of class. It is possible, of course, to say what classes exist and who belongs to them according to some measurable and objective standard. What does that procedure mean, however, if the individuals so allocated to the several classes are unaware of class or do not subjectively fit in the class? Nor is this the only problem. There may be no consensus on the standard used for determining class position, nor any agreement as to the relative importance among the several criteria of that standard. If that is the case, and it is not entirely inconceivable, there is little sense in simply assigning individuals to the several classes by a standard that has meaning for no one other than its creator.

Most research on social class moves quietly around these questions. A frequent procedure is to let the specific problem under study determine which concept of class is to be used without specific attention given to the consequences of the choice. For example, if the research is on social mobility, the design usually depends upon some objective determination of class, such as changes in occupations. Mobility is measured by the movement that has taken place between occupations arranged in the form of a prestige hierarchy. Or, if the interest is in attitudes determined by class, the research procedure might well call for the respondent to identify his own class position. In this way, presumably two subjective responses are compared. This easy shifting between alternatives and perspectives may be justified in part by the demands of research, but clearly no theory can afford this kind of laxity. The responsibility of a theory is systematically to recognize these several dimensions and to incorporate them unambiguously into a conception of class.

A theory of class faces a second set of obstacles that emerges from the fact of the close relationship between social structure and its accompanying system of stratification. Class, as a fact of social life, is interwoven throughout the institutional fabric of a society. Each institutional sphere, whether the family, education, religion, or the economic and political orders, exerts some influence in setting the individual's class. That position, in turn, can be thought of as the sum of the combined effects of all institutional spheres. Furthermore, not all of these institutions are of equal importance; some are more important than others in determining class.

The ready presumption, stimulated by Marxian theory, has been that the economic institution predominates and therefore determines class position. Economic relationships, above all, determine all other social relationships whether in politics, religion, or education. This is a tempting argument, the more so because economic matters obviously are so central for an industrialized society. However, the tempting simplicity of this logic must be more realistically modified. Political affairs, for example, cannot be fully understood from the economic perspective alone. Political power, although it may be heavily dependent upon the market place, can also be independent of it. The reverse may also hold: economic power can be a consequence of political power. The ward boss, as Weber noted, is a man generally without social standing and often without wealth, yet he is a power within his bailiwick. More recently, the military has moved into positions of enormous political significance not through economic channels but as a consequence of the dependence upon its skills and knowledge. So great has its prestige become that military men have been co-opted by large corporations, in part for economic gains, in part for political and prestige gains.[6] Similarly, religious elites command social positions that make little sense in an exclusively economic interpretation. The prestige gains of religious spokesmen in an era of personal insecurity, cold war, and impending destruction are explained more meaningfully from the social psychological perspective of human behavior than by economic cost accounting. In short, though there are close resemblances and interlocking consequences between institutions and their ability to confer status and power, each institution maintains some autonomy not directly affected by the others.

The problem for a theory of class becomes one of bringing order to the variety of effects that are exerted by institutional segments of the social order. Phrased another way, the problem is one of specifying the relationship between a position held in one institutional order and that held in another; a problem in establishing a prestige currency with a constant exchange value.

A third difficulty encountered in a theory of class is the proper demarcation of the social limits to which it is meant to apply. The system of stratification defined by the theory can be applicable only to a community or to a whole society. The first alternative limits social stratification to those elements that are set by interpersonal relations within the community. The rhetoric and symbols of class are restricted to an area that can be no larger than that in which these symbols have meaning. "Hilltop" as a section of upper class residence, for example, can only have class connotations for those who live in the community where "Hilltop" is located, who know the name and for what it stands.

For some purposes, it is legitimate and sensible to limit a study to the single community and to its consensus about the standards of class. The thing to recognize, however, is that a theory so devised is restricted to a narrower range. It cannot go beyond those limits. There are social processes affecting the class structure that originate and operate only at a national level. The economy, for example, is not community-bound. Economic decisions made at the national level set trends and produce immediate effects within every community. These decisions cannot always be discerned by looking at them through community relationships. Similarly, nation-wide class power is much more than simply the total of the separate powers that can be found within separate communities.

As noted in the preceding instance, research requirements may dictate either alternative. An adequate theory, however, cannot choose but should, ideally, be able to explain the phenomena of class at both the community and national levels. Weber, for example, has supplied a possible solution. The class relations of the economic order belong at the level of the national society. Relations at the community level, as a separate analytical dimension, involve the "status" order.

Even Weber's analytically ingenious distinctions leave unsolved the precise character of the relationships between a community system of status and a national system of class. The class system is more than the total of all community status systems. Nor is there the clue in Weber's theory for a way of comparing the status system of one community with that of another. Yet, there must be a measure of such comparability if only because all communities share values in common with the society of which they are a part. Some minimal national consensus must exist about class else the idea of a society, somehow integrated and whole, is overlooked.

These and other lesser difficulties have not yet been adequately solved. No wonder then that "class" has been interpreted and handled so differently in each of the four theories discussed in this chapter. Marx's view of "class," for example, is a universe distant from Warner's view of "status." The difference is more than semantic. It is a basic difference in conception, in attitude, and in intent. The theoretical architectures differ; so do the orientation and the stance toward the subject; and finally, the ideologies differ, as differ they must.

Rather than becoming bogged down in what is a form of definitional bookkeeping, no attempt has been made here to define a single meaning of "class" or to insist too obviously upon neat distinctions between "class," "status," "prestige" and other terms currently in the vocabulary. The definitional problem is never going to be solved by a glossary of terms. Once the orientation is made explicit, once the theory is formulated, then the vocabulary can be established if need be. Fortunately, the communication of ideas is not seriously threatened by using the terms of class without a pseudoscientific definition at the beginning. Definitions, like research conclusions, depend upon the theory and the method used. Hence, "class" and its several variants are used interchangeably except where specific comparison requires somewhat more rigorous handling.

This is as logical a place as any to make explicit mention of a point that is to be applied to all of the theorists discussed here, with the possible exception of Warner. In setting forth the basis for an analysis of stratification these men were more concerned with developing and validating the criteria and general principles of class systems than with the number of separate classes that might be distinguished. The number of classes that might be designated, after all, was likely to vary between societies and between time periods. What Marx, Weber, and the functionalists were seeking was a *theory* of class that had universal application. They were not concerned, and rightly so, with specific class descriptions that would be meaningful only for a specific society.

The four separate theories—Marx, Weber, functionalism, and Warner—have been selected because they represent a range of different answers to the difficulties that have been enumerated. There have been others that might have been included. Yet, each of the theories selected has been a bench mark in the development of the intellectual interest in class. Each has differed from its predecessor. Each in a way has typified the intellectual concerns of its time, from the revolutionary cosmology of Marx to the community-centered, status vocabulary that Warner has developed for American consumption, which is essentially middle class, status-involved, and ethnocentric.

Marx: Economic Determinism and the Class Struggle

MARX should be read today with understanding rather than with misplaced pedantic precision; an attitude, by the way, that must be granted to Freud as well if either of them is to speak sensibly in the present. The comparison is worth continuing further. Both men were polemicists as well as theory builders on a grand scale, and their analyses should be studied partially as heated arguments that have cooled. Freud in the earlier years moved over uncharted intellectual ground, against the current of accepted medical and psychological traditions. Marx, who lived through an era of social revolution, fought on the academic front as well as on the political. The polemics of Marx and Freud that today can more calmly be appraised were heated by intellectual battles and by the practical concerns of manipulating followers.

The deliberate oversimplification was sometimes required to make a point for political control rather than for intellectual requirements. Marx's reduction of social causation to a single source—the means of production—was the kind of simplification demanded of the polemicist and the politician. Probably no other single idea in Marx's writing, what he and Engels labeled as a "vulgar economic interpretation," has led to so much later misinterpretation; for that hypothesis taken literally was, and is, a gross simplification. Read today in a calmer perspective it can be taken for what it was intended: a deliberate emphasis upon economic forces in shaping the relationships and character of industrial society.

Freudian psychology, especially in its conception of the role of culture upon personality, makes many errors when read literally. But it too, like Marx's theory, yields astounding richness when read sympathetically. The reader, in both instances, must consciously be willing to translate mere words into proper meanings in order to resolve the gap in years and in social tone between the writing and the reading.

Marx, very much like Freud, constructed a theory that was most useful in what each of them might have considered as peripheral insights. Marx's historiography of dialectical stages in human societies and Freud's instinct pyschology depended too much upon assumptions that are strange today. What saved each of them from the intellectual graveyard to which naive historians and instinct psychologists are sent by succeeding generations was the rich quality and the hint of timeless universality in the ideas that they generated; ideas that were able to stand independently from the theories out of which they were developed. Marx read history through the turmoil of Western society as it moved through a major economic phase, a phase that was radically altering the structure and social relationships of that society. Forced on by his own ideology as much as by his scholarship, Marx projected the tremendous changes into the future, and predicted, erroneously, the overthrow of industrial capitalism; at least the revolt did not come as he thought it would. Yet, at the same time he saw the beginnings and much more successfully forecast the character of the social relationships that were to come. By distilling out the elementary requirements of an industrial economy and social organization, he could project some of the consequences.

In a like manner, Freud saw in his early contacts with hysteria a pattern that led him on to a somewhat oversimplified theory of personality, one that depended heavily upon instinctual drives and metaphysical notions of psychological transmissions. Yet, at the same time, he encompassed a wide range of personality dynamics into a more meaningful and systematic pattern than had ever been achieved before.

Perhaps it is in the nature of the genius that he cannot settle for anything less than a universalistic explanation. Apparently he has little patience with establishing a few limited facts. In any case, the genius can be forgiven the gross error where the same error would mean intellectual death for smaller minds. It is in this spirit that Marx's theory of class should be considered.

Social classes for Marx were the inevitable consequence of social and economic forces set in motion by the prevailing system of production in society; hence, the label of "economic determinism." But classes for Marx were not simply scientific abstractions, nor merely categories of convenience. Class was a reality. It divided individuals into social categories so basic that their relationships with one another were determined by it as were their lives and destinies. Class was not simply a device for social analysis, but a material set of conditions that surrounded real human beings and established the tone and pattern of their affairs.

Marx's reading of history established a central fact for him. Beneath the apparent variation between one society and another, between one historical era and another, there was to be found a characteristic common to all societies in all periods: each had to satisfy the minimal requirements of human existence by supplying the necessary goods and commodities needed for life. The system of production, Marx's summarizing term for the process, was the social manifestation of a basic biological fact. The manner in which goods were produced and distributed, of course, varied between societies; for each had devised its own cultural means for organizing the process. However, in all cases the central consequences were identical. The productive system necessarily divided society into two antagonistic classes, each with its own characteristic interests and needs. One class owned the means of producing these life necessities, while the other class owned nothing but its own labor. "Freeman and slave, patrician and plebian, lord and serf, guild-master and journeyman, in a word oppressor and oppressed. . . ."[7] Furthermore, Marx found the elements of a natural political antagonism in these class relationships which made them much more than economic positions alone. As the opening statement from the *Manifesto* continued, these classes "stood in constant opposition to one another, carried on an uninterrupted, now hidden, now open fight, a fight that each time ended, either in a revolutionary reconstitution of society at large, or in the common ruin of the contending classes."[8]

A second fact was established for Marx in his interpretation of history. There was a pattern in the struggles between classes: a dialectical progression over time by which the system of production in every historical epoch not only created the ruling class of the moment but set the conditions for the development of the ruling class to come into power in the next historical period. The forces of social and economic necessity evolved the thesis, antithesis, and the resulting synthesis in each era as the latent pattern of economic and social antagonisms inherent in social organization emerged. Under capitalism, for example, the sharpest class antagonisms in history were developed from the requirements of capitalism itself. The constant expansion, the drive toward national monopoly and then to international cartelization were inherent forces in capitalism. The operation of these forces, Marx predicted, would decrease the size of the ruling class and thereby swell the ranks of the proletariat. This power added to the proletariat, symbolic of the contradiction under capitalism, would eventually destroy capitalism. Capitalism had necessarily nurtured the forces of its own destruction and it could not be otherwise.

The "system of production," upon which a good deal of Marx's theory rested, was a complex category that included not only the technical features of production but more importantly the values, social relations, and social institutions that surrounded it and were created by it. Money, credit, profit, and the contract were basic components of the "capitalistic system of production." Yet equally basic were the social relationships between bourgeoisie and proletariat determined by the economic process. Marx's reduction of social organization to the core of its system of production, therefore, was not simply a naive oversimplification. He intended by that concept to include the more subtle nuances of the whole social and economic complex that characteristically emerged under a given production system. The class structure was the single most outstanding manifestation of that complex. It organized social life into significant constellations arising from the productive system.

It should be clear that Marx's theory of social stratification was tied to a philosophy of history and to a theory of society. Classes were basic features of social organization for they were the immediate and direct expressions of the relations created by the productive process. One class owned the means by which life's basic necessities were produced and their distribution governed; another class owned only its own labor. This basic polarity, this fact of class struggle and antagonism, has always existed in human societies, although the productive system in each historical period has distinctively created different classes. Slaves, after all, did not live under the same conditions as the proletariat, nor should they be exactly compared. The master was not entirely the prototype of the bourgeoisie, although each held superior class power. The nature of class relationships under feudalism, for example, differed in many essentials from those found under capitalism, as did the class relationships between the early and later periods of capitalistic development itself. These differences clearly needed to be recognized for the theory of class with the universalistic range that Marx propounded. The differences in existence between social classes in different historical and social periods had to be systematically ordered. Marx implied that two criteria were needed for that purpose.[9] The first criterion for class distinction was the difference in property ownership already mentioned. One class owned the property required in the productive process and by its ownership was able to exert power. The other class did not own property and could only sell, exchange, or forcibly give its labor to produce the goods needed for subsistence.[10] This criterion permitted the identification of the extreme class poles in all societies.

The second criterion distinguished classes in different productive orders, or different historical periods. Neither the slave nor the proletariat owned property, but still they could not be considered as belonging to the same class. The difference was to be found in the degree of personal freedom that each possessed. The master owned the slave, but the bourgeoisie did not own the proletariat in the same sense. The worker under capitalism was in some sense a free agent, where the slave in social fact was not. The former could sell or choose not to sell his labor, even though the latter choice might have meant starvation. Nonetheless, the analytical importance of the alternative was crucial for the identification of subordinate classes in history. Clearly the slave had no rights. He was himself property and as such was owned by his master. The serf was bound to the land, but with a measure of more personal freedom than that of the slave. The proletariat was, in a relative degree, more free to move and to select his place of work than either the slave or the serf. Commensurate differences appeared, of course, in the relative power that could be exerted by the dominant classes. The control of the master over his slave was greater than that of the bourgeoisie over the proletariat.

One further point needs clarification. Marx recognized that under capitalism there were more than the two classes he had identified. First, he made note of the fact that, in the earlier stages of capitalism, the bourgeoisie included the "remnants of absolute monarchy, the landowners, the non-industrial bourgeois, and the petty bourgeoisie." These "remnants" were fought and destroyed by the proletariat even though they were the enemies primarily of the growing bourgeoisie. This was how Marx interpreted the struggles in France in the middle of the last century; the proletariat was misled, he felt, from fighting its real enemy.[11] He also recognized the existence of the lower middle class, the small manufacturer, the shopkeeper, and the artisan. These groups, he believed, were only temporary class participants whose position was doomed. Struggle though they would to preserve their middle class status, the weight of social forces set in motion by the contradictions of capitalism would finally force them into the ranks of the proletariat. This process of "proletarianization" was an inherent effect of capitalism—one of its contradictions—that added to the numerical growth of the proletariat. Another class, "the social scum" (*lumpenproletariat*), was also to be found under capitalism. Marx wrote of them as "that passively rotting mass thrown off by the lowest layers of old society, [that] may, here and there, be swept into the movement by a proletarian revolution; its conditions of life, however, prepare it far more for the part of a bribed tool of reactionary intrigue."[12] These several class variations, Marx predicted, would disappear as the destiny of capitalistic society unfolded.

With this background it is possible to consider further refinements. Marx's conception of class had three interrelated dimensions—economic, political, and social. Had he considered class in economic terms alone, many of the further—indeed the rich—implications of class might never have been developed. Although class relations were economically determined in his analysis, the value of the theory was increased to the extent that Marx carried his class analysis beyond the economic realm. In part, this was accomplished by treating classes as groupings of political consequence, upon which much of Marx's political ideology was hinged. The class, in other words, was an agent in history because it played a role in the political process. Indeed these two dimensions could be separated only analytically for they were inseparable in fact. In the political process, classes historically evolved through two key stages. In the first, the class did not exist as an integrated group but only in the more or less private awareness of the individuals of the class. The individual recognized the difference between his position and that of others. This relatively loose collection of individuals could be called a class more because of its future potential than because of its present common economic position. It lacked the cohesiveness of the group that was to develop later. The recently established system of production, say early capitalism after feudalism, had not yet emerged to the point where class differences were polarized; nor were the political destinies of the separate classes yet apparent. In time, however, the latent characteristics of the productive system and the class relations it engendered became manifest. At that point the individual was forced to realize that he was not alone; others shared the same conditions of life and the same fate with him. The class was then a "class for itself," a real group with a developed consciousness of itself, its position and its destiny.

Much of Marx's contribution to the study of social stratification stemmed from his sharp analysis of the social dimensions of class. Class was pivotal for understanding the economic process, as in the theory of surplus value; it was pivotal for understanding the political process, as in his theory of revolution; so too, class was pivotal for understanding the social process—the dominating ideology, the social institutions, and the interpersonal relations that were engendered. Class was the primary filter through which Marx saw society. It was the basis from which he interpreted a society's characteristics and dynamics.

The logic for this analysis of the social consequences of class was found in his early assumption that class position determined a set of all-inclusive life-conditions for the individual. The person never fully escaped his class. Further, it was groups of individuals acting as classes that set the path of development for society itself. These social dimensions of class were peppered throughout Marx's writing, and when collated they show a startling range of effects attributed to classes:[13]

CONSUMER BEHAVIOR

The bourgeoisie has through its exploitation of the world market given a cosmopolitan character to production and consumption in every country. . . . In place of the old wants, satisfied by the production of the country, we find new wants, requiring for their satisfaction the products of distant lands and climes.

WORLD ART

In place of the old local and national seclusion and self-sufficiency, we have intercourse in every direction, universal inter-dependence of nations. And as in material, so also in intellectual production. The intellectual creations of individual nations become common property. National one-sidedness and narrowmindedness become more and more impossible, and from the numerous national and local literatures there arises a world literature.

COMMUNICATION

The bourgeoisie, by the rapid improvement of all instruments of production, by the immensely facilitated means of communication, draws all nations, even the most barbarian, into civilization.

URBANIZATION

The bourgeoisie has subjected the country to the rule of the towns. It has created enormous cities, has greatly increased the urban population as compared with the rural, and has thus rescued a considerable part of the population from the idiocy of rural life.

MONOPOLIZATION

More and more the bourgeoisie keeps doing away with the scattered state of the population, of the means of production, and of property. It has agglomerated population, centralized means of production, and has concentrated property in a few hands.

TECHNOLOGY

> The bourgeoisie, during its rule of scarce one hundred years, has created more massive and more colossal productive forces than have all preceding generations together. Subjection of nature's forces to man, machinery, application of chemistry to industry and agriculture, steam-navigation, railways, electric telegraphs, clearing of whole continents for cultivation, canalisation of rivers, whole populations conjured out of the ground—what earlier century had even a presentiment that such productive forces slumbered in the lap of social labour?

Those activities, some desirable and others not, that Marx attributed to the bourgeoisie were materialistic in character, or at least were more directly traced to the economic demands of that class. Marx reserved some of his most venomous writing, however, for the social relations that the bourgeoisie created in their drive for power.[14]

> The bourgeoisie, wherever it has got the upper hand, has put an end to all feudal, patriarchal, idyllic relations. It has pitilessly torn asunder the motley feudal ties that bound man to his "natural superiors," and has left no other bond between man and man than naked self-interest, than callous "cash payment"! It has drowned the most heavenly ecstasies of religious fervour, of chivalrous enthusiasm, of philistine sentimentalism, in the icy water of egotistical calculation. It has resolved personal worth into exchange value. . . . In one word, for exploitation, veiled by religious and political illusions, it has substituted naked, shameless, direct, brutal exploitation.

> The bourgeoisie has stripped of its halo every occupation hitherto honoured and looked up to with reverent awe. It has converted the physician, the lawyer, the priest, the poet, the man of science into its paid wage-laborers.

> The bourgeoisie has torn away from the family its sentimental veil, and has reduced the family relation to a mere money relation.

Writing in a more analytical moment[15] and less as a political pamphleteer, Marx specified more deliberately the social consequences of class as he saw them to stem from the production system.

> The production of life, both of one's own in labour and of fresh life in procreation, . . . appears as a . . . social relationship. By social, we understand the co-operation of several individuals, no matter under what conditions, in what manner and to what end. It follows from this that a certain mode of production, or industrial stage, is always combined with a certain mode of co-operation, or social stage, and this mode of co-operation is itself a "productive force." Further, that the multitude of productive forces accessible to men determines the nature of society, hence that the "history of humanity" must always be studied and treated in relation to the history of industry and exchange.[16]

> Language is as old as consciousness, language is practical consciousness, as it exists for other men, and for that reason is really beginning to exist for me personally as well; for language, like consciousness only arises from the need, the necessity, of intercourse with other men. Where there exists a relationship, it exists for me: the animal has no "relations" with anything, cannot have any. For the animal, its relations to others does not exist as a relation. Consciousness is therefore from the very beginning a social product, and remains so as long as men exist at all.[17]

Marx then proceeded to tie consciousness down more firmly to the materialistic base of what he believed to be the "real" world, and to argue that valid intellectual endeavors began from that base and not from some "pure" or "detached" world as some philosophical idealists would have us believe. His argument and his theory should be sufficiently clear by this point, even though many more examples might be given of how he applied the theory and expanded it.

The quotations convey Marx's insistence upon the intimate nexus that existed between class and social structure. Although he arrived at this conclusion through a path filled with strong, personally-held ideologies and with intense political involvements, he argued cogently for that interrelationship. This insistence, for whatever reason, was a contribution of major consequence to the study of stratification for it placed class in a proper perspective. Class was not simply "another" dimension of social life, but indeed the most basic to it. Class by this view became the outstanding characteristic of the social structure that produced it. At the same time, it was a social fact so real that it determined the individual's behavior and motivations.

Marx's insistence upon the economic character of class was also a contribution of merit. He left that stamp upon class study; one that is immediately evident today, although at times it is mincingly circumvented or else naively interpreted.

Marx's outstanding weakness was one of omission. In part, because he did not have time to fully explore the subject as he was on the verge of doing; in part, because he was politically and ideologically committed to a program of action, Marx did not give fuller attention to the psychological consequences of class for individuals. Class consciousness, for example, he considered as dependent upon changes in the productive system, never as an attribute that might stand independently or develop in other ways. Tied as he was to a theory of economic determinism, Marx did not explore the possibility that class position could produce a set of attitudes and motivate behavior in ways that were not to be shrugged off simply as epiphenomenal consequences arising from the economic order. The striving for social recognition, the aspirations for upward mobility in the status hierarchy, the concern with matters of status, and the irrationalities produced by status consciousness, received only a glancing tap. Marx did note that some would fight to retain their middle class identities even as they were losing them. However, that statement, and the implications that might be credited to it, did not tap the full psychological depth of what "striving" and the "desire for status" can mean for individuals.

It seemed at times that Marx foresaw the variations that

would appear in the class structure of a highly industrialized society, and would have explored them further had a whole series of impossible conditions been satisfied. Yet, for all of his political involvement in trying to organize a revolutionary party, for all of his involvement in the immediate affairs of his day, he managed in his theory to break loose from temporal ties and arrive at ideas and conclusions that transcended the immediacy of the time in which he wrote.

Weber: Class, Status and Party

THE heading of this section is taken from the title of one of Weber's major essays on social stratification.[18] The title was descriptive of his theory at the same time that it intimated the nature of his intellectual relationship with Marx. Indeed, Marx's writing was clearly an important stimulus to Weber both in the subject and in the direction given to the analysis. "Part of Weber's own work," Gerth and Mills noted in the introduction to their volume, "may . . . be seen as an attempt to 'round out' Marx's economic materialism by a political and military materialism."[19] And, it must also be added, to "round out" Marx's theory by a more systematic emphasis on the social psychological elements that Marx had underplayed and by a more comprehensive analysis of social structure and social dynamics. For Weber, human intent and motivation were relevant facts that belonged in the analysis of the larger social processes that Marx preferred. What was more, the social process could be analyzed by means of individual social psychology. Economic organization, for example, was not only a force that controlled human behavior but was at the same time itself a consequence of that behavior. Weber's writing, especially about class, must be read with Marx in the wings. For Weber began with Marx, in an intellectual sense, taking the rich elements of the latter's sociological insights, adding to them valuable original dimensions, and finally incorporating the whole into one of the best statements on stratification.

"Class" in its Marxian usage did not exhaust for Weber all its relevant dimensions as a phenomenon of social organization. What was more, Marx's definition tended to read an economic determinism into some facets of class behavior that were better understood by another vocabulary. Analytically, Weber argued, two additional dimensions had to be identified: those that he termed "status" and "party"; the first concerned with social honor or prestige and the second with social or legal power. The three often were intermingled in fact, both in the criteria that identified each of them and in the social forms by which they were typically expressed. Yet, by insisting upon this three-fold separation, Weber was able to explain behavior in a direct and parsimonious chain where Marx's explanation often required a circuitous appeal to economic factors alone as the sole cause. Weber's deliberate expansion of the Marxian concept of class, then, was justified by the greater range of meaning and understanding that it brought to the analysis of class. The hard structure of a stratification system as well as the dynamics that propelled it could be accounted for more parsimoniously and could be handled with greater analytical ease by Weber's analysis than by that of Marx.

Perspective on Weber's view can be attained by seeing it as fitting between the extremes of an "objective" theory on the one side and a "subjective" one on the other.[20] Marx represented the first.[21] By that view, individuals were pushed into classes by economic and related social forces. Relatively little emphasis was given to the opposite view; to the self-conceptions of individuals and how they evaluated their own position. At the "subjective" pole it was the view that classes existed finally only in the consciousness and awareness of individuals, both as to their own class position and that of others. Weber considered both dimensions necessary. Neither one by itself was exclusively valid. On the subjective side he held that the individual's own evaluation and interpretation of his class situation were clearly valid, for the effects of those self-conceptions would be reflected in behavior. At the same time, however, he also recognized that the personal goals and interpretations of the individual were not always realistic or realized. Frequently, greater social forces stepped in, "objectively," to determine class regardless of what persons might like to believe. These distinct nuances were systematically recognized by Weber and were basic to his whole view of social organization. Briefly, "class" was objectively determined by the rational economic processes of the market; whereas "status" and "party" reflected subjective judgments more clearly, and were determined by social norms and consensus in a community setting.

Weber's theory of social stratification was phrased around two basic pivots that set its orientation. First, whatever its form, stratification was a manifestation of the unequal distribution of power. Position in any social hierarchy, in other words, was finally established by the power it could command as compared with the power held by those in other positions. Power was defined as "the chance of a man or of a number of men to realize their own will in a communal action even against the resistance of others who are participating in the action."[22] It was not necessary, by that definition, for power to be actually exercised. The probability of its success was sufficient, for the power was just as potent and real if its possible use caused persons to alter their original intentions as it would be if actually employed. In truth, there would be but little difference. Interestingly enough, this emphasis upon power, upon which the meaning of Weber's theory of stratification depended, has been almost totally overlooked by many sociologists. Few theories and fewer research designs have done anything with Weber's system, nor has either picked up the cue of power as the central focus for the study of class.

From that first orientation toward power, Weber advanced to a second analytical distinction. He distinguished three orders, or systems, within society—the economic, the social, and the political or legal. Each created its separate hierarchy, its arena where the form of power peculiar to it was expressed. In actuality, of course, the three were interdependent. A position held in one order could provide the basis and hold consequences for the exercise of power in another. For example, a "high" position in the economic hierarchy might also support a "high" position in the status hierarchy —but not automatically so, and herein lay Weber's central point. Each order was sufficiently unique to require separate analysis and description. Marx had commingled all three under the rubric of economic determinism. Weber contended, instead, that each order was characterized by its own distinct criteria and by its own distinct distribution of power, to which he applied the terms "class," "status," and "party."

"Class" referred only to position in the economic order, and all persons were in one class who shared (1) similar life chances as represented by (2) common "economic interests in the possession of goods and opportunities for income," under (3) the conditions of the commodity or labor market. The operation of forces in the market, in other words, distributed individuals into a class hierarchy measured primarily by economic criteria.

Weber's handling of class closely resembled Marx's analysis. Still, Weber was more meticulous in spelling out the economic foundations of class rather than piling up everything on a "system of production." Both men designated the ownership of property, for example, as a significant criterion of class. Similarly, both recognized that the kind of property that was owned varied from one economic system to the next; that the economic elements of a slave economy were not the same as those under capitalism. Yet, brief as his writing was on the specific subject of stratification, Weber specified in greater detail than did Marx what some of those elements were and what their analytical importance was. Where Marx reduced economic variations to what he believed were its simplest elements, Weber retained the variations as a means of identifying the channels of economic power. The kind of property owned, for example, whether it was men, land, fixed capital equipment or money assets,[23] indicated at the same time how power could be manifested.

Marx barely had touched the point. Property ownership could confer a means to power through a monopoly and control over (1) the purchase of high-priced consumer goods, (2) the sale of economic goods, (3) the opportunities for the accumulation of property through unconsumed surpluses, (4) the opportunities for saving and accumulating capital, and (5) socially advantageous kinds of education where these would involve expenditures. These distinctions were analytically significant for they specified the form and the shape of economic dominance that could be conferred by property ownership.

Those who did not own property, of course, were powerless. They were the slaves, the debtors, the poor and the proletariat, each of them part of the numerically large subordinate class in various historical periods.

Had Weber stopped at this point, his definition of class would have added little to Marx's. Property for Weber, however, was but one kind of commodity, so to speak, that had meaning in the market place, and it served to distinguish essentially among "property classes," as indicated above. A second commodity, that of human services, could be offered or exploited in an economically relevant manner and formed the basis for what Weber termed "acquisition classes."[24] Capitalism in particular led to a proliferation of these classes. Merchants, bankers, financiers, entrepreneurs, professionals, and others with economically valuable skills were able to offer their services, which in turn gave each a measure of monopolistic control in the market, especially where the demand was great and the services limited. The proletariat held no such skill monopoly nor was its service especially in short supply. Where labor was available and relatively unskilled, there was little possibility for economic control. Furthermore, unlike those specialists mentioned who could organize their smaller numbers to gain greater control over their specialty in the market, the proletariat was numerically massive and the obstacles to its effective economic organization were that much the greater. Where Marx saw the proletariat as gaining power automatically in the future,

Weber was more pessimistic, for he saw only a proletariat subjected to the hard economic laws of the market. Only by organizing into an effective group with commonly recognized goals, that is, by the development of a "class consciousness," could the proletariat gain power.

Somewhere among these property and acquisition classes were the middle classes. They were very much a residual category in Weber's analysis, much as in Marx's. They might or might not own property, might or might not hold some measure of monopoly on their services in the manner of acquisition classes. Weber recognized that this middle stratum existed but did little about them in a systematic analysis.

One effect of Weber's distinction between property classes and acquisition classes was to increase the number of variations of class interests that might exist in the market. For Marx, it should be recalled, two separate, antagonistic and rather monolithic structures of class interests were defined, somewhat reminiscent of Adam Smith's neat logical system primed by rational motives. Weber, on the contrary, implied that there were different interests pursued in the market. To reduce the variation down to but two types of class interest was to oversimplify the real situation without special gain for the analysis. Each of the classes that Weber defined was presumed to pursue its own economic goals, which at times were like the goals of another class but at other times were different and clashed with the goals pursued by others. The aim of professionals to get more income, for example, was as real and important as that of bankers for a higher interest rate. The two might often conflict. The goal of some to monopolize high-priced consumer goods for status reasons could conflict with the purposes of the producer of those goods. The interest of the bourgeoisie, finally, clashing with that of the proletariat, was but one possible set of market relationships in Weber's analysis, although it was singularly all-important in Marx's.

Weber similarly differed from Marx in what he believed to be the prerequisites for unified class action growing out of common interests. Where Marx simplified, Weber held on to the complexity of the real situation. As noted above, the variety of differing economic interests between the several classes could create dissension rather than harmony; dissimilar rather than common class interests as Marx believed. Furthermore, even assuming a communality of class interests generated by economic relations in the market, the unifying of those interests into a coherent form as a basis for class action depended on other equally important requirements. Among those Weber noted were: (1) the state of satisfaction with existing conditions; (2) the extent of the contrast observable between classes; (3) the transparency of the connection that could be made between one's class situation and its cause; and (4) the feeling that one's position in the market was a direct and immediate consequence of the existing system of property distribution. Weber refused to accept, even if only for purposes of analysis, the rather naive view that a common economic situation by itself was sufficient cause to spontaneously generate a common interest and mobilize it into action. After all, mass movements of the scope visualized by Marx depended upon sustained and directed human motivation towards a most difficult goal. Such activity, like any other, whether it was buying soap, voting for a president, choosing an occupation, or striving for higher status, depended upon a complexity of personal and social factors. What Marx might have thought was a sufficient basis for class action was possibly not at all recognized by the individuals concerned. Marx tended to follow a classical economic tradition in this regard, by assuming that rational self-interest was a sufficient explanation of human conduct. There was more to human action, as Weber knew, than met the economically rational eye.

Primarily with that view in mind, Weber held that economic classes were not communities; that is, they had no basis upon which to command united and sustained action of the sort that would be needed to revolt against a social order or to defend that order against revolt. The economic motives of men in the market place were not the stuff out of which revolutions were made, although economic inequalities might be used as a rallying cry and an organizing symbol. Still, in the past those in the same class stratum have risen in mass actions in response to common economic stresses, as for example in the general strike or in consumer boycotts. However, Weber maintained that this did not justify the conclusion that such action was inevitable, automatic, or traceable solely to economic motives. Neither did it justify a belief that the class, rather than individuals as such, possessed a mystical infallibility about its destiny that transcended human failures and miscues. In a gentle statement, Weber noted that that kind of "pseudo-scientific operation has found its most classic expression in the statement of a talented author *[sic]*, that the individual may be in error concerning his interests but that the 'class' is 'infallible' about its interests."[25]

To summarize: class for Weber referred to position and common life chances in the economic order. Class struggles and class interests emerged from economic relations in the market and applied therefore only to market relationships. They could not be extended to cover the kind of united action that depended upon a "community of interest," where the latter had to include such socially complex matters as group allegiances, human emotions, and sustained motivations.

The principal meaning of Weber's objection to Marx's grossly inclusive class category was incorporated into the concepts of "status order" and "status," the second of the three dimensions Weber distinguished in his theory of stratification. "Social honor" and "prestige" were the currency of the status order by which positions were distributed in a hierarchy that conferred social power differentially. Individuals held positions in the status order according to the prestige that they commanded. Because it was prestige that was accorded, the status order existed only in a community setting. Judgments of prestige and social honor, after all, depended upon a common standard of evaluation that was accepted by the group. Status judgments required consensus. In the final analysis, these social evaluations could only be made meaningfully by a "community," which meant that continuous and integrated relationships existed between persons governed by accepted norms. Unlike the market situation in which class position was objectively determined by rational and knowable economic facts, a status hierarchy rested finally upon the accepted social prestige estimates that were accorded to persons within their community.

Weber was not unmindful of the fact that the basis used by a community to judge status might depend rather directly upon the market situation; that status distinctions, in other words, were reflections of class distinctions. "Property as such," Weber pointed out, "is not always recognized as a status qualification, but in the long run it is, and with extraordinary regularity."[26] Yet, Weber's separation of the two dimensions allowed for the possibility that persons in different economic classes might be members of the same status group. By the same token, status and class positions need bear no relationship to one another. Innumerable examples of that situation have been reported in community studies; of those who were once wealthy but now almost destitute still retaining positions of high status. Or the reverse: the man of wealth unrecognized in his own community. The essential meaning of democracy could fit perfectly into these terms—the recognition of economic differences but insistence upon status equality. All men are social equals although they are not and need not be economic equals.

Status groups were distinguished by their different life styles, which reflected prestige differences. The mode of living Weber advanced as the first basis for distinguishing status groups, but he included as well the "formal process of education" and the "prestige of birth or of an occupation."[27] Each of these criteria provided a basis for the expression of different styles of life that distinguished between social strata in the community.

Status equals were socially accessible to one another. They

tended to maintain free social interaction between themselves at the same time that they tended to limit interaction with others in lower status positions; a characteristic that Warner and other community analysts of the American status scene have frequently reported. Even more, status groups sought to monopolize the goods, the opportunities, and the symbols that conferred honor so as to maximize the social distance between themselves and others. The barriers of exclusiveness, the defenses against unwanted social intrusion, could thus be raised higher. The goal could be achieved by sumptuary laws controlling the expenditures for dress, food, or other items of consumption, thereby reserving status privileges to a few. The same goal could also be achieved by using custom and convention to maintain a status exclusiveness; an institutionalized snobbery. The status group, in any case, attempted to stylize its own life patterns so that they became a distinctive and symbolic mark of its position. A necessary component for all of these actions, however, was not only the desire for prestige exclusiveness by a status group, but also the concomitant recognition by others in the community that such aims were legitimate, deserved, and worth the desired symbolic meaning that was accorded them.

Weber's differentiation between status and class orders is highly meaningful for understanding American patterns of stratification, and it is surprising that American sociologists have overlooked his theory. Here it is frequently the case that individuals hold prestige positions that are not fully coordinate with their economic class. The white collar employee, for example, illustrates a fairly common instance where status is relatively higher than income alone would indicate. Similarly, in the older established communities in the United States, as Warner and others have shown, persons oftentimes hold high social status by virtue of their family background alone, even after they are no longer wealthy or hold economic power.

Weber also indicated some of the utility of his analysis by projecting a possible future trend initiated by upper status groups to guarantee their position. Such groups, Weber noted, have attempted to close off the channels into their stratum, a move which, if successful, would change an open class system into a caste-like hierarchy implemented by law and social convention. In the case of the United States, Weber intimated that some upper status groups were moving toward the caste extreme by establishing prerequisites for entry that were no longer accessible to late comers. The First Families of Virginia, the Daughters of the American Revolution, or the Society of Mayflower Descendants were examples of status organizations using qualifications for entry that were no longer available. One's family either was here at the right time or they missed the boat—in both meanings. Where such practices become institutionalized, then economic criteria lose importance for determining status. Indeed, Weber held that when economic relations became stable, then distinctions based on status came to be preferred instead. The voracity of the human appetite for greater and greater differentiation from his fellow man seemed to be insatiable. Caste and aristocracy were the final goals.

Weber's analysis, it should be pointed out, was not so much directed towards trying to prove that status and class must be different, as much as it was in showing the utility of treating them as analytically distinct. The examples given above are some proof of that utility. Similarly, his theory offers one of the best explanations of the social dynamics of caste systems.[28] What is more, that explanation was tied into the same set of principles of stratification that were applied to less rigid status systems. This, too, is another instance of the parsimony of Weber's theory of stratification.

The explanation becomes even richer and more creative in those instances where the economic and status order are not coordinate. The comparative importance of the two, the relationship between them, and the effects of one upon the other become more easily understandable from Weber's theory than from that of Marx. Marx, after all, was not unaware of the status overtones in the class system he described. He implied, however, that those were but temporary manifestations; part of the facade overlaying the more basic set of class relationships.

Weber's own statement might be used as a summary of the points raised above:

> With some over-simplification, one might thus say that "classes" are stratified according to their relations to the production and acquisition of goods; whereas "status groups" are stratified according to the principles of *consumption* of goods as represented by special "styles of life."[29]

The political order comprised the third and final dimension in Weber's analysis of stratification. Weber developed this part of his theory least of all. Social power was the key principle operating in this order, and it yielded essentially separate "parties," or, if one preferred, separate political groups. As in the case of the status order, the political order also depended upon community actions and for the same reasons. Furthermore, Weber stipulated that it depended upon the existence of political bureaucracies with some form of governing staffs. This latter characteristic appeared to be included so as to omit those societies governed by monarchies or other types of one-man rule where, almost by definition, divided and competing political groups could not exist.

Position in the political order was interpreted, then, according to the degree of social power that was held—"that is to say, [the power of] influencing a communal action no matter what its content may be."[30] The way by which such action was influenced might include everything and anything from naked violence to the more subtle manipulation of others within the rules of the existing political process. Parties could use money, social influence, suggestion, or obstruction through parliamentary tactics to attain their goals. The degree of success attained by the party was an indication of the extent of power it commanded and thereby of its position in the political hierarchy.

On the question of the relationship between parties and the other two dimensions of stratification Weber was brief. It was clear, however, that he recognized that the interrelationship could be a close and functional one. "Parties," wrote Weber, "may represent interests determined through 'class situation' or 'status situation,' and they may recruit their following respectively from one or the other."[31] Once again, as in the discussion above on status and class, the distinction had analytical utility.

The analytical separation of this political category was useful because it provided the means for identifying individuals within the community who held power—the basis of his approach to the subject of stratification—yet had no "standing" in either the status or class orders. An outstanding example of this type for Weber was the ward boss in American cities. Here was an individual, Weber felt, who held power in the political decisions of a community, yet was not highly regarded by others and did not necessarily possess great wealth. He was content to manipulate from behind the political scene. Political power was its own end.

The utility of the distinction was also evident in the greater precision it allowed for identifying the type of power used and the goal sought by the use of power. The activities of a party, of a status group, and of an economic association are all data for stratification study; yet it is obvious that each has its own unique social manifestations and its own peculiarities. Nothing is gained and much is lost by lumping them together. Weber strongly disagreed with the Marxian proclivity of reducing most social processes to an exclusively economic base. If nothing else, Weber looked for more solid analytical ground to justify his insights and suspicions. In the example of the ward boss or the leader of a political machine, Weber's analysis could make more meaningful their possible attempts to convert their political power into economic advantage or into status advantage under certain circumstances. He also recognized that economic power carried with it direct advantages for political power, once again justifying the utility of keeping the two distinct. The owners and managers of corporations, for example, have become grossly involved with the political process, as Mills for one has shown,[32] and as has been documented in instance after instance in a study of the political power of international cartels in setting policy for the American occupation abroad after World War II.[33] The flow of power from the economic to the political sphere, Weber implied, was characteristic of industrial society where rational bureaucratic structures dominated the government both of politics and of corporations.

As has been intimated throughout, Weber's analytical distinctions offer the most meaningful framework for interpreting and understanding stratification in a modern industrial society. The theory is broad, ranges far, and includes a variety of different manifestations of stratification under one explanatory roof. Its principal shortcoming seems to be not so much due to Weber as to succeeding sociologists who have failed to take up the cues of his theory and to give them the empirical testing they need and deserve. As it now stands, the theory does have, at many crucial points, an airy abstractness about it that cannot always be related to reality. The very important question, for example, of how the three aspects of power are interrelated, needs explicit testing. So too does the matter that Weber never fully settled as to the priority among these aspects; is economic class, for example, the dominating characteristic of stratification in industrial societies, and do the others simply follow from it? Research developed from Weber's formulations no doubt would yield conclusions to modify the theory itself, and the result would be an immeasurable gain for the understanding of the many facets of stratification and of its operation in society.

Functionalism: Stratification, Survival and Social Values

THE functional theory of stratification, at least as expounded by Parsons and by Davis and Moore,[34] conveyed a special quality of its own. This quality emerged from the total concern by the functionalists with the manipulation of formal categories of analysis, with abstract qualities, more so than was true of other theorists. Marx, Weber, and Warner began from a concrete basis: the forms and character of classes as they were found to exist in modern industrial society. Each of the three, in his own manner, went on from there to a more general analysis that was meant to have wider application. The functionalists, on the contrary, began from the opposite direction. They started with more abstract concepts that carried a cross-cultural tone and a sense of universality. Thus, American patterns of stratification were viewed as a single case, and even "industrial society" was only one variation among several possible types of social organization. In part, this approach was anthropological in orientation and especially close to the cultural views of Malinowski.[35] Culture was seen in its most universalistic expression with little attention to any particular society. Concepts were purposely kept abstract enough to be so widely applicable. The more familiar realities used by other theorists of stratification were translated by the functionalists into more general terms. The loss of dramatic and dynamic realism that the other theories conveyed so well was a cost paid with apparent willingness by functionalism in exchange for its theoretical gains. The more familiar descriptive terms in the vocabulary of stratification were exchanged for less specific and therefore more applicable terms in keeping with the attempt of functionalism to be a universal statement containing all possible variations in stratification systems.

Parsons' essay, "A Revised Analytical Approach to the Theory of Social Stratification," is discussed first because its theoretical canvas is more detailed. The Davis and Moore paper was intentionally less ambitious. The two papers are complementary, however, and taken together present the functional position satisfactorily.

Stratification, according to Parsons, was considered as a necessary element of social organization, *i.e.*, to be found in all societies. All organized social groupings had to fulfill that requirement if they were to survive. Stratification, in short, was as universal as society itself. Although its empirical forms varied, the systems of stratification were to be explained by a single theory. Hence, the occupational prestige structure of the United States, the caste system of India, or the age and kinship hierarchies of primitive societies were viewed only as concrete variations; each fitted into a proper category, and all were analyzed by the same general theory. Briefly, this goal was accomplished by viewing stratification as a means of social ranking based upon and justified by the paramount values of a society. If the constellations of values could be categorized, then the forms of stratification could similarly be accounted for.

This theoretical orientation required Parsons to reduce stratification down to its barest essentials, down to the least common denominator of events present in all societies. That element was contained in his concept of "social action." The final and irreducible element upon which the whole analysis of social systems depended was this concept of "social action," by which Parsons understood the goal-oriented activity of individuals carried out within the set of institutional norms of a society. It was activity that was guided, motivated, and directed towards goals that were socially desirable and through means that were socially sanctioned.

Social action, Parsons next postulated, always implied a standard of evaluation. Not all actions could be considered as equally preferable or as undifferentiated in quality. There was variety in life. Whatever humans did was judged as more or less desirable, as more or less useful, or as more or less important according to some standard that each society had adopted. Stratification, thereby, was wedded to the most elemental social process, for stratification was the result of this evaluation of human activity.

Parsons defined stratification as "the ranking of units in a social system in accordance with the standards of the common value system."[36] This definition forged a particular theoretical stance with several consequences. First, it was apparent that any system of stratification, whatever its specific form, was the expression and implementation of the central values of a society. These values provided the basis for evaluation, which in turn necessarily produced a hierarchy of positions, rewards, individuals, or whatever else was to be ranked. Secondly, stratification was intimately related to the very mainspring of society itself because stratification was an immediate and inescapable consequence of social action. The social forces that created and supported organized social relationships at the same time established stratification as an inescapable product. It was an inevitable feature of social existence. Finally, the theory of stratification, like the larger theory of social systems itself, was stated in terms that were abstract enough and general enough to apply to all societies. Parsons' choice of the vague term "units" rather than some more specific referrent, for example, was deliberate. Without any empirical referrent, "unit" pointed to no particular item of stratification. Occupational prestige would be one of the "units" in the American system, while kinship or race might fill the concept for other systems. Parsons justified his choice of terminology partially because of the confusion in our understanding about the nature of stratification; a legitimate decision for one who has embarked on a task of clarifying that confusion.

The next step for Parsons was to analyze the process of evaluation, upon which stratification was so obviously dependent, and to break it down further into its elemental components. This goal was to be achieved by categorizing the general properties about which evaluative judgments were made.

Qualities are "those properties of a unit which can be evaluated independently of any change in its relations to objects in its situation, but may be ascribed to the unit as such."[37] They were characteristics that were ascribed, let us say to the individual, such as intelligence or noble birth. They "belonged" to the individual in the sense that they could not be altered. These "qualities," of cource, must be endowed with some meaning for the ranking of individuals.

In some societies, noble birth provided a major basis for stratification based upon such qualities and was expressive of their central values. A quality such as intelligence, too, might be incorporated into the evaluation of an individual's position in other societies.

Performances referred to judgments of the activity of an individual relative to that of others. In this case, stratification would depend upon evaluations of what individuals have accomplished or have achieved. The occupational hierarchy of American society exemplified this dimension where persons were judged by the occupations they had attained; individuals were ranked by their occupation. Other societies have emphasized such achievements as prowess in war or the attainment of religious visions as the basis for evaluating an individual's position. The particular standard used, of course, depended upon the values that were considered important by the society. In other words, one had to do well in some activity that was considered important for the performance to have any meaning in placing the individual in his niche in the hierarchy. A highly proficient gardener in a nomadic tribe, for example, would have as useful an accomplishment as an equally talented spear thrower in our own society.

Possessions, finally, referred to the objects which individuals owned or over which they had control as these were relevant for stratification. Included here were not only material possessions but talents and skills as well. The prestige of any occupation, for example, in our society is associated with some estimate of the level of training and skill required to perform it. Similarly, persons might own objects which tended to confer prestige upon the owner, such as works of art,[38] or they might even possess more directly economically valuable goods. These objects, as in the case of performance, had to be socially valuable if they were to have relevance for a system of stratification. Sentimental mementos may mean a great deal to their owner but usually have little value in the prestige currency of the community.

At this point in his analysis, Parsons interjected an aside. For purposes of clarifying his orientation and specifying some of its limits, it would be well to follow him. In effect, Parsons re-emphasized his earlier declaration that he was primarily concerned with building an abstract theoretical model rather than with the immediate description of existing systems of stratification. The model was deliberately an ideal one, specified by certain conditions, and one which assumed a social system that functioned in a consistent and logical fashion. In actuality, of course, no society met the requirements of the model fully, nor was it necessary that one should. In actuality, individuals might hold positions that were not systematically explained only from the values of society. They might hold power and exert authority in terms which were not directly related to the values of their society, or they might capitalize on these values in unintended ways. For example, persons who hold national reputations, deserved as they might be, can translate that reputation into power in a variety of social areas where they have no special competence or upon which their reputation does not depend. Again, every era has produced its charismatic leaders who hold power because the strength of their own personalities can command a mass following, which in turn has opened the gates of power to them. Such leaders might embody values that were unimportant before. Their rise to power would be "accidental" and could not be explained from the kind of model Parsons had constructed. These instances would constitute empirical deviations not within the range of Parsons' view.

In short, the implementation of the "common value pattern" that occurred in reality might deviate sharply from the ideal standards by which a society was analytically described. From the standpoint of a theory, such as Parsons has constructed, these real manifestations remained outside the range of explanation. It is one of the costs of any abstract model of empirical phenomena, and Parsons' theory is no exception. His justification was that of any model builder. Only by a "technical theoretical analysis," he maintained, was it possible to establish a formal basis upon which any existing system of stratification could be described. "Empirically, the imperfections of integration of social systems formulated by . . . the power of a unit may be extremely important. However, the point of view from which we approach the analysis of stratification prescribes that analysis should focus on the common value-pattern aspect."[39] In one stroke, Parsons had cut his analysis loose from the empirical concerns that had dominated Marx and Weber. Parsons preferred the more abstract and more ideal social value system as the focus for his analysis instead of the concrete class phenomena of industrial society. He has attempted to reconstruct the social system, in a sense, and derive the character of stratification from the functional expression of those values. Davis and Moore, as is to be noted, established their theoretical orientation on the same ground.

Given that emphasis, the next step for Parsons was clear: the classification of "common value-patterns" into an ideal typology that would categorize the possible standards of evaluation and, simultaneously, the resulting forms of stratification. Each type summarized the central value orientation of a society. By this classification, any society was typed by the priority and the importance it gave to each of these four value standards. Further, this order of priority at the same time defined the evaluative judgments for ranking and specified the form of stratification. The assumption was clear, but unstated, that the values Parsons had selected exhausted the possibilities, although it was hard to know exactly why.

1) *Universalism* referred to those values that were relatively free from ethical or emotional restrictions. The emphasis was upon the effective utilization of an object. "Efficiency" as a value in its own right, for example, conveys the meaning intended. In some measure, Parsons here had reference to what Weber meant by "rationality," where what was important was only that efficient means be selected to achieve given ends without regard for tradition or similar emotional encumbrances. Later, in this essay, Parsons has

equated "universalism" with "adaptiveness," by which it can be presumed he meant, similarly, the emphasis on the manipulation of means to achieve a given goal without other considerations.

2) *Goal Definition* or *Goal Gratification* referred to those values that emphasized the importance of the goals of a society in their own right. The emphasis upon realizing those goals set the dominant social direction and motivated individuals to direct their activity in that direction. At the same time, the limits of permissible "private" goals were also set, thereby restricting the amount of deviation by individuals from the accepted social norms. Within the analytical meaning of this category there was to be no reference to the means or the instrumentalities by which these goals were to be achieved.

3) *Integration* referred to the maintenance of social solidarity as a central value. A society thereby defined its expectations in terms of a devotion and adherence to the system itself and in its own right. Actions were judged primarily on the basis of whether they tended to increase or to decrease the integration and solidarity between individuals within the society.

4) *Pattern Maintenance* referred to the value emphasis upon maintaining existing definitions and standards within a society. The existing values, in other words, were judged to be the most desirable, and action was evaluated accordingly as to whether it supported those values or not. Similarly, any change in the value pattern was itself regulated and formalized. Where, for example, change was necessary, as in the socialization process, the emphasis remained upon maintaining and inculcating existing values. This standard conveyed a traditional tone, by which the social emphasis was placed upon the unquestioned adherence to existing forms and patterns as a desired end in itself.

According to Parsons, each of these four types represented possible central values of a society, which could then be analytically described by its pattern of preference. Indeed, theoretically, it should be possible to categorize any society by its ranking of these four values. The United States, for example, generally would be characterized as giving paramount place to "universalism" with the other values following, while India might be described as emphasizing the maintenance of existing patterns. These were relative judgments, to be sure, since every society must pay some heed to each value mentioned else it would lack continuity and would have its existence threatened. Internal solidarity and the maintenance of existing patterns, for example, were to be expected to some extent in all human societies. The problem for the analyst was to establish the relative priority of these four central value patterns for any society. Societies must differ, of course, in that respect. Inasmuch as the priority pattern varied between societies, so too would the basis of evaluation and the form of their stratification systems.

Parsons' next task was to match up the dimensions underlying the evaluative process with each of these four central value patterns. Each type of value pattern, in other words, required its own type of "quality," "performance," and "possession." The categories used for stratifying members and the criteria employed, therefore, were to be analyzed on the basis of the paramount value pattern of the society. It seems plausible that if individuals were ranked in terms of qualities that they possessed, then these qualities themselves must be judged according to the central values, just as would be true for "performances" and "possessions." By this type of categorization, finally dependent upon the common value pattern, Parsons hoped to achieve a model classification within which any system of stratification could be placed, and at the same time, by which the supporting values of that system could be discerned.

At this point, Parsons included an additional consideration that he had not mentioned before. *Sanctions* were expressions of "attitudes toward the action or performance of others through reward and punishment." They were to be considered along with "performance" as a social judgment of that activity meant to encourage or inhibit the actions of individuals. Parsons classified such sanctions along two dimensions. First, whether they were "specific" and directly related to some particular goal, or instead were "diffuse" in not being so immediately tied to the goal. Secondly, the sanction could carry an attitude that allowed the individual to be rewarded relatively soon upon the attainment of the desired goal, or an attitude that delayed the reward and stressed the goal more emphatically. "Affectivity" and "neutrality" were the terms used respectively for these two states. The accompanying schematic plan indicates how Parsons related the several dimensions he has specified:

> . . . the formal composition of the stratification aspect of a social system may be summed up as follows. The categories in terms of which social objects (actors) and systems of them in roles are analyzed, are categories which in one aspect are value-standards. Value-standards, then, are in terms of the same dimensions or variables which differentiate units in the social system in a structural sense *and* which define the types of sanctioned performance of those units and hence the appropriate sanctions relative to those performances. The evaluation of qualities and performances has inherently a hierarchical aspect because according to any value-standard some will rank higher than others.[40]

It was Parsons' intention to use the schema first to classify a society by its paramount value standard and the relative priority given to the succeeding standards. Once this step was accomplished, then various institutional subsystems within that society were to be analyzed by the same set of categories. In the example given by Parsons, the American value system was characterized as holding universalism as its paramount value. One of the "strategic subsystems" below this would be the occupational; that is, "the subsystem organized about the adaptive problems of the total system."

Parsons indicated some of the problems and difficulties that remained unsolved or untouched by his model. First, although the theory did provide a rubric for classifying any social system, it did not provide the means for identifying the paramount value standard—that elementary first step in the application of the model. Parsons has suggested that this be accomplished by identifying the performance norms and their related consequences, from which the value standard might then be inferred. Performance was considered as more amenable to empirical investigation and hence could provide the necessary clues to the central values. In other words, Parsons suggested that the central values could be inferred by seeing what actions a society seemed to evaluate highly; the reverse of which he has hypothesized as the proper sequence of events. This suggested procedure, however, denied the independence of the value standard as the model has assumed. Further, as Parsons himself noted, this procedure assumed that performance norms would indeed incorporate the paramount values. If any single proposition was crucial to Parsons' theory, it was precisely that the paramount values were incorporated into the norms of performance and into other aspects of the system. The inability to identify those values made it impossible to test that assumption satisfactorily.

A second problem was that of "spread," as Parsons has labeled it. "Spread" referred to the relative independence of various subsystems in the total society from each other and the relative importance of these separate subsystems for a "general prestige continuum." The theory cannot designate a single total prestige position for individuals, arrived at as the sum of their position in various recognized subsystems, for no technique was provided for evaluating the relative importance of these several subsystems. The problem is closely related to that of "interlarding," by which Parsons meant the relative comparison between a position in one subsystem with that in another. How does the social standing of a high-ranking executive, for example, compare with that of a middle-ranking politician? What is the comparative importance of wealth with that of "proper family background" in establishing the status of an individual? Neither the problem of "spread" nor of "interlarding" was settled by Parsons' theory, as he has himself indicated.

The complexity of the Parsons' model derived from the very complexity of his ideas as well as from his intention of

Table 1—Schematic Presentation of Parsons' Categories of Value Standards and Related Stratification Components

		VALUES EXPRESSED IN:			
VALUE STANDARD	Performance Norms Refer to:	Sanctions Produce Attitudes of:	Qualities Evaluating:*	Possessions as Facilities for:*	Rewards*
Universalism	Technical efficiency	"Approval" Neutrality and Specificity	Competence of individual	Adapting norms of performance	Approval
Goal Definition	Goals to be attained and permissible private goals	"Response" Affectivity and Specificity	Goal-orientations held	Goal attainment	Response
Integration	Maintenance of solidarity	"Acceptance" Diffuseness and Affectivity	Loyalty to the system	Integrative functions	Acceptance
Pattern Maintenance	Maintaining existing definitions and regulating change	"Esteem" Diffuseness and Neutrality	Residual status qualities	Pattern Maintenance	Esteem

* These categories were mentioned by Parsons, but not developed to the same length as those of performance norms and sanctions.

maintaining as broad and universal a level of analysis as possible. In spite of this recognition, however, it is still doubtful if the theoretical gains have justified the deliberate departure from the more concrete and realistic facts of stratification. If this presentation and interpretation has been correct, then Parsons has finally reached the uncomfortable conclusion of undercutting a central assumption with which he began. Apparently, the paramount values of a society are not ascertainable except through effects that logically should appear only after the determination of those values. Even determining those effects, it should be noted, is a questionable research operation for which no clues are provided. If the values of a society are not directly knowable, then there is no way of testing what is a basic assumption for Parsons—that stratification systems incorporate and express the paramount values of a society. Plausible as the assumption may be, and it is one which underlies much of functional theory generally, it clearly needs its own independent testing. The hope of realizing that goal is considerably dimmed by the difficulties that have been encountered in utilizing similar theoretical orientations in the study of simpler societies. Even in those instances, apparently, the neat analytical structure of functional theory has encountered rather formidable barriers in reality.

The problems that Parsons chose to exclude from consideration may, from one point of view, be advanced as precisely the ones that are most germane and crucial for an adequate theory of stratification. In a complex industrial society such as ours individuals do hold simultaneous positions in a number of different institutional settings. Any realistic determination of their status would have to depend upon some systematic procedure for allocating the influence and importance of each of these spheres relative to one another. Furthermore, the cross-effects of one upon the other would also require some systematic handling for a realistic analysis of American society.

Finally, a serious reservation concerning the theory must be made explicit. The exclusion of power and authority as elements in stratification tends to keep Parsons' theory at an abstract level without the possibility of its coming down to earth easily. No matter what the paramount value standard of a society might be, and assume for the moment that it can be ascertained, some individuals will hold a high-ranking power position in spite of those values and not because of them. This power need not be legitimately open and public, in which case it might be possible to classify it under one of the categories Parsons has provided. Rather, power can be much more subtle and covert as in an economic monopoly or behind-the-scenes political manipulation. In neither case need power become public enough so that negative sanctions would be applied against the individuals commanding such power. The era of the robber barons may never again be repeated in the same form, but the intrigues for economic and political control probably have not ceased entirely. What is even more to the point, the complexity of modern society and its legal forms tends to elevate the process of grabbing power to a highly technical plane not easily understood by anyone but the specialist. The robber barons were crude in comparison with the subtle manipulations required today.

There are, in other words, in any existing society many things done and many more attempted that manage to stay outside of the formal structure of the norms and rules ordinarily governing behavior in that society. One has but to recall the voluminous information about bureaucracies, where established practice appears to be set by informal definitions rather than by formal rules of the organization. Furthermore, it cannot be argued, as Parsons has implied, that these manifestations of power are random and unique and hence outside of the systematic scope of a theory. On the contrary, the deviations may follow a well-recognized pattern in reality, needing only another theoretical approach to systematize their consequences. After all, Parsons' emphasis upon values as the touchstone of human activity leads towards only one possible theoretical solution. As the other theories discussed in this chapter should have made clear, it is possible to begin from some other basis yielding different theoretical results and consequences.

The Davis and Moore paper undertook a less ambitious excursion into functional theory than did Parsons'. They were concerned with setting forth *some* of the principles of a functional theory of social stratification. Yet the two essays were closely related. Both have begun with the assumption of the functional orientation; essentially, an emphasis upon the functional importance of values for social integration. Both have tried to formulate a theory of stratification at an abstract and general level. Both have more or less shunned the path of concrete characteristics that would have limited the applicability of the theory. Further, both essays have conceded a central importance to stratification as a necessary and basic feature of social organization. The Davis and Moore paper was developed principally by plausible extensions of certain basic assumptions that were inherent in a functional view of society.

The first of these assumptions was that stratification was functionally necessary for organized social existence. The assumption was handled as just that; it was not to be proven, but to be used for spelling out some of its implications. The entire intent of the paper was set forth early and the later details could logically be traced back to the key sentence. "As a functioning mechanism a society must somehow distribute its members in social positions and induce them to perform the duties of these positions."[41] Congruent with this requirement was another: society must induce the *desire* in individuals to fill these positions and to perform the duties connected with them.

The second assumption Davis and Moore made was that the social positions in a society were not equal. Socially significant and socially relevant differences between positions were to be expected because the duties associated with those positions would vary as to their social value. Positions would vary then in the importance they were judged to hold for the survival of the society. Secondly, positions would differ by how pleasant or unpleasant were the duties associated with them. Finally, variations would be found in the degree of ability and talent that was required of persons to qualify for the position. These were axiomatic descriptions and generally characteristic of the functional orientation, as the discussion of Parsons' model should have made clear. Some problems, by no means picayune, are raised by these assumptions and are discussed later in this section.

However, if these assumptions can be granted for the moment, then much of the succeeding detail follows readily enough. Davis and Moore's conception of stratification, its causes and manifestations, can be traced rather directly to these assumptions. Societies must provide rewards in order to induce individuals to fill the positions required by the society; positions that must be socially necessary if only because they are recognized. Rewards must be distributed unequally to the various positions because those positions are not equally pleasant nor equally demanding in the training required. The attractions of the positions, in short, are not of equal strength. The conclusion is clear. "The rewards and their distibution become a part of the social order and thus give rise to stratification."[42]

Davis and Moore next moved on to an analysis of the rewards that could be offered by society—the next step logically. Of several types, rewards could contribute to sustenance and comfort. Some could provide humor and diversion. Finally, others could contribute to self-respect and to ego expansion. These rewards, and presumably others that had social value, became built-in features of social positions. They were viewed as "rights" and as prerogatives that were associated with given positions. The consequences, necessarily, led to the creation of a system of social inequality based immediately on the differential rewards attached to positions, and based finally upon the inescapable requirements of social organization itself. Some positions in every society were judged as somehow more important and more crucial for the values of that society, and consequently required that they be filled by the most qualified. In turn, those who performed such vitally necessary duties were rewarded with greater prestige and with other socially valued benefits that society could confer. The total effect was the creation of a social hierarchy, in which generally the rank of a position was an index of its importance and was matched by rewards that were commensurate with that level of importance. This did not mean that the form or the extent of inequality would be the same in all societies. Each society, after all, defined its own needs according to its own standard of values. It did mean, however, that inequality to some degree existed in all societies. Furthermore, the rationale was clear; inequality was a functional necessity for continued social existence.

Davis and Moore proceeded next to amplify and translate their two assumptions into analytical criteria for identifying the relative ranks of positions: (1) the functional importance of different positions; and (2) the ability and talent needed to fill them. In the first instance, it should be clear from their opening statements, those positions which were allowed to contribute more directly to social survival were at the same time positions holding relatively higher rank than those that made lesser contributions. This proposition was logically consistent with the initial assumptions. However, as Davis and Moore have pointed out, ". . . functional importance is difficult to establish."[43] The bugaboo of reality and empirical proof apparently plagues functional theory at the same vital point repeatedly. Davis and Moore suggested, however, that one index of functional importance was the degree to which a position could perform those functions not duplicated by other positions. A second suggested index was the degree to which other positions were dependent upon any one position. In spite of these clues, the solution is by no means easy. One-of-a-kind functions might be fulfilled by some positions that otherwise do not seem to have the sense of functional importance. A safecracker would fill the bill, but the position contributes little to general social survival. The second index suggested, similarly, is as difficult to establish as the functional character of a position itself. The formulation of Davis and Moore on this point is logically tempting but empirically hard to practice.

The variations in the levels of ability and talent required by different positions was a second analytical criterion suggested as a possible lead to help establish the functional rank of a position. The longer and more demanding the training, the more likely there was to be a scarcity of qualified personnel to fill positions of importance. This scarcity in turn, they argued, tended to confer a relatively higher rank than otherwise. On the other hand, if the required skills were few and not especially difficult to learn, large numbers of people would be able to meet the requirements, and consequently such positions could claim only relatively little prestige. The formula was simple: positions that required long and difficult training and considerable expenditures of money and time for such training must be made sufficiently rewarding in the end to induce individuals to go through the training period in order to become qualified. "This means, in effect, that the position must be high in the social scale—must command great prestige, high salary, ample leisure, and the like."[44] This conclusion and its logic are strongly reminiscent of classical economic theory. After all, this defense of functional importance and its consequences for social stratification are not far different from a classical supply and demand analysis applied precisely to the same phenomena. Indeed, Adam Smith reached almost the same conclusions, and for almost the same reasons, when he discussed why certain occupations should command a higher remuneration than others.

With this basic orientation, then, Davis and Moore moved next to an analysis of major societal functions and their relationship to stratification. The extent to which any given society emphasized one or another of these functions, they proposed, would determine the particular form that its system of stratification would take. This argument strongly resembled the basic thesis that Parsons had advanced; namely, that the paramount values of a society, the core around which it was organized and in a sense to which it was dedicated, would dictate the basis and character of its system of stratification. Davis and Moore advanced the same general idea, although with different categories. The logic that supported these categories, however, was the same as Parsons': the outstanding function of a society (*i. e.,* its central values) set the mold and the basis for stratification.

Religion was the first function considered. Its functional necessity in all societies, Davis and Moore have traced to "the fact the human society achieves its unity primarily through the possession by its members of certain ultimate values and ends in common."[45] In societies where religion was paramount, all social duties connected with it would rank high in importance. Religious functionaries would be powerful figures under those circumstances. Furthermore, power might be enhanced even more by surrounding religious positions with elaborate rituals and endowing them with a mystical and supernatural content that would separate them dramatically from other positions. Such power could also be used to control accessibility to those positions by emphasizing special skills and technical competence to a degree that would discourage all but the most dedicated. At the same time, the religious functionary would add to his own prestige by making his position ever more wonderful and ever more necessary in the eyes of others. It would all depend, to a great degree, upon the willingness of others to accept the importance of religious values as paramount. The medieval social order exemplified the extreme emphasis on religion. A society centered on science and technology would exemplify the opposite extreme. In the first, the strong religious emphasis obviously enhanced the positions associated with that function. In the second case, the priesthood had lost status as the values of traditionalism and the dependence upon the supernatural were replaced by rationalism and science.

A second institution that Davis and Moore specified was government. "The main functions of government are, internally, the ultimate enforcement of norms, the final arbitration of conflicting interests, and the overall planning and direction of society; and externally, the handling of war and diplomacy."[46] As was the case for religion, governmental functionaries have held power because of the importance their position was believed to hold in social organization. Similarly, social inequality was an expected consequence in this sphere as in others because the interests of society were so much at stake in these positions and because the number of such positions was relatively limited and demanding in loyalty, sincerity and skill. Hence, the power and authority associated with the tasks of government were commensurately higher. This was not to imply that such power was unlimited, for by the very fact of its potential, that power was carefully restricted by such rules and norms as were necessary to protect the general interest from selfish personal interests.

The same reasoning was applied to other functions related to wealth, property, and labor and to technical knowledge, which Davis and Moore considered as areas of great functional importance. In each case, they indicated the importance of the function for social organization and then inferred that relatively higher rank would be accorded to positions thereby involved. As was noted above, where any one of these functions became paramount, it would be expected that positions associated with its performance would simultaneously gain and hold greater prestige and power than those of other positions.

Davis and Moore concluded their exposition with a statement of five general propositions that they believed could characterize the basic differences between various systems of stratification. To a great extent, these characteristics fall within the logical framework they have detailed.

(1) The degree of specialization will affect the number and extent of gradations of power and prestige in a society. Presumably, the more specialized tasks that were recognized in a society, the more the proliferation of prestige and power positions, with finer gradations separating them from one another. (2) The type of functions emphasized will vary between societies, generally according to whether

sacred or secular matters are stressed. An emphasis upon sacred concerns will produce a social rigidity that tends to limit both the specialization of positions and the social mobility between positions. A primitive society probably would exemplify the sacred type. In a secular society, the tendency is toward a proliferation of positions usually as a consequence of the increased division of labor required by advanced technology and economic organization. (3) The extent of invidious distinctions made between positions will vary between societies and will be measurable. (4) The degree of opportunity typically available within a stratified system is another characteristic that would vary between societies. At one extreme there can be an open and highly mobile set of conditions in which individuals can move with relative ease between strata. At the other extreme, positions will be relatively closed and rigidified so that social mobility becomes relatively difficult and frozen. (5) Finally, there is variation to be expected in the degree of solidarity found among the occupants of a class or stratum. At one pole, a class can be tightly organized, while at the other there is a total lack of such organization.

The intention behind these five propositions was to provide clues as to the basic variables determining stratification. Further, these clues were presented in terms that had enough empirical reference to allow for measurement, and thereby for comparisons between societies. The variables mentioned, then, would possess theoretical relevance as well as be highly susceptible to research procedures. Although its research accessibility is certainly a desirable feature for a theory to have, the assumptions that make the criteria relevant to begin with are themselves sorely in need of testing and analysis. It would be illogical from almost any point of view to proceed to a research on the criteria Davis and Moore have enumerated without first establishing the validity of the theoretical defense of the assumptions upon which the criteria themselves depend for their meaning.

The Davis and Moore argument, and thereby the functional view as a whole, has been challenged from two different quarters and in two different ways. Tumin[47] has questioned their basic premises, especially the one that assumes stratification to be an inevitable feature inherent in social organization. Although he readily admitted that stratification and inequality have been the ubiquitous mark of human societies since antiquity, Tumin voiced considerable doubt in using that historical fact as proof for the necessity of stratification. Specifically, he questioned the criterion of functional importance upon which Davis and Moore have built their case. Tumin's criticisms can be condensed to several basic counter-arguments, which, if correct, would seriously shake the propositions of the functionalists. First, the functional importance of a position was admittedly difficult to ascertain in fact. As Davis and Moore have suggested, the procedural answer was to consider matters in reverse order: those positions with higher prestige and power were by that fact functionally more important than those with lesser rewards. The dead-end was the same one encountered by Parsons and answered in the same way. In his theory, as well as in the present case, as Tumin has pointed out, the suggested procedure is a tautology which does nothing to strengthen the supposition, let alone to validate it. What is or is not functional for a social system cannot be established by using the same basis as that employed for establishing the functional contention in the first place. Yet, the thread of argument that runs through functional theory is of that order.

A related point raised by Tumin was that it was equally possible for *dysfunctions* to develop from the social process, even as Davis and Moore have used that process to explain *functional* consequences. Possibly, Tumin argued, those who occupy positions of privilege might use their power to restrict the further recruitment of new occupants. In this way, the supposedly smooth flow of inducements and motivations to attract the best qualified would be seriously interrupted by those who wanted to keep the advantage all to themselves rather than sharing with others. Davis and Moore have replied that this criticism did not apply because they were primarily concerned with the stratification of *positions* rather than of *individuals*. In other words, the possibility that individuals under certain circumstances might try to insure what they had by keeping others away, did not affect the propositions concerning the manner in which *positions* were analyzed. Indeed, Davis and Moore themselves had admitted in their discussion of religious functions that individuals might well raise barriers against the entry of other qualified persons by manipulating the power at their disposal. Yet, one seriously wonders what a theory might be losing by its insistence upon abstractions of this order. The question of power and its social use, as already indicated in the criticism made of Parsons' theory, is a real one that properly belongs in the analysis of stratification.

Finally, Tumin has objected most strongly to the statement of Davis and Moore concerning the continued inevitability of social inequality. Although ready to concede that a society must distribute power and property unequally in order to get necessary tasks performed, Tumin has denied the conclusion that such distribution must always result in social inequality. Is it not possible, he argued that ". . . under propitious circumstances, . . . the tradition [is developed] that each man is as socially worthy as all other men so long as he performs his appropriate tasks conscientiously?"[48] Davis and Moore have refused to take up the ideological gambit thus presented them and have preferred instead to steer clear of that dimension raised by Tumin's question. Instead, they have replied that Tumin has confused the idea of differential rewards with that of the inequality of opportunity. They were totally concerned with the first. Individuals, even under the conditions Tumin has suggested, would still be distributed in some manner to perform the necessary tasks of organized social life. The growth and maturing of social inequality based on invidious distinctions, Davis and Moore have correctly maintained, need not develop in all societies. Even within their framework there is nothing to prevent some society from achieving social equality in spite of the dissimilarity of tasks that must be performed by the individuals in that society. That this goal has only been a utopian fantasy thus far in human history, however, does little to support any optimism as to its eventual realization.

From another quarter, the functional view has been criticized for its assumption that stratification must result from functional differentiation.[49] Just as Tumin had indicated the *social* dysfunctions of stratification, Foote and Hatt in their paper on social mobility and economic advancement have raised the matter of *economic* dysfunctions. The growth of a mass market with its "massification" of tastes, coupled with the leveling of the income distribution that has been taking place in the American economy, have operated to increase the demand for social equality. "We may as a society," Foote and Hatt have noted, "be on the verge of discovering that general economic advancement and social equalitarianism are interdependent, while retention of steep stratification and rivalrous personal mobility is economically stultifying."[50] The social demand for equality in consumption, whether of automobiles or college educations, would lead to increased economic demands that could possibly be met as income levels rise for more and more people. This increased demand, in turn, could stimulate greater production. One major consequence would be the trend toward economic equality as products became less expensive and more available to an even broader market.

The implications set forth in this proposition go contrary to some of the assumptions made by Davis and Moore and others. If economic equality is near, as Foote and Hatt have contended, both in income and in consumption patterns, then a basis for rewards presently important at least in American society, would be seriously modified. Money, and the opportunity to consume it in a way that can publicize an individual's status to the community, is an important part of our reward system. The needed incentive and motivation visualized by the functionalists, therefore, must be modified as these particular rewards no longer would serve their purpose. The counter argument that can be raised by the functionalists, of course, would simply be that other rewards would be substituted. However, the social channels whereby this modification is introduced, if all the supposed conditions do occur, are not clearly delineated within the framework of their theory.

Even more basic to the whole argument is the possibility that Foote and Hatt have raised, that the economic requirements of equality—greater markets, increased productivity, new capital ventures, and the like—might well demand social equality, especially in a society that is economically advanced. Where the economic basis for social distinction is removed, and, we might add, for functional reasons, the result possibly might produce equality as a social consequence.

The major difficulty with the functional view of stratification centers around the definition and interpretation of "functional importance." It is a concept that is difficult to define and even more difficult to measure, yet it is central to that view. The functionalist tends to assume that what exists in society must, almost by definition, be socially important. There are few, if any, survivals of practices or customs that are maintained out of habit alone. Further, there is a belief in a social logic by which greater prestige and power must be given for some purpose. The real problem is caused by the lack of any independent standard by which functional importance can be evaluated. "Function," as used in biology, can be ascertained with some clarity, and "functional importance" can finally be determined by the contribution of an organ to the maintenance of life. If death results without it, then the importance of that organ is quite clearly established. There is really no analogy in the study of social forms. The life or death of a society would be a poor standard for establishing the importance of a social function, even if it could be ascertained. Furthermore, it is hard, if not impossible, to determine just how necessary any function is for the continuance of society. The fact that a function—such as religion, government, or the family—is universally found in human society, is not finally proof of its necessity.

The determination of what is functional and what is dysfunctional in a social system is another difficulty. It seems to depend very much on the perspective that is assumed by the analyst. The criticisms by Tumin and by Foote and Hatt are important because they have described possible dysfunctions within the same analytical system that Davis and Moore had stressed as functional. Undoubtedly, there are other such exceptions. If there is no unequivocal standard for determining the functionality of some social form or practice, except by the arbitrariness of one analyst's logic, then here lies theoretical quicksand.

In conclusion it should be noted that the general procedure of functional theory appears to be to begin with existing social forms and then to account plausibly for their existence in a systematic fashion. A good deal of Parsons' and Davis and Moore's conclusions can be reconstructed in that fashion. The direction of this logic, almost in the very nature of the case, omits the possibility of dealing with social change in the system by the same theory. Aside from some notion of equilibrium—the tendency of a system to integrate and to establish an internally consistent set of practises—there are no theoretical categories by which change can be taken systematically into account in functionalism. Both functional theories discussed have deliberately omitted the dimension of power precisely because it can produce changes and variations which the ideal model cannot handle. By any social analysis it seems evident that change, and not continued stability, is the mark of human society.

Warner: Status by Community Reputation

WARNER'S contributions to the study of social class in America have been significant, by volume, by the research he has stimulated, and by the interest he has helped to create in the subject.[51] Throughout it all, he has been heavily criticized, more so than any other writer on stratification.

Yet, at the same time, his ideas have managed to spread wider and to have greater appeal than those of any other. In part, that appeal has been helped by a style of reporting that was descriptive and almost fictional in tone and by the careful avoidance of weighty abstractions and a sociological vocabulary. His books read with a homey intimacy as if he were writing about a town in which he had lived most of his life. The reader is forever recognizing familiar touches which make him feel more at home. In addition, the phrasing of his studies within such popular values as "democracy" and the "American Dream," has strengthened the appeal even more; even the striving for status fits snugly into the American's self-conception. This appeal is even stronger in an era of relative economic security and political conservatism, whereas it would have been miserably out of place in an earlier decade of protest.

Warner was trained as a social anthropologist. He did his field work with an Australian tribe before he moved in on the New England community of Yankee City and his first investigation of class. The training was evident throughout his work, in the concepts and methods he used and, more significantly, in his orientation. It was not so much that he eschewed theory as that he operated with only a minimal number of rather gross organizing categories in mind that became explicit after the data were collected. For the most part, these were the traditional categories of the field-working anthropologist and were adapted to the study of primitive societies. Rather than comprising a theory of class or social systems, the categories were more a device for classification meant to sensitize the observer to certain constancies in human social organization. What Warner did was to describe the events of stratification as he found them in such towns as Yankee City and Jonesville, and within such social units as the family, age and sex groupings, cliques and associations. The description was specifically bound to the particular community he studied in much the same way that an anthropological monograph is meant to describe one society and its practices. Warner went into Yankee City with the same orientation that he had used in studying the "simple horde of Australia," as he himself granted. This approach has led Warner into the greatest difficulty with his critics, who not unjustly have insisted that Yankee City, or any other American community for that matter, was not the simple, isolated and self-sufficient community that Warner was ready to assume it was. These towns were part of a national economy, a national polity, and a national value complex.

This theoretical looseness, this sense of unanticipated discoveries and surprises, was indicated again and again. The clique, for example, was "discovered" in Yankee City late in the field investigation,[52] and a chapter in that same book was entitled with the same feeling of exploration: "How the Several Classes Were Discovered." The initial research on class, Warner explained, began with a "general economic interpretation of human behavior," but evidence "began to accumulate" that made the acceptance of the hypothesis difficult.[53] It sounded like the dirty linen of scientific honesty, but what the initial hypothesis was, or what proof there was to reject it, was never made entirely clear. This is not the procedure of social science, no matter what concessions have to be made to expediency and ignorance in the actual investigation itself. For Warner, the research arena and the conclusions gained seemed to be endowed with a life and vitality all of their own. The events set their own framework, so to speak, while the researcher supposedly remained as a passive but sensitive recorder of their unfolding. This is neither good history nor good anthropology.

Warner's theory must be understood as a method, antithetical as that statement might appear at first. His conception of social stratification was developed principally from the repeated characteristics he observed within several American communities. The theory assumed an explicit structure, it appeared, only after he started to make sense out of the information he had collected. Therefore, that explanation contained a number of assumptions and conclusions that he had not explored systematically. Instead, "class" was and is what he "found" it to be.

Class was a social reality that people within a community recognized. Its reality was located in the consensus of the community about where individuals belonged in the local class hierarchy, and in the general agreement on the criteria that were used to place them there. "By class is meant two or more orders of people who are believed to be, and are accordingly ranked by the members of the community, in socially superior and inferior positions."[54] A "theory" of social class, then, involved making those judgments systematic and objective; a fair statement, on the whole, of what Warner in fact did. The job of the social scientist, furthermore, was to discern the vocabulary, read the symbols, and designate the occupants of the several classes in the community he studied. The number, the designations, and the characteristics of the classes were to be identified by the citizens themselves, not "determined" supposedly through the independent knowledge of the observer of that community. Hence, in Yankee City, Warner "discovered" in this manner that there were six classes, two in each of the upper, middle, and lower, from the information supplied by his respondents. In Jonesville, only five classes were found. Jonesville had no division of the upper class into those from "old" families and the more successful, recently mobile arrivals from the middle class, as in Yankee City. Certainly, the sociologist or anthropologist was active in identifying these categories; it couldn't have been otherwise. Warner, however, continued to underplay that role of the social scientist.

Warner's method was to move in on a community and interview it concerning a wide range of its activity—what were its clubs and associations and who belonged to them, what churches there were and their membership, the occupations and incomes of its citizens, family histories, the character of different sections of town and who lived in them, and above all where people ranked other people they knew according to their standing in the community. From all of this information, Warner identified several social segments, or strata, consisting of all those who were in the same prestige position, by what others said of them and by the social characteristics they possessed. A person's social standing in the community then was a function of his income, occupation, where he lived, and most importantly, his reputation.

An individual's class position became for Warner synonymous with the judgment of how the individual was known to others and how he was ranked by them relative to other persons. In later studies, Warner objectified this procedure in the form of two measures—Evaluated Participation (EP) and the Index of Status Characteristics (ISC)—but they came from what he had observed. The first was based upon interview data secured from community informants. These "judges," drawn from what was suspected to be the entire class range, placed other individuals that they knew about in what they believed were the true class positions the individuals occupied in the community. The lists were then compared with each other and by comparing the judgments made, some measure of agreement was obtained that put persons in their proper class; that is, the social stratum that most persons in the community would agree upon. The final list represented the consensus among the informants as to the real class structure, detailed by the names of the occupants of the several classes.

The ISC was a more objective device that could be constructed independently with a minimum of background information about the individual and without relying upon community judges or informants. It consisted of a summation of an individual's score on four sub-indices: occupation, source of income, house type and dwelling area. Each of these was divided into a seven-point scale, on which a person was scored for the kind of work he did, the kind of house he lived in, and the section of town in which he lived. A physician, for example, who was self-employed, who owned a fairly comfortable home in a good neighborhood, would rank rather high by his ISC score, as he probably would in the estimation of his community. One of his patients, say, who was a day laborer, working for a local building contractor, and who rented a three-room house near the railroad yards, would score very low by his ISC. The total score, in both examples, would be the sum of the points each had measured on these four characteristics. Class position was then presumably derived from that score.

Both measures, EP and ISC, have been subjected to a heavy critical barrage for their rationale, their methodology, and their validity.[55] The major shortcoming of these measures was that they remained quite arbitrary in their derivation and use in spite of the patina of numbers and measurement scales. In his use of ISC, for example, Warner gave no indication where the scale was to be divided so as to be translated into class terms without using the most arbitrary set of estimates. Furthermore, the measure itself was highly questionable because the way the "points" were allocated depended upon arbitrary divisions not upon an independently ascertained cutting point.

Some impression of the tone of Warner's class categories can be obtained by briefly describing the six classes he "found."[56] The upper-upper class was, naturally enough, at the top of the heap. It held a superior position principally because its occupants came from families that had been in the community for some time and had come from a line of wealth and social standing that had had the time to age properly. They were a social aristocracy. They knew it and the community accepted it. They remained exclusive about their membership and as far as possible kept their marriages within the clan. The lower-upper classes, immediately below, consisted of those who were wealthy, oftentimes wealthier than those of the upper-upper stratum. However, their wealth was new, much too new, nor did they have the proper family background, and both factors operated to exclude them from membership at the social summit. By income, residence, and the extent of their social participation in the community, the lower-uppers resembled those above them, but they lacked the proper graces, the right tastes, and the accepted social mannerisms. The Phillip Starrs, for example, one of the fictional lower-upper class families described in Yankee City, were looked down upon by members of the upper crust for doing things too perfectly, too elaborately, and too much for effect.[57]

The upper-middle class consisted of professionals and substantial businessmen. Although they had a comfortable income, it was less than that of the upper classes. They lived as their income allowed—comfortably, but they could not afford the expensive tastes of those in the strata above them. They were, nonetheless, respected in the community and carried their share of community responsibility and time given to good works. The lower-middle class included the white collar employees and the smaller businessmen of the town. They were those of whom it was said they approximated the Protestant ethic, "being careful with their money, saving, farsighted, forever anxious about what their neighbors think, and continually concerned about respectability."[58]

The two lower classes were separated from the class structure above them principally by occupation and income. They were workingmen of all types and smaller tradesmen with relatively low incomes. The upper segment of this class, however, counted among their virtues cleanliness, honesty, and respectability, all of which were important for them to maintain. The lower-lower class at the very bottom, on the other hand, lived in the slums and were not considered as at all respectable; instead, they were thought to be immoral and generally anti-social. Without respectability, without ambition for success, and without the desire to improve themselves, the occupants of the lower-lower class almost did not belong to the community except in the most negative terms.

These then were the classes that Warner found existing in the American communities he studied. There were variations to be sure, but on the whole, class distinctions were drawn along the dimensions that were noted in these descriptions.

A further characteristic of Warner's view was the belief that the prestige position of the individual was manifested in each of the several institutional facets of the community's social structure. The social participation of individuals, as well as the very structure of the community, therefore, became class conditioned from the start. Clearly, class for Warner was a feature so basic that its manifestations wove themselves throughout the structure and fibre of the community.[59] The rituals of family living were influenced by the class of the family. Voluntary associations were class-graded; who participated and who held power in them was class-determined. Church congregations similarly showed the same class effects. The school was not immune from the mark of class, for it served as the ladder for social mobility to those who learned the skills and the aspirations for such class travel. At the same time, the school could also frustrate those from the lower classes, for it was dominated and dedicated to middle class values, which lower class children could not or did not care to share. The factory was a museum for class because it was by the work that a man did that his class position was symbolized for all to read. Increasing mechanization, at least in the shoe factories of Yankee City, had leveled the traditional skill hierarchy to a common denominator and at the same time increased the gap between those who worked and those who owned and managed. The once proud craftsman had been overwhelmed by the machine tenders.

Warner's orientation was not a theory, although it may be convenient to label it as that at times. What he has done is to describe in relatively free fashion certain relationships that, at best, hold true for single communities. Such description falls far short of the systematic unequivocal statements of relationships that are the very character of theory. His conceptualization remains fuzzy, and the use of "class" shifts with each different phrase, piling up a mixture of meanings that should have been carefully separated in analysis.[60] At best, Warner's orientation commits him to studies at the level of single communities rather than to a theory of stratification with broader scope. For the community is the real limit of the class symbolism and class vocabulary that Warner depended upon. The placement of individuals by personal knowledge, the class meaning of street names and neighborhoods, and the class significance of cliques, clubs, and associations were criteria that could only have meaning within relatively limited geographic boundaries. Neither the large city, nor the national society, could be handled within the compass of his method or conceptualization. It was not accidental, therefore, that Warner's studies, and others like them, have been conducted in small towns with populations of not more than 17,000, as in Yankee City, and more often closer to 6,000 as in Jonesville. For that reason, Warner's findings have remained as localized, temporal descriptions, with some suggestions for a theory of social stratification but with no hard theoretical lines to follow.

Pfautz and Duncan, in their critique, have demonstrated that not only does Warner's work fall far short of "portraying the stratification structure of American society," that not only does it suffer from serious methodological deficiencies in the reliability of its findings, but "that their [Warner and his associates] conceptual formulations are inadequate to account even for their own findings, are theoretically uninformed in relation to the existing literature on social stratification, and further, are ideologically suspect."[61] Yet, Warner's work seems to have had a greater impact upon more people than any other in the study of class. Marx and Weber remain almost unread, while the functionalists remain too esoteric to be understood except by the most willing. Warner's orientation, more than any other, is most evident in the voluminous research on class, and this in spite of its inherent and recognized shortcomings and deficiencies. It has indeed been a long century since Marx to watch the shifting emphasis from Marx's class analysis to Warner's status and prestige descriptions.

Summary: Some Comparisons between Theories

THE preceding pages of this chapter have detailed the structure and orientation of four theories of social stratification. These four were selected because their combined impact has been considerable and because they represented the range of theories that have been devised for the study of stratification. Combined, they portray all of the facets and elements of the subject that are significant. The ideas they presented have in some form or other provided the basis for most of what is known about class and its place in social organization. Some of those ideas have even become a relatively permanent fixture in the popular thinking about the subject.

It was clear almost from the first that not all of the theories were equal in their sophistication or analytical skill. Each of them has considered class differently. They have a range not only of ideologies, but also of abstractions. In different ways, the theories shared some similarities and presented some contrasts. It seems advisable, therefore, to devote this summary to a few central questions raised in the study of class and to compare the theories on these points.

The first question that might be raised concerns the sources of stratification. How, in other words, did each theory conceptualize the causes and the basis for stratification in society? Marx's answer was clear, direct, and unequivocal. The economic system, broadly defined, was the source of class divisions and the force for continued stratification. The means of production, which for Marx constituted the central and basic fact of social organization, created a set of relationships that flowed out to color and define all other social relationships as well. Those who owned the means of production were the ruling class in every era of human history and those who did not were the oppressed and exploited. All social facts for Marx stemmed from this basic and inevitable class dichotomy. Social position, power, wealth, and all relations between men were finally colored by their relative positions in the economic order. The source of stratification for Marx then could be traced back to the very production of those life's necessities from which all other social facts followed.

Weber constructed a revised view of Marx's economic determinism. He recognized, with Marx, the importance of economic processes, economic values, and economic relationships for society. "Class" was for him the special concept meant to describe those relationships of the market. In addition, and this constituted his unique contribution, Weber defined two other dimensions, "status" and "party." The first referred to social differences based on life-chances and life-styles and was the product of community relationships. A status structure, therefore, no matter how closely it might be tied to and determined by market relationships, was planted firmly in the social life of the community rather than in the impersonal and rational affairs of the economy. The social power that derived from these status relationships had its own sphere of operation and its own reality, just as did the economic power that derived from economic organization. Similarly, political power represented a third dimension of stratification. It too was a consequence of community relationships and might be closely bound in actuality to both class and status hierarchies. Analytically, political power was a phenomenon of the "party," which was organized for that purpose. Hence, the source of stratification for Weber came from each of these three central elements of organized society.

The answer of the functionalists to the question came from their basic assumption that society must satisfactorily meet certain basic requirements for organized existence. To accomplish this, societies were conceptualized as organized around certain positions that served to meet these needs. These positions, in turn, came to be evaluated differently according to their importance for social organization. Not all were equally valuable nor equally worthy. Not all required the same training to be filled. The differentiation gave rise to a system of stratification, which essentially organized these positions hierarchically according to the importance and value they were believed to hold. Generally, those positions considered to be the most vital for existence and those that contributed most to the social values that were highly cherished, were endowed with the highest rank and the greatest prestige. The result, finally, was a stratified social hierarchy based on the values, needs, and indeed the survival of society itself.

Warner was not fully explicit concerning the source of stratification. What he stated in various ways was that stratification resulted from community judgments made about individuals. These evaluations were the basis for determining an individual's status and were themselves based upon a complex of factors evaluating occupation, social participation, family background, and style of life. Stratification, for Warner, proceeded directly from an estimate made of the individual *qua* individual. Although it depended upon a number of what might be considered as objective criteria, the judgment itself was personal. Status was a real category, according to Warner, that affected all relationships between persons in the community. Unlike the others who rested the bulk of their theory upon the operation of rather large, essentially impersonal social forces, Warner located the source of stratification finally in the personalized judgments of a community about its own members.

A companion question to that concerning the source of stratification is one on the presumed social necessity of stratification. As noted earlier, this question carries with it an ideological commitment that has been indicated in the discussion of each theory. If the theory concluded that stratification was a necessary and inevitable feature of society, it has expressed one possible set of social beliefs concerning the nature of social organization and its purposes. Just as at the other extreme, to have maintained that stratification was not and need not be inevitable created an opposing ideology.

For Marx, stratification was inevitable by the very nature of the historical process itself. Linked as classes were to the basic elements of existence, he had no other consistent choice but to hold that classes were always present. Indeed, his survey of history was meant to prove just that, as well as to set forth the developments he read in the historical changes in class composition. Since man must constantly produce to live, some men must inevitably own the means of that production while others must labor to obtain the necessities for their subsistence. Yet, Marx held on to the firm conviction that in the future classes and class antagonisms would disappear when all men labored for the benefit of all.

In somewhat similar fashion, and for somewhat similar reasons, the functionalists also defended the inevitability of stratification, but without the eschatology. Because they went back analytically to the basic components of survival to find the source of stratification, such division was as inevitable as social life itself. Distinctions between individuals in society must always be made because certain positions will always lie closer to the core of that which is socially necessary and the occupants of those positions therefore will wear the mantle of power, prestige and importance.

Weber also implied that stratification was an inevitable social feature. He based his conclusion, however, upon necessary consequences produced by the operations of the economic, social, and political orders in social organization. The competitiveness that was characteristic of the market situation must produce differential success for the various participants. Not everyone can achieve the same stratum because the market operates for some to succeed and others to lose. Similarly, the distribution of prestige in the community and the distribution of political power must also result in a hierarchy of status differences. The values of the community upon which status depended, created different life styles and different opportunities according to the means and talents of individuals. The inevitability for Weber, therefore, was not found directly in a survival component, as was true for Marx and the functionalists, but rather in the operation of organized social existence itself.

Warner made no explicit statement about this question. However, there was implicit in his writings a strong belief that stratification was a necessary social phenomenon. In his later writing, which is much more ideologically explicit than was true for the Yankee City studies, he looked upon stratification as a problem for a democracy and at the same time has tried to prove that opportunities for entrance into the upper status positions were as available as ever before.[62] What was implicit in these views was that stratification existed although its anti-democratic features could be counteracted by maintaining an open class system with sufficient opportunities for upward mobility.

The answers to the questions on the necessity of stratification have touched upon a third question that can be addressed to each of the theories. What does each foresee as the future trend of stratification? This question, more clearly than the preceding one, brings forth the ideology that each theorist has assumed. For, in commenting upon the direction that stratification was expected to take, especially in industrial societies, the theorist had to indicate the implications and latent consequences of his theory.

Marx, of course, built his views of class and stratification around this point. His theory of dialectical materialism as an historical dynamic traced in a detailed manner what he anticipated would happen in the future. Up to and including capitalism, stratification has always been marked by conflict between the polarized classes in society. The conflict was inevitable, for the interests of each class were brought increasingly into direct and glaring contradiction. The inherent requirements and demands of capitalism forced the creation of a proletariat, whose position was to become degradingly worse until such time as the proletariat became aware of itself as a class and revolted against the existing social order. Beyond that point, Marx hypothesized, class conflict would cease and stratification would emerge upon more socially worthy ground than that of class antagonism.

Just as the inherent dynamics of a capitalistic economy must drive it to its own destruction, Marx felt class-inspired struggles must cease with the triumph of the proletariat.

Weber saw continued conflict as a mark of class differences in the economic order. This, for him, was simply the result of the inherent logic of the market. While the market was dominated by rational values, Weber saw the status structure of the community as dominated by traditional ones. Those in upper status positions attempted to insure their position by increasingly greater reliance upon irrational criteria. The tendency, initiated by those in high status positions, was to move toward a caste system where status became an hereditary position bolstered by ritual and tradition. This was possible within the personalized context of the community, where it was not in the more impersonal context of the market situation. As long as status remained dependent to any significant degree upon the market, it was possible for individuals to attain status through their successful efforts in the economic sphere. This could mean a continual turnover among the occupants of the various statuses. The insecurities of this situation plus the attainment of economic stability in the later phases of capitalism, turned the eyes of the successful toward those means which would freeze the system to their advantage. Entry to the upper status positions became closed, principally by appeal to such irrational criteria that were no longer accessible, as proper family lineage or membership in necessarily exclusive organizations, as the D.A.R. and similarly restrictive groups. The status structure thereby would be separated from the economic. As this movement was completed, high status positions no longer would be open to late arrivals. Status thereafter was to be defined as an hereditary position rather than one to be attained solely by means of the individual's own accomplishments. Exactly how probable Weber felt that process to be, he did not indicate. Yet, he noted the evidences for it, and he presented a highly plausible defense for its development.

Functional theory, as has been noted, had no explicit

position with regard to change in or dynamics of social systems. Its only stand in respect to future developments was one based upon notions of equilibrium. Contradictions within a social system tended to be balanced and corrected, for the tendency was towards attaining consistency between the value structure and the ranking and rewards of positions reflecting those values. Should the inconsistencies become too great, the functionalist implied, the system would have to change and become organized around a new set of values that could integrate the society. The bases of stratification, of course, would similarly change. When a religiously-oriented society, for example, moved toward such guiding values as competition and economic rationality, the formerly high status positions based upon dominant religious institutions would lose their standing to positions that were based upon the institutions organized around the newly emerging values. Whatever the direction of movement, however, the functionalist would hold that "proper" adjustments and modifications would occur in the bases of stratification.

Warner made no statement concerning the future character or quality of social stratification. He tended to assume that the system would continue with minor modifications in the degree of mobility or in the particular occupants of any one class in any given community. Individuals, he implied, will continue to strive for status under the existing set of social values and they will be accorded their just rewards within the judgments of their communities for that effort. Since Warner was not concerned with basic analytical properties of stratification systems and the place of those systems within a theory of society, he obviously could not extend his views to cover future possibilities and emergent trends.

One final question might be posed in this summation that has been more or less explicitly considered in each of the theories. Because of its importance to a theory of stratification it should be included again at this point as a final comparative device. When the theories are considered as to the limits of applicability of a stratification system, clear differences emerge. This can have two connotations, both of which are evident in the theories under discussion. First, it can be interpreted as, what is the range of applicability of the categories and the analysis used in the theory? Or, it can refer to the range that any given empirical system of stratification is intended to cover. For Marx, the two connotations were merged into one universalistic view. His theory was deliberately intended to apply to all human societies, regardless of time or place, since he had placed them within an all-encompassing evolutionary historical process. All societies, in effect, must progress through the necessary historical stages, each with its own clear forms fitted to its particular stage of development.

The two connotations noted above were kept separate by Weber. On the one hand, his categories were meant to be universally applicable insofar as they referred to characteristics of social organization regardless of its specific form. On the other hand, Weber recognized explicitly that the limits of a given system of stratification extended only to the boundaries of the national society itself. The market, for example, covered the economic order of a society and was necessarily limited to those boundaries. The status and political hierarchies, on the other hand, were placed within the community and hence were confined to limits narrower than those of the society. Status and party, within Weber's definition, depended upon communal actions, and hence a system of stratification based upon them could only go as far as the meaningful limits of those actions. Yet, it was also evident that the categories Weber used were meant to have universal applicability, at least to industrial societies.

The functionalists followed a similar differentiation of meanings and came to conclusions similar to Weber's. Their categories were meant to have universal applicability, since the functionalists were concerned with stratification in the abstract. However, any one system was limited to a given society, for it was the organizing values of that society which finally determined the content, character, and basis of the stratification hierarchy.

Finally, Warner was explicitly concerned with the community as the effective range for the application of his notions. The dependence upon personal judgment and upon a consensus of specific class symbols meant that a stratification system could only extend as far as the knowledge about those judgments and symbols applied. His theory was not adapted to deal with the peculiar elements of a national society, or indeed, even with those of a large urban area. Whether his categories could have universal applicability, in the sense that it has been used above, is doubtful. Certainly, at best, Warner was concerned with the peculiarities of American class structure and not industrial societies generally. Since he did not consider the institutional units of a social system as abstract categories, say in the manner of the functionalists, his theory did not contain those elements that could give it meaningful application beyond the community.

It would be foolish and to no purpose to make a single decision as to the utility of each of these theories. The discussions and critical points raised for each of them should provide sufficient material for anyone to come to his own conclusions about that decision. There is still a long way to go to attain a feeling of security with any single theory of social stratification. Part of the difficulty, as is discussed in the next chapter, is tied to methodological problems. In other words, it does little good to have a wonderfully consistent theory that can never be applied to reality nor ever be tested against things as they are. A good theory, in short, will be the one that systematizes all we know and suspect about the nature of class in society and sensitizes us to other aspects of that phenomenon that formerly were clouded in ignorance.

CHAPTER III

The Methodology of Class

THEORY IS BUT ONE SIDE OF THE coin of scientific knowledge. Method is the other. Theory requires the imaginative reconstruction of the world to organize and to order our perceptions of that world. The aim of methodology is to phrase and justify the procedure for getting reliable knowledge about that world. The two scientific acts are intertwined. For as theory dictates a methodology, methodology in turn modifies a theory by the empirical relationships it discovers. There is no priority of one over the other in the scientific process, for they are complementary.

In the study of social class these specifications of the relationship between theory and method are concretized. No document, no piece of research reporting can evade the double-barrelled question. If it be a conscious and systematic construction of theory, such as discussed in the preceding chapter, methodological questions intrude: how is the theory to be tested and what procedures for testing does the theory demand? Similarly, the most cautious and limited research into class uncovers questions of theoretical orientation and theoretical commitment, even though the researcher may try to sidestep these matters quietly without nudging them into active consideration.

As a way of illustrating the scientific kinship between theory and method in the study of class, two points that were discussed in Chapter Two as problems for theory can here be re-analyzed as consequences for methodology. The first is the nagging question of the social limits of a system of stratification. How far does the system extend? Do the symbols, criteria, and functions of a class system apply only to a local community or do they extend to the structure of the national society? Marx, Weber, and the functionalists used the wider social aperture; Warner, and Weber in part, narrowed down to the community. The choice between these two alternatives would carry consequences for the method used. If class was defined in the first way, as position in a community, then the procedure used to determine class would have to reflect the intent of that definition: people would be asked to rank others in their community according to some class hierarchy. The very nature of the procedure would make it useless for the large city and impossible as a technique for studying the class structure of a national society.

The same reasoning would apply where the wider scope of a national society was selected as the theoretical orientation. If classes are seen as products of the economic order, as Marx saw them, then the notion of prestige in the community would be irrelevant. Marx's theory demanded a methodology that could keep pace with it. The same was true for Weber's definition of class, and for functional theory as well. The methodology would have to be able to encompass class as a national phenomenon, not as a local life style.

A second example of the tie between theory and method

is highlighted by another set of alternatives. Does class depend upon the subjective awareness by individuals of their position, or rather is class defined by the objective social features of an individual's position? If the former was to be emphasized by theory, then clearly the implementing research procedure required that the individual's attitudes be tapped. If class was defined by objective criteria, then a method was needed to translate these criteria into an index of objective measurement such as occupational prestige, consumption patterns, or social power.

The reverse also holds true because of the ties between theory and method. Research can, and does, establish empirical relationships that force modifications and revisions in theory. Whether research begins from established theoretical propositions or from simple hunches and intuitions, the findings can pay off at times in significant theoretical revisions. The use of occupational prestige measures, for example, in class studies has greatly enlarged the sphere of knowledge about class and its importance for a whole range of social behavior. Simultaneously, these findings have presented important modifications for all the theories of class.

The point is clear: theory and method are handmaidens. It is as useless to have a theory of class without empirical referents as it is to have a wonderfully prolific methodology that pours forth facts without any clue as to their interrelationship within a systematic theory.

Methodology, like theory, has its own special problems and dilemmas. The single outstanding methodological problem is that of identifying classes by means of valid, reliable, and unequivocal measures which also make sense within a theoretical fabric. To be sure, there are other problems as well, including those of class-consciousness, measures of social mobility and its effect upon class relationships, and the content and intensity of status aspirations. All of these, and many more, are admittedly matters that are vital for the understanding of class. Yet, determining what class is, how to identify classes, and how the several classes differ, is the generic methodological issue from which all others stem.

How, in other words, can classes be measured, and once measured, how valid and reliable is that measurement?

Four kinds of criteria have been used to identify social classes—four related, yet distinguishable methodological stabs at the key problem. They can be entitled: (1) How the person lives; (2) What others think of him; (3) What he thinks of himself; and (4) What he does. Each concentrates on a particular feature of class, yet all four turn around a common axis—the determination of some central index of class, some simple key measure that captures the true dynamics of class in its full social reality. Not one attains that goal. Instead, each measure enjoys its own particular advantages and suffers its own disadvantages. The total effect, however, has been to broaden the limits of knowledge about class; error can be as much a teacher as success.

The discussion and analysis of each of these indices, which is the purpose of the present chapter, should recall the preceding discussion of the theories of class. Methodology and theory have much in common here too. There is no neat cook-book procedure whereby the recipe of class can be easily and unambiguously set down, complete with theory and methodology to go along. Both theory and methodology attempt to answer the problem from their separate, yet related, tangents: what is class and what does it mean for social organization?

A word about the journalistic descriptions of class that have had an increasingly popular vogue as Americans have become, and been made to become, more class-conscious. In their own way, the journalist and the novelist have probed the subject of class based for the most part upon personal impressions. In recent years, this genre has added some brilliant as well as some muddled comments on life in middle class suburbia, on the tastes of intellectual pretenders, on the monotonies of middle class civilization, and on class conformity in American society. These accounts make good reading, and at times show strikingly provocative insights into the habitat and conduct of the class species. Still, these are personal reports, not scientifically based conclusions, no matter how good they seem to be; and this is no dictatorial demand for the sanctity of science. Just as an untrained bird watcher's report of what he has seen has to be taken cautiously and checked against the reports of more experienced ornithologists, so too the part-time preoccupation of some with class must be subjected to a similarly rigorous check. It is not so much that these semi-scientific class watchers are wrong in what they see, as it is a matter of how much they see and what they do not see. Fiction, feature articles, and popular books operate under their own logic of argumentation and literary craftsmanship. The sociologist, looking at the same social phenomenon, must satisfy a more rigorous scientific logic, and again the term is not used to bedazzle. That he does not always achieve that goal, that he sometimes belabors too hard what seems most obvious, that he raises more questions than he answers, or that he forsakes the wide dramatic spread for a more limited pedantry are merely comments on the style of the sociologist, not on his purpose. Although many clues can come from literary productions, the social scientist must translate these finally into testable and tested conclusions. For every portrait of Apley, Babbitt, or Lester, there are hundreds of well-written but badly informed literary works. The sociological yield has been much higher although at times less glittering. In the last analysis, the Sunday bird watcher, sooner or later, has to consult a reliable bird book to tell him what he saw.

Life Styles: Living Rooms and Living Standards

AMONG one of the earliest techniques in the study of class was a so-called "living-room-scale."[1] It was developed from a recognition of the very apparent fact that life styles generally, and the things people owned in particular, were different for different classes. The path that finally led to the construction of the scale began with Chapin's formulation in 1926-27 that status "... is the position that an individual or a family occupies with reference to the prevailing average standards of cultural possessions, effective income, material possessions, and participation in the group activities of the community."[2] This definition required the use of four scales, one for each of the elements that contributed to status. However, it was found that the four components correlated so highly with an independent measure of living-room furniture, that the latter alone could do the job statistically of measuring class. This conclusion was further rationalized by what Chapin felt were sociological axioms. The axioms instead were *ad hoc* explanations that should have been left alone, as is apparent when they are read several decades later. First he suggested that the living room was "most likely to be the center of interaction of the family." Secondly, the items to be found in the living room, more than in any other, were thought to reflect the "cultural acquisitions, the material possessions, and the socio-economic status of the family." Finally, and this assumption causes the greatest discomfort today, "the attitude of friends and other visitors, and hence social status, may be advantageously influenced by the selection and proper display of cultural objects in the living room."[3]

The rationale sounds specious and outdated today, although it seemed to make sense at the time. Styles and patterns have changed and so have many of the commonly accepted axioms about class. Neither the living room nor what it contains is the same today as it was then. The point to be made, however, is not alone that styles do change and fads become outmoded, but also that a method to study class must depend on a deeper perspective and a more stable theoretical base than that of currently popular modes of thought and belief. Otherwise, what soon becomes methodologically clear is that one is forever writing a history without catching up to the real dynamics of stratification.

The dated quality of the scale is soon evident. The original living-room scale contained some fifty-three items, each assigned a separate weight to reflect its relative importance for measuring class. A family's status, then, was represented by the total score of its living-room possessions gotten by summing the weights of all items. Six years of experience, gained from administering the scale in some 1500 homes in nine states and analyzing the findings, were distilled into the final Social Status Scale 1933. It consisted of twenty-one items: seventeen that gauged and ranked "Material Equipment and Cultural Expression"; and four that measured the condition of the articles found in the living-room. The interviewer had only to check the articles he found and their condition against the Scale. Some of the items that were included and the weights given them, shown in parentheses, give a good idea of what the Scale was like:

Floor, softwood	(6)	Bookcases with books	(8 each)
hardwood	(10)	Sewing machine	(−2)
Windows with drapes (each window)	(2)	Alarm clock	(−2)
Fireplace with three or more utensils	(8)	Newspapers	(8 each)
Armchairs	(8 each)	Periodicals	(8 each)

The condition of the articles was evaluated as to cleanliness (−4 if spotted, +2 if spotless), orderliness (−2 if disorderly, +2 if in place), condition of repair (−4 if broken, +2 if well kept), and on the general impressions of the observer (−4 if "bizarre, clashing, inharmonious, or offensive," +2 if "attractive in a positive way, harmonious, quiet and restful").

It was further suggested that the total scores could be grouped into six class categories from 0-24 as "destitute," and 125-149 as "upper middle class." The scale was judged to hold up consistently for a wide variety of homes in different sections of the country. It is difficult to know what supported that evaluation of the scale's efficacy, for when compared with occupation and income the Social Status Scale 1933 correlated at a rather low .52 and .38, respectively.

In 1942, Guttman computed a factor analysis for a correlational matrix of the original scale scores, occupations, income, and participation scores for a sample of 67 Negro homes in Minneapolis.[4] His purpose was a statistical one rather than an intention to test the plausibility of the scale. From his analysis of the intercorrelations between all of the items on the scale plus the four other variables, Guttman derived a set of revised weights for the living-room articles that Chapin had used. For example, "floors" were increased in relative value by several points, the status value of the "arm-chairs" was cut in half, the "sewing machine" was shifted from the minus to the positive column of this status ledger, and the "alarm clock" penalized a family's status to an even greater extent than it did in the original scale. These revised weights, however, as Guttman himself noted, were not "to be interpreted as the 'contribution' of the respective items to social status," but represented rather an expression of the statistical fit between these items and what was defined for the sample studied. If another sample were studied, or new items were added to the scale, it would be necessary to recalculate the entire analysis again. The sample was, after all, admittedly small and admittedly limited to but one group of a heterogeneous urban population. Other than showing a use for factor analysis, it is still quite unclear what Guttman had in mind. Whatever it was though, his analysis did not do much to vitalize the scale.

A scale similar in method and intent to Chapin's was constructed for farm families by Sewell,[5] although his was not the first nor the last variation. With a precision that was somewhat misplaced considering that there was much about the basic idea that needed serious thought, Sewell correctly reasoned that a farmer's status must be measured by different criteria than an urbanite's. Using 800 farm families from three sample counties in Oklahoma, Sewell started to work with 123 items that covered household possessions, education, reading, participation in organizations, and even whether a musical instrument was played or not. After weeding out those items that did not discriminate statistically between families in the sample, Sewell was left with

36 items that did. To enhance the use of the scale without sacrificing its original reliability, a short form of 14 items was distilled out of the longer scale. The short form scale was based on five items of possession (power washer, refrigerator, radio, telephone, automobile); four that related to the physical characteristics of the home (type of construction, ratio of persons to number of rooms, lighting facilities, and running water); and the remaining five items to education, newspaper reading, and church attendance. The shorter scale seemed to be a statistically adequate substitute for the longer one. Furthermore, the intent had remained unchanged from the original working hypothesis: that socioeconomic status, as defined by Chapin, could be applied successfully to farm families when proper changes were made in the possessions and characteristics considered as indices of that status. The line of reasoning did not necessarily end there, and Sewell, perhaps inadvertently, opened the breech by which it could be argued that any distinct social group would require a special adaptation of the scale—Westerners, Easterners, suburbanites, Negroes, and immigrants.

There are a few advantages to scales of the type just described. Principally, the gains are of a mechanical sort, derived from the techniques that are used. The scales are short and simple to administer. In the abbreviated versions of both Sewell's and Chapin's scales, the interview probably could be completed in less than fifteen minutes by someone familiar with the technique. A second advantage is the statistical reliability of the scale, or what can more loosely be called its objectivity. The private and personal judgments of the interviewer are minimized and his job is limited. He performs mostly as a clerk who looks around, asks some questions where necessary, and checks the proper blank on the form. Indeed, both scales have reported high reliability, by which is meant that the scores for any one home obtained by different interviewers have been very close. A final advantage of the scale is that it can be used with a fairly large number of persons. Community size, for example, does not present an impossible obstacle to the use of this technique.

It has worked in the large city as well as in a large farm area. Since the scale does not measure status by interpersonal knowledge of the kind that develops in the small community but only upon what the interviewer can see himself or what his respondents can tell him, community size does not matter here. Whether these advantages are significant or not, of course, depends upon other features of the scale.

These more or less mechanistic advantages, as a matter of fact, are quickly cancelled by more serious disadvantages. Some of these are technical shortcomings. The selection of the items for the scale and the weights that are assigned to them remain uncomfortably arbitrary. Experience and a feel for the situation have something to do with the selection of items, but it is finally the scale constructor who must decide what goes in and what stays out. This is a weak link in the chain of procedure. The use of statistical refinements, such as Guttman's, for paring down the original scale or altering the original weights, are, after all, based entirely upon information obtained from the use of the scale and are not independently devised. Such statistical manipulation, at best, can only reveal which items are consistent with one another or with some other arbitrary standard. Nowhere is there any assurance that the scale makes sense to begin with or that what it measures is at all related to the reality of class. It is very possible, as attitude testers have bitterly learned, that the time and effort spent on making a scale snugly fit one group might be wasted when the scale is used for a second group. Statistical symmetry is too unsteady to be a sufficient basis for prediction, although it is often a necessary part.

These scales also falter seriously when used to distinguish between those near the middle of the class hierarchy, although they seem to stand up fairly well when describing those at the extremes. This criticism, by the way, applies to other class measures as well. In the present instance, for example, the well-kept home, obviously expensively furnished and in harmonious and acceptable taste, is clearly distinguished from slum housing at the other extreme. The respective scores of the two on a living-room or a living standard scale would differ sharply, as expected. But this difference is obvious enough without any measure. Trying to separate, on the other hand, the differences between, say, an upper middle class and a lower middle class home is usually where such scales do not work, and where they are most needed. The differences are not as evident as those separating the extremes and are difficult to measure objectively although the feel for the difference and the sense of difference are present.

A related criticism has been raised by Wirth in his review of the literature on stratification: "... because of their selection of items such scales cannot discriminate between the social status of individuals who have similar standards-of-living but who have different social status because of differences, say, in occupation, family background or political power, or between the status of newly-rich and impoverished members of 'old families.' "[6] This perhaps unavoidable, but surely unwanted, feature makes these scales even more unsatisfactory as measures of class because they do not fit in with other measures, as Wirth has noted. By confounding rather than separating those obvious class features mentioned by Wirth, the living-room and living standard scales become burdened by disadvantages too great to be readily overlooked.

Wirth has mentioned another disadvantage that appears to be an inherent feature of these measures of class.[7] It is quite possible that the persons interviewed might disagree with those who constructed the scales as to the relative importance assigned to the scale items. In that case, Wirth has rightly concluded that the meaning of the scores becomes somewhat obscured. Is the rich old eccentric who insists upon having a cheap alarm clock atop an expensive antique table to be "penalized" for his eccentricity? Perhaps so. But at a somewhat lesser extreme, cannot "bizarre" and "inharmonious" tastes be traced to an oddly evidenced individualism, or simply to a disinterest with the whole matter, or even to a misreading of popular taste preferences? By any other criterion such persons might rate higher than their living-room indicates. Finally, from the other direction, what of the family that maintains a visibly high standard of living precisely for its status effect and at the same time is getting along without some other less visible necessity? The motives behind the consumption patterns and the status goals of American families are wonderfully complex and variable, and only some of the more obvious class motives are tapped by the rationale of the living-room and living standard measures.

If these were the only disadvantages, they might possibly be remedied by more experience, more testing, and standardization. However, there are difficulties of a more serious order that permanently impair the effectiveness and validity of these scales. Simply phrased, these are difficulties produced by the faddish and variable tastes of American consumers. As has been implied before, what a representative family at any class level would have considered as a tastefully furnished living room that was "harmonious" and "restful" in 1933, certainly would have become "bizarre" and "clashing" within two decades. Periodic revisions would be necessary to keep the scale up-to-date. Further, the focus of family living even seems to have shifted to other rooms in the house. The conception of modern residential architecture, and with it the indoctrinated residents of its products, has moved away from the idea of the living room as the show place of the home. We are now entreated to live functionally throughout the whole living area, and Chapin's assumptions about the living-room become inevitably as outdated as the scale items he depended upon.

Neither are farm families immune to these changing patterns, for the influence of urban tastes has spread beyond metropolitan boundaries. The consumer habits and taste preferences of rural dwellers are as much conditioned and affected by the mass media as those of the city's residents. Hence, the criticism applies with the same force to Sewell's scale as well.

The rapidity of change in consumer preferences, which

forms the basis for measures of living rooms and living standards, creates unwanted analytical havoc. Additionally, the steady trend toward standardization of those preferences vitiates the measures even more. Advertising, the studied development of the feeling that they "need" certain items among a large proportion of the population, the lowering cost of many consumer items, and the use of consumer credit, all added together have produced an amazingly high degree of similarity in the furnishings of American homes. Riesman and Roseborough[8] have coined the apt phrase, the "standard package," to denote the parcel of consumer's goods that most Americans seem driven to own. *Fortune's* survey of the American market, similarly, supports the impression of a steady move by many different class levels in the population toward purchasing the components of that standard package. In the case of furniture, for example, *Fortune* concluded that the taste preferences set by interior decorators in the industry have filtered down to the mass audience.[9] What are the chances, then, of widely different consumption patterns where standardization has become so typical, so widespread and so intentional?

The possibility of devising a measure that can identify different classes by means of their living standards grows ever smaller. To the considerable difficulty of keeping such measures up-to-date, there is added the effects of industrial standardization by which the mass market necessarily counteracts the justifying rationale behind such scales. Not everyone in America is living exactly like everybody else; but, too few people are living differently enough to distinguish one from another according to the living-room scale.

Prestige Judges: What Others Think

A PROCEDURE for determining class that seems to be attractive by its methodological simplicity depends upon the evaluations made by community "judges" about their fellow citizens. A group or a sample of informants—"prestige judges"—is selected in the community to be studied. They, in turn, rank everybody else in the community into as many class categories as they consider necessary. All of those placed in the same category, therefore, belong to the same class, according to the estimates of the "judges." If these community informants between them know everyone else, and further, if they agree with one another as to their evaluations of persons they know in common, then the class structure of the community and the occupants of each class are rather easily identified and located. Class, according to this operational definition, then, is nothing more nor less than what people in the community say it is.

The rationale underlying this technique is temptingly plausible. An important feature of class, it may be granted, is that there exists a consensus within the community as to the characteristics and the composition of the several classes. By using community prestige judges, the researcher has been able to tap directly into the main line without stumbling over nasty particulars. The consensus of the community is expressed totally and at once through the evaluations of the prestige judges: which classes are recognized, by which names the several classes are locally known, the criteria used for class placement, and finally, who belongs where among the various class strata. No other technique apparently draws upon this consensus so directly nor so reliably, assuming of course that there is a unitary consensus in the community, and more importantly, that the prestige judges can make reliable estimates.

The procedure has been used by Kaufman in a study of a small township in central New York.[10] Fourteen prestige judges were used to rank some 1200 residents and apparently the judges were almost unanimously agreed in their evaluations. Furthermore, Kaufman reported that the ratings of eleven of the judges showed correlations of from .74 to .88 with a composite of other measures of prestige, such as occupation, participation, education, and ratings on the Sewell socio-economic scale. There was also some agreement, but somewhere less than unanimous, on the number of classes there were in the town. Kaufman reported that ". . . fourteen prestige judges used from four to ten classes in ranking community members in terms of prestige; ten judges employed six or more classes. The writer was able without difficulty to place the community population in eleven classes. Several of the judges, who possessed a keen sense of prestige distinctions, probably could have ranked the community population in more than eleven prestige classes had they been requested to do so."[11]

The quotation, which indicated a sizeable variation on an important point, creates an uncomfortable suspicion about what consensus means and how valid is the use of prestige judges as a research technique. There is something unexplained that badly needs elucidation when a measure can turn up eleven or more distinguishable classes in a community with a total population of some 1200. Either the technique is spurious in spite of its apparent plausibility, or it forces a suspicious refinement of the population when used. A closer analysis of this technique in actual application indicates that it has its own problems that are not perhaps immediately apparent. The simplicity and plausibility of the rationale behind the technique cannot easily overcome some of the serious disadvantages inherent in its use. These are discussed shortly.

Warner too has used community judges beginning with his first study in Yankee City and in later studies as well. Drawing on that experience he has tried to regularize the procedure, based on the propositions ". . . that those who interact in the social system of a community evaluate the participation of those around them, that the place where an individual participates is evaluated, and that the members of the community are explicitly or implicitly aware of the ranking and translate their evaluations of such social participation into social-class ratings that can be communicated to the investigator."[12] This so-called method of "evaluated participation" depended upon six techniques:

1) Matched Agreements, *i.e.*, comparing the evaluations

of several prestige judges and partitioning the community into classes as directed by these evaluations. This technique is a restatement of what has been described above.

2) Symbolic Placement, *i.e.,* determining the class of an individual by the symbols people use when referring to him, such as "poor white," "one of the 400," or someone from "the wrong side of the tracks."

3) Status Reputation, *i.e.,* determining class by the "good" and "bad" references to an individual's behavior in the community.

4) Comparison, *i.e.,* noting comparative evaluations made by informants of an individual as higher, lower, or in the same class as someone whose class position is already known.

5) Simple Assignment, *i.e.,* determining an individual's class by some direct reference made about his class position.

6) Institutional Membership, *i.e..* determining an individual's class position by the organizations he belongs to, assuming that the class character of those organizations is known.

These so-called "techniques" can hardly be thought of as full-fledged procedures for analysis. At most, they are nothing more than cautions to read the interview materials carefully and they offer some hints, based on experience, of the way that class might be mentioned in that material. Furthermore, these six hints hardly differ; certainly not enough to be considered as separate procedures. The "method of evaluated participation" really comes down to a ranking by prestige judges as previously described.

The intent and the rationale behind both Warner's and Kaufman's use of community judges is the same, notwithstanding the variations each of them has introduced: to get a relatively direct and explicit delineation of the class strata and the people in them for any community by means of the evaluations of community representatives. The technique can be assessed by how well it does that job and by what it cannot do.

There are a few ready-made advantages in using prestige judges; advantages that can avoid some of the difficulties not as well handled by other measures. The judges, because they live in the community under study, are likely to reflect the thinking about class that is accepted in the community. In effect, they are being asked to characterize their own community, which they should know well. Unsophisticated though they might be about relationships in class terms, perhaps never having thought in those terms, community judges usually are aware of the accepted social differences by the symbols that have local currency, whether those differences have formal class names to them or not. The doubt that always hovers over other measures, which sometimes never finally establish whether class is a fact or not in the consciousness of a community, can be more easily settled when prestige judges are used to voice a community's views of a set of real, reliable, and operative social categories.

A second advantage, and one as critically important as the first, is that the evaluations made by prestige judges are likely to express an individual's total social position in the community. There is the likelihood that the judgments represent a balanced assessment of all relevant characteristics that might set an individual's position in the prestige hierarchy—personal characteristics, occupation, education, organizational memberships, community participation, family background, and life style. This social arithmetic depends upon an intuitive balancing and weighting of the individual's relative standing according to several prestige dimensions simultaneously. These values are summed by a special social logic that can handle each dimension as if it were comparable to all the other dimensions. Only by this method can income be added to occupation, family background to power, and participation to life style. Yet, this would seem to be closer to the real nature of class at the community level. Other measures that must stay within a mathematical logic, not permitting the addition of apples and oranges, cannot begin to duplicate the malleability of personal judgments. The prestige judge, making his intuitive additions and subtractions in line with what the community would do, can total the class position of individuals in a way not available to other measures.

Finally, the use of prestige judges produces as an end

product a hierarchy of discrete social classes. Most other measures, starting with some continuous variable such as occupational prestige, or income, or living standards, must end by drawing arbitrary dividing lines to separate the several classes, a process that is always open to some doubt. Prestige judges, on the other hand, think in terms of separate class categories because they are evaluating people, not working from statistical variables. To be sure, there may be disagreement among the judges about the number of classes and the placement of individuals in those categories. This possibility creates one of the major disadvantages of the technique, and is more fully discussed below.

These advantages, it should be reiterated, succeed in overcoming some of the major stumbling blocks in the way of most other measures of class. It is not so much that the use of prestige judges solves these problems, as it is that these problems never become issues at all. For example, no stand need be taken as to the major determinants of class in a community; the assessments of the community informants can be taken at face value as expressing the place an individual occupies in the structure. Or again, the question of whether class is real or is only an artificial category never has to be met; if the prestige judges use class as a social dimension then it exists as far as the particular community is concerned.

Although the advantages of this technique are tempting by their plausibility and by their avoidance of complex problems, they are sobered and tempered by some formidable disadvantages. Three such disadvantages are obvious, and they are as inherent to the technique as are the gains noted above. It is clear that prestige judges can be used only in small communities, with probably not much more than five thousand people. It is not simply a matter of using more judges for a larger community, for it is the logic of the technique that collapses. The range of social intimacy decreases in the populous city. The fragmentation of urban populations into separate and insulated social worlds makes the very notion of prestige judges nonsense. Few know the large community in all of its facets, let alone know enough about enough people to evaluate their prestige. The urban community must rely more upon symbols than upon personal knowledge for class identification.

A second inherent disadvantage is the difficulty, if not the impossibility, of comparing the findings from one community to another. Neither the criteria used to evaluate class nor the relative importance between criteria need be the same for any two communities. The prestige judges can only judge their own community and not another. Even if the criteria could be converted into a more objective form, the intuitive judgments would be lost in any inter-community comparison. The major gain of the technique, then, produces its own major limitations.

A third disadvantage is more mechanical perhaps: how to reconcile differences between the estimates of the several judges. Neither Kaufman nor Warner have reported unanimity among the judges they have used. Although the degree of consensus between judges was appreciable, there was always some disagreement. The problem, then, was to balance the differences in some way so as to get the best single estimate. The evaluations of several judges could be averaged, if that is possible. Or, the disagreement could be settled by using an independent measure, such as occupation or length of time lived in the community. Neither alternative, however, was satisfactory. If an independent measure was used, then there was not much sense in using prestige judges to begin with. If an average was used, then methodological difficulties emerged. A statistical average has little meaning for this kind of problem. To pose an extreme case, is an individual in the middle class because one judge puts him in the upper and another insists he is lower class? The average, perhaps unjustifiably, assumes that the estimate of each judge is as accurate as that of any other judge. This was hardly the case. The people selected as judges could have different sensitivities to class, or differ in their knowledge about the community, or be capable of different levels of objectivity about the whole matter. There is no easy way of digging out these differences in the estimates made by informants, especially where serious discrepancies are revealed.

Even if these difficulties were to be solved, two additional questions still remain. How does the researcher get, and make sure that he has gotten, a representative sample of the population to serve as judges? Not only do those individuals have to know their community and its residents, but equally important, that knowledge must be accurate. People see the class structure from different perspectives, depending upon their own positions in it. Those at the bottom often fail to discriminate the nuances separating those at the top. Similarly, those at the top tend to overlook the distinctions that make sense for those at the bottom. This might be overcome in a small town, but it is just as likely that pretensions and inaccuracies are permanently built into the gossip channels of small communities to distort the real situation. A panel of judges overweighted at one extreme or the other can produce serious errors and discrepancies in the final estimates.

It was this kind of error that seemed to be partially involved in the discrepancies that Warner found in his study of Jonesville, and that has been further criticized by Pfautz and Duncan.[13] The latter have computed the errors found in Warner, and this information is reproduced below, where ISC, "Index of Status Characteristics" is a combined score based on such variables as occupation and rent, and EP refers to the "Evaluated Participation" index discussed earlier.

Table 2*—Errors in Predicting Class Level (as Determined by EP) from ISC Scores, for a Sample of Old Americans

Social Class (as Determined by EP)	Number in Sample	Number of Errors†	Percentage Error
Upper	44	8	18
Upper-middle	50	11	22
Lower-middle	44	3	7
Upper-lower	28	9	32
Lower-lower	43	2	5
All classes	209	33	16

* Taken from Pfautz and Duncan.[13]
† The number of errors is given for only 200 of the 209 cases in the sample

The size of the error for the upper-lower and the upper-middle classes was large enough to be serious, indicating that the relationships between the two measures were far from perfect. In part, it is suggested, the failure can be traced to the erroneous judgments of "evaluated participation," the errors made by the judges themselves. Though judges may report what they believe, they cannot fully avoid the bias of their own class position, especially when it comes to judging others. The upper-middle class saw its own distinctiveness in a way that was not appreciated as much by others. Similarly, the upper-lower class, fighting for its respectability, may not have been given enough prestige credit for its efforts.

The caution is clear. Whether the judges are selected as Kaufman selected them, or where the judgments of everyone interviewed must be culled for relevant material as Warner suggested, the matter of who does the judging remains as a difficulty. Their biases, their shortcomings, and their own aspirations enter in and color their estimates of others.

A final criticism needs to be stated. In using prestige judges the problem remains unsettled of precisely what it is that is being judged. Even a full exploration of the criteria that are used gives no assurance that the criteria mean the same things to the different judges. What is "class position" to one, may mean something importantly different to another. After all, even among professionals in this subject there is less than full agreement about that term. To make the whole matter even more worrisome, the judges might appear to come to similar conclusions but by different routes, by weighting different criteria in different ways. The route is as important as the conclusion. Over a period of time it is likely that some individuals will move between several classes, but the criteria that determines their place will change more slowly, bound as they are to a relatively stable base of community sentiments and values. The judges must somehow keep up-to-date with those class changes and with the more subtle shifts in the criteria of class. Without this guarantee, the analyst is likely to be left with a dated list of class designations for a community but without any certain knowledge of what it represents, or indeed, if it represents what he thinks it does.

Subjective Identifications: Class Consciousness and the Psychology of Class

ONE element of class and its effect upon behavior centers around the individual's consciousness of class and his identification with a class. With that emphasis comes the involvement with questions of attitudes, feelings, sentiments, and subjective awareness.

Taking this orientation as the guiding rationale, some have insisted that it is precisely the subjective identifications of individuals and the psychological consequences of those identifications that convert class from an abstract category into social reality.[14] Kornhauser has stated the position as one of finding out to what extent objective class differences were accompanied by "significant psychological differences." A social class, thereby, was defined as "those sections of the population which *feel* similarly concerning their position and interests, which have a common outlook and a distinctive common attitude."[15] In short, the defining feature of class was the common psychological identification or set of attitudes held by individuals.

Of course, class must have subjective correlates woven into the orientations of individuals. What is distinctive about the emphasis upon subjective factors, however, is the priority given to such awareness as a class criterion. In effect, class *means* the identification of individuals with such a group. The objective criteria, occupation or income, say, are considered more as indices of class but do not strictly determine it. This particular insistence upon subjective elements as class determinants is different from Marx's idea of class consciousness, or indeed, from that of any of the other structural theorists that have been discussed. For Marx, consciousness developed as a consequence of social forces operating outside of the individual, but it was clearly the social fact that created classes. In the psychological interpretation, however, class consciousness gives class its reality; the social force may or may not be contributory.

A study by Centers, *The Psychology of Social Classes,*[16] exemplified the subjective definition of class. It was a detailed and deliberate statement within that orientation; further, because it was concerned with the methodology of determining class, it fits in with the purpose of this section. Centers' findings, by the way, are not unanimously accepted even by those who share a similar psychological emphasis. The disagreement, however, at least in one case, is more with research procedures than with the logic of the argument. Kornhauser,[17] for example, seriously questioned the adequacy of the method of self-classification Centers used to determine class, and also questioned the causal tie that Centers imputed between such classification and the attitudes expressed by individuals. Although the research itself is of interest, it is still the general argument that is of concern at this point, and Centers can still be taken as representative.

One of the first clarifications that Centers wished to set right was the distinction between the "objective" and the "subjective" dimensions of class. The former, which he labelled a "stratum," referred to the "social and economic groupings and categories of people distinguished on the basis of occupation, power, income, standard of living, education, function, intelligence [*sic*] or other criteria."[18] "Class," on the other hand, was a subjective component defined as ". . . psycho-social groupings . . . essentially subjective in character, dependent upon class consciousness (*i.e.,* a feeling of group membership)."[19] Subjective "classes" may or may not be the same as objective "strata," according to Centers, but there was little doubt that his interest was predominantly in the former and that "class" was also prior.

For it was the subjective identification with a class that gave class its reality, and that identification struck deeply.

"A man's class is a part of his ego, a feeling on his part of belongingness to something: an identification with something larger than himself."[20] Class achieved reality as a psychological phenomenon by what people believed, by their class identification, and by the class-conditioned attitudes they held. Centers criticized Marx and others who would follow the same theoretical channel because, he argued, they and not the people they studied have predetermined what class was to be. The preconceived categories of the social analyst, in other words, have been imposed from above, rather than the reverse: deriving those categories from the psychological material itself, as Centers would have it. Centers wanted to approach the phenomenon of class somewhat *de novo*, to find out what individuals believed and only then, and only from that information, to designate class categories.

Naturally, there must be some basis from which to begin; some theoretical footing no matter how temporary. Otherwise there would be no justification for any research into class, for one could do little more than admit total ignorance. This was no reasonable alternative. Centers retrenched, therefore, from the notion of a completely fresh start and began instead by recognizing that objectively determined "strata" might precondition the psychological dimensions of class he was interested in: the relationship to be tested by research. He labelled this pattern of reasoning, the "interest group theory" by which he meant, ". . . that a person's status and role with respect to the economic processes of society imposes upon him certain attitudes, values and interest relating to his role and status in the political and economic sphere." Further, that position created by social processes ". . . gives rise in [the individual] to a consciousness of membership in some social class which shares those attitudes, values, and interests."[21] Briefly summarized and sharpened, Centers maintained that those in the same economic circumstances held common interests, beliefs and attitudes about their position. The latter, he chose to call "class."

At first glance, the "interest group theory" seems to avoid

some of the problems encountered in measuring class. Centers, by definition, has strained the objective facts of class—position in the political and economic sphere—through the subjective orientations of the individual. In this way, apparently, premature assumptions about the nature of class and its effects upon the behavior of individuals were to be avoided. If class made any difference and had any reality, then apparently it should be manifested in the attitudes and conceptions that individuals hold. Certainly, the bulk of social psychological theory would support this general contention.

There is not much disagreement with Centers' theory up to this point. The question might be raised: just how was position in the political and economic sphere to be assigned and by what logic were individuals to be considered as in the same "stratum"? This criticism, vital as it is, can be left aside for the moment. What is more to the point, however, is that by the time Centers had analyzed his materials and reached his conclusions, the subjective dimension had been elevated to the position where it determined and defined classes. The earlier recognition of economic and political forces as *causes* of the subjective components of class seemed to have been intended only as a temporary research assumption; something to get him off the ground. He had, after all, to begin somewhere, to assume that classes existed as social realities in order to set in motion the distinctive attitudes and identifications of each class that he wanted to describe. That assumption, however, was dropped like a first-stage rocket. Midway through the study, class had become "no more or less than what people collectively think it is."[22] At the conclusion, "Social classes in their essential nature can be characterized as psychologically or subjectively based groupings defined by the allegiance of their members."[23]

Centers' proof was based upon a nationwide public opinion survey conducted in 1945 of 1100 white male respondents over twenty-one years of age. A major interest of the survey was in a battery of some six opinion questions that were used to establish political conservatism or radicalism. These were utilized as indicators of a set of attitudes common to a class. One question, for example, asked: "Do you agree or disagree that America is truly a land of opportunity and that people get pretty much what's coming to them in this country?" The respondent agreed, disagreed, or indicated no opinion.

The feature of the survey that provided the main basis for conclusions on class identifications and expressions of affiliation with some class was presented in one question:

> If you were asked to use one of these four names for your social class, which would you say you belonged in: the middle class, lower class, working class or upper class?[24]

The reponses obtained to the question, as well as those obtained in a re-check six months later, were as follows:

Those Answering:	*July 1945*	*February 1946*
Upper class	3%	4%
Middle class	43	36
Working class	51	52
Lower class	1	5
Don't know	1	3
"Don't believe in classes"	1	—

As Centers has correctly pointed out, the inclusion of the alternative of "working class" was significant, and his findings have strongly contested those of other surveys that concluded that everyone in America believed he was "middle class." Other surveys in omitting "working class" as an alternative thereby left "middle class" as the only possible response for many. Both "upper" and "lower" class choices carried such negative connotations within American values that most people rejected both in favor of the "middle" class alternative. What was also clear from the above findings was the close agreement in the distributions of class identification obtained in the two periods.

Class affiliation, as indicated by the responses to the question above, correlated rather highly with other variables related to class. The tetrachoric correlations between class affiliation and occupational group was .69; between affiliation and economic status, .65; between affiliation and responses to the conservatism-radicalism questions, .49;[25] and between affiliation and education, .56.[26] Other relationships found in the study are not of direct concern here. However, one other statistic should be presented to round out the picture, for it tended to support Centers' theoretical view of class. When asked what criteria, *other than occupation,* people used to determine who belonged to their class, almost half answered that beliefs and attitudes were most important. Centers interpreted that finding, naturally enough, as support for his view that "common ideologies, attitudes, values and interests" were basic to the formation of class consciousness. Still there was a measure of inconsistency left unexplained. The reason given by individuals for placing someone in a class *other* than their own showed a dependence upon such criteria as possessions and skills rather than upon ideologies. Wealth, income, and education were most frequently mentioned as the bases for upper class membership. "Money, income, etc.," were distinguishing criteria for the middle class. "Working for a living" and a direct reference to occupation were what most persons considered as typical of working class occupants. "Poverty" and "poor education" were most frequently mentioned as the criterion of lower class placement.[27] These two sets of findings, when juxtaposed, imply a double standard by which the "finer," the more genteel, and the more subtle qualities of personality were used as criteria for defining class peers, but by which a more "crass" materialism was used to define others. This difference was left unexplained, although it was a most suggestive finding.

All in all, Centers concluded that subjective identification was somewhat vindicated by the study, not only as a measure of class, but even further as part of that psychological force that Centers had proposed gave meaning to class. He concluded that there was a communality in feelings and attitudes among members of the same class. The range of phenomena covered under the communal tent was indeed broad. It supported a number of conclusions that Centers was ready to make. The communality meant that "the working class as a group tends to be distinctly more frustrated than the middle class."[28] It meant that the "middle class appears to be somewhat more liberal than the working class with respect to the economic freedom of women."[29] It could even be interpreted to show that "while this working-class group as represented in labor unions does constitute a definite social movement, it is as yet a class and a movement lacking in a clearly defined and well organized ideology and program in the sense and degree to which the middle class possesses these attributes and employs them to defend itself."[30]

As Kornhauser has pointed out in his criticism of Centers' study,[31] these conclusions based on subjective identifications extend dangerously far, considering that they were dependent finally upon the single question: "What social class would you say you belonged to?" How valid it was to call this question and answer, "class identification," and what interpretation could be made of the responses, were never fully established. However, leaving this particular methodological point aside, what can be said about the broader question: the subjective determination of class?

One point favoring the subjective view has been mentioned at the beginning of this section. Clearly, as Marx and Weber had recognized, class, or something like it, must come to have meaning within the psychological orientations of individuals before it can be expressed in their behavior. Whether individuals consciously labelled themselves by class or not was not the point. But if they behaved in a manner that was consistent with a designated class type, it must finally be traced to some self-conceptions that were held pertaining to class. Whatever the individual believed his class to be, determined in large measure the way he would think, the attitudes he would hold, and the things he would do.

Evidence of this relationship between self-identification and behavior is apparent in many psychological correlates of class. For example, the aspirations that an individual holds for upward mobility, in some way must be related to the estimate he has made of his own class position and the class with which he would identify. Even the lack of such aspirations, not at all too infrequent an occurrence even though Americans idolize the opposite, is itself indicative of the acceptance of certain class identifications and values. The conscious attempt of a middle class striver to emulate the behavior of those above him springs from a particular psychological set that he holds toward class. In the same way, the refusal of a lower class person to set his aspirations too high can be viewed as a response to his class situation and what he thinks about his own abilities and chances for success. The psychological fact, to paraphrase Durkheim, must be explained by other psychological facts. The psychological identifications with class are behavior determinants. But, at the same time, the individual is not a free-floating entity. He is pushed and pulled by larger social and economic forces about him that are not of his making nor necessarily of his choice. He must also react to those forces, if only to explain himself to himself, and his identification with class, or the lack of it, reflects some of the effects of those forces upon him.

Still, recognizing the importance of subjective elements for class does not open a completely free path; other issues automatically arise and intrude. It can be agreed that what an individual thinks is his class helps to explain his behavior. Unfortunately, for research purposes this datum is not enough for either the measurement or understanding of class. Self-evaluations do not always match the evaluations made by others. For various reasons, be they ignorance, bias, or delusion, some place themselves in a higher class than others would, just as some class themselves lower. After all, those self-evaluations rest upon an interpretation of social clues and social symbols, not upon public discussions of comparative standing. There are bound to be errors in interpretation under such conditions. Centers found, for example, that there were instances where self-judgments did not match the judgments based on more objective criteria. The largest percentage of those who said that they were middle class also said that doctors, lawyers, small business owners, and managers were in that class. However, some 24 per cent who said they were middle class included factory workers, 18 per cent included laborers, and 11 per cent mentioned waiters and bartenders as part of the middle class as well. Similarly, the majority of those who said they were working class included, as expected, farmers, factory workers, laborers, and waiters in their own group. Unexpectedly, some 8 per cent also included doctors and lawyers, 20 per cent included small business owners, and 17 per cent included store and factory managers.[32]

The fact that some do hold class identifications that do not correspond with the estimates of other persons was a discrepancy that made it difficult to build a systematic picture of the class structure. No one can say how prevalent these discrepancies were, but given American class values they must have been significantly large. The delusions of the paranoid must be considered for therapeutic reasons, but no one except the paranoid really believes them. "Class consciousness," by similar reasoning, cannot be determined only by taking as fact what the individual says about himself, nor can his class be established only by that criterion. His evaluations must be considered, but along with other objectively established factors and criteria. Marx, for example, was aware of the possible discrepancies between self-judgments and social reality as reflected in his notion of a "false" class consciousness; the individual's conceptions did not fit the facts. For if class means only what the individual himself thinks, then we have no class structure, but at best, a collection of class-thinking persons who may or may not agree with one another. To admit, as a general principle, along with Centers that a person's attitudes reflect his socio-economic position should not becloud a recognition of the many instances where attitudes may reflect other personality needs. People come to believe many things about themselves for many and varied reasons, and what they believe cannot always be taken as simple, objective truth. Where, for example, the success emphasis is heavy and unrelenting, people may be psychologically ready to confuse actualities with wishes and aspirations, no matter what their socio-economic position may be.

Another criticism of this method of subjective identification is the ambiguity in the idea itself. There are at least three quite separate meanings of subjective identification. It can mean the awareness of the existence of classes as a social fact. Regardless of their evaluations, individuals differ in their conceptions of whether classes do or do not exist to begin with. For some, the class structure is a hard reality that they live with and to which they train themselves and their children. For others, class is a myth preached only by radicals. A second meaning of subjective identification refers to the awareness about one's own class position. The person who says, "I work with my hands, and am proud of it," is stating a class fact about himself. So too are those who live a middle class existence near the financial brink, earning more prestige than money and maintaining a status-consciousness almost to the point of disaster. These are instances of class consciousness in the sense that people identify themselves as belonging within a class segment. Finally, the psychological identification can mean consciousness of a class as a group to which the individual belongs; that he shares a life style and a class fate that binds him to others in the same situation. In this sense, the individual has not only identified his class, but has come to identify with others as class equals. The consciousness of class, so to speak, has been broadened to make class a distinct social grouping integrated by common interests and goals.

The difficulties that have been mentioned are probably not insuperable. With experience, the nuances behind the separate meanings, intentions, and connotations of subjective identification could be clarified. Even so, there still is a residual sponginess when the psychological dimension is relied upon as the sole, or even the primary, criterion of class. The sponginess comes from the fact that class varies in its importance for different sections of the population. Not everybody lives the class life with the same intensity. At one extreme, class can be an all-pervasive reality that burrows into all personal calculations and conceptions. At the other extreme, there are those who can take class or leave it alone in the way they would react to a game. There are addicts and non-addicts, buffs and non-buffs, in every phase of human existence, including class. Some are aware of their class position and even know that they are not alone, but they accept these realities without emotional heat. All other variations on this theme also exist. The intensity of class involvement varies between individuals. What is more, these intensities probably do not vary consistently by class; no class is consistently the same, since variations are by personality. Taking these variations in the concern and involvement with class as an inevitable feature of the class structure, means that subjective identifications can never be wholly depended upon as a reliable index of class. The identification may be only an expression of class concern rather than a valid index of class identification.

The technique of subjective identification then, like other techniques, is supported by some validity in its general rationale, but at the same time also contains many inherent disadvantages that nullify its utility; or at least limit its use.

Occupational Prestige: The Job as Status Symbol

Occupation has become the most frequently used index of class. It has been used by itself as a simple index; it has been combined with other measures into a multiple index. What is more, occupation has been frequently relied upon as an independent measure to test the validity of other measures of class. For example, Centers compared the subjective identifications given by respondents with their occupations. Living standard scales have relied upon occupation in the same manner. Few studies of class omit a reference to occupation and most of them incorporate occupational measures into the research design. In short, occupation and occupational prestige have become the symbols of class, not only in the scientific but in the popular mind as well.

Occupational measures of class, more than others, have been accepted so universally and so unreservedly that they have been able to avoid the intense criticism to which most other measures have been subjected. However, measures of occupational prestige have their own peculiar limitations even though their justifying rationale is usually strong. Apparently those measures do the job effectively and give results that look good and make sense. Yet, these clear credits must be evaluated against their disadvantages, for occupational measures can make sense under some circumstances but not under all.

Two general methods for using occupation as a class index have been developed. Although they differ by the particular operations employed, they are clearly compatible in their logic and intent. By one method, occupations are classified according to the judgment of the classifier into a limited number of occupational groups, arranged hierarchically. By the second method, a "prestige score" for a number of occupations is determined by the judgments of a sample of persons and the occupations are then ranked by their relative scores.

The technique of occupational classification of the first type based upon some socio-economic dimension is most often associated with the work of Edwards[33] for the Bureau of the Census. What he wanted, apparently, was a classification that could (1) fit all occupations reported in the census into (2) a relatively limited set of categories, that (3) would combine occupations together insofar as they connoted a common life style and common economic and social characteristics. Generally, Edwards seemed to accept as the primary distinction the division between "head" and "hands" types of employment.[34] The result was a classification of all occupations into six major groups, described as social-economic classes:

1. Professional persons
2. Proprietors, managers, and officials
   2a. Farmers (owners and tenants)
   2b. Wholesale and retail dealers
   2c. Other proprietors, managers and officials
3. Clerks and kindred workers
4. Skilled workers and foremen
5. Semiskilled workers
6. Unskilled workers
   6a. Farm laborers
   6b. Laborers, except farm
   6c. Servant classes

"It is evident that each of these groups," Edwards noted, "represents . . . a large population group with a somewhat distinct standard of life, economically, and, to a considerable extent, intellectually and socially. . . . Each of them is thus a really distinct and highly significant social-economic group."[35]

This made a rather large claim for the classification, especially in view of the distinctions that were to appear in a succeeding decade of research on class. Only as a first approximation do these occupational groups reflect the differences that Edwards claimed for them. As soon became evident by the further analysis of occupational measures, the differences *within* each of Edwards' categories were almost as great and as significant for class analysis as the differences *between* categories.

Still, variations on Edwards' general theme have not been lacking, apparently a sign of confidence. Many of these variations have been styled to fit the particular research needs of the moment, but the underlying intent has remained the same. The simplest variation has been to condense all occupations into but two or three groups, dividing those occupations that deal with "things" from those that deal with "people," or those that use "hands" from those that use "heads." The Lynds' study of *Middletown* was an excellent example, although it was made some ten years before the Edwards' classification.[36] Other variations expand or otherwise modify the original categories designated by Edwards. Centers, for example, followed Edwards' classification for the lower class categories, but rearranged the other categories according to his own logic.[37] He separated urban occupations from those in rural communities, the latter including only farm owners and managers, tenants, and laborers. The urban occupations were divided into:

1. Large business owners and managers
2. Professional
3. Small business owners and managers
4. White collar (clerks and kindred workers)
5. Skilled manual workers (and foremen)
6. Semi-skilled manual workers
7. Unskilled manual workers

"These categories," Centers stated, "form a hierarchy in terms of skill, responsibility, and complexity of the occupational function."[38] This rationale, like that of Edwards, rings a plausible tone. Yet, both classifications, in reality, assumed rather than proved the existence of such differences. Furthermore, by what objective logic does the "large business owner" move into the first category for Centers but remain in the second category for Edwards? The arbitrary character of such classification is clear when the variations are compared with one another.

Warner produced yet another variation on the Edwards' classification that is worth noting because it differentiated between occupational groups in a different manner.[39] Warner's addition was to consider that occupational groups could overlap, unlike the insistence upon a clear-cut separation that both Edwards and Centers implied. In his classification, Warner sought to incorporate that overlap in a systematic fashion. Furthermore, Warner's classification provided a logical bridge leading to the more detailed occupational prestige scales. In other words, if finer distinctions within each category are introduced, then it is but a short analytical step to considering all occupations as part of a single continuous structure rather than a series of discrete occupational groups. An abbreviated version of Warner's scale is presented in Table 3.

These various occupational groupings, whatever the specific form, cannot avoid being products of arbitrary decisions. There is no procedure to designate which occupations are to be grouped together, nor indeed, how the several groups are to rank. Each variation certainly seems plausible enough, but plausibility or immediate research demands are not enough to establish validity.

That disadvantage is largely corrected by the second form of occupational ranking, which depends upon some form of computed "prestige score" for individual occupations. Briefly, the technique consists of translating the evaluations made by a sample of individuals about the relative prestige, desirability, or importance of each occupation they are asked to judge. The number of occupations presented for such evaluation have varied from as few as twenty-five to as many as two hundred. Ideally, of course, the number should be large enough to represent the occupational range, yet small enough not to become burdensome for the respondent. It should be immediately apparent that the scores that are obtained in this fashion are only as good as the sample that does the evaluating, and only as good as the list of occupations the sample is asked to evaluate. The fact that the results are expressed as scores that are measurable and apparently continuous does not endow them with any halo of validity. The persons that give the evaluation might be representative of no identifiable group, or perhaps of a limited and atypical world. Their ratings, in that case, if used in other contexts, are questionable no matter how plausible they may appear. On the other hand, the occupations presented for evaluation might be unrepresentative of the diverse range of the occupational structure. The results, in that case, are similarly limited.

Table 3—Warner's Occupational Rating Classification*

Rating Assigned to Occupation	*Professional*	*Proprietors and Managers*	*Business Men*	*Clerks and Kindred Workers*	*Manual Workers*	*Protective and Service Workers*	*Farmers*
1	Lawyer, doctor, judge, etc.	Business valued at $75,000 and over	Regional and division manager	CPA			Gentleman farmer
2	High-school teacher, undertaker, minister	Valued at $20,000 to $75,000	Assistant manager	Accountant, insurance salesman			Large farm owner
3	Social workers, grade-school teachers	Valued at $5,000 to $20,000	Minor official	Auto salesman, bank cashier	Contractors		
4		Valued at $2,000 to $5,000		Stenographer, bookkeeper	Foreman	Drycleaner, butcher	
5		Valued at $500 to $2,000		Dime store clerk	Carpenter, plumber, electrician	Barber, fireman	Tenant farmer
6		Valued at under $500			Semiskilled	Night-watchman, gas station attendant	Small tenant farmer
7					Heavy labor, miner	Janitor, newsboy	Migrant farm laborer

* Adapted from Warner, *et al.*, "Social Class in America."[39]

One of the earliest attempts at constructing a scale based on comparative occupational evaluations was that by Counts in 1925.[40] Others followed at what seemed to be almost regular intervals. Most of the studies were alike, varying principally in the number and titles of the occupations used. Several studies depended upon students or teachers as raters. Aside from the advantage of their availability, there was little else to recommend the use of students for this kind of research, in which the aim was to generalize to a national society. The occupations that were included were relatively well chosen although in some instances socially marginal occupations were listed. The rationale for including such an occupation as "prostitute," for example, was to set the lower prestige limit of the scale. In point of sociological fact, however, that and similar occupations fall completely outside the intent of a prestige scale for they cannot be considered as socially "legitimate" jobs.

Most of these methodological objections were corrected in a study of occupational prestige by North and Hatt, which remains as the best scale of its type.[41] The North and Hatt scale was based on the evaluations given by a nationwide sample of almost 3,000 adults for a list of ninety occupations. The sample itself was well chosen and the list of occupations covered the range quite well. One of the authors of the study claimed that "the prestige ratings of between two-thirds and three-fourths of the gainfully employed can be either identified exactly or estimated accurately" by the use of this scale.[42] Additionally, the list was so constructed as to encompass the obviously high and the low prestige occupations, as well as to provide checks on the internal reliability of the procedure. The study was conducted in 1946 by the National Opinion Research Center on their regular national sample. The instructions asked the respondent to evaluate the general standing of each occupation as "excellent," "good," "average," "somewhat below average," or "poor." Indicative of the care given to research detail was the fact that the order of presentation of the occupational list was systematically varied to avoid the bias of a tired respondent answering at random just to finish in a hurry. The effects of tiredness and impatience were thus randomized. The five-point rankings were expressed as percentages for each occupation and then transformed so that a maximum score of 100 represented the occupation with the highest prestige.

From the point of methodology, the North-Hatt study was careful, too, for the attention it gave to the reasons behind the evaluations and to the analysis of the pattern of differences by various segments of the sample. The reasons most often mentioned as making an occupation "excellent" were the pay (18 per cent), its "service to humanity" (16 per cent), its social prestige (14 per cent), and the education, work and money required to prepare for it (14 per cent). Other reasons that were thought to be less important nevertheless still showed the same mixture of materialism and idealism.[43]

There was a fair amount of agreement among individuals in their evaluations, yet some differences did appear. These were analyzed according to the social characteristics of the sample itself.[44] Scientists and lawyers were rated lower in the South. Priests were rated higher in the Northeast and lower in the Midwest. County judges, psychologists, sociologists, economists and bartenders were rated higher in the Northeast. For about four-fifths of all occupations, however, no significant differences were found between the ratings of those living in different sections of the country.

Some differences in evaluation were evident when analyzed by the size of the community where the respondent lived. Metropolitan residents gave higher ratings to the so-called "sophisticated" occupations such as artist, musician, author, bartender and night club singer, and to the scientific occupations. Rural dwellers, on the other hand, gave higher ratings to such occupations as farm owner and operator, railroad conductor and mail carrier.

Young people rated most jobs lower than did their elders, but the relative ranks given to the occupations were remarkably similar between the age groups. Some differences, however, were noted. The bartender, interestingly enough, was ranked highest by those between the ages of twenty-one and thirty-nine, and lowest by the older age groups. A lot of time could be spent speculating on that one point alone. Almost equally worth the time of speculative reasoning was the finding that the undertaker was ranked lowest by those under twenty, and rated higher by older people.

Men and women showed little differences between their ratings, although men picked the bartender and the factory owner for somewhat higher prestige kudos than did women. The prestige appeals of the bartender were as interesting as they were consistent.

Other differences appeared by education. The college group gave a generally higher standing to the professions. Those who had only been to grammar school rated carpenter, railroad conductor, building contractor, and union official higher instead. High school graduates gave rankings that tended to place between these groups. Differences by socio-economic level also appeared: wealthier persons rated the scientific occupations and the arts higher, while the lower income groups gave higher ratings to the skilled and semi-skilled occupations.

As might have been anticipated, the occupation of the person doing the rating made a difference. Generally he ranked his own occupation consistently higher than did others. Yet, what must also be recognized was that this upgrading of one's occupation stayed within bounds. Not everyone placed his own occupation first. Apparently it was recognized by most respondents that other occupations could carry more prestige than their own. On the whole, agreement was fairly close throughout the sample.

The evaluations were checked in part for reliability by planned controls. For example, "garage mechanic" and "automobile repairman," two names for the same job, differed by only one point in prestige scores. "Public school teacher" was paired with "instructor in the public schools" and similarly showed a difference of only one point. A partial test of validity was devised by including some occupations that were not ordinarily well-known. A little more than half of the sample did not know how to rate "nuclear physicist," which was a relatively new occupation in 1946. Similarly, "psychologists" and "sociologists" drew blanks for some respondents. This admission of ignorance was in fact desirable for it could be interpreted to mean that individuals ranked only those occupations about which they had knowledge; that they were not responding automatically nor afraid to admit ignorance.

Table 4—North-Hatt Occupational Prestige Scale*

Rank	*Occupation*	*Prestige Score*
1	U. S. Supreme Court Justice	96
2	Physician	93
3	State governor	93
4	Cabinet member in the federal government	92
5	Diplomat in the U. S. Foreign Service	92
6	Mayor of a large city	90
7	College professor	89
8	Scientist	89
9	United States Representative in Congress	89
10	Banker	88
11	Government scientist	88
12	County judge	87
13	Head of a department in a state government	87
14	Minister	87
15	Architect	86
16	Chemist	86
17	Dentist	86
18	Lawyer	86
19	Member of the board of directors of a large corporation	86
20	Nuclear physicist	86
21	Priest	86
22	Psychologist	85
23	Civil engineer	84
24	Airline pilot	83
25	Artist who paints pictures that are exhibited in galleries	83
26	Owner of factory that employs about 100 people	82
27	Sociologist	82
28	Accountant for a large business	81
29	Biologist	81
30	Musician in a symphony orchestra	81

* From North and Hatt, "Jobs and Occupations."41

Table 4—North-Hatt Occupational Prestige Scale (continued)

Rank	*Occupation*	*Prestige Score*
31	Author of novels	81
32	Captain in the regular army	80
33	Building contractor	79
34	Economist	79
35	Instructor in the public schools	79
36	Public-school teacher	78
37	County agricultural agent	77
38	Locomotive engineer	77
39	Farm owner and operator	76
40	Official of an international labor union	75
41	Radio announcer	75
42	Newspaper columnist	74
43	Owner-operator of a printing shop	74
44	Electrician	73
45	Trained machinist	73
46	Welfare worker for a city government	73
47	Undertaker	72
48	Reporter on a daily newspaper	71
49	Manager of a small store in a city	69
50	Bookkeeper	68
51	Insurance agent	68
52	Tenant farmer (one who owns livestock and machinery and manages the farm)	68
53	Traveling salesman for a wholesale concern	68
54	Playground director	67
55	Policeman	67
56	Railroad conductor	67
57	Mailman	66
58	Carpenter	65
59	Automobile repairman	63
60	Plumber	63
61	Garage mechanic	62
62	Local official of a labor union	62
63	Owner-operator of a lunch stand	61
64	Corporal in the regular army	60
65	Machine operator in a factory	60
66	Barber	59
67	Clerk in a store	58
68	Fisherman who owns his own boat	58
69	Streetcar motorman	58
70	Milkman	54
71	Restaurant cook	54
72	Truck driver	54
73	Lumberjack	53
74	Service-station attendant	52
75	Singer in a night club	52

Table 4—North-Hatt Occupational Prestige Scale (continued)

Rank	Occupation	Prestige Score
76	Farm hand	50
77	Coal miner	49
78	Taxi driver	49
79	Railroad section hand	48
80	Restaurant worker	48
81	Dock worker	47
82	Night watchman	47
83	Clothes presser in a laundry	46
84	Soda-fountain clerk	45
85	Bartender	44
86	Janitor	44
87	Sharecropper (one who owns no livestock or equipment and does not manage farm)	40
88	Garbage man	35
89	Street sweeper	34
90	Shoeshiner	33

The irrationality of some of the scores, however, was disturbing. Hatt himself was aware of that feature. "While this continuum [of occupational prestige scores] seems usable for many purposes," he noted, "the presence of similar scores for such dissimilar occupations as 'airline pilot,' 'artist who paints pictures,' 'owner of a factory employing about one hundred people,' and 'sociologist' raises the problem of whether or not the continuum holds together."[45] Trying to overcome this objection, Hatt combined the occupations into what have been called "situses," or occupational groups with similar prestige components. Eight situses were designated, which in turn were further subdivided into occupational "families":

1. *Political*
   - National
   - Local
2. *Professional*
   - Free professions
   - Pure sciences
   - Applied sciences
   - Community professionals
3. *Business*
   - Big business
   - Small business
   - Labor organization
   - White-collar employees
4. *Recreation and Aesthetics*
   - High arts
   - Journalism and radio
   - Recreation

5. *Agriculture*
   - Farming
   - Employed on farms

6. *Manual Work*
   - Skilled mechanics
   - Construction trades
   - Outdoor work
   - Factory work
   - Unskilled labor

7. *Military*
   - Army
   - Navy
   - Marine Corps
   - Coast Guard

8. *Service*
   - "Official Community"
   - "Unofficial Community"
   - Personal

The Guttman scaling technique was used to find if there were separate prestige scales, "quasi-scales," when occupations were grouped by situses or families. In this manner, the inconsistencies that Hatt had noted in the notion of a single continuum might be explained by a consistency within the smaller subdivisions of that continuum. The results of the scaling analysis were not statistically definitive, although plausible groupings among the occupations did emerge, which supported Hatt's interpretation "that each situs does include only jobs and occupations which can be compared consistently by most people."[46]

An intriguing idea, developed from the scale analysis, indicated that there was an overlapping of prestige scores between situses rather than a simple hierarchy by which each situs built on top of the one below. The lowest rated occupation in one situs, thereby, could be equal in prestige to the highest ranked occupation in another. The path of prestige scores was a weaving line, and not a straight one from top to bottom. For example, the prestige score for "carpenter" was higher than that for "clerk in a store," although the business situs as a whole, including the clerk, stood higher in prestige than the manual work situs to which the carpenter belonged. Hatt has suggested that the occupational history of an upwardly mobile individual from a job of low prestige to one of higher prestige might be a broken field run rather than a straight climb from "rags to riches." In this example, the individual could give up carpentry for a clerk's job with lower pay and lower prestige, with the intention of then being able to rise through the business situs where his ceiling would be much higher than it was for manual work.

The description of the two methods of occupational classification, exemplified by Edwards' classification and the North-Hatt scale, should indicate how occupation has been used as a basis for class measurement. With that information for background, it is now possible to weigh more critically the gains and limitations inherent in the use of occupation or occupational prestige as measures of class.

The rationale supporting the use of occupation as an index is attractively plausible. Occupational measures seem to catch and concretize the impressions that most people have of the class structure. This function of occupation has also had distinguished support in the past. Adam Smith deduced the social nature of occupations and the basis for their inequality, which he described in various sections of *The Wealth of Nations*. Durkheim, too, in an analysis of "organic solidarity," which he saw as a function of the division of labor in industrially advanced societies, noted:

> In effect, individuals are . . . grouped, no longer according to their relations of lineage, but according to the particular nature of the social activity to which they consecrate themselves. Their natural milieu is no longer the natal milieu, but the occupational milieu. . . . In a general way, classes and castes probably have no other origin nor any other nature; they arise from the multitude of occupational organizations. . . .[47]

Occupation has a social reality, especially in an industrial society. It is a real category of social classification that has direct meaning for status and class. Occupation, undoubtedly, is interpreted as an index of social position not only by social scientists but by non-professionals as well. To know that a person is a professional, for example, is to bring to mind an apperceptive mass about the kind of person he is —what he thinks, what he wants, and what his interests are. What is more, the professional himself has internalized these same expectations about himself, holding a view of professionals that is similar to that of others in the community.

Occupation can also be a summary indicator for other class characteristics, especially income and education, which in turn also reflect upon other class characteristics such as life styles and attitude patterns. The correlations between occupation, income and education are high and any or all of the three are important symbols to categorize people in the necessary shorthand of social interaction. That Americans are coming to live more and more in occupationally-based and occupationally-dominated social worlds only lends further credence to occupation as a class measure.

The rationale is supported not only by impressions, but by the formal theories of class, as presented in Chapter Two. Functional theory, for example, placed occupations at a vital point of social structure; prestige inequalities between occupations were explained as the results of differential contributions made by occupations to social existence. Those occupations, as Davis and Moore noted, that were considered most valuable within a society were given the higher rewards, including higher prestige. The generally high prestige position of the professional, as all measures have found, could be traced functionally to the increased dependence upon the technical and idea skills of the professions in an industrial society. Warner's theory, with a like emphasis, supported the view that occupations were a valid index of class. In the communities he studied, occupation was always used both by him and by his informants as a central index of class. Nor can Marx or Weber be excluded from mention as supporting this strong orientation toward occupation. At the very least in Marx's view, the bourgeoisie and the proletariat could be identified occupationally. Weber, even more explicitly, established occupation as a symbol, commonly used to identify status.[48] In short, the defense of occupational measures of class is almost unanimous and most formidable and impressive.

The case for using occupations as class indicators can be made even more solid, for such measures have clear methodological advantages. An occupation is inherently an objective characteristic. Occupation, although not always directly observable by some symbol—except for collar color—can be ascertained with directness and without difficulty. It is a category which most individuals understand and accept. Objectivity also implies that occupation can be measured. Enough has been said of that feature. Questions can be raised about the validity and reliability of the measures that have been discussed, but such problems are not inherently impossible to answer satisfactorily.

A third advantage, already implied, is that measures of occupation or occupational prestige can be used in a comparative fashion, within limits, to contrast changes through time and from place to place. Changes in the ease or difficulty of moving in and out of occupations, for example, have been studied and compared between two time periods, a matter to be discussed in detail in Chapter Six.[49] The occupations of sons have been compared with those their fathers held as a means of measuring differences in occupational mobility over a generation. The prestige of occupations has been compared between countries, as in a study by Inkeles and Rossi.[50] They compared the occupational prestige of a number of occupations in the United States, Great Britain, the U.S.S.R., Japan, and New Zealand, based on separate studies conducted in each country. In international comparisons it is necessary that the countries compared be near the same level of industrialization. The occupational setting and occupational values are different as between a highly industrialized nation, say, and one that is predominantly agricultural. However, this does not require that nations be at precisely the same level, as Inkeles and Rossi have pointed out. Indeed, variations in industrial ages can be significantly reflected in the differences in prestige accorded a number of key occupations. Occupation, in short, is extremely adaptable as a measure for such wide-ranging comparisons where no other measure would do as well.

A final advantage to be noted before closing this discussion is that occupation lends itself both to studies at the national level as well as to the study of the small local community. As a feature of economic institutions in a society, occupation extends throughout the social structure. This fact supports the use of occupational measures for a study of class that considers the society as a whole. At the same time, the same measure makes sense within the narrower boundaries of the community, for occupation also has relevance at that level.

The limitations of occupational measures, and there are some, have received very little systematic attention. Yet, it is as necessary to determine these shortcomings as well as the measure's utility in order to fix its potential as an index of class. The principal objection to the use of occupational measures can be phrased by a question: What is the relationship between an occupational index and class? Most stratification studies that depend upon occupational prestige as a measure of class reach an uncomfortable denouement; one sentence ends on a reference to occupation and the next picks up with a reference to class. From there on, class becomes the major, sometimes the only referrent, and the occupational measure used to reach that analytical plateau is seldom mentioned again. The plot might vary. Occupation and class might be used as interchangeable terms, or though the intention is class, the data presented in support of the conclusions depend entirely on some occupational measure. The problem and the question still remain: What is the relationship between an occupational index and class?

Admittedly, occupation and class have something in common; there is a strong theoretical linkage between the two. For example, occupation has been found to correlate significantly with a host of other indices of class, such as the prestige evaluations by community informants, the life styles of individuals, their education, their home, and their social participation. However, "having something in common" is a very general statement. The nature of the relationship between class and occupation requires greater precision, else there is no security, no stability, in what it is that is being measured.

The problem cannot be skirted by simply defining class in operational terms as a social segment that includes all those with occupations of similar prestige. The contention is not always, nor even generally, true. Nor are the measures of prestige exact enough or stable enough to lend a reliable and valid meaning to that contention. On the contrary, the use of occupation as an index of class often becomes a means to avoid taking a clear stand on one's theory of class and social stratification. In a great deal of research, occupation is depended upon not so much to index class as to define class entirely, oftentimes yielding an inconclusive set of findings precisely because the class phenomenon itself has not been independently determined and analyzed. Rather, it is often descriptions of an *occupational* group and not a *class* that occupies a great many studies in stratification, contrary to the stated intent of the authors.

The question is not naive. To be sure, there is little trouble in making occupation fit with some notion of class at the extremes. A shoeshiner, for example, is undoubtedly lower class on any type of scale and by any type of definition. By the same reasoning, the member of a board of directors of a large corporation is very probably upper class, or close to it. However, the major difficulty appears not so much in explaining the extremes of the occupational hierarchy, but in explaining and understanding the great and expanded middle range of that distribution. White-collar workers are not all middle class, for example, with the same assurance that permitted the class typing of the shoeshiner and the board member. Any number of exceptions come to mind. The financially successful salesman and the manager of a store are both white-collar and show almost no difference in their prestige scores according to the North and Hatt scale, but they could not be considered as class peers for many purposes. The money they make and what they do with it can be tremendously different between the two. The same holds true among professionals as a group. The successful physician in a large city and his professional counterpart in a small town may be class worlds apart. Yet, from the standpoint of a straight occupational comparison they are considered in the same category.

Although these examples essentially stress income differences, the case could have been presented just as easily using education, family lineage, class consciousness or any other dimension that has some meaning for class placement. Occupational prestige, in brief, does not exhaust the relevant dimensions of class. Nor is the occupational structure the same thing as the class structure. Therefore, occupation cannot always serve as an adequate class index, especially if the dimensions of class itself have not been fully established nor systematically related to a theory of stratification.

At the methodological level the problem becomes one of establishing the cutting points of an occupational measure to make it coterminus with a class definition, assuming that the measure is a demonstrably valid index. There are no reliable clues as yet to accomplish that goal. Hatt's suggestion of using occupational situses for the purpose might have some merit, but thus far the suggestion has not been explored. Instead, most studies using occupation as the basis for class determination apparently are content to use the most arbitrary set of operational cutting points to fit the immediate distribution. The particular sample under study is divided into two or more classes on the basis of the distribution at hand. Obviously. this method cannot be used as a general technique without at the same time making class anything more than whatever any one person thinks it is.

Another difficulty hampering the use of occupational measures is that the evaluations made of occupations can mean different things. Some of these differences can be equalized by proper sampling, as in the North and Hatt study, whereby a lack of knowledge about all relevant variables can be balanced by randomization, by including as many different types of people in the sample as possible. However, even from the North and Hatt findings it was clear that there were variations in the evaluations. Education, income, geographic region, and age were some of the factors that were found to affect the prestige evaluations of occupations. There are others as well that create special attitudes among individuals and affect the views they hold concerning occupations. Some occupations are so specialized that only those in direct contact with them would know what the occupation involved. Again, some occupations rate higher in some social segments than in others. In an industrial plant, for example, individuals who are considered as no more than, say, skilled mechanics by the outsider, in reality can hold positions of greater responsibility and higher prestige than the title of the occupation alone indicates. These shifting bases for evaluation can become important where, for example, the study was concerned with the community in which that plant was located.

The same order of dissatisfaction also holds for international occupational comparisons. Although prestige ratings of occupations can be compared, as in the Inkeles and Rossi study mentioned earlier, this does not mean that such ratings can be simply translated into a comment or description of the class system and social structure. The evaluations and interpretations of occupations in *class terms* are not fully reflected within an occupational prestige scale. The cultural history of each society is sufficiently unique to create various and subtle differences in what the evaluations of occupations really mean.

A final point needs to be raised in this list of general objections to occupational measures of class. There is no certain knowledge of how occupations do determine class actions. It is not enough to say that those in different occupations participate in varying degrees in the social life of the community, when the intended implication and intent is that differential participation is a function of class. An occupational prestige measure, of any sort, is much too thin to support propositions at the level of attitudes and personality. Persons differ in their behavior along several dimensions, and not completely along occupational lines as some studies have assumed. There are variations due to differences in income, in community position, in social philosophy, in responsibility, and in education. Yet, many studies presume to explain what is essentially class-conditioned behavior on the basis of occupational data alone.

In short, instead of using occupation as an *index* of class with all of the shortcomings and limitations that any index inherently contains, the unwitting tendency has become one of using occupation as a *synonym* for class which is a methodological step of a vastly different order.

Conclusions

THESE last remarks, as well as the whole discussion of class measures, are calls for methodological caution in the use and development of those measures. Each type that has been presented possessed its unique advantages as well as its own inherent limitations. The same will undoubtedly be true for those measures that are yet to be devised.

Each measure has its own range of usefulness. Each can be adapted in some manner to fit the particular needs of a research study at hand. However, they have all been used in the past with some degree of relative abandon, especially where the primary interest has been in class and in class matters. It is precisely at that point that such indices must be cautiously interpreted.

The dominant assumption in most work on class appears to be that any available measure, usually occupation, can serve as a class indicator. In the next step, class, so measured, is correlated with whatever characteristics the study has included, such as aspirations, achievements, participation, and political behavior. The conclusions which are taken from that procedure then purport to speak of *class* behavior, when in reality, class has hardly been defined or considered. It is a sloppy research procedure that in effect seems to say, "We can find out something about class if we just keep studying it, no matter how poor or how inaccurate are the basic tools that are used." Not only is this a downright suspicious rearrangement of the sequence in scientific inquiry, but it is also misleading. A mountain of facts can be collected by this order of procedure, yet truly there is little basis upon which to make comparisons between the facts. There is only a doubtful scientific benefit in knowing that some classes aspire more energetically than others and that some classes are more community conscious than others, if the definitions of class in the two instances really allow for no comparison. In that case, just what is the utility of stock-piling these so-called facts about how class affects behavior, attitudes, and personality? Kornhauser has made an extremely telling point in this connection:

> Investigations of social class as determinant of public opinion or of anything else must deal with class in such a way as to go beyond reliance on a simple rating of occupation, an index of social participation, or a self-classification. . . . The appropriate procedures for this task must certainly include far more than the correlations among measured characteristics of people.[51]

Two positive suggestions emerge from this critique. The need to devise a systematic theory of class is greater than ever. Only in this way, can the problems of definition and the problems of relationship between relevant variables be placed within a logical and stable perspective. The research effort intended to add to an understanding of class-based phenomena thereby would proceed from a firmer foundation, one that would bring order and system into the study. The theoretical suggestions of Weber, for example, as noted in the preceding chapter, have been almost completely overlooked either as a guide to research or as a basis for theoretical modifications. Yet, in spite of some of its shortcomings, Weber's theory does much to clarify the confusion that arises when the attempt is made to compare the many and disparate facts that are known about class.

The second suggestion is that more deliberate effort should be made to revise and refine the methodology of class. In part, this goal is tied to finding an adequate theory of class.

In part, too, is needed the testing and analysis of alternative measures with the intent of overcoming some of their purely technical problems. It is not enough to compare occupational prestige measures with living standard measures, or with some other type of measure, to ascertain how much they agree with one another. Rather, what is needed is to go on with the problems raised by any one measure and seek to remedy them. For example, as has been already noted, the inconsistencies found in the North and Hatt scale of occupational prestige have not yet been subjected to systematic investigation. Yet, here is a matter that requires some serious work to account for and explain those inconsistencies.

As long as the major effort in the study of class is centrally concerned only with proliferating facts that can be correlated with some measure of class, however defined, it is unlikely that any significant gains can be made except to uncover another selected item that still cannot be fitted into a tight framework of knowledge about the subject.

CHAPTER IV

Class and Social Structure

CLASS IS PART OF SOCIAL REALITY, part of the fabric of society, and is not simply an abstraction devised by the social analyst for his own convenience. Class, it can be shown, has dimensionality; it makes a difference for a very wide range of social relationships.

Class is expressed in social reality in two ways: through the institutional structure and through the behavior of individuals. The two aspects are related, of course, but like most complex matters must be handled separately if they are to be adequately understood. The first expression, which is the subject of this chapter, affirms that class can be traced throughout the organization and the ideologies of American society. The second, which emphasizes the role of class in behavior, is considered in the following chapter. What is documented and analyzed there is the wide spectrum of human activity that is touched, shaped, and modified by class: levels of aspiration, mental health, birth and death, and attitudes, frustrations, and prejudices. Perhaps class does not affect and modify every phase of human motivation and activity, but it does influence a range of behavior that is enormous in its scope and significant in its effects.

The social institutions of society are elemental points where the impact of class is most significant. "Social institutions," in the vocabulary of the sociologist, refer to the basic dimensions of social organization that are common to all societies, although the specific content of the institutions obviously must vary from one society to another. Each institution, in short, is the cultural answer to a universal need of social organization. The need to maintain order, for example, is met by explicitly delegating power to a recognized and legitimate authority; and the norms of the political institution specify the manner by which that is systematically accomplished. The family, another institution, controls the manner of human reproduction and orders the method of socializing new generations into the society. Similarly, the economic order, education, and religion are other institutions, each concerned with meeting other vital demands of social organization. "Institutions regulate the modes of meeting important recurrent situations such as birth, death, marriage, acquiring economic goods, dealing with power relations, maintaining social consensus, and training the young, and at the same time help ensure that these situations will recur."[1]

In ways that are particularly adapted to each of these institutional spheres, then, class enters as a defining characteristic that establishes the tone and sets the format for social relationships. Whether it is the prestige aspirations of the family, the social consciousness of a religious denomination, the ethos of the market place, or the symbols of a political ideology, class intervenes as a force of importance. As was recognized by each of the theorists discussed in Chapter Two, class has a ubiquity and a pervasiveness that strikes deep to the very basic organizing elements of society itself.

In that sense, class is part of the American culture, in spite of the formal ideological denials. Some of the possible reasons for the denial of class have been discussed in Chapter One, but other dimensions of that ideology have yet to be described in the context of the present chapter. In any case, behind the formal vocabulary of the American creed, class differences have persisted and have been recognized. Whether social inequality was considered as the will of God or simply as evidence of differences in talents, personal qualities, or individual accomplishments, the facts of such inequality were in evidence. America is not the first society, nor probably the last, to maintain such discrepancies between its social ideology and social actuality.

In short, class has been, and is today, a real and present feature of American social structure, in its institutions and in its ideology. Class is a social fact to be found in the local communities of America and in the national society as well.

Class and Culture

Before the documentation and analysis of the place of class in American social structure can be approached, two notions regarding class and culture need to be discussed. Both have a measure of popularity. Both are, furthermore, highly relevant for the perspective one assumes toward the analysis of class structure in American society.

The first view contends that American society is primarily middle class; that middle class values, tastes, and life patterns are the dominating cultural feature. In education, in politics, and in religion, it is contended, the American middle class is the dominant influence. Even suburbanization is pictured as primarily a middle class population move stimulated by the desire to attain the predominately middle class values of a home and a fitting environment for children. By this view, the average man as the mass man is middle class.[2]

In some measure, this cultural ascendancy by the middle class is explained as the consequence of its numerical superiority. By any criterion—occupation, income, education, or subjective identification—the proponents of this view argue that America has become a society bulging in the middle ranks.

However, it cannot be size alone that would account for this dominant hold over American culture. Rather, this dominance is part of the heritage left by many generations of middle class control. It was the "old" middle class that initiated and successfully carried through one of the most extensive social revolutions in all of human history. It was the "old" middle class that won out over the landed nobility and at the same time introduced a radical revision of the philosophy and ideology of politics, of social relations, of family life, of religion, and of education. The pervasiveness and the impact of this revolution in social organization did much to fashion the character of contemporary Western culture. The modern era was entered, therefore, with a set of beliefs and values fashioned by a once middle class.

To be sure, the proponents of this view would recognize that the middle class and the entire class structure have changed considerably. A lesser social revolution, perhaps, has taken place. The "old" middle class of independent entrepreneurs and proprietors, the "bourgeoisie" of early capitalism according to Marx, has in part been transformed into the "new" middle class of salaried clerks, professionals, and managers. The "new" middle class depends upon a new set of social relationships and new cultural forms even though many of the values and ideologies of the old are still evident. However, these are more evident in the formal ideologies that the "old" middle class did much to develop than in the actual working ideologies and values of the "new" middle class.

In spite of the shift in composition and ideologies of the "new" middle class, there are those who contend that the cultural dominance of the middle class still continues; that it rests upon the cultural heritage of the past, upon this strongest commitment of any class to things as they are, and upon the loud cultural voice of the class. The middle class dominates many of the channels for expression in the community, whether it is in voting, guiding welfare activities, discussing changes in local government, steering the PTA, or just keeping informed about current affairs. It is middle class values that are taught to the young in school, and it is the middle class that most conscientiously keeps tabs on the conduct of that education. The middle class votes and discusses campaign issues. The middle class, in short, is loudly vocal in its demands, sophisticated about its responsibility and educated about its environment and what to do about it.

On historical grounds, on the grounds of numerical superiority, and on the basis of greater social involvement, therefore, the argument is made that American society is a middle class society. Nor is the trend likely to abate. The forces pushing towards a mass middle class culture are strong and continuing; the push toward conformity, and a middle class conformity at that, is almost inevitable.

This argument that American culture is middle class cannot be fully proven or disproven, for it is a rather sketchy generalization that really depends for its proof upon a piling up of examples and incidents rather than upon assessed facts. It is easy to point out the symbols and the means of typical middle class dominance: the emphasis upon education, upon the success ideal, the noisy middle class involvement in community affairs, or the infiltration of middle class tastes into consumer patterns. Yet, counter instances are just as evident: the startling absence of middle class effect in the decision-making processes at both the local and national levels, the easy way in which middle class tastes can be manipulated in consumer purchasing and their faddishness, or the many instances of failure of middle class values to filter down to the lower class in the hierarchy.

Little is gained by a blanket characterization of this sort. Indeed, as is indicated later, much may be lost by adopting this suspiciously ready generalization. It is a spongy contention that covers over too much, that ends up by telling very little either about the middle class or its relative effect on the class structure. It should be enough that the study of class is generally a middle class preoccupation; the tendencies toward bias are sufficiently probable as it is without deliberately heightening them even more by adopting this kind of orientation.

Class has been tied to culture in a second way. Briefly, this is by the view that classes are themselves separate "sub-cultures," or "part-cultures." The several classes, it is contended, live in distinguishable and separate cultural worlds, even as they share certain common elements of the general culture.

The theoretical basis for the formulation of a class sub-culture is that the values, life styles, goals, and behavior of the several classes are distinct and different. Even further, the assumption is made that the cultural expressions within any one class are sufficiently cohesive and consistent to distinguish them from those of any other class. The class sub-culture, then, is a cultural unity, and there arises the distinct reality of a middle class culture, an upper class culture, and a lower class culture—or as many other variations as can be found and identified.

Nor is class the only type of sub-culture. Kroeber,[3] for one, has applied the concept to racial groups, to age groups (the adolescent sub-culture, for example), and has described a male sub-culture and a female sub-culture. The identification of sub-culture, as implied by these examples, can be carried to startling extremes. A sub-culture exists by this definition whenever a definable criterion can distinguish any group of individuals from others. Apparently, the anthropologist has found this conceptualization meaningful. However, what are class cultures and what do they mean?

This view of classes as sub-cultures is not simply a semantic or definitional matter, for the view carries with it a baggage of assumptions that is crucial. It is true, of course, that individuals in the different classes do behave differently and are motivated by different values. Social class does make a difference for human behavior. However, to conceptualize these differences as sub-cultures goes beyond a recognition of class differences alone and transforms the very character of a class.

One assumption of this sub-culture perspective is that each class has some unity as a group. The members of a class, in other words, share a recognition of their class membership in much the same way that members of a racial group, or ethnic group, or age group recognize those of their group and those outside it. Although there is a consciousness of class in the United States, there is very little evidence of class consciousness in the sense of a cohesive group. Without this shared awareness by members of a class, the designation of sub-cultures becomes questionable, for there is no ready identification with a recognized and unequivocal set of cultural norms. There is too much variation in the ways that so-called class norms are interpreted. There is confusion and disagreement over the way individuals label themselves and identify others by class. To refer to classes, then, as "sub-cultures" implies much more consistency, class cohesion, and agreement than exists at this level of subjective class identification. This is not to deny that there are differences between class strata, but there is relatively little consensus about these differences in all particulars; at least, little enough so that most Americans do not belong to a self-conscious class group.

A second consequence in the use of the sub-culture notion is that heavier stress is thereby given to the value systems within the several classes instead of to the effects of the social structure itself. There is the tendency, although not an inevitable one, to consider behavior as the result of the value system of class rather than as the effect of, say, economic factors, social power, education, or political forces. The crux of class distinction, thereby, becomes one of values, which in turn become the presumed causes of class difference in behavior. The middle class in this manner would be distinguished by, say, its heavy emphasis upon prestige and upward mobility, the lower class by its acceptance of a kind of social inferiority, and the upper class perhaps by a belief in its own inherent social superiority. The particular motivating values are open to many other interpretations, of course, depending on one's view of the class system.

To some extent this emphasis upon the difference in value systems between the classes is a cultural variation on an old theme. At one time it was maintained that some classes were biologically inferior and some superior. Later, the base was changed to a religious one, and some were thought of as chosen, others as damned. The use of the concept of sub-culture in this area follows the same logic, but with reliance upon a supposedly less loaded criterion of cultural difference rather than of biology or religion. Instead of seeing classes as cultural variations around a central cultural norm, classes come to be interpreted as different cultural units. Instead of seeing class differences as effects of a set of common causes—economic life chances, educational opportunities, or control over positions of power—such differences become rigidified into distinct cultural patterns revolving around separate value systems. This path leads away from an understanding of and an appreciation for an American class system, and instead fragments the study into a concern with sub-cultural units.

This latter point raises another objection to the notion of class sub-cultures. Clearly, the free employment of that concept might go to rather minute extremes. Why stop at only three sub-cultures for class? Why not distinguish six or nine, or more? Further, because there are regional variations, why not step up the pace of sub-cultural designations to include a northern, upper-middle class sub-culture, a middlewestern, lower-middle class sub-culture, and so on for many more categories? There is no indication where such needless proliferations should stop. The notion of a single culture that gives coherence and unity to national society is lost in a potpouri of many "sub-cultural" units. Under such circumstances, the theorist of culture is faced with an even more formidable task than before: to explain how these sub-cultures are welded together into the single unit that obviously must exist if we are to recognize "an American society."

Furthermore, the concern with sub-cultures leads away from a recognition of how society-wide forces operate. How is one to understand the function of national power, say, if the class system is seen as composed of many separate sub-cultural units? What are the effects of changes in the economic institutions of American society upon the class system and how are these realized, if that system is but a congeries of separate cultural groups? Clearly, the issues raised by these questions become only peripheral ones in the sub-culture view of classes. This would then throw out the major concerns in the study of class.

This approach, therefore, carries with it its own particular bias. It tries to counter the complexity of social structure by splitting it up into more manageable sub-units, rather than by studying the complexity itself for the basic unifying features that bind that social and class structure together. Social classes in an industrial society cannot by any stretch of the imagination be thought of as cultural units that are comparable to primitive communities. Yet, one suspects, that is precisely the rationale behind the anthropologist's tendency to think of class as a sub-culture. To consider the several classes in American society as somehow distinct cultural entities is to transmogrify class into a bizarre cultural enclave.

Class Structure: The Local Community

A SIGNIFICANT proportion of the literature on stratification, in the United States and elsewhere, is taken up with descriptions of the class structure in the small community.[4] The towns vary in size from a thousand people to fifty thousand or so, averaging somewhere around six thousand. In the United States the communities that have been so studied cover a wide geography including New England, the deep

South, the Midwest, the Southwest, and the Plains area. This is not to say that the places that were selected were always representative of the surrounding region; more often, the selection depended on more incidental factors rather than upon a rigorous sampling procedure. Nonetheless, the character of the region usually has infiltrated the community under study; sometimes in the sense of the tradition of older regions, or in the crackling newness of the regions more recently settled; sometimes as an ethnic dominance in the farm regions, or as a racial separation in the South.

In spite of widespread geographic differences, the differences in the importance of tradition, and differences in population composition, there is a recurrent monotone in class features in all of the community descriptions that may be dull, but that is scientifically comforting nevertheless. The cliché that "people are the same everywhere" might be let loose here. The cliché applies. "We don't have classes in our town," almost invariably is the first remark recorded by the investigator. Once that has been uttered and is out of the way, the class divisions in the town can be recorded with what seems to be an amazing degree of agreement among the good citizens of the community. Each town has its own set of class symbols; its own terminology for "high," "middle," and "low." What is more, almost everything of social significance—friendships, marriages, morality, education and religion—are drawn into the vocabulary of class and into its frame of reference. The upper classes are respected by all and emulated by some; the middle classes are respectable and dedicated; and the lower classes are sometimes immoral and shiftless and sometimes decent and poor. The cast changes, the scenery shifts from town to town, but the plot and the outcome are as standard and predetermined as an old time melodrama.

Yet these community studies are useful. They provide a microscopic image of class. These descriptions give a feeling for class textures; for what class is like on a personal and intimate level. The total of these studies taken together, and even multiplied several times, reads as a meaningful integer for the national class total. Economic and political trends, the locations of power, and the decisions that can only be national in scope, are difficult to comprehend only from a knowledge of what class is like in the small community. The nation, after all, exists as an entity in its own right, and many social processes make sense only within this broader scope. However, it is senseless to demand answers from these community studies that they are not designed to give. Instead, it is more reasonable to take such studies on their own merits and for what they are—detailed glimpses of the way class operates at a local, interpersonal level in the daily life of a community.

Because these communities are so much alike in their class structures, it is possible to combine them into a single description. In this way, too, much of the monotony of repetition can be avoided. In the description that follows, some corners have been cut and a few liberties have been taken; each point mentioned might not hold true of every community. Such inaccuracies, however, are relatively unimportant and do not really threaten the validity of the description. Let this composite community be called "Hometown," simply to name it. Hometown is not representative of the United States, but is only a composite of some of the communities that have been studied.

Hometown is a small town, not a suburb. Although it is not economically self-sufficient, Hometown tends to be socially self-sufficient. The mass media reach the community, of course, but most people are concerned with local affairs, both political and social. There is a small industrial plant or perhaps an agricultural processing plant in Hometown that dominates the economy, and the community is heavily dependent upon it. The plant, though, is absentee-owned and is managed by an outsider sent into Hometown and trained for his job. The manager tries to find his proper niche in the social structure of Hometown but it isn't at all clear whether this is for good public relations or because he has to live in the town and somehow be part of it. Even with the intrusions of managers, corporations, and political events from the outside, Hometown scales everything down to size and the illusion of community self-sufficiency is maintained. People know each other, or at least know about one another. Living in Hometown, in other words, is a full-time occupation.

This personal knowledge, which sets the basis for much of the social relationships in Hometown, is formed by definite symbols in Hometown. These symbols, especially those of class, are stable, conceded and unambiguous. There is general consensus about what the symbols are and what they stand for. The upper classes form a small percentage of the population, and are known variously as the "Tops," the "Elite," or the "Society People." It is believed that the members of the upper classes think of themselves in the same symbolic terms. The lower classes are known variously as the "Bottoms," or the "No-accounts." It is unlikely that the lower classes think of themselves in these negative terms although they do recognize the social gulf that separates them from others. Most of the people in Hometown are middle class. There is no special terminology for them but they do have a near monopoly on such adjectives as "respectable," "decent," and "dedicated." The middle class also likes to think of itself in these terms and does so.

The symbols of class extend to the streets and homes of Hometown. Almost any resident of the town could draw a class map that ecologically would locate the several classes by where they live. All of the children of Hometown are socialized early into this residential class difference, and as adults they live with this class mapping firmly fixed. The address of a family is as much a symbol of its class as a coat of arms. This symbol, above all others, is kept up-to-date, which means that if a family goes up or down in the class heirarchy of Hometown, change of residence is required. When moving up, the family itself is motivated to change addresses; when the move is down, economic circumstances as well as the unrelenting social pressure of the small town force the change in address. The class symbol, "the other side of the tracks," was minted in Hometown and is still honored currency.

Symbols induce stereotypes, especially when used continuously, and Hometown has its share. Indeed, most social intercourse is conducted automatically through the social shorthand of stereotypes. The middle classes, as already noted, are the respectable members of the community. They are the social bedrock upon which the organized community depends. They are the most loyal Hometowners. Civic responsibility is the noisy concern of the middle classes, whether the job is to build monuments, publicize the town for new business, collect money for a worthy charity, or organize for civil defense. The middle classes are there first, stay the longest, and work the hardest.

The upper and lower classes show the extremes. The former live above the town's social life, so to speak, and never become too noticeably involved with it. They are gracious, sometimes friendly, but above all, the current and supreme conveyors of whatever tradition the town has. They are the direct descendents of the founders of Hometown, and they never let anyone forget it. They stick together, and succeed in keeping their circle select. But they are looked up to by most people in town, even though they live in a social world that is often hidden from direct view. This screen serves to enhance the position even more.

The lower classes live just as much in a social world screened from view, but not by choice. They are stereotyped as habitually lazy, inherently immoral, and socially impossible. Considered to be without ambition, they are doomed to remain at the bottom of the class structure. Some lower class Hometowners, though, are clean, honest, and try to lead decent, *i.e.*, middle class approved, lives. These individuals, of course, are more socially worthy even though they probably will not rise either.

Hometowners, no matter how small their community, live their public lives within relatively insulated class worlds. It is somewhat amazing, the divisiveness in even the smallest community. Although necessarily there are points of social contact between classes in the daily business of Hometown, most people spend their private lives within their own class. Except for patriotic celebrations, perhaps religious worship, some organizations, and the necessary jobs of the work world, most Hometowners spend their time by themselves or with their peers.

The number of classes that is recognized varies, depending on the number of social differences that Hometowners can detect and agree upon. For those who stand either at the very bottom or at the very top of the class hierarchy, there is the tendency to think of Hometown as consisting of only two groups: people like themselves and everyone else. The more subtle criteria for differentiation either escape them or are considered unimportant. Those who belong in the middle ranks are more perceptive to those above and below them. On the whole, however, the following are more or less distinguishable after a time:

1) An "upper-upper" class whose title and privilege stem from its position as the class composed of the descendents of Hometown's past and tradition—the founders of Hometown and the men who gave the town and themselves whatever success can be claimed. This class is Hometown's version of nobility, and consequently, a high social wall has been built between this class and would-be aspirants to these ranks.

2) The "lower-upper" class includes those who have managed to achieve many of the symbols of status, such as wealth, education, and the proper home. However, they are denied admission into the uppermost rank because they lack the prime requirement—a long, respectable, and traditionalized social standing. They are newcomers, or, if long residents, without the proper family background. Their gains are too recent. They are not yet socially aged to the proper mellowness that would properly condition them for upper-upper class membership. Although they try to emulate the upper-uppers, their mimicry is poorly executed, pathetically overdone, and manifestly gauche.

3) The middle class is also subdivided into two segments, principally on the basis of wealth. Less wealthy than those above them, the upper-middle class at least is a notch above others in the community. These are the upwardly mobile individuals who are ready to approach the next hurdle into

the upper class itself. The lower segment of the middle class includes those individuals of solid respectability with a steady, sober life pattern. They are the average citizens of Hometown, its stable element, who never do anything outstanding or out of the ordinary. Respected in the community, they have little else to mark them.

4) The lower classes include those who by occupation, income, and education stand lowest in the hierarchy. They perform the skilled and semi-skilled work. They have modest incomes, and socially are the most invisible class of all. They are the honest and steady citizens of Hometown, differing only from the class immediately above them by occupation and income. At the very bottom of the class hierarchy are the lower-lowers. They do the unskilled labor. They don't amount to much of anything, most people in Hometown believe, and they never will. If the upper-uppers are the contemporary versions of aristocracy, then the lower-lowers are the American version of the untouchables rejected by a caste system.

This class description is admittedly general. There are some variations between one community and another, but those are not especially important. One version of Hometown, in other words, might not have an upper-upper class because the town was only recently settled. Another Hometown might not have as many sub-segments of the three major classes as have been here described. Nevertheless, it is important to note that even in those instances, the trends can already be seen that in another generation will produce as many, if not more, class segments as here described. In one such community, for example, the nucleus of the upper class is only some fifty years away from the founding of the town and already it seems clear that "ancestry" is being emphasized as the prime mark of elite membership.

This description of the classes in Hometown has only intimated other features of the community's social structure that can be further specified. Interpersonal relationships seldom breach class lines. Friendships and cliques follow class boundaries rather strictly. In turn, the social intimacy or the social distance that these patterns create are institutionally preserved by endogamy within classes. Such closely personalized judgments, of course, are to a large extent the mark of small communities like Hometown where social control by gossip and ostracism can be effectively exerted.

The social institutions of Hometown also carry the stamp of class. The one that has been the most studied is the school, and in many ways it provides a good example of the way the classes function in Hometown. Education, in spite of the equality preserved for it in a democratic ideology, is predominantly an upper and a middle class institution in Hometown. Simply put, schools are staffed by the middle class, and controlled by both the upper and middle classes. As property owners contributing to the financial support for the schools of Hometown and as conscientious parents, the persons in those two classes exercise effective control. The officials of the Hometown Board of Education are elected, as in most communities, but very rarely does an individual seek or win election without the support of the upper classes. Not that many upper class Hometowners send their children to local schools, especially at the high school level; instead, children of the upper classes are sent elsewhere for their training. But, the control of the school system is important because it requires a major portion of a Hometowner's taxes and it can affect the values and ideologies of impressionable youth. Hence, the Board of Education is usually headed by someone legitimatized through the informal selection of the upper class leaders. Other members of the board come from the sober sections of the middle class as well as from some upper class group.

The educational philosophy that seems to pervade most of the Board's thinking is that the high school is especially designed for those who can most benefit from it. Lower class adolescents, it is believed, would be better off working at a paying job than wasting time in school, for they probably will have little use for their education as adults. In any case, high school is the terminal educational point for many of them. Children from higher class levels, however, benefit from high school both as a preparation for college as well as for "living," whatever that might mean. What the Hometown students learn is pretty much the things that Hometown upper and middle class adults believe: the values of property, of initiative, of community responsibility, and of the need for adjusting to the world one is in rather than changing the world to fit some other set of ideals. These are the ideas that the Hometown Board of Education wants taught. These are the ideas that Hometown teachers are expected, and want, to teach. To insure this goal, teachers are chosen from qualified local Hometowners, and additional teachers are imported only as needed. Since teaching is a respectable occupation for many in Hometown's middle classes, there is some assurance of a continued supply of certified teachers.

Those who pay the taxes for the school system call the price on Hometown's educational facilities. Modernization, textbooks, teachers' salaries, and school equipment must all be approved by the Board of Education, and their responsibility to Hometown citizens is clear. People don't want to pay more taxes, especially those who are paying any taxes now. Hence, change is not really welcomed in Hometown schools because it is new and because it usually costs more. The only counteracting force, without which Hometown schools would remain forever in the past, is that schools must be accredited by organizations outside of Hometown's influence. Such organizations at least keep Hometown schools from lagging too far. This real pressure is implemented further by the fact that state funds to the school depend upon continued accreditation. To lose such funds and to be forced to rely solely upon Hometown's own financial resources is infinitely worse than changing the school system and its facilities where needed to keep an accredited rating.

In short, then, the education of Hometowners is effectively dominated by the upper and middle classes. The lower class cannot and does not apparently want to challenge that control. Generally, they are apathetic, recognizing that their future is not closely tied to schooling. A job in the mill or the plant, a family, and perhaps a modest home are the real elements in the future of those lower class Hometowners that don't want to remain at the very bottom. Hence, they lose any voice in the educational institution by default.

Religion in Hometown is as much affected by the class structure as is the educational system. Like education, religion is an important area of life in the society of Hometown; it involves something that Hometowners think about, consider important, and to which they are socially sensitive. Little wonder then that religious practices and the religious style in Hometown reflect status differences.

Hometowners take their religion seriously, although this attitude is differently defined within each class. Churches in Hometown are ranked by the class of their parishioners. Some religions and some churches are considered by many to be somehow more respectable than others. This is not to say, as most Hometowners would be quick to add, that others are not as good or are less respectable. Still, it is one of the unceasing wonders of social logic that it need never obey the principles of formal logic; that some churches are better regarded apparently does not imply that other churches thereby be regarded as worse. Leaving these semantics aside and looking only at the kinds of people that belong to the several churches and denominations, there is little doubt that an individual's class has a good deal to do with which church he attends. Perhaps this is only the coincidental result of free choice, but it seems unlikely in view of the sharp class cleavages between churches. It is more than likely that informal pressures have been exerted upon those who would be "unwelcome" if they made a choice inconsistent with the accepted norms.

Class also affects the degree of participation in religious activity in Hometown. Generally, there is a high correlation between the two components: the higher the class, the greater the religious participation. The principal exception is that the upper classes are not as active in the church as are the middle classes. The former keep their religious activity down to a minimal and formal level. They marry in the church, conduct funeral services there, and hold their religious affiliation in front of them as a formal symbol that they recognize the values of religion as every good Hometowner and American should.

The middle classes, on the other hand, try to manipulate their religious affiliations for social advantages. They are active in the church, as directors and as leaders in the many activities that most American churches have had to include in their programs. Wherever possible, ambitious middle class people try to join upper class churches, thereby using religion as another channel for upward mobility.

The lower class participates less in religious activity than others in Hometown. More among them than among any other class have no religious affiliation, and attendance at religious services is kept to a minimum for those that do belong. Religion is not a satisfactory form of social participation—another evidence of the lower class person's general withdrawal from the social life of Hometown. However, there are those in the lower class that do go to church, and they go with typically lower class motivations. Religion and church-going are approved social escapes for the lower classes in Hometown, the more so for individuals who otherwise participate very little in the community. As one woman told the Lynds in Middletown, "I like to go to church. It's the only place, about, I ever do go." This attitude is prevalent among lower class Hometowners that do have some religious affiliation.

Religious institutions in Hometown, then, are not so sacred that they are above the secular class rivalries. Churches are dominated typically by one of the several classes, and religious participation and affiliation are heavy with class overtones.

The differential degrees of participation and control between the several classes in Hometown as already shown in education, religion, and formal organizations continue throughout the social structure of the community. The pattern seems to be always the same: the upper classes in control, dictating policy insofar as they wish to become involved in the affairs of the community; the middle classes showing the greatest fever of community activity and involvement as the means for currying favor with those above them and somehow accumulating a reserve of social goodness that might some day be cashed in for a more material status advance; finally, the lower classes centrifuged away from the core of most community activity out to the periphery, where they have the least say about any Hometown matters. The pattern is the same throughout most of the social institutions of Hometown.

This then is Hometown: the composite picture of local community life in the United States, and the enormously important role that class plays. The pattern is repeated in almost every real counterpart of Hometown, and is repeated in almost exactly the same terms as outlined here. That these facts do not fit the idealized values held for our society—especially its rural phase—is not surprising because formal values are often retained intact long beyond the existence of their real life. All that flourishes is the discrepancy between ideals and actuality. The pervasiveness of class in so many social niches of community life is not surprising either.

One community has not been included in the composite Hometown portrait. The place has been called "Regional City." What makes this community study different is that it was a study of power.[5] Hunter was interested in finding out who were the leaders of Regional City, those who made the decisions within the legitimate channels of the community structure and by these acts, in effect, directed much of the activity and community energies of Regional City. The study is discussed at this point because it is a community study and because it offers an importantly different perspective on community structure as it is affected by class.

Locating the leaders of Regional City was a relatively straightforward process. Hunter looked for the prominent persons in civic, governmental, business and status circles by the names that were mentioned in newspapers, that appeared on the rosters of organizations, and that otherwise received publicity. Interviews with a cross section of "judges" provided the means to narrow the list and also to rank the leaders in order of their presumed importance in the community. This group, finally narrowed down to forty names, included individuals who it was generally agreed were the leaders in the four spheres just enumerated—civic, governmental, business and status. Included were the executives of local banks, insurance firms, and commercial establishments, the top officials in local government, labor and professional leaders, and finally, the social leaders of Regional City.

There are levels of power just as there are class levels, and from among the forty persons designated as leaders a few stood out as leaders of the leaders. These few men formed the apex of the power hierarchy. They made the policy decisions and designated the personnel in most instances to convert those decisions into action. The top group consisted primarily of the leading businessmen in Regional City. The top seven men, as picked by the leaders themselves, included three top executives from utilities and an oil pipe line company, the mayor, two top executives from manufacturing plants, and an attorney. These men, and others near them, held and exercised the power in Regional City whether it was the power of decision to build or not to build a new municipal auditorium, to alter the tax structure, or to use political pressure at the national level where it might affect Regional City. Indeed, as Hunter found out, the top leaders in Regional City have a range of influence far beyond the limits of their own community. "Regional City cannot be isolated from state, national, and international affairs." Power, unlike a locally based status hierarchy, can be extended to the larger national society.

What the study of Regional City adds to the status picture of Hometown is the dimension of social power. The two together reveal a greater depth of meaning to the idea of class within the social structures of American communities.

The two are woven together, as the description of Hometown implied again and again. The control of education and of the life styles in Hometown by the upper classes is an indication of social power. Similarly, the knowledge gained from Regional City leaves little doubt that the top power leaders could and did have something to say about the conduct of affairs in that community. In short, all of these community studies taken together really reveal a harmonious composite, in which class must involve both power and status dimensions. What is more, status and power follow class lines in precisely the same manner. Upper status groups produce and support the men of power. The other classes stand further away from that power. Indeed, all of these elements are aspects of the same social universe.

For that reason, it should be reiterated, there has been no attempt made here to become embroiled in and thereby hindered by the terminology of stratification. To insist upon an abstract differentiation between "class," "status," or some other term is pointless. The context in which the terms are used should make it unequivocally clear whether it is fashions, life-styles, power, or economic position that is being referred to. The central point that needs to be made is only that all of these terms and concepts belong to the same vocabulary. "Class" has been used here as the generic term, although it might have been any other acceptable term. Instead of stumbling over the semantics, however, the crucial need is to explore the many manifestations of class at both the local and the national level with the aim of finding interconnections between those manifestations rather than attempting to separate them, even if the ostensible purpose is that of research convenience. The merging of the Hometown studies and Regional City is a beginning in the proper direction.

The recognition of another fact must be made: the local community is not the national society. Obvious as this sounds, and it is obvious, many seem to believe that class at the national level is the same as class in the local community. The differences are enormous.

Class Structure: The National Society

THE IMPLICATION that there is a national class structure has been latent throughout this book. The discussion of values, of the theories and methodologies of class, and even of the class structure of the local community have assumed the existence of a national class system. Few would disagree that there is a national dimension to class. However, there is some question as to whether it is a class *system,* and if so, how it operates. The periodic polls of national samples on opinions of class assume at the very least that class has some meaning nationally. Similarly, the analysis of the dominant elements of an American ethos as it reflects upon class, assumes that beliefs about class extend beyond the limits of the local community. What is still left unsettled, however, is the way that class is manifested at the national level, the channels for a national consensus about class, the relative importance of class, the procedure for measuring class, and the interrelationship between the several dimensions of class.

The difficulty appears because the class structure of a small community is not the same as a national class system. The ease of personal identification and knowledge of the class participants in Hometown, for example, is not possible in large city populations or on a national level. Nor is there such consensus on the national level as to the characteristics and criteria of classes. Symbolic criteria, not personal knowledge, must be depended upon more heavily in judging an individual's class and all that goes with it, on the national scale. Nor are the symbols as clear and unambiguous at the national level as they were for Hometown. The same symbols may be used in both, such as the home, occupation, or consumption patterns. These are, however, approximations of an individual's class, and the nuances missed and misinterpretations made could be numerous. In Hometown, personal knowledge could be used to adjust these symbols realistically. Finally, the total position of the individual at the national level is seldom known. Where an individual's standing on several dimensions of class in the local community could be calculated simultaneously for a single placement, the complexity and impersonality of class at a national level make such evaluation often impossible.

These difficulties add up to an obvious conclusion: a national class system does exist even though it does not look the same as the local class system. Qualitative differences between the two are brought about, in part, by their differences of sheer quantity. The American class system is not only more complex than that of a local community, but also depends upon a different set of social dynamics and social processes than those at the local level. The national economy, for example, is something more than simply a collection of local community markets. The functions of the federal government and the arena of national power are quite different from the functioning of local governmental units and the sources of legitimate power that they contain.

A discussion of a national class structure, therefore, cannot proceed from the same orientation or the same kind of knowledge that have informed the study of class in the local community. They are different social phenomena.

One of the principal bases upon which an orientation depends is the ideological stance that is taken when considering the structure of American society. That stance is pivotal for the consideration of an American class system. Some commitment, whether explicit or not, seems to be necessary in the study of class, but nowhere is it quite as important as in the present instance. The reason is relatively clear. The complex structure of American society requires that the observer pre-select certain phases or aspects for study, for the totality cannot be encompassed at once. This requirement in a sense forces him to become sensitive to one set of phenomena rather than to another, and that selection in turn tends to be determined by the orientation he consciously or unconsciously has assumed. The act of research selection, in other words, is itself a value preference, an expression of an evaluated choice from among alternatives.

Two opposing ideological conceptions are current today as regards the class character of American society. The one generally chooses to emphasize the dominating middle class character of American society tied to a broadening process of social conformity and of the leveling of social power. By this view, Americans are living in an "age of conformity." The countering stance pictures American society as dominated more than ever by an elite that holds power in the political, economic, and status spheres of American society. Even though the elite in each sphere may include different individuals, they share a common perspective and are socialized within a common background to see things in the same way. By this view, Americans are living in an "age of power."

At times, perhaps, the two orientations do not seem to be so much antithetical as they appear to be talking past one another—concerned as it were, with two quite different levels of description and analysis. Yet, this is only a surface effect, for the implications inherent in each orientation yield two antagonistic views of the same basic data. That one chooses to concentrate upon conformity at the middle level and the other upon power at the elite level is a real difference and a reflection of basically opposed ideologies and philosophies of social structure, social class, and the role of the individual in society.

The view of America as in an age of conformity is represented by the writings of Riesman and Whyte, authors of *The Lonely Crowd* and *The Organization Man,* respectively. America as in an age of power is detailed in the writings of Mills and Hunter, *The Power Elite* and *Community Power Structure,* respectively.[6] The identification of books and authors should not be misinterpreted to mean that the discussion that follows is but a documented exposition of what Riesman, Whyte, Mills, and Hunter have to say about the United States. To do so would place a most unwanted restriction upon that discussion. The four authors and their writings are used instead as a core from which interpretations and extensions are made to fit the purposes of this discussion. In other words, there is less concern here with the detailed documentation of the ideas that these four have presented, and more with what are believed to be the consequences and implications of their ideas for a view of the American class system.

Those who see Americans caught in the strengthening grip of conformity generally tone down the importance of class. Not that we have reached a utopian goal of egalitarianism, they would argue, but because the Marxian theories of class and class struggle do not apply for whatever reason. Their argument has two aspects. The postwar decade has been characterized by a leveling of class differences in American society; the upper class peak has been worn down as the lower class level has been raised. This process, the proponents of conformity claim, has been accomplished partially through a redistribution of income forced by labor union wage demands and government taxation policies, and partially by the osmosis of middle class values, consumption patterns, and life styles. "America is a middle-class country," Riesman has stated at one point, "and . . . middle-class values and political styles of perception reach into all levels except the fringes at the very top and the very bottom."[7] Indeed, the almost complete encirclement of American society by a middle class ethic, or what Whyte labels the "social ethic," is simply another way of labeling the "age of conformity."

The belief in the pervasive middle class character of American society is coupled with a second proposition that similarly functions to play down the influence of class. This is the contention that traditional class values have been seriously altered in their form and manifestation; "class" today is no longer the same thing that Marx was writing about. The meat of this orientation intends much more than an obvious comment that the middle class, primarily, has shifted from its "old" entrepreneurial form to a "new" salaried, white-collar version. The shift in the meaning of class phrased by this argument sees a redefinition of the motivating values of class; from the hard economic purposefulness of the "inner-directed" to the soft interpersonal competence of "sociability habits and consumption styles"[8] of the "other-directed." Whyte agrees with the judgment of Riesman and sees the "breakdown of the old divisions of class [that] has left people vulnerable to other kinds of webs, and these too have their tyrannies."[9]

In short, the outstanding current feature of American social structure is its classlessness; a classlessness developed from the leveling of and the shift from traditional class divisions and antagonisms to a "middle classless" conformity and harmony.

The opposite image of American social structure that is drawn by those who contend we are in an age of power is sharply different from that of the conformists. Essentially, what the power proponents see is evidence of more sharply drawn class differences rather than less. The power consequences of class are now more sharply different rather than leveled to unity. Instead of a middle class domination, those who believe in the age of power see signs of increasing elite dominance. The "enlargement and the centralization of the means of power now available," Mills has argued, have given the decisions of the power elite greater "consequences for more people than has ever been the case in the world history of mankind."[10] The "middle levels of power" are characterized by a "semi-organized stalemate, and . . . on the bottom level there has come into being a mass-like society which has little resemblance to the image of a society in which voluntary associations and classic publics hold the keys to power."[11] In a concluding phrase critically directed toward those who see only conformity, Mills reiterated his position. "The top of the American system of power is much more unified and much more powerful, the bottom is much more fragmented, and . . . impotent, than is generally supposed by those who are distracted by the middling units of power which neither express such will as exists at the bottom nor determine the decisions at the top."[12]

American society by this view, then, is incorrectly and inadequately conceived of as a conforming one. Its dominant feature is not conformity, but the steady institutionalized funneling of power into the hands of an elite. At the local level, the same process goes on, and with the consent of the community, as Hunter found in Regional City. "The situation, as observed in this study, is that the policy-makers have a fairly definite set of settled policies at their command, which have been historically functional in the community."[13] The acquisition of power, thereby, at both the national and local levels, is not so much a deliberate and conscious plot, but an historically imposed consequence. The elite, whether military, political, or economic, has acceded to power, in large measure because of functional necessity rather than by deliberate manipulation; through ignorant acquiescence rather than force.

In both images, conformity or power, the American class system is seen as transformed from what it was. The traditional features, characteristics, and social functions of class have been altered. Those of the conformist persuasion see this change essentially as the disappearance of the old class lines in favor of a new middling equality, achieved by the demands for conformity to a few norms and standards. The power argument, on the other hand, sees the change as the growth of deeper class cleavages and class antagonisms nurtured by developing differentials of power available to those in different classes.

The outlines of these opposing images are enough to indicate some of the differences in emphasis and orientation. The two views contrast, too, in other ways. The conformity argument depends primarily upon a psychological exposition; the power one upon a structural analysis. *The Lonely Crowd,* significantly, is sub-titled, "A Study of the Changing American Character." "Character" is a representative symbol for the heavy attention given to psychological phenomena. Conformity, in other words, is above all a psychological event. This emphasis, of course, creates a pattern of consequences throughout—for the presumed causes of conformity, the results of conformity, and the suggested solutions to overcome or neutralize conformity. These features are to be analyzed presently. A word of caution, however, first. Although the emphasis is heavily psychological, it does not mean that those who hold this view overlook completely the effects of social structure and process. However, it is a matter for them of relative stress and they choose conformity essentially as a psychological event in preference to considering conformity primarily as a structural phenomenon—as a social event.

The other view, that of power, is not blind to psychological correlates even though it is predominately concerned with matters of structure and with the operation of the larger social processes in the economic, political, military, and status spheres. Still, the relative stress is upon structural variables rather than personality variables. Just as questions of conformity tend more toward matters of personality, questions of power tend in the opposing direction toward matters of social structure, that is, how power is legitimated and what forces contribute to its expansion.

Where "character" and "ethics" are the pivotal concepts for those who see conformity in American life, the institutional structure of power and its attendant social processes are pivotal concepts for the power analysts. This difference in stance and orientation is again evident in the assessment each makes as to the central trend in American society.

Those who see conformity place the genesis of the trend in the sphere of motivations, as might have been expected from their overall psychological emphasis. What is important in this view is the basic shift that has taken place from the individualism of the Protestant ethic and its "inner-directedness" to the "belongingness" and "togetherness" motivations behind the "social ethic" and its "other-directedness." This shift has nurtured the strain toward conformity. The reasons for the shift are located in several simultaneous and interdependent social developments: the growth of bureaucracy and the large corporation, the dominance of the mass over the individual, and both of these coupled with the rising insistence upon social adjustment and exaggerated gregariousness. By this conceptualization, Americans supposedly have been catapulted into an era of beckoning contentment, bolstered by high productivity and higher incomes that encourage them to consume more lavishly than ever before.

At the same time, these analysts see Americans as under

pressure to rid themselves of the individualistic and competitive ethos in favor of the social ethic of the organization. Americans have, in other words, shifted the responsibility for their own success or failure away from themselves as agents, to society, to the corporation, and to the organizations that stand above them. The social guilt of success and the personal guilt of failure that once were by-products possibly produced by the fierce individualism of the Protestant ethic, now can be avoided by an identification with the larger, mass society and with its institutions. Individuals have accepted the contentment, the apathy, and the conformity that beckons from the organizational heights. "In the Protestant Ethic," Whyte concludes in discussing the matter of budgetism, "morality was identified with savings because of the idea that man, rather than society, was ultimately responsible for his destiny. . . . As our society has grown more beneficent, external forces, like the corporation personnel department, have assumed much of the protective job, and it is this defensive alliance, not a slackening of moral fiber, that has robbed saving of its moral imperative."[14]

To the analysts of power the important dynamics and the nature of the shift lay in a wholly different sector of the social structure. It is not the individual, they maintain, as much as it is the larger social forces that account for the current patterning in American society. Instead of seeing the shift as a psychological one from the Protestant Ethic to the Social Ethic, those of the power persuasion see principally the increase in economic concentration and the steady institutional merging of economic with political forces as shaping the main outlines of American society. The factors that stimulated the growth of the organization are the important data, not the consequences for personality engendered by the organization. From the period of the entrepreneur, the privateering capitalist, and the robber baron, American society has moved toward increased centralized controls located in the gigantic economic enterprises. With economic power, has come political power, as wealth provides the means for making major political decisions. The more that the conduct of national politics has come to depend upon wealth and the men of wealth, this view would hold, the more has economic power provided a passport to the domain where political power is exercised. Hence, what appears as a psychologically conforming mass is, by this view, a mass that has lost power. A contented mass is, by this view, a mass that has lost its economic initiative, incentive, and reward. The individual is not to be blamed. The basis for this tremendous social revolution is to be found in the social processes to which our economy, our polity, and our way of life have been committed.

The view of America as moving toward conformity emphasizes psychological effects. The opposing view concentrates on the structures and processes of power that move toward the creation of a unified power elite. The differences between the two views, and the consequences that follow from these two different images of American society have been detailed sufficiently. Further consequences could be described, but they are already implied in what has been said. For example, in the sphere of politics and political action, the view of the conformists leads to a characterization of the political situation as one where political apathy or the neutralized effects of opposing veto groups is dominant. The other view, beginning with the power dimension, sees instead greater political control settling in the hands of a relative few, who in turn are intimate with the men of power in other spheres, such as the economic and the military.

In rounding off this comparison, it would be enlightening to consider the two views as to the ends they foresee for American society and their solutions for escape. Those who see conformity, quite naturally enough, foresee the extension of apathy, "other-directedness," and the concern with "togetherness" extending to all corners of American society; a mass leveling of individuals to the lowest common denominator, to the great average. The solution suggested by this view, since such massification is undesirable, is expectedly in the hands of the individual himself. "The organization man," Whyte concludes, "is not in the grip of vast social forces about which it is impossible for him to do anything; the options are there, and with wisdom and foresight he can turn the future away from the dehumanized collective that so haunts our thoughts. . . . He must *fight* The Organization . . . for the demands for his surrender are constant and powerful, and the more he has come to like the life of organization the more difficult does he find it to resist these demands, or even to recognize them."[15]

Riesman's conclusions and those of Whyte are identical both in content and intent, although Riesman does not see that the goal is to be attained as easily as Whyte implies. "I have set forth some thoughts about the middle-class world of work and play, in the hope of finding ways in which a more autonomous type of social character might develop," says Riesman in the opening of his final chapter.[16] "Is it conceivable that these economically privileged Americans will some day wake up to the fact that they overconform? Wake up to discover that a host of behavioral rituals are the result, not of an inescapable social imperative but of an image of society that, though false, provides certain 'secondary gains' for the people who believe in it? Since character structure is, if anything, even more tenacious than social structure, such an awakening is exceedingly unlikely. . . . But to put the question may at least raise doubts in the minds of some."[17] Riesman and Whyte, in short, look for a Utopia of individual autonomy, of the new individualism recast for the necessities of the twentieth century, but achieved and maintained by the individual in the teeth of whatever social forces he encounters. They see the individual as *less* in the grip of social forces and as more in the trap of his own inaction and reaction against those forces.

The opposing power view of American society does not conclude with any neat solution to what it sees as an equally undesirable situation. However, the implications of this view are clear—change must occur at the level of social structure and social process, not at the level of individual reflection and reassessment. The unattended social processes have led to the creation of a power aristocracy, which, although not fully known nor fully formed, can only move in the direction of greater articulation. Although America has avoided feudalism, America is moving toward that end by another path. This will be accomplished by the gradual merging of all social power into the hands of an integrated well-knit elite. This state, for most sociological purposes, is a duplicate of feudal society.

"The men of the higher circles are not representative men . . . their fabulous success is not firmly connected with meritorious ability. Those who sit in the seats of the high and the mighty are selected and formed by the means of power, the sources of wealth, the mechanics of celebrity, which prevail in their society. They are not men selected and formed by a civil service that is linked with the world of knowledge and sensibility. . . . They are not men held in responsible check by a plurality of voluntary associations which connect debating publics with the pinnacles of decision. Commanders of power unequaled in human history, they have succeeded within the American system of organized irresponsibility."[18] The elite has attained its pinnacle by the operation of social forces, yet as a violation of the formal guiding ideologies of those forces. American society, in Mills's view, is approaching the stage where the elite will soon have few ties of responsibility to the rest of the population, except perhaps for a *noblesse oblige*. To effect any change or modification, therefore, action must take place at a level that is close to the social mainsprings. The effort for change must be total and society wide, not simply individualistic or personalistic. What makes the successful development of counterforces more difficult is the fact that this power concentration is legitimate. It has developed almost without plan and through the unfolding of inherent features within our social structure. Nonetheless, the power is still real.

The central differences between these two orientations toward American society should be clear. From the initial identification of the social dynamics involved, through to the final conclusions and remedies offered, the two views have shown considerable differences in their concepts of American social structure and in the consequences each foresees as a result.

These opposing views mean that an answer to the question: "Does a national class structure exist?" is above all contingent upon the particular alternative that is chosen. The orientation and the posture that are taken toward the question itself, the way that social structure and its dynamics are phrased, is of enormous importance in answering the question.

A further clarifying assumption must be made, for it is in this light that much of the evidence throughout this chapter is presented. Power as well as status components of this social category called "class" must be recognized; the more so when the arena of description is the national society. Perhaps status does play as large a role in the thinking, aspirations, and values of Americans as those who advance the ideas of a growing conformity believe. This does not mean, however, that American society is not at the same time shaped by the consequences of power in its social relationships and in its institutions. Therefore, the theme of power as a vital component of class must be threaded throughout almost any full discussion of the subject.

The matter of valid evidence to support generalizations about power and stratification at the national level is obviously a crucial one. There is an astounding lack of such data. In fact, there is much less information about the characteristics of class and power at the national level than about class and status at the local level. The research techniques and their supporting conceptualizations about a class system are sorely lacking. The national system of class division cannot simply be a composite of the systems found in smaller local communities. Interpersonal communication, consensus, class symbols, and identification are qualitatively different at the national level. This kind of complexity has been the perennial problem of the social scientist, and there is no need to become involved in discussing possible solutions for it at this point. All that requires to be said here is that the kind of generalizations to be offered or suggested in the following pages must remain limited.

The realization of this situation, of course, reflects back again on the alternatives presented by the "conformist" and the "power" views of American social structure. Both of them, clearly, are more interpretative commentaries from given orientations than they are systematically derived conclusions from research data, in spite of the fact that some data are presented to some degree in both views. Riesman's handful of interviews and examples, or Mills's necessarily limited frequency counts of elite memberships fall short of the kind of information both they and other social scientists would like to have at hand. Hunter's study alone comes closest to fulfilling the more exacting requirements of social research. In short, the generalizations that are made are far broader, oftentimes far richer and more dramatic, than the available data could validly allow. This fact does not, however, destroy the nature of the ideas they express or the contribution they have made to the study of class. It does seem, in very large measure, that one chooses from between the two alternatives on the basis of preference, taste, bias, or whatever mystical source one cares to rely upon in such matters. Neither view is at a point where it can be proven or disproven entirely; nor is there sufficient data to allow such an objective determination to be made.

The American Class System

THE PRECEDING remarks have set the tone for the discussion that is to form the remainder of this chapter. This is not to be a discussion of formal theory, or a manipulation of formal theoretical categories for a so-called "theory of class" in society. Those have been sufficiently considered in Chapter Two. Nor is this to be a discussion of social structure in a formal theoretical sense, although much of social structure is involved here.

Before assessing the characteristics and evidence for the existence of a national class system, it would be advisable to list, briefly, some of the dimensions that might be expected ideally from a coherent and recognizable class system:

1) There should, in that instance, exist a relatively high degree of consensus among the members in the system about the criteria, characteristics, and dimensions of the several classes.

2) Associated with the first dimension, is that of value cohesiveness. In other words, not only should there ideally be an almost unanimous acceptance of the meaning and character of class, but in addition the values supporting class should, ideally, fit in with other values held by the society. The recognition of classes and the recognition of the dimensions and criteria of class should mesh with other values that have currency in the society. Hence, class position becomes the symbolic equivalent of the successful attainment of these values that the society considers crucial, important, or worthwhile.

3) Class consciousness should also be evident, in that individuals are subjectively aware of their own class and that of others in the system. Individuals, by this requirement, should be aware of classes as significant and meaningful social groupings, though they may or may not at the same time be cognizant of the fact that many other individuals are in the same class circumstances as they are.

4) The class structure should also mesh with all institutional spheres of social structure. This is but the structural counterpart to the second requirement mentioned. If class values tie in with other values in a society, then it follows that the class system should also show the effects of its operation in the institutions of a society. In other words, class is in the nature of an individual's total standing in the hierarchies of the several institutions. This is relatively evident in the case of the economic and political institutions, say, where a position of relatively high power in the one usually means a comparable kind of standing in the other. Ideally, this kind of complementariness should pervade throughout religion, education, leisure, or any other institutional segment.

5) Finally, one might expect the existence of relatively

unequivocal, unambiguous criteria of class and their symbolic interpretation. The class standing of individuals should be evident, objectively determined, and commonly accepted by the majority. This is a counterpart to the requirement of consensus.

Obviously, these requirements are ideal in the sense that they are not realized in fact in a complex national society. The limited social visibility of class created by the large numbers of people involved, the fragmented and discrete social worlds that are present in the national society without immediate and cross-personal interaction, and finally, the disjunctures in status position between the several institutional dimensions—all mean that class at the national level does not fully approach the detail set forth in these five requirements of a fully articulated class system. This is not to say, however, that some of these elements do not exist, for they do.

The Economic Dimension

THERE is no doubt that the economic institution provides the major dimension for stratification in American society. Although there are other modes of stratification—by prestige, by political power, by race and ethnicity, and by family background, for example—it is the economic base that is generic and all others are derivative. The one outstanding conclusion that comes out from the mass of materials on the subject of stratification clearly is that the economic processes set the primary and elemental molds of class. This dominance of the economic institution, Lynd has correctly noted, is a consequence of the special case of capitalism and is not part of the inevitable character of the economic institution.[19] Since the study of stratification really began with the interest in the structure of an industrialized capitalistic economy and has continued with that primary focus, it is not coincidental that economic criteria have played such an important role in the determination of class. Lynd goes on further to explain that this priority of the economic institution in capitalistic society stems from the close identification that has been created between economic and social structure. Capitalistic enterprise and society have been intimately united in our social ideology whereby the economic good has always been interpreted as a necessary social good. In keeping with this ideology, social position has been first and foremost dependent upon the economic role one plays and from which other roles take their cues. "Classes [have been] erected fundamentally on economic interest and power; and it has been the fact that this social structure of classes has been primarily economic . . . that has made it possible for economic institutions so largely to 'determine' the other institutions."[20]

In spite of the clear centrality of the economic institution for any reasonable analysis of social stratification, few sociologists have studied this phenomenon. Whatever their reasons, whether the subject is methodologically difficult to handle or that questions of economic power are volatile, the result is the same: a severe lack of information about the character of economic classes. Yet, because of the enormous significance of the economic dimension for understanding stratification at the national level, some speculations must be attempted.

The central question of concern is as follows: What are the economic dimensions of class? This question can be further sub-divided: What is class, how is it to be designated, and how does it function? Two assumptions inform the subsequent discussion. The first is that individuals are forced into their class niches primarily by economic processes. The matter of class consciousness or similar counterparts to class placement are pushed aside for the moment.

The second assumption is that the generic criterion of class is economic control and power, by which is meant the relative degree of economic potency an individual commands by reason of his position in the economic order. Power is interpreted here to include the real or potential ability of an economic position to affect the behavior of those in other positions, as well as the interests and economic goals that typically are associated with each of those positions. By this interpretation all economic positions are differentiated by the degree of power they can command: the producer, the consumer, the professional, the labor unionist, the executive, and the like. Furthermore, the grouping of positions into classes by the criterion of economic interest, as Weber has suggested,[21] must be expanded to include the probability of a class realizing its interests in the market place. In other words, that several positions have common economic goals can become the basis for their formation into a class only when there is some estimate made by those affected of the probability of achieving those goals. Without any chance estimated to achieve success, such economic groups would not form into a class even though their goals were similar.

It should be clear from this interpretation that power derives from an institutional position rather than from any accidental or idiosyncratic characteristic of particular individuals. The directorship of a large corporation, for example, commands power and the power resides in the position. It is certainly evident that different personalities can realize the potential power of their position to different degrees, in much the same way as the president can be spoken of as a "strong" or a "weak" president. However, these individual variations are presently beyond the methodological range where they can be dealt with systematically.[22]

The determination of economic classes on the basis of power differentials is an impossible task at present, for the information needed is not at hand. Income, wealth, and occupation have been used as criteria of class within the meaning specified here, but they are not fully satisfactory. These criteria have been chosen more because of methodological desperation than because of theoretical soundness. Although each does reflect upon an economic characteristic, none of the criteria is usable to define class because its functional relationship to matters of economic power and control is unclear. Income classes, for example, can be arbitrarily designated from a distribution of income, but except at the extremes, there is little justification for equating such classes with economic classes. Other problems also arise by the use of an income criterion that complicate matters further. Income information is often unreliably reported; the definitions of income can vary as in the expense account, the bonus, or payment by shares of stock, all of which make comparison difficult; and finally, income levels change over time and the computation of "real" income becomes a nasty problem of methodology that must first be settled. All of these conditions would seem to create more difficulty than value in the use of income as a criterion. Similar objections could be raised against the validity of occupation as well, and these have been detailed in Chapter Three.

Returning to the main argument, the central stratification feature to be determined in the economic dimension is that of the distribution of economic control and power. Classes, in the economic sense, are groups of individuals who hold similar degrees of power and control by reason of their position within the economic institution. Unfortunately, the only class which can be reasonably identified on this basis is the one at the top, and by implication the powerless class at the bottom. Various procedures have been used for this purpose. Hunter, in his study of power in Regional City, relied upon community judges to identify the men of power and he has suggested that a similar technique could be employed at the national level as well.[23] Mills has identified the class of the very rich by using a figure of $30 million and has traced through some of their characteristics.[24] Studies of executives of large corporations have recently appeared which identify those that belong to the class of power.[25] The Temporary National Economic Committee in 1938 and the Federal Trade Commission in 1947 published findings on interlocking directorships of large corporations, both of which provide firm data on the positions of control in the economy.[26] These represent important beginnings for devising procedures to identify and analyze the positions of power classes, not only at the top but throughout the hierarchy.

A closely related matter, of course, concerns the matter of economic concentration, for as greater concentration occurs, greater power is bequeathed to the positions that control. The extent to which economic concentration is or is not occurring is itself an area for investigation large enough to demand its own independent study. A recent government publication on concentration in American industry, based on the 1954 Census of Business, has produced a mass of information on this issue,[27] but with no clear-cut conclusions. For example, the largest 200 companies added 30 per cent of the total value by manufacture in 1947 compared with 37 per cent in 1954.[28] However, there were evidences of different degrees of concentration in industry during the period, not all proceeding in one direction.

From all these sources, the conclusion is inescapable that economic classes do exist at the national level. What is more, the simple measures of income or occupation are insufficient to index the underlying complex reality of these classes and their memberships. In short, the structure of the economic institution is necessarily such that classes are created and differentiated from one another by the access to and potentialities for power that each can command. It it within this kind of dimension that class at the national level becomes the basic feature of social stratification.

It is the purpose of this section to indicate additional features by which the functions of class can be discerned. Occupation can be utilized to determine class types, although it is necessary to add hastily that this is meant to include much more than the notion of occupational prestige alone. In the present context, occupation is taken not alone as an index to prestige but as an index of the relative access it typically allows for the exercise of legitimate power in the economic institution. The power feature is perhaps implied in occupational scales of other types but seldom explicitly so, nor is it usually intended in that sense. Here again is a possible area for more intensive research to achieve a functional grouping of occupations, rather than relying upon prestige alone.

From another direction occupations play an important role in the matter of power distribution in the economic structure. This is primarily through occupational organizations[29]—unions, professional societies, and businessmen's groups. A prerequisite for the exercise of power by such organizations is the existence of "a social structure where the vast majority of the people recognize and have no choice but to recognize that their position in a certain social stratum is a permanent, life-long fate."[30] Where this condition does not exist or where it is not accepted, then the solidarity and strength of an occupational organization loses its potential effectiveness. The point has been raised, for example, in connection with the failure of unionization of the white-collar occupations. Individuals in these occupations tend to identify more with those above them in the economic structure and do not feel sufficiently committed nor fated to their present job to feel the need for unionization.

A second prerequisite for an effective occupational organization is the recognition by individuals that their economic interests can be best served by such organization. Under such circumstances, the organization can effectively move into the political sphere where essentially economic decisions affecting their self-interest can be influenced.

Occupations, in the sense just implied, clearly are part of the picture of economic classes as they have been interpreted here, although they have not been so utilized in the usual study of class. In short, classes are organized around the positions occupied by distinguishable economic groups within the structure and by the relative access to economic power commanded by those groups. The point suggested here is that occupational groups may serve to index this power aspect when they are interpreted as being more than prestige groups alone.[31] Similarly, income might be employed as an index of economic power, but few studies relying upon an income index have used it in this manner.

In addition to the dimensions of class suggested above,

there is another perspective from which the class dimension can be considered: the consideration of the shift that has occurred in corporation leadership. The business hero and the man of power have changed from the entrepreneur hero of the past to the executive hero of the present decade.[32] That shift is linked to an ideological shift that has supported the rise of the new hero, and is supported by a modification of the economic goals of big business from the singular pursuit of profit to the recognition of public relations as an important facet of that goal.

The entrepreneur was the business type of the nineteenth century. He was the business leader who attained his position by virtue of his personal qualities and abilities to take full advantage of the economic situation. In many respects, he was the "inner-directed" type of Riesman's typology in that he made his own rules more or less and was able to dictate those rules to others by the position of control he held. He reigned in a period that was dominated by the philosophy of classical economics; the unfettered individual left alone to pursue his own economic self-interest would produce not only for himself but for society as a whole. The economic enterprise and the social enterprise were inextricably intertwined.

The entrepreneur was the self-made man *par excellence*. By his own efforts, by his character, by his stamina and perseverance, he achieved economic success and earned the rights and prerogatives of economic leadership. "The source of success . . . is conceived of as lying in personal qualities; character determines destiny. So long as he [the entrepreneur] has the requisite qualities, success will be his at any time, in any place, under any circumstances."[33]

The entrepreneur was known publicly, in part, because he epitomized the dominant economic ideology and the value it was supposed to have. His power, his achievements, in short, were primarily tied to him as an individual and only secondarily to the economic enterprise he had created or developed. Rockefeller, Mellon, Morgan, Vanderbilt—these names and their biographies remain even though exactly what they did may be unremembered. Even less was known about their private affairs since the belief in economic individualism also implied the rights of privacy. At a much later period did the concern with public sentiments, in a sense, force the lives of these men into public print.

These nineteenth century entrepreneurs were individual giants who had the good fortune to be living as they did in a favorable economic environment. Their rise to positions of eminence and their conduct reflected the tenor of the period. Their activity, for most people, was above comment and above judgment—it was the success that mattered. They were the last of their breed, for with the growth of the corporate empires these men had created, the individual was to become subordinate to the corporation name and to the corporation team. The entrepreneur was expected to be a snob and he was. He moved within the small circle of his own society and lived as expensively and sumptuously as he cared to with little concern about public reactions. Later generations have gained some from that way of life, if only by the donation of the former mansions and estates to the public for art museums and the like.

The change in business structure and in the supporting ideology from that of the individual entrepreneur to that of the community-conscious corporation also necessitated a shift in the dominant business type—from the entrepreneur to the manager. The manager was the product of the first decades of the twentieth century. The entrepreneurial era had passed and the economy had moved into a different stage of complexity. In the rise of the manager, the shift away from the economic individualist was clear. As the name connotes, the manager was a coordinator within a bureaucratic setting. There were rules to be followed: rules created by boards of directors, rules imposed by the government, and much later rules demanded by labor and by a complex of different economic agents. The manager's job, then, was one of guiding the organization through the rule maze, to keep the organization functioning, to maximize profits and to keep ahead of the yet unwritten rules the future might write.

The manager was also a success hero, but unlike the entrepreneur, he attained his success through the organization. His was not a success that was as dependent upon personal qualities as it was for the entrepreneur, or the qualities were not the same. The corporation at this point had already taken steps to rationalize its leadership by removing control from the hands of a single, irreplaceable person. The entrepreneurial type would have been dysfunctional in this period. With the establishment of training programs to co-opt potential managers, and the subdivision of authority and responsibility among several top positions, the channels for the emergence of the entrepreneurial type within the structure of the corporation were closed.

The manager moved into a functioning enterprise that was not of his own creation. His role was more of a helmsman than of the ship's designer and builder. His role was less one of founding new enterprises, and more that of coordinating and directing the economic empire in which he had been promoted. Whatever expansion did take place was primarily from the base of economic operations he headed and had acceded to.

Coupled with the rise of the manager was the now dominant view that business was not everything. The manager more and more was presented in his non-business roles, to make him more recognizable, more human, and more accessible to public view.[34] The personal life of the entrepreneur had been hidden. He had been publicly unapproachable. People perhaps read about him and his family in the local society pages, but he appeared there in surroundings so fabulously different that to the ordinary man it was a world beyond his comprehension. The manager, on the contrary, was portrayed more frequently in roles that the public would understand and with which they could empathize—as a community leader, as a parent, as a philanthropist and doer of good deeds. The manager needed public acceptance and approval more than the entrepreneur, not so much for himself perhaps, but for the economic benefit of the corporation. Community public relations had become a necessary facet for the conduct of business enterprises. It was one of the costs of doing business. The manager, as the titular head of the enterprise, had to portray its virtues in his own person and by his own behavior. Social distances had to be lessened rather than maximized, for business had begun to worry about the images that the public held of it.

The dominant business hero now seems to be the executive whose emergence on the economic scene dates around World War II. If the entrepreneur could be typified as the pioneer who took the risks of establishing and running the corporation, and the manager typified as the specialist who coordinated the operation of the corporation without any economic risk except for his own job, then the executive can be typified as the one who executes orders in an operating organization. The executive has to incur the least risk of all in the economic enterprise. He is more the bureaucrat than even the manager was. Profits, although still obviously important, are no longer his central concern nor the only measure of the man, as they clearly and predominately were for the entrepreneur and even the manager. The executive's principal task is to guide interpersonal relations. To a great extent, the corporation has achieved a plateau of comparative economic smoothness. Many new economic frontiers are closed, and the chances for a newcomer into the field are increasingly small. Where there is economic expansion it is principally by the older firms that may branch out into other economic ventures, or through the merger which has become an outstanding form of economic growth.

The principal residue of concern that is left is the concern with morale, with the "team," with intra-organizational communication, and with interrelationships between members of the administration. At these points, the expertise of the executive is called upon. His primary function is less directly economic than any hero before him, and more one of guiding, steering, and executing decisions in such a way that a certain tone and quality in interpersonal relationships are maintained. He is the leader personifying a new and subtle economic dimension.

This definition of the new corporation hero is evident in the frequent articles and books written about the executive. The editors of *Fortune,* for example, have compiled a book on *The Executive Life,*[35] which describes the type and offers some clues for the handling of the executive. It was almost inevitable that the executive would begin taking himself seriously, and precisely in terms of his area of specialization. He is well on the way to becoming as much concerned about himself as he is with others in the corporation. "Their [executives'] capacity for self-examination and introspection has itself become a notable facet of the executive life," the *Fortune* survey concluded.[36] He must learn to adjust to the world of the expense account and to its psychological consequences as well as to the role confusion it can create. "The expense account man inhabits two quite disparate worlds, one when he is with his family and another while he is courting his clients. This, the moralists have pointed out, leads to a sort of national schizophrenia and a curiously garbled standard of personal values."[37] Not only that, but he must even learn to live without a desk and to handle the consequent psychological problems that its removal apparently induces. His symbol of separation from the outsider, his crutch being so removed, requires a major readjustment. Yet, the removal of the desk is symbolic of his function—he must be ready to see, understand, and relate to individuals.

A further example of the shifts in organization caused by the dominance of the excutive role is the growth and rationalization of a "corporate caste" system.[38] According to the *Wall Street Journal,* the status symbol is increasingly evident. "From the parking lot to the executive washroom, the special privileges denoting corporate rank are more prominent and more frankly acknowledged than ever before."[39] This conclusion was based upon interviews with more than 50 businessmen in 12 cities. Crown Zellerbach Corporation, the *Journal* reported, has been seeking to achieve what it calls "scientific stratification." The manager of the building and office services' division of the corporation has announced that in their new office building "we'll be able to arrange walls so that the offices for executives of equal rank can all be built within a square inch of one another in size."[40] These are among the present concerns in the world of the corporation. The tone of profit has been muted, though not stilled; the entrepreneur would not be recognized in this new land of "corporate caste," expense accounts, and the constant emphasis upon the adjustment of interpersonal relations.

What these developments imply, as the present context suggests, is that the executive as an economic type is in a world removed from the entrepreneurial type. The economic structure, apparently, has reached a strange and wondrous maturity—it has become socialized in its own way after decades of much fiercer competitiveness. Executives who can worry about status symbols—parking space, drapes, carpets, and other status trappings—are the new heroes serving a corporation that can afford the luxury.

Furthermore, the very character of the economic structure must itself have changed, of course, to permit and to foster the emphasis upon this type of talent. From an emphasis upon the personal qualities of the entrepreneur, we have come to an emphasis upon the interpersonal skills of the executive.[41] From an individualistic economic philosophy, we have come to demand a socially responsible philosophy. The economic environment, as Diamond concluded in his study of the obituaries of businessmen from Stephen Girard to Henry Ford, is now "presented as synonymous with the nation itself, and nation and economic system are interchangeable parts of the same mechanism."[42] Society has at least achieved an equality with the economic institution rather than being its servant as it was by the earlier economic philosophy.

In this environment that has been created, the executive and what he does are understandable enough. His task is to ease the psychological blows, to coordinate the motivations and morale of organization people into a smoothly functioning group.

The importance of this shift in economic heroes is seen in its effect upon class definition and composition. The formerly clear divisions of the entrepreneurial era into the economically chosen few and the economically and socially damned has given way to new definitions. For one thing the channels of access to the executive levels are more open than before. The channels are also different. The chances of building an economic empire on the scale of, say, Rockefeller or Morgan are slimmer, but the chances of rising through the bureaucratic hierarchy of the corporation are better. The way stations on the way up and the procedures for such movement are clearer and more structured than in the past. In the past, there were no rules. The struggle was idiosyncratic and the economic land was wild. Now, however, education and training, a certain degree of loyalty, some imagination at the higher levels, and proper friendships properly formed can mark the path to success in the organization.

The executive represents a new class type. Those who inherited the wealth and sometimes the corporate control from the earlier entrepreneurs are still at the top as an economic elite. These are the $30 million people that Mills has identified. Closely allied, but still distinguishable, are the top level executives. They are newcomers who have risen in the system according to its demands or else may have inherited their positions from manager-fathers. These executives stand high in terms of corporate control and wealth, but they remain essentially company employees who are regularly rewarded by stock or some other bonus.

The white-collar and professional groups of the middle class have not gained greatly by this shift. Their material economic position has been bettered, in many instances, but their relative economic standing, economic power, and class position have remained unchanged, or perhaps even worsened. The working class is also still identifiable. They have through unionization bettered their working conditions and their income position, but they are not really any closer to the centers of control and power than before. The effective range of their power remains limited to working conditions and the like, even with union organization, although they have in a few instances moved closer to some of the managerial prerogatives.

In spite of the shifts in economic personnel and changes in the structure and composition of the classes, the economic ideology has remained relatively static and committed to a reiteration of traditional values. Hence, in a recent analysis of the institutional advertising of large corporations,[43] it was found that the emphasis upon free enterprise, free competition, and the unfettered operation of the market place was still clear, as if the economy were unchanged since *The Wealth of Nations.*

Of course, these advertised expressions are a form of economic patriotism rather than an accurate reflection of the current state of economic affairs. Large corporations are owned, technically, by many people who by virtue of their stock pass upon the management of "their" corporation. In actuality, however, it is abundantly clear that the ownership of a block of stock can mean actual control even though it is but a small percentage of the total shares available. The fact that the remaining shares are subdivided thousands of times among thousands of individuals and more, means that such small stockholders would need to organize and agree unanimously upon their actions to be able to challenge the single large stock holder. However, it is not this economic dimension that is of concern here.

A major consequence of the existing economic ideology for stratification is in its statements of equality and of equal opportunity for mobility and achievement. Implicitly, the ideology recognizes that inequalities exist but these are explained away as the result of differential rewards given to the economically successful and denied to the economically unsuccessful. Some individuals will necessarily be more adept and successful than others in their economic pursuits. The equalitarian dimension of that ideology only avers that opportunities are equally available; the stratified end-result represents achievement differences, not inheritance.

In any case, it seems clear from what has been said that economic classes exist, no matter what the ideology may say about how they were created or how they were filled. These are nationally important, even though members in the same class measured by economic ownership and control may not know one another. The operation of the market place, as Weber noted, places individuals in a common position as to their economic interests and access to economic controls. The fact that there may be no total consensus about who fits where or by what criteria, is relatively unimportant at this level. What is crucial is that the potential is there, that if it were converted into actuality by some process, the recognition of economic peers would take place. Furthermore, those who insist upon consensus as a measure of class structure sometimes overlook the relatively high degree of consensus that does exist on the *criteria* for class placement. Consensus exists on what constitutes economic wealth, power, and control. Very few may know the specific people that fit each class by those criteria, but the placement of specific individuals is relatively unimportant; *someone* fits those criteria. After all, the economic decisions that are made can be made by a few, yet affect the society as a whole, and the majority of the population remains totally ignorant of the process whereby all occurs even though it is directly affected by the consequences of these decisions.

The Political Dimension

THERE can be no attempt in this section to detail the political ramifications of social stratification. They are as varied as the manifestations of political behavior itself, including under this rubric voting, attitudes towards politics, office-holding, and even the unconscious motivations that guide an individual's politics. In large measure, the assumption that "the ideas and actions of men are conditioned by their social and economic position in society"[44] is fairly widely accepted in the analysis of political motivations and behavior. As indicated above, this assumption is clear in a wide spectrum of political analysis beginning with the Marxian thesis that economic classes are simultaneously political classes, and up to the present decade where emphasis has been placed upon the influence of class variables on voting behavior.

Little would be gained by a recapitulation of that information, since the intent of this book is less one of a catalogue and more one of pointing out questions that might be asked and directions that might be taken by social stratification study. It should be recalled, therefore, that the primary purpose of the preceding section on the economic institution as well as the present one on the political situation is to highlight some of the ways in which a national class system can be said to exist. Additionally, the informing purpose is to indicate how the analysis of stratification must at some points deal with the national society as the proper unit for study rather than the small community.

To that end, two ideas are presented here, quite speculatively, to convey the tone that stratification study might reasonably sound in analyzing the consequences of class for politics. It is assumed, furthermore, that the body of information that now exists in this area, as alluded to above, has gone far in this direction. The two notions that are taken for discussion are these: (1) to note some of the effects of status as they are seen to condition political beliefs; and (2) to indicate a preliminary analysis of nationalism as a middle class ideology.

In the first instance, some have noted that the status struggle affects political behavior.[45] In brief, the thesis presented by Hofstadter[46] states that there are two political motivations that are operative, both inextricably connected. The first is "interest politics," which is the "clash of material aims and needs" among various politically significant groups. The second type is "status politics," which is the "clash of various projective rationalizations arising from status aspirations and other personal motives." During times of economic depression, interest politics tend to dominate; during prosperity, status considerations become the motivating element of political behavior. In the present period, for example, Hofstadter and others have argued, the "pseudo-conservative" in politics has dominated; one who has been driven by his status aspirations to demand "conformity in a wide variety of spheres of life." The psychological rationale behind the demand holds that "conformity is a way of guaranteeing and manifesting respectability among those who are not sure that they are respectable enough." This desire for conformity and respectability also includes within its psychological scope an all-out attack upon others who either are non-conformist or who have gained a secure position of status and respectability. McCarthy found his support, it is reasoned here, among the status-discontented because he led the attack upon the people and institutions of high status and tried to cut them down to the size, at least, of the status aspirants. In the same way, he attacked any kind of "liberal" nonconformity, the "eggheads" who, by threatening conformity, threatened precisely those who felt their status to be insecure.

By this argument then, political behavior and political attitudes are expressions of the status struggle and inextricably tied to it. The rush toward pseudo-conservatism by a status-threatened middle class that is uncertain and anxious about its position, is one political possibility. Another is the turn toward radicalism of a sort when the position of the middle class has deteriorated so badly that it is faced by both economic and social ruin. Under such conditions of stress, the middle class might follow the first demogogic appeal that would hold out the hope of reclaiming its former position.

A second political aspect of stratification involves the relationship between nationalism, as a political ideology, and the interests of the middle class. The thesis advanced here can be thus summarized: nationalism, the belief by which the conception of loyalty to the nation becomes the dominant and central political theme, has been and is the ideology that is nurtured and sustained by the middle class. As Hans Kohn, one of the leading scholars on the subject of nationalism, has explained, nationalism emerged as a political reality only in the seventeenth century,[47] closely tied to the rise and development of industrialization and the middle class.

It is still impossible to document adequately the reasons for the growth of nationalism as the dominating political ideology where a numerous or a growing middle class is found, but it seems historically clear that nationalism has found its major support among the middle classes of industrialized countries. Not only has this been true in the past, but also appears to be following similar paths in countries now proceeding toward industrialization. In Guatemala, for example, Silvert has concluded that nationalism has its strongest appeals among the numerically small but politically active middle class.[48] Similar occurrences can be found in other presently under-developed countries moving through the industrializing phase.

The rationale, though not fully substantiated, is that the middle class is the true offspring of industrialization and, further, that nationalism is the one ideology that gives it the most nutritive ground for its existence. In under- or pre-industrialized countries, the aristocracy and the peasantry both have a place in what is typically an agricultural economy. With the growth of industry, and thereby with it the subsequent growth of cities, the middle class emerges—the merchant, the professional, the bureaucrat, and the banker. Their newly won economic role is dependent upon the economic success of industrialization, for if the attempt to industrialize should fail, they have the most to lose and the farthest to fall. No other single class stands to gain so much; the aristocracy must seek new sources of power in the new order, and the peasantry most usually is converted into an urban proletariat with a higher standard of living after several generations but with not much greater power or commitment.

Nationalism, as a political and social ideology, shifts the loyalties and allegiances of the citizenry away from the nobility and the king to the nation-state itself, with whose destiny the middle class has identified. Furthermore, nationalism also helps to turn the orientations of the individual away from the fixed limits of a small agricultural locale to the broader international sphere for trade and world markets. Yet, throughout this move toward internationalism, the ideology seeks to maintain the nation as the central symbol. In this way, the older middle classes of highly industrialized nations won their way to economic and finally to political supremacy. In a like manner, the newly created middle classes of under-industrialized countries support the ideology of nationalism as their political banner. For whatever gain the nation makes serves to bolster the status and insure the position of the middle class. Whatever success industrialization has in those countries finally comes to mean a more prosperous middle class.

Also, because the middle class in under-developed countries is usually the only educated segment aside from the aristocracy, it is able to make an impact upon political affairs far in excess of its numerical strength. Evidence from Latin America, Puerto Rico, and India indicates that the growing middle class is playing the same historical role that it once played earlier in England and the United States.

A great deal more must yet be done in the study of this nationalistic process and the shifting powers of the stratification system in the change. Whatever the conclusions, however, it seems clear even now that the class features of nationalism are an integral part of that ideology; one that involves the national polity as a whole.

Conclusions

THE preceding discussion of economic and political dimensions of stratification should be sufficient to make the central point of this latter section; namely, that there are national dimensions to stratification that are not tapped by the studies of small communities. Other institutional areas could have been discussed to give substance to that point. For example, the educational institutions are national in scope and impact as far as their influence upon a national system of stratification is concerned. Educational values are nationwide, and their impact upon occupational selection and occupational placement are similarly nationwide in scope, and are not bounded by the local community scene. However, this matter is to be discussed in Chapter Six on social mobility.

Leisure might also be pointed out as an area of national impact for a system of stratification. The creation of leisure demands is national in scope. Similarly, the taste and consumption patterns in leisure and of leisure goods are determined much more at a national level than at a local one. In this sense, social status can be seen to derive in part from the way that an individual spends leisure. Activity in voluntary associations, fashioning furniture in a solitary but expensive home workshop, or watching mass sport spectacles are all current ways of spending leisure, and class plays a discriminating role in that expenditure.

In concluding this chapter, the following observations seem justified, concerning the subject that has informed the latter sections. To the question, "Is there a national class system?" the answer must be given in the following manner: if by that is meant a clearly differentiated system of class levels, with full consensus and awareness of the criteria and the occupants of the levels, then the answer is, "No." However, these requirements are taken substantially from smaller social groupings where they might be met. There is no necessary reason why a class system must indeed have all of those characteristics in order to function.

If, however, the question implies that only selected basic elements need exist that can differentiate individuals into more or less favored positions within the institutional structure, then the answer is emphatically, "Yes." The descriptions of the economic and political structure, to the extent that they are acceptable as accurate and valid descriptions of the real state of events, is proof of that positive response. If the question considers that there is a process of stratifying individuals or groups in terms of their differential access to power and its sources—whether economic, political, or prestige—then the answer is once again, "Yes."

The structure of stratification nationally does not look like a small community structure, and indeed it could not, for it must function differently and by different modes. Because its functions are qualitatively different, too, it cannot simply be a congeries of local systems. The national dimensions of a class system are unique and not simply a repetition of many local ones. The fact that American sociologists have done relatively little about studying the national dimensions of stratification may be more an indication of the limited tools they have available than a comment upon the features of class at the national level.

CHAPTER V

The Social Psychology of Class

CLASS BECOMES TRANSLATED INTO social reality through its effects upon human behavior, and the range of behavior so influenced is broad. The class position of the individual establishes important conditions for his existence and sets the style for much of the spectrum of his personal horizon. His personal interaction, his experiences, and his impressions of what his life is all about are all styled by class to a great extent. In greater or lesser degree, class has been found to influence child-rearing practices, political attitudes and political activity, sexual patterns, consumer behavior, social participation in the community, social ideology, physical and mental health, and fertility. The list could be expanded but it should be evident that class impinges on behavior at many points. Class creates a social mold that is so inclusive that the individual is seldom free of it. Often, his attempts to escape it are hindered because others continue to appraise his behavior in class terms even when he does not .

A reason for the heavy class pressure in the public world of human interaction and even in the private world maintained by each individual—and it is more a descriptive labeling than an explanation—is that class is a primary social category. That is to say, people depend upon a class label in order to categorize others and thereby to style their own responses to others. For example, a man's occupation has become his symbol of distinctiveness at the same time that it categorizes him for others. Not only is it asked for on application forms where it might be useful or necessary, but increasingly, a person's occupation is among the first questions that strangers ask of one another in order to find their social fit. More and more, too, occupation has become the core around which individuals have styled their own self-images. Occupation and, by implication, class are today the ubiquitous marks of belonging. It is little wonder then that class has dominated so much of our thinking, planning, imagery, and activity.

The purpose of this chapter is to document the impact of class on behavior by describing selected instances of such impact. The selection has been guided first by the scope of the behavior so affected, by its importance and its consequences for broad areas of human activity. A second factor in selection required that several substantive studies be available for consideration. The validity of the conclusions might not be any better for that reason, but at least there is an increased probability that it will for having several independent research studies upon which to rest.

The study of class-conditioned behavior as it is to be surveyed here has its advantages and disadvantages. From one point of view the study of class and behavior is easier than that of class and social structure. The manifestations of class at the behavioral level are more apparent, both to the individuals involved as well as to the sociologist. The class symbols and the class vocabularies that are used may differ, but on the whole people are more prepared to recognize class within the ken of their own experience where they can see it, than they are to generalize or to consider class as a society-wide phenomenon. People know about class and live with it even though they may not be aware of it. Like Molière's M. Jourdain who had been using prose without knowing it, Americans live class in the same kind of ignorance. Whether their children go to college, the home and neighborhood they live in, the kind of work they do, their tastes in furniture, art, or friends—all of these characteristics and many more serve to build and style the class worlds within which people live and move. Whether they know about them or whether they can see out of them is, for many purposes, quite unimportant, for their behavior obviously does not depend entirely upon the awareness of where and what they are.

The fact that class can have reality within the experiences of individuals means, for the sociologist, that the material has greater accessibility. The research design can be more simply fashioned. The study can be more direct by specifying the variables involved. Consequently, the investment in a broad theory of class, such as those considered in Chapter Two, can be kept to a minimum, although this is not to say that theory is superfluous. In the typical study of the type to be considered in this chapter, a test is made of some segment of theory converted into a research operation. The research findings, in turn, should be traced back to their theoretical origins, and the theory modified if necessary. In a very real sense, the kinds of studies reported upon in this chapter represent the basic building blocks, which, together with a coherent and consistent theory, can be used to systematize our knowledge about class and its effects.

The relatively simpler design for the study of class effects on behavior also means that the research techniques presently available to the sociologist can do the job reasonably well. The materials do not outrun the statistical tools nor practical sampling considerations. Neither do they greatly overtax the methods of survey design, attitude testing, questionnaire construction, or interviewing. In most instances, the task can be handled validly and with reasonable dispatch.

To admit that the research problem in this case is somewhat easier than in the study of social structure is not to say that it is all without difficulties.

A recurring difficulty, it would appear, is the definition of class—a problem that must be faced in every class study. In most research, a definition of class is used that steers between the theoretically meaningful statement and the measurable one. It is not often that the two demands can be satisfied at the same time. Nor is it an easy task. Who is middle class and why, or what are the major dimensions of class, can be handled in an abstract sense, but such questions encounter enormous difficulties when subjected to the harder demands of research. The solution, in most cases, is to settle upon any available criteria that have class connotations—occupation, residential area, income, or education. Classes are then designated quite arbitrarily, and frequently on the basis of the distributions found in the particular study. Although this is far from an ideal procedure, there is no other immediate alternative. If the research problem is to test certain relationships between class and behavior, it is somewhat unfair to expect the research to concern itself entirely with definitional problems, especially since the problem is not easily settled. As indicated in Chapter Three, operational definitions of class are necessary at present for research. All objections cannot be overcome at once, and the information gained in this way about class is not at all without merit or importance. The definitions of class that are currently used in most research studies are plausible, as far as our knowledge goes. They make sense. Perhaps by accepting them, if only temporarily, further insight into class and its effect might be gained.

A second related difficulty in the studies of class and behavior, concerns the people who are studied and whether they are representative of some larger group. The objections to the use of students as captive substitutes for adults have been noted in an earlier chapter, and there is no need to do more than mention the point here. It is this kind of procedure, however, that restricts the sense of some studies. The general fault is to be found in many guises. For example, a study of class and its effects upon fertility cannot make do with a sample of women who come to a birth control clinic; the sample is not representative of the female population. A sample of patients in a state mental hospital, again, can at best only represent mental hospital patients at a certain class level in a study of the relationship between class and mental illness. Fortunately, however, the deviations from broader representativeness in one study might be corrected in another, and the effects of studying a limited group can sometimes be traced to the final results more specifically. In other instances, even the study of a special population can add importantly to the knowledge about class. For some research purposes, even the population of a state mental hospital may be an excellent group to study.

Definition and sampling are technical difficulties that can be corrected; there are other difficulties that cannot. The dependence upon an *ad hoc* explanation in some of the studies to be considered is a case in point. Suppose that a study of the relationship between class and some facet of behavior comes out with results which are statistically significant. What does this mean about the nature of class? To answer that question requires an interpretation that must necessarily go beyond the bounds of the research itself. Greater stress is placed upon the interpretation of findings and less upon the actual data collected. Is class indeed the cause of the phenomenon being studied, or is it possibly a chance correlation, a fortuitous juxtaposition? The answer to that question requires not only a more rigorous research design, but also a more detailed theory that can map the path of reasoning to be followed in interpreting results. The more rigorous design is seldom possible and the detailed theory is not yet developed.

The decision made by many researchers is to follow a hunch and then look around for interpretations to explain the results. The argument they make is that one way to find out about class is to pile up studies of the relationships between class and a whole range of other so-called dependent variables and see what these all add up to. Certainly, there can be no doubt that studies conducted from this perspective have added to our understanding. However, we are at a point where contradictory findings have emerged, as for example on the relationship between class and psychoneurosis. The undesirability of constructing plausible explanations to account for the findings of each study *de novo* is that a unified system of knowledge about class is not created, but rather, a potpourri of disjointed, if clever, bits of information emerges.

There is an allied problem as well. By these *ad hoc* explanations in which class is presumed to be the cause of some behavior, there is no room to consider other contributing causes. What is not put into the research in the beginning cannot be found in the conclusions. For example, assuming that class position is important in setting the manner in which children are raised, how does it compare in relative impact with other factors related to the child-raising: ethnic background, religion, parental aspirations, and parental personalities? It is tempting to give class the major credit, especially if one is primarily interested in and sensitized to class. But how valid is that? Important as class undoubtedly is as a social determinant and as a condition of social life, class is not the only determinant nor the only condition. The proliferation of class studies without standards may serve only to compound a basic error rather than yield a more balanced view of the role of class.

Just why there are so many studies of class simply correlated with some other characteristic is an interesting speculation. Doubtless, the narrower limits of these studies as compared with, say, a cross-cultural study of class, is appealing to many researchers with limited research budgets and facilities and heavy pressures to produce something in print. Similarly, the greater simplicity with which such studies can be designed and completed tends to attract research talent to this kind of study. Valuable as these kinds of studies undoubtedly are for providing a mass of data about class, it is unfortunate that so few of them try to grapple with some systematic theory that, after all, gives any study its real significance. Numerous as these simple correlational studies are, they have yet to be gathered together into more meaningful bundles of interrelated facts.

The research studies to be analyzed here share a major characteristic in common. Each is concerned with the social psychological impact of class; the difference, in other words, that class makes for behavior. Class, however it is defined, is presumed to style the individual's environment and experiences in such a way that certain phenomena hit him differently than they do individuals in other classes. The social psychological dynamics are not always fully known, but that there are differences traceable directly to class is a basic postulate for each of the studies.

Class, in short, creates a significant social milieu in which the individual moves and thereby predetermines a wide range of what the individual sees, experiences, and does. The tie to social structure is evident. It is the structure that is responsible for the creation of the class worlds to which individuals belong and in which they move.

These last statements are not meant to create an image of a mechanistic social world in which individual choice and decision are totally absent. It is true, even in class terms, that the individual has some say over his destiny and over his actions. Nevertheless, it is equally true that if class means anything for the individual it means that class position creates a series of broad boundaries within which individual action is conducted. The way in which the indiivdual comes to see and to define his world is part of his personal history—the influences of his parents, his siblings, his peers, his teachers, his idols, and his demons. In adulthood, by some complex social chemistry, these influences are ingrained into a personality style and translated into ways of meeting the environment. Class enters at almost every significant point: in the influences the individual is exposed to and in the evaluations he learns to make of his own experience; in the values of the people whom he contacts from infancy throughout life and in the values he comes to take on as his own. Class is not the only significant social psychological influence. There undoubtedly are others. But class as a fact of modern life is of enormous importance; and as individuals come to be class conscious in their own values and in their evaluations of others, then the importance of class as a determinant of behavior increases even more.

Class and Childhood

CLASS begins with childhood. Here, where personality begins in seriousness to take on the outlines of its later mold, where the individual learns the culturally approved responses for the roles he is to play, the traces of class can be discerned. Culture—through the family, the play group, and the school—impinges upon the developing personality, shaping it and directing it along certain lines of conduct rather than others. An important feature of this socialization process is supplied by class values. The family, which is a pivotal agent in this cultural indoctrination, transmits to the child many class-tinged values that become enmeshed in the basic interstices of the personality. The class concepts of the parents as well as the class-influenced values they hold determine a good deal of the ways in which they raise their children. These parental values are unconsciously or consciously implanted. Since the child's world is severely bounded by his parents, his playmates, and later his teachers, there is little contrast and less choice for a comparison of values such as an adult might be able to make. What the child learns—the rules of the social game, the roles he must play, the bases for judgments of his own as well as of others' actions, and his conceptions of self—is in a real sense a series of absolute rules and formulas for managing his environment and getting along in it. These brook no interference and cannot yet be tempered by the judgment which will come with maturity and experience. This is a regular stage in the development of the child and, as Piaget has described it, is dominated by this character of "absolutism." "Having little understanding of the rationale of the rules, the child accepts them as a part of the universe—like the law of gravity, which he also does not understand. They become incorporated into his social motive patterns." This is a stage of personality development in which "the child becomes increasingly aware of the ways of the world, but in which he has very little sense of reciprocity between himself and others. [Other persons] are all simply parts of a newly discovered world, parts of which have to be recognized and coped with in order to get along."[1]

This does not mean, however, that personality development is an assembly line product in which you pour in so much class at the beginning and come out with a finished class result by adulthood. No one would argue that personality processes are not complex. Social psychology is far from secure in its theory of personality and in the dynamics of personality development. But class is a factor in the development of the individual because it is expressed through so many of the agencies that shape and control his personality growth. To say we do not know all of the facets involved in the process is correct. To say that class has an enormous, if not fully known, effect upon personality growth is equally correct.

All of this is by way of entering into an analysis of child-rearing practices—an initial and crucial stage of personality development in which the effects of class have been discerned. There are some who might disagree that weaning, toilet training, and feeding schedules are for the infant psychologically important events having personality repercussions. The more cautious position, however, would be that these are important, although to an unknown and as yet unmeasured degree.

If it can be granted, then, that such child-rearing practices are important, here is a package of behavior that has clear ties to culture. The manner in which children are socialized is culturally determined. The way in which this process is generally carried out, the specific family members that are held socially accountable for it, and the legal and moral obligations upon adults for the socialization of the new generation are all fixed in the cultural fabric. In turn, some of the variations within these limits imposed by these society-wide mores can be explained as class differences. Middle class parents, for example, would be differently oriented toward the child and toward his upbringing than parents from the lower class, or so the rationale would run for these studies.

There are two questions involved here that must be separated, and it is only the first that is discussed here. First, the question can be asked: does class initiate significantly different practices in child-rearing? Do parents at different class levels, in other words, raise their children differently? The second question refers to later personality consequences: what are the effects of class-based differences in child-rearing upon the adult personality? The latter question depends upon a more developed theory of personality and upon research into this matter in order to be answered, though it is by far the more significant of the two.

The study of child-rearing practices and class, fortunately, has received systematic attention. It has been the subject of four studies of good research caliber.[2] These studies have paralleled one another so closely in design and purpose that reasonable comparisons can be made between them as to their findings. The guiding rationale behind them, as stated by Ericson for her study, was "to test the hypothesis that, since differing social classes represent different learning environments for children, systematic differences in child-rearing practices could be found."[3] "Child-rearing practices" has come to mean the ways in which infants, and later children, are fed, weaned, and toilet trained, and later still the ways in which parents discipline and punish the child. These practices are universal requirements that are believed to influence the personality of the child; and the ways in which they are handled by the parents are believed to be indicative of the kind of parent-child relationship that exists at a deeper psychological level.

A feature that threads these several learning situations together is the degree of permissiveness, or lack of it, that guides the parents' behavior toward their children. At one extreme, the child is given maximum latitude, within bounds presumably, while growing up. He is allowed to set the pace at which he learns. He is given attention, but is not catered to; he is appreciated and "understood," but is not over-idolized. Parents who are permissive let the child feel that the pace he is setting is acceptable. The situation of teaching and learning is kept clear of overtones of parental anxieties about the child, and the main business is to let and to help the child mature. For example, the child is weaned when he appears to be ready, rather than at a time set by parents who either are anxious to have the child move closer to independence as soon as possible, or who are upset if their child does not conform to or exceed the expectations they hold for him.

In a permissive environment the child is allowed to exhibit a "reasonable" amount of aggression towards others, parents included. The notion is that the healthy personality requires a certain measure of autonomy that is partially satisfied by an individual's revolt. The child in American society, unlike his Victorian predecessor, is thought to be a person and be entitled to certain rights at an early age.

The psychologically demanding environment is at the opposite extreme. As the term implies, the parents take the lead and set the pace for the child's development. The child is reared according to the demands and time schedules of the parents' standards rather than one set by and adjusted to the child. The child is toilet trained earlier and weaned earlier, and is expected to conform at an earlier age than he might otherwise be ready to. Aggression towards the parents is not tolerated. Punishment is severe and discipline is enforced. In extreme forms, the parent threatens the child psychologically, dangling love as the bait.

No one seems to be very sure just how these opposing environments and the numerous variations between these extremes affect and shape personality, although there is agreement that these environments do shape the person. As far as class is concerned this matter of personality environments has two aspects: (1) to find whether there are class differences in child-rearing environments and practices; and (2) if such differences do exist, to find what consequences they may have for the adult personality in a class setting.

The conclusions of four studies on class and child-rearing do not show that there are consistent class differences, but there has been some disagreement among some of the authors about that point. Havighurst and Davis, most notably, have contended that class differences exist but that the differences they found do not agree with those found in other studies. The reasons for this confusion in interpretation are hard to locate, although one reason can be traced to a greater willingness by Havighurst and Davis to accept certain differences as statistically significant where others are not so willing. From the content side, and leaving statistics out of it for a moment, it is still unclear why other authors contend that the findings of these several studies are contradictory. The asymmetry of the research variables in the several studies makes for a tricky comparison, but there is little question that the several findings are consistent with one another.

The first of the four studies in which one hundred mothers were interviewed was conducted in Chicago in 1943. It concluded that lower class mothers generally were more permissive toward their children in the first infant years than were the middle class mothers. Lower class children were more often breast-fed, were weaned later, and were fed on demand rather than by the clock. Middle class children, on the other hand, were often bottle fed, weaned earlier, and fed on schedule. Middle class children were started on toilet training at an earlier age than lower class children, but both groups were finally trained at about the same age.

The atmosphere became more permissive for middle class children as they grew older. What is more, this occurred in areas of important psychological weight. Among the significant findings on this point were such differences as these: (1) middle class mothers were more willing to ignore "accidents" after toilet training had begun; (2) middle class mothers, more often than lower class mothers, allowed their children to show aggression; (3) middle class children were more frequently disciplined by reward and praise rather than by physical punishment as was more the practice in the lower class; and finally, (4) middle class fathers spent more time with their children than lower class fathers did with theirs. "Middle class children," Ericson concluded, "are taught ways of living that will prepare them to . . . assume positions of responsibility in the home and in the community. The lower class children are reared in families in which life is less strictly organized, and fewer demands are made upon them."[4] The first part of this statement was somewhat beyond the limits justified by the information gathered in the study; the second was reasonably supported by the evidence.

The Boston study, conducted almost ten years later, reached similar conclusions, although it found statistically significant differences in child-rearing practices between the middle and lower classes in some situations where the Chicago study had not. Conversely, in some situations it found no significant differences where the Chicago study had. Nevertheless, the general tone of the findings impresses one as similar. The pattern of differences yielded very similar images in both studies. The lower class in Boston, as in Chicago, was more severe than the middle class in punishing the child for soiling after toilet training had begun. The middle class, in both studies, was more permissive in allowing children to show aggression towards others, was more permissive in the area of sex and sex attitudes, and the middle class father showed a warmer and less rejecting attitude toward the child than did the lower class father. There seemed to be but two points in which the Boston study departed from the conclusions of the Chicago study: (1) in Boston, lower class mothers said that toilet training was completed earlier for their children than was the case for the middle class mothers; and (2) middle class mothers said that they used the threat of withdrawing love as a discipline technique, while lower class mothers relied on physical punishment. These two practices and their class differences, more by direction than by solid fact, seemed to imply that the middle class parents are somewhat less than completely permissive, especially in the use of love as a reward. The Chicago study, on the contrary, did not find signs of such ambivalence.

Unless these two studies have been badly misread, the pattern of class differences in both studies generally seemed to be consistent. In both, the middle class created a generally more permissive environment in such situations as punishment, discipline (with the Boston exception), responsibility given to the child, and the amount of aggression that the child was permitted to show. The relatively greater permissiveness by lower class parents in beginning toilet training later and in being more relaxed about feeding the infant, does not seem to carry too much weight psychologically. Both studies concluded that lower class parents were not as "natural" in their behavior as was the middle class, taken all in all. The children of the lower class were treated almost as if they didn't exist for the first years of life and then came up sharply against strong discipline and firm demands. Middle class parents, on the other hand, according to these studies, showed somewhat greater confusion about how they should treat their children in the first years, but settled down after that to giving the children as much of their head as could be allowed. Yet, Havighurst and Davis, the authors of the Chicago study, concluded after a comparison between their findings and those of Boston that "the disagreements between the findings of the two studies are substantial and important."[5] Whatever these disagreements were was not apparent from the data except in the two points mentioned and in essentially minor statistical variations.

The confusion introduced by Havighurst and Davis in their evaluation has been somewhat further increased by two more recent studies of the same subject but with some variations. In one, a study of 206 parents in Eugene, Oregon, the authors concluded that there were almost no statistically significant differences between the child-rearing practices of the two classes. The situations studied were generally the same as those already reported. Their results, they believed, "point quite clearly to the absence of any general or profound differences in socialization practices as a function of social class."[6] The comparisons between their study in Eugene with the Chicago and Boston studies led them to conclude, furthermore, that the number and direction of statistical differences in all the studies did not support the hypothesis of differences. Out of 108 comparisons between the middle class and lower class groups in the three cities, they found that only 21 were significant. "In 14 the MC [middle class] were more permissive or less demanding and in 17 the LC [lower class]; the null hypothesis that differences are evenly divided cannot be rejected. . . ."[7] This says quite clearly that there are no class differences at all in the child-rearing practices that they studied, thereby departing considerably from the Havighurst and Davis findings.

The second of the two studies was carried out in California where 74 mothers were interviewed. The author there concluded that her findings generally agreed more closely with the Boston rather than with the Chicago results. She found six statistically significant differences out of thirty-one comparisons, again dealing with the same matters. The judgment that there was closer agreement with the Boston study, as the author indicated, however, was more a matter of agreement on selected variables rather than on the sum of these variables. The California findings appeared to establish the same general impressions conveyed by both Boston and Chicago results, even though the author of the California study favored the former.

There is little point in arguing interpretation as between the studies. It is not really important whether these findings from several studies agree with one another, but instead whether these findings are consistent and whether they are significant. The authors of the Eugene study, Littman, Moore, and Pierce-Jones, very cogently have commented on this matter.[8] Some of the variables used as indices of permissiveness in child-rearing practices are so equivocal that it is unclear which is the permissive action and which the demanding. By what criterion, for example, is breast-feeding any more "permissive" than bottle-feeding? Indeed, feeding practices—and a good many other practices of raising children—go through cycles, depending on the child authority accepted at the moment. Spock, either because he believed it or because he believed that anxious parents are not good parents, has argued that the kind of feeding is less important than the amount of affection shown toward the infant during feeding. The differences between the Boston and Chicago findings in this respect might be due more to faddism than to basic differences between the classes.

The statistical bases of the findings, even of those differences found to be statistically significant, might be questioned. The samples studied were small, and some were doubtful samples. Further, the number of significant differences were few in relation to the number of such comparisons that were made. The findings, therefore, were not as firmly substantiated as one might wish, even though one is left with more than a suspicion that class has something to do with the manner in which the child is reared.

Whether or not these differences were class determined or class induced is also left unsettled, yet is the most crucial point of all. In part, the inability to settle this matter stemmed from the muddy notions about the nature and meaning of class. In part, the matter was unresolved because it was not determined whether the parents acted as they did primarily for class reasons or rather for other reasons. Parental attitudes were the results of their individual histories as well as of their current experiences. Their own childhood experiences, for example, may have been much more a determinant in how they raised their own children than was their current class position or their class aspirations for the future. The absence of significant differences in some of the comparisons might have meant that factors other than class were of importance—the number of children in the family, for example—and that class became important only within those conditions.

Finally, the objection might be made that the variables

that were studied were poor indices of the complex psychological dimension that was really at issue. In other words, could feeding, weaning, and toilet training adequately portray the psychological environment and whether it was permissive or not? There was reasonable doubt that they could. Added to this equivocation is the fact that studies of class and personality do not fully agree nor fully extrapolate the psychological tendencies found in childhood. There is some question about the degree of permissiveness supposedly present in middle class homes in which older children are raised; such children show their own neurotic strains. Yet, studies of class and mental health among adults have indicated that the middle class environment was a somewhat better bet than the lower class one. In short, there are many equivocal points that are peppered throughout this entire area of study.

The final feeling which this analysis leaves is that it is very much up to one's point of view as to what is valid. The studies do not provide firm enough findings to point the way. It still seems plausible to assume that different class environments created important differences for the socialization of the child, even though none of the studies fully substantiated that assumption. What is needed, therefore, are fewer studies replicating the same designs used in the past, and more attention given to the testing of other variables that get at the dimensions tying class and personality together—if they are so related.

What has been suggested in the present discussion and in the conclusions of the Littman, Moore, and Pierce-Jones study in Eugene, has been that the research techniques as well as the theoretical specifications must be sharpened to fit the goals of research into this aspect of class, not only of the class concepts but of the personality concepts as well. Except for the California study, for example, none of the research has considered the *source* of child-rearing ideas as having an important bearing on the matter. Class attitudes are in some measure the results of social contacts with others and with their values. The fact that a significantly greater proportion of the middle class mothers in the California study got their information from "expert books" (Spock, Gesell, etc.) and from friends, whereas lower class mothers depended on "common sense," is a datum of some importance in this kind of study. Class is not alone a determination of where one stands on some statistical scale, as so many studies of class have tended tacitly to assume. Class is very much a set of dynamic social relationships that have consequences for human behavior. Where parents get their information from—whether they read about it or hear about it or just play it by ear—could be an incisive class difference with direct consequences for child-rearing practices, the socialization environment, and the stance taken by the parents.

Further knowledge about the relationship between class and childhood is obtained by considering the older child, beyond these first years. What are the consequences of a class-conditioned child-rearing for the later personality development of the child?

One study of personality consequences traced to class differences in socialization has become something of a minor classic in the literature of stratification, Arnold Green's "The Middle-Class Male Child and Neurosis."[9] It attempted to explain why neurotic conflict could develop in middle class homes and be absent in lower class ones, in this case a Polish lower class group. The generating situation of conflict, Green has argued, was to be found in different child-rearing practices; specifically the use of physical punishment for discipline in lower class families and the threat of withdrawing love as a control device in middle class families. The psychological effects of these different control techniques came through to the children, further heightened by the feeling tone with which such punishments were administered. Green has argued that there was less neuroticism among the lower class children, in spite of the physical punishment, because the personality of the child could remain relatively free for its own development. "Parental authority, however harsh and brutal, is, in a sense, casual and external to the 'core of the self.' "[10] Polish parents could not "absorb the personality" of their children because their children picked models other than their parents as standards for behavior. Thus, children were able to escape parental domination if not punishment and ended up judging their parents in negative and harsh tones according to the American standards that the children had accepted. The lower class Polish parents could and did lay hands on their children but did not get through to the psychological level.

Among middle class children, on the contrary, neurotic symptoms developed because of the "personality absorption" of the child by the parents, by which Green meant "the physical and emotional blanketing of the child, bringing about a slavish dependence upon the parents."[11] The dominant tone in middle class socialization, Green argued, was the need for love, which the child has been conditioned to accept as supremely important. Perversely then, the effective means of discipline was to threaten the child with that love by possibly withholding or withdrawing it. Love was at once the goal and the means of middle class socialization.

The psychological difficulties of an already heavily laden condition were complicated even more, Green argued, because middle class parents were ambivalent in their feelings towards their children. They wanted children, but this desire was confounded with the fact that children interfered with the attainment of dominant middle class values such as a "career, social and economic success, and hedonistic enjoyment." The ambivalence was passed on to the child as part of his heritage of socialization in the form of a conflict between the needs for being submissive in the home and competitively assertive in his peer groups outside the home. The middle class child under such circumstances emerged from these cross-pressures and counter-demands with the burden of neurotic conflict heavy upon him even though he came from an American home with a good living standard. The Polish child, on the other hand, shorn psychologically of his parents at an early stage in his personality development, emerged relatively free of cross-pressures and of neurotic conflicts on that score.

The final answer to this, of course, is not to avoid parents in order to avoid neurotic conflict, but rather that the middle class parents with their children are caught in a web not of their own making. Pursuing contradictory values and without a sure hierarchy of relative values that is sincere and honestly believed, the middle class person—as boy and man—works himself into a psychological corner from which there is not much chance to escape.

The conclusions are more in the nature of plausible hunches that are psychologically consistent than they are fully verified findings. A major question is: how valid is this as a characterization of middle class styles and middle class socialization? On the latter point, the studies of class differences in socialization left some doubts. On the first point, there is still no full measure and description of middle class mores in parent-child relationships.

The Polish group, of course, shares certain traits in common with all immigrants: the generational split of parents sticking to the old world norms they knew best and of children pursuing the newer American standards. The so-called rejection of the parents by the children, therefore, might not have been so much a lower class feature as one of immigration and the acculturation experience. Even so, Green would have argued, the character of the middle class group remained, whatever the explanation for the lower class Polish group.

An outstanding feature of this study and its analysis was its dynamic character. It was not a study of simple correlations between socialization practices and class levels, but more importantly, an hypothesis about the dynamic interrelations between those variables. Furthermore, it was a study that probed below the surface manifestations of class and tried to cope with the significance of class at the level where personality was formed and developed. As such, it provided some clues to the psychological dimension of class; competitive striving for success by the middle class was a mixed blessing which could tie the individual into a neurotic's web. Damned by the loss of friendship and warmth if he succeeded and damned by the possible destruction of his own ego if he failed, the middle class child might pay a high psychic price for the sake of his class position.

Unfortunately, there have not been enough attempts to get at these kinds of dimensions, and the hunches about the psychological environment of the middle class, or any other class, cannot always be substantiated. Research studies of the personality adjustment of the child have been of a relatively limited scope, limited both in design and in the measures used. In one, for example, a small community was chosen as the locale and paper and pencil tests of personality were used. No significant relationship was found between the child's scores on these tests and his social status.[12]

These tests, like the measures used in the studies of child-rearing practices, required large concessions to objective measures of personality. Content and interest were sacrificed for a measure of objectivity. Perhaps personality cannot yet be measured objectively by any other device. However, it should also be noted that negative findings from these tightly objective studies cannot be taken as full proof. The absence of a casual relationship between class and personality as measured by short answer, paper and pencil devices, may only indicate that the techniques are at fault. It would be analogous to arguing that the galaxies that cannot be seen by the naked eye do not exist even though there is theoretical ground to believe that they do. In a similar fashion, the theory and internal systematics of the available knowledge about class lead one to suspect that class plays an important role in the formative years of personality development. Green's conclusions about the neurotic conflicts in the middle class may not be fully substantiated yet, but there must be more to come in the shape of better studies on class with better techniques.

The analysis of class and childhood can be further rounded out by reference to the studies of school-age children. There have been several studies in this respect, but the discussion here is limited to one relatively lengthy and carefully detailed study by Stendler.[13] Interviewing 107 children in the first, fourth, sixth and eighth grades in a school in an industrial town of 15,000 fictitiously named "Brasstown," Stendler wanted to learn what symbols of class the children recognized and at what age they came to identify them. In addition to an interview, each child was given a picture test consisting of pictures cut out of several national magazines of home scenes, clothing, recreation spots, and people working. The children were thereby tested on their knowledge of class differences in the pictures shown them. Additionally, each child completed a "Guess Who?" questionnaire in which he filled in the names of other children to such inquiries as "Who is the best ball player?", "Who has the most spending money?", "Whose clothes often need mending?", "Who has a maid to help at home?", etc.

By the sixth grade, children were aware of differences between rich and poor; by the eighth grade, their distinctions followed the stereotypes of adult attitudes. By the time they had reached this level in school, children were able to rate pictures by the class they represented and were additionally able to give reasons for their ratings in terms of "the exclusiveness of what they see, or the money involved, or the privileges accompanying a particular class station."[14] Like their parents, they were able to rate their classmates in terms of the kinds of homes they had, their fathers' occupations, clothes and manners.

This knowledge takes years to accumulate. The first grade child, it seemed, was aware of differences between people but had not yet learned to relate these to class. The process of learning class symbols, Stendler concluded, was "part of the whole developmental process; it is not a separate and disparate learning but is interwoven with, and dependent on, such aspects of growth as becoming a member of a social group and learning the mores of the society."[15]

The consequences of class awareness in young children showed up in several ways. Friendships were chosen on the basis of class, especially in out-of-school friendships, and the first clear lines of staying within class boundaries were evident at an early age. Stereotyped attitudes towards the classes were already emergent; favorable behavior went with the upper class, unfavorable with the lower. In the earlier grades, children noted class diflerences, but they also tended to defend the poor and criticize the rich. This did not seem to be much more than a case of repeating the ideal values, much as adults do; and like adults, the children rejected working class children more often as friends than they did those from the middle and upper classes. In short, the groundwork of adult class attitudes and behavior was set fairly early in life, aided by the school and the playground, and condoned by the parents.

The sum of this information on class and childhood leaves an indelible impression: class makes a difference for the attitudes and behavior the individual exhibits and, furthermore, is a feature of the most formative years of personality development. This conclusion is ragged, as has been pointed out several times before. The methodology and the techniques do not provide as much validation for these points as should be required to consider them substantially correct. Yet, the sheer consistency of the composite image that they created is there. Perhaps this is the result of a middle class bias of the investigators. Perhaps it is due to a repeated bias in the sampling and the interpretations of results. Even those possibilities, not too highly probable in this limited research area, do not destroy the image of consistency. Furthermore, any coherent theory of class, coupled with the most minimal theory of personality and psychodynamics, bolsters the general impression these studies have created. The middle class child is prepared for his class role, and prepared for it early. The lower class child, by the relative inattention paid by him and his parents to class matters, does not have that identification. What is at stake, are two highly different ways of life, beginning in childhood and extending deep into adulthood.

Class and Fertility

THE studies of the relationship between class position and demographic behavior have a mixed tone. On the positive side, the statistical clarity and objectivity of the measures of fertility, mortality, and migration give the investigator a sense of security. A child born, a person dying, or a family moving are real events that are collected with greater completeness than is any other sociological phenomenon. The resources of local and national governments, bolstered by legal requirements, insure that births and deaths are officially noted and recorded. The census provides information on migration in a similarly detailed manner. In other words, unlike many other areas of sociological interest, demography yields the kind of objectivity and measurement that permits comparison and analysis of great reliability.

There is a negative side, however, that muddies the clarity demographic measures might otherwise have. No matter how reliable a measure may be, it is only as useful as the categories it measures. It is at this point that demographic variables sometimes give rise to a misleading and unjustified sense of security. Counting up the number of births and deaths is relatively simple, even though there are the usual problems of assessing the accuracy of such statistics. However, the demographic interest is not in sheer numbers of births and deaths but in their meaning for future trends and consequences. This requires the apportionment of births and deaths into meaningful sociological categories. What is wanted is information on demographic differences—births, deaths, and migrations—among different segments of the population, no matter how these segments are defined.

Class is clearly one of the more significant dimensions by which a population can be divided and separated. What are the differences in birth rates among the different classes? What are the mortality differentials by class? Are there significant migration differentials as between one class and another?

It is clear that the answers to these questions are as good as the definition of class that is used, but this is a familiar reservation by now. It is on precisely this methodological rock that many of the demographic studies of class have foundered. Almost without variation, the procedure followed has been to define class by such measures as income, occupation, and education. Of course, in this respect, the demographic studies of class are no different from many other studies of class in other areas as has been already documented in earlier chapters. The problem that arises here, however, is that the relationships between class so defined and a given demographic variable are never quite clear. Even though the statistics show an inverse relationship to exist between class and fertility, say, by which lower class persons have a higher birth rate than middle class families, there is little indication as to just what these differences are supposed to mean. For example, does such a finding imply that lower class persons really want more children than middle class persons? Does it imply, as most studies in this area have suggested, that middle class persons only have as many children as they believe they can raise properly according to a set standard of living? The answers to these questions are not found in the data usually collected; they are still beyond the figures. Yet, finding such significant statistical correlations often lulls the investigator into a feeling of scientific security, the more so when the evidence seems to be so objective and so clear-cut.

These notes of caution are justified if only because proper demographic data can give important indices to differential class motivations. Variations of the several demographic characteristics provide a solid check to the orientations and behavior of each of the several classes. It is to that subject matter that the present section on class and fertility is oriented.

Fertility alone among the several possible demographic characteristics has been selected for analysis here. Information on migration factors is not complete enough nor detailed enough to be useful for class analysis, although it is potentially so. Hence, the 1950 census included a question about residence of the respondent in 1949 as a means of measuring migration. From the answers it was possible to analyze some of the characteristics of those who had moved during that one year period. This is insufficient for any detailed class analysis. Other data on the characteristics of migrants do exist, of course, but are usually quite limited by the nature of the samples studied. The migrant, by his very mobility, is a difficult subject to study.

Mortality differences are not to be considered. First, a number of the conclusions of such studies are too apparent to require any elaboration: those in the upper classes tend to outlive those in the lower classes; those with greater incomes and more education are healthier and live longer than those lower on the income and educational scales. An appreciation of health and of preventive medical practices, which usually goes with education and money, increases the chances for life over those who pay no such careful attention to their health. Secondly, mortality differences do not as unequivocally represent matters of choice that are reflections of class as does fertility. People do not choose to die, aside from suicide. People do have some choice about the number of children they will have. It is this choice element—whether deliberate or unconscious—that can make demographic analysis a pathway to some elements of class behavior. Finally, mortality, unlike fertility, does not show an unequivocal relationship with all the criteria of class thus introducing an unwanted element of confusion. By income and education, for example, there are relatively consistent mortality differences; by occupation, on the other hand, there are not. Occupation, when used in this way, comes to include more than prestige characteristics alone. Occupations differ in how dangerous and demanding they are to the individual, and differential death rates by occupation, therefore, reflect several facets other than class.

The study of class differences in fertility, then, remains

as a demographic variable that can provide some insight into the social psychology of class.

The trend in middle class attitudes toward fertility has been an impressively consistent one for a long time. The quickened pace of industrialization after its establishment in western Europe and the United States was matched by two effects upon the industrial middle class. First, the gains in medicine increased the efficiency of populations; more of the children that were born lived and they lived longer. Secondly, the productivity of the industrial economy in consumer goods and services raised the standard of living at the same time that it heightened the desires and aspirations of the industrial population for the many goods that it produced.

The middle class—the social product of industrialization—was most sensitive to these advances in the standard of living. It assimilated the attitudes to limit its birth rate and was further encouraged to do so by the remarkable gains in medicine and in the control over the causes of high mortality rates. This tendency was further abetted by the fact that the middle class was urbanized. In the cities it was more expensive to raise large families than in the country, and from a hard and materialistic point of view children were even less of an economic asset in the city. Children were competitors in the labor market and tended to depress wages in the earlier decades of industrial development before the initiation of child labor legislation.

A falling birth rate for the middle class was already noted by the middle of the nineteenth century.[16] The birth rate continued to decline in succeeding decades and there appeared to be strong and consistent evidence that class and fertility were inversely related; the higher the class, the lower the birth rate. This relationship was found not only in the United States, but in England and throughout western Europe as well. It seemed to hold, furthermore, regardless of class index, whether occupation, income, or education. Heavily industrialized countries were dismayed at the pattern because of the population consequences of a lowered birth rate and a lowered death rate, at the same time as the spread of middle class values was considered desirable in other areas of social belief.

The rationale that was widely employed to explain the inverse relationship turned out to depend upon a view of human motivation that was quite rational and economic in tone. The middle class person, it was argued, more than any other had the strongest aspirations for social and economic success in an industrial economy. In order to realize these ambitions and to enjoy the higher standard of living that industrialization made possible, the middle class individual was forced to make an economic choice. He could economize either on children or on expenditures. By limiting the number of children, he could live more comfortably within his middle class means and retain his middle class values.

This economic rationale for middle class behavior was almost exactly the advice that Malthus had offered to the educated classes over a hundred years before. Malthus had argued for a victory of reason over animal instinct, for those capable of reasoning, in order to escape the traps of misery and death that nature visited upon those who blindly defied the natural laws of overpopulation. Now, many demographers were using the same logic to explain the reasons for a falling birth rate, albeit without preaching. The middle class married late, it was argued, because it took them longer to achieve the social position that was their prerequisite to marriage. They had fewer children in order to raise them by middle class standards, including a better education and a more prestigeful occupation. Malthus certainly would have agreed with that choice.

In spite of the seeming plausibility of this explanation of events, there remained disturbing elements that did not fit the facts. At the most technical level, some demographers were dissatisfied with the explanation because it left some questions unanswered. Typical of the objections at this level were those raised by Notestein, who generally accepted the validity of a consistent and inverse correlation between class position and fertility rates. It was still unknown, he argued, to what extent the differentials in birth rates were reflections of differences in age at marriage, of difference in marriage rates themselves, or of differences in the proportion of childless couples in the several classes.[17] These and similar questions pointed to a need for analytical refinements but not to the questioning of the basic hypothesis itself.

However, there were more basic and critical doubts that were raised. It seemed clear, even from the early data, that a perfect inverse correlation did not always appear. The upper class, in almost all studies, did not show the lowest birth rates as a consistent correlation would have predicted, but instead that class often had among the highest birth rates and always higher than that of the middle class.

Even more upsetting to the widely accepted formulations, however, was the marked change that occurred with the start of World War II when birth rates climbed, and the evidence of an inverse correlation between class and fertility rapidly began to alter. Middle class people married earlier and were parents at earlier ages than had been true for decades. This shift apparently caught demographers unawares, and their earlier explanation, based on the rationality of the middle class, needed serious revision. For a short time the argument was made that the changed birth rate situation was temporary, brought on principally by the war. All that was happening, some argued, was that people were marrying younger, but that in the long run the family would remain as small as before. The birth rate, however, continued to rise even after the end of the war, further stimulated by prosperity. Family sizes continued to expand as greater proportions of women than for decades before were having their third, fourth, and even fifth child.

An inherent error in the demographic explanations of the pre-war low birth rates was generated by a naive view of human nature. The explanation assumed a kind of rational economic man, one who chose between clear-cut and simple alternatives, children being one element in that choice. Children, in this sense, were apparently categorized as a consumer item which families chose or did not choose to buy. Raising children, by this formulation, was like undertaking time payments; so much down, so much a year. This greatly oversimplified the psychological and sociological complexities of human behavior. The demographic explanation had to go wrong as a prediction because it had not properly tapped the choices nor the decision process behind the behavior. Not only was human motivation oversimplified, but so were the effects of social customs, social definitions, traditions and the dynamics of class. Both factors in the equation—class and fertility—were more complicated than the demographic indices had shown.

Not all demographers were caught short by an inadequate formulation. Some had earlier disagreed with the general interpretation of an inverse correlation between class and fertility. Heberle,[18] for one, in an article in 1941 had argued that the inverse correlation was a misleading statistic that obscured a generally *positive* correlation. In his data, as well as in the data for Stockholm by Edin and Hutchinson,[19] there was strong evidence for that positive relationship between class and birth rates. The argument of this opposite view was that the dynamics of class position were obscured by the simple index of class, through the use of income, education, or occupation as measures. Although the figures were correct, the conclusions of an inverse relationship were not, because insufficient attention had been given to the logic of class and what it meant for behavior. Heberle's argument can be taken as representative.

Heberle contended that the period of industrialization was not a uniform one as regards its effects upon the class and fertility relationship. Only in a relatively late period did the typical attitudes associated with industrial society have a chance to take hold and to affect behavior. In the demographic argument, the assumption was usually made that almost from the first the attitudes of an industrial society were in power—desires for upward mobility, for increased standards of living, for urban residence, and for limited fertility. On the contrary, these attitudes took time to infiltrate the class structure and to become internalized in the aspirations and ambitions of individuals.

Even more cogently, Heberle argued that the decisions concerning children must be analyzed not only between classes as other demographers had done, but more importantly within each class itself. Each class might be thought of as further subdivided and in the lowest level of each class were those who had just begun to move out of lower class origins. The struggle was costly and still incomplete. Still, the standard of living, the tone of the class, was generally set by the more secure and longer residents of the class; those who were economically secure and had had the time to stabilize their position.

The recent class immigrants were, therefore, caught in a psychological and economic squeeze. They were caught between the higher standards of living that they felt they had to duplicate and the low incomes that they received with which to do it. They had to live beyond their means, forced into an economically tight and frustrating position. Obviously, they could not cut down on their living standards for this was the principal symbol that tied them to their new and wanted status. Their children had to be properly raised, properly dressed, and properly educated. The parents had to maintain a proper home, automobile, and all the rest. Their style of life came at a high cost, but it could not be sacrificed without knocking them off their class perch. "Suppose a father of five or six children, who is a clerk in a department store or bank, should move to a working class district of his town in order to make ends meet, wear his suits six years or more, and drive an old car. Would he not be censored by his fellow clerks for disregarding the standards of living of his occupational group, and would he not even be criticized by his superiors?"[20] If he had to economize, and economize he must to hold on, he did it by having fewer children. To compete in "displayed consumption" with those whom they recognized as peers, the insecure lower levels of each class limited their fertility as one means of getting economic breathing space between their status demands and pocketbooks.

Heberle's explanation has the merit of including reasonable psychological dimensions; of creating an image of behavior, molded by class, that makes more sense than does the classical economic argument. His explanation, quite importantly, could interpret the rise in the birth rate during the present decade more meaningfully and could explain the current positive correlation between class and fertility.[21] During the decade of post-war prosperity most families have not felt the pressure of economic insecurity. Following Heberle's interpretation, this sense of security has not made pressing the need to limit births. Middle class families, especially, seem to have found that they can afford homes and appliances as well as children. The effect of an economic recession may slow down births but this further substantiates the explanation that fertility is tied to feelings of economic security and not simply to class position alone. This decision to increase family size has further snowballed by effecting changes in values and norms. It has become fashionable to have larger families in the suburbs, for example, as compared with the family sizes of city dwellers two decades ago.

Further support for the social psychological realism of this comes from one of the most intensive studies ever made of the factors connected with fertility—the Indianapolis study of 1941 based on interviews with 41,498 native-white couples.[22] Kiser and Whelpton were the main investigators and two of their many research reports are used here. Rather than classifying individuals on the basis of a single class index such as income, education or occupation, and then comparing birth rates between those categories, Kiser and Whelpton in one phase of the analysis classified couples according to the success of family planning. Within these several categories showing relative success in planning fertility, families were further classified into broad socioeconomic groups. Comparisons of differences in fertility rates were then made. What they found was a direct rather than an inverse relationship. For those families that were successful in planning and spacing children, the more frequently was there a positive relationship between socio-economic position and the number of children. In other words, this finding implied that there was not a simple choice between children and goods, but a choice based on the attainment of economic security.

In a similar manner, the authors analyzed fertility rates according to expressed feelings of economic security and by the extent to which families planned the number of children they had.[23] Once again, among those families that planned and spaced their children most successfully, there was a positive correlation between family size and feelings of security. Where there was planning, in other words. the families with more children also evidenced feelings of greater economic security, although it was impossible to label which was cause and which effect. Among those families that did not plan, on the other hand, those with fewer children showed feelings of the greatest economic security.

These later conclusions relate very directly to Heberle's explanations. It was not socio-economic status alone, according to the Indianapolis study, that explained differential fertility rates. Rather, the psychological assessments and aspirations of the married couples played a decisive role. Where there was rational planning of family size, there it was found that large families went with feelings of economic security. It was not a question simply of the number of children in an absolute sense, but more importantly, the individual's estimate of his economic and social position that mattered. Once the individual believed his position was secure, then family size tended to increase.

What this comparison between class and fertility has tried to show is that fertility is an important consequence of class position—of class dynamically interpreted. As individuals assess their position in the light of their expectations and aspirations, then the rate at which they will produce children is directly affected. This would seem to be a rather basic matter to lay at the door of class determinism.

Class, Neurosis and Psychosis

THE effects of class upon mental health are important not only for the study of class but also for the study of neuroses and psychoses. It must be clear by this point that class might be expected to make a difference for the success of individuals in handling themselves in their environment. The environment of socialization, the parental attitudes toward children and the child's adjustment to these forces, all set the groundwork for personality and shape its development. Of course the process does not end with childhood. The aspirations of the adult personality and his ability to live in an adult social environment are equally important components of the situation that can determine the psychological health or illness of the personality.

The usual image painted of the middle class is derived from what are thought to be the dominant features of the middle class—competition and striving in the way children are reared and in the way adults must work for success. Hence, the middle class occupant appears as highly neurotic, highly disturbed, and perpetually dissatisfied. The lower class image, on the other hand, stereotypically composed of non-strivers and non-competitors, makes that class a calmer psychological type with few instances of mental breakdown. In the case of the upper class little is said about their psychological life, except for some mention of boredom, snobbery, alcoholism sometimes, security of course, and dissatisfactions perhaps. These are crude, though. Much surer is the view that the middle class is neurotic, the lower class placid.

Horney, for example, as well as other psychiatrists turned social analysts, has supported the image of the "neurotic personality" as typical of the competitive middle class segment of American society. This class, more than any other, has been raised and has lived in an atmosphere of competition with its inevitable product of continuous anxiety. Anxiety, in its turn, becomes the force behind neurotic conflict. These interpretations of American society—principally middle class society—fit in with the main strains of the life patterns of this class. From their first contacts, middle class children are taught to compete and taught to give the search for status first priority. They, more often than the children of any other class, are expected to adjust earliest to their social world. The difficulty is, however, that the social world can seldom be stable for those who are upwardly bound, for such persons seldom remain long enough nor do they have the orientation of adjusting to their positions of the moment. The alternative is just as bad, for to remain in one social place too long is a mark of failure which provides no psychological escape either.

The psychiatric particulars of the process, that develops in the adult class world the psychological consequences of childhood, have been set forth in considerable detail by Ruesch.[24] These can be usefully summarized here to match the class images generalized above. According to Ruesch, each class typically has trained its children in the social techniques of adjustment "which are not very modifiable during the mature years of a person's life."[25] When confronted with the repetitive frustrations arising from the very nature of his class position, the individual follows the path of least resistance, following the techniques he knows, as to the form of psychological protest he will manifest. To that extent, then, personality is determined by experiences that are common to a class rather than being only experiences unique to the individual.

In the lower-middle class, psychosomatic complaints were among the most predominant, Ruesch suggested, because in that class the individual has been raised within a pattern of conformity and excessive repression. "Because of lack of expressive facilities, the only possible solution for unsolved psychological conflicts seems to remain in physical symptom formation."[26] The greater permissiveness sanctioned in the lower class, on the other hand, toward physical expressiveness allowed the individual to show his anger and rebellion openly. The lower class encouraged protest because of its position of relative deprivation compared with other classes. "Therefore, we are not amazed to see that the diseases of the lower classes are connected with exposures to machines and expressions of hostility as found in the incidence of fractures, accidents, and traumatic disease."[27] Finally, Ruesch contended that in the upper class there was a "relatively large incidence" of psychosis and psychoneurosis because individuals in that uppermost stratum were victims of strong superego controls and overbearing cultural traditions. Each class, in other words, favored its own particular psychological outlet for frustration and failure; an outlet that was in a sense predetermined by the social techniques inculcated during the socialization of the child.

Although a number of studies have documented a relationship between class and mental illness, Ruesch's conclusions were not among those that were substantiated. Even coming to an assessment of Ruesch's findings through the studies of child-rearing practices, it was noted earlier that there was much unclarity about what were the typical characteristics of the different class environments. Middle class children, for example, were not reared as strictly as Ruesch seemed to suggest, nor were the lower class children reared as permissively as he suggested. Evidence from other studies apparently has shown that schizophrenia was significantly characteristic of the lower class, and that the middle and upper classes were relatively free of serious mental illness.[28] One study in fact has concluded that the psychoses, as measured by admittance rates to public and private mental hospitals, were most frequent among lower class persons.[29] The only exceptions to these findings of mental illness as being most prevalent in the lower class were that the neuroses rather than psychoses tended to be more characteristic of those in the middle and upper classes,[30] and tangentially, that the manic-depressive psychosis was not class linked at all.[31]

These findings tend to be more convincing than those proposed by Ruesch because of the systematic and repetitive fashion in which they have been studied. For example, the possible objection that the relationship between class and psychosis was a spurious one because psychotics have "drifted" down to the lower class has been effectively controlled in the designs of several studies. Through the use of control groups and extensive checks on the life histories of psychotic patients, it has been established that psychosis apparently has little relationship to social mobility. The schizophrenics who were studied were found to have lived in the lower class areas of the city not as recent migrants from upper class neighborhoods but as long-time residents, longer than the onset of the disease itself.

The objection that the relationships between class and psychosis were the artificial results of studying mental hospitals that drew only from the lower class has also been invalidated by careful research designs. In the study of New Haven, the universe of study included patients from every psychiatric source—public and private psychiatric institutions, clinics, and private practitioners; and not only in Connecticut but in surrounding states including metropolitan New York. The only possible exceptions, from what was in effect a census, were those who may have been mentally ill but had not as yet sought professional psychiatric assistance. The possible bias then that might have resulted from considering only those resources typically open to the lower class, could not affect these conclusions.

The fact that these studies were conducted at different times and in different places, and yet are all in close agreement, would seem to take care of any objection that these were unique or exceptional findings.

Where the findings did tend to fulfill expectations about the effect of class was in the analysis of psychiatric treatment and patient-doctor relationships; not so in the matter of the incidence of psychoses. In general it was found that the higher his class, the more adequately the individual was treated. Concluding their study of a psychiatric out-patient clinic in New Haven, Myers and Schaffer found that "acceptance for therapy and the character of subsequent clinical experience were related significantly to the patient's social class; the higher an individual's social class position, the more likely he was to be accepted for treatment, to be treated by highly trained personnel, and to be treated intensively over a long period."[32] Upper class persons more frequently were treated by private practitioners or in private hospitals, which they entered of their own volition; lower class individuals were more often coerced into hospitalization, usually a public facility. The higher the class of the individual, the more likely it was that he received psychotherapy; the lower his class, the more likely that he received organic therapy or no treatment at all.

These latter findings turn out to be more of a commentary upon the middle and upper class bias of psychiatrists towards their patients than of the prevalence or incidence of mental illness among the different classes.

Most findings on the incidence and treatment of mental illness and its relationship to class leave some psychological dynamics untouched. The relationship between being lower class and suffering from schizophrenia, on the contrary, has at least been partially explained in terms of a possible etiology. Faris and Dunham, for example, have argued that "seclusiveness" was characteristic both of schizophrenia as an illness and of the lower class environment from which most schizophrenics came. In these areas, more than in any other, individuals were socially isolated. The relatively greater isolation of lower class persons has also been supported by other studies, which have shown them to be less concerned with and less active in their social environment generally. That this isolation, in effect, removed the individual from "the social control which enforces normality in other people," was the interpretation given by Faris and Dunham, and they went on to contend that isolation and seclusiveness were distinctive traits of schizophrenia.

The findings and interpretations presented here account for the prevalence of one type of psychiatric disorder—schizophrenia—among the lower class, but do not really comment upon the psychiatric conditions of the middle and upper classes. Presumably, the frequency of severe disorders in the middle and upper classes is lower.

The New Haven study by Hollingshead and Redlich has suggested just that conclusion. They found the neuroses rather than the psychoses to be positively correlated with class. Middle and perhaps upper class persons somehow have learned to control or narcotize their psychological weaknesses and have presumably kept them from emerging in anything more severe than neuroticism. As Horney has suggested, perhaps individuals in these classes are able to submerge themselves psychologically in their work or in their social relationships to such an extent that potentially severe disturbances are kept in check. The lower class individual, on the other hand, has little opportunity and no supportive values that would present such escapes as reasonable alternatives for him. Neither intensive social interaction nor neurotic work drives are part of his life style or occupation.

Middle and upper class environments typically surround the individual in a web of social involvement and social responsibility—to the family, to the work group, and to friends. Seclusiveness and isolation are not elements in the way of life in these classes. The conclusion that follows, then, is that the very forces that might be conducive to psychotic breakdowns in the middle class—competitiveness, fear of failure, and continuous ego comparisons with others—are at the same time forms of psychological insurance against such disorders becoming more severe than neurotic conflicts. The presence of others is at once a cause and a preventive.

For reasons which are unknown, and perhaps are unimportant, there has been very little research concern with the causes of such neuroticism and their class character. To be sure, the writings of Horney, Fromm, and others have dealt with this matter but by the sweeping interpretation rather than by the more detailed specification of relevant causes. However, there are more than enough of such interpretative essays presently available, but a dearth of the kind of research testing that has characterized the studies of class and psychiatric disorders reported on here. One major exception to this generalization was a study by Leavy and Freedman that analyzed five hundred case records of patients in a psychiatric dispensary and in a private psychiatric hospital.[33] Their research, although it leaves some doubts as to the methodology, was importantly directed toward analyzing the psychological effects of economic life upon individuals.

The questions they asked were most reasonable, and one wonders why they had not been considered to any intensive extent as a legitimate focus of research before. "We may ask whether experiences of adult life related to getting a living have a determinative effect in the appearance of neurotic symptoms. We may also ask whether neurotic people show their neurotic symptoms in specific ways in their economic life."[34] To answer these questions, Leavy and Freedman studied case records in terms of three general headings: economic insecurity, relationships to work, and competition.

As regards the first, they found that it was impossible to separate clearly the factors making for economic insecurity from other factors that might have created family tensions. It seemed evident that economic insecurity could provoke deeper psychological insecurities by creating an environment where such psychological insecurities were almost certain to occur. Poverty, unending financial difficulties, and the repeated inability to find work were intimately interwoven with the neurotic syndromes of the cases reported by Leavy and Freedman. It is probably true, as they pointed out, that emotional concerns might be displaced to economic concerns, that economic values may only be manifest expressions of strong emotional value, but this does not greatly detract from the importance of economic insecurity as a cause of neurosis.

Work, as they pointed out, was an important stage for the neurotic drama. In our culture the healthy person is supposed to work, and we have caused individuals to internalize this belief to such an extent that their inability to work was turned back negatively upon themselves; they judged that either they were sick or they must lack the capabilities. Work was sanctioned and idleness condemned to such a clear degree that "patients themselves usually . . . stress as complaints . . . their inability to carry on their work."[35] Patients reported that their self-respect was shaken when they were unable to continue working because their symptoms made it impossible.

> Not working in a community where nearly everyone works is itself sufficient to arouse feelings of guilt and depression. It stirs up old anxieties, that may have been long latent, concerning one's ability to achieve and maintain independence. . . . He adds to his existing feelings of inadequacy the picture of himself, drawn from reality, as one unable to meet a fundamental demand of the society.[36]

For others, work turned out to be a neurotic escape, such as Horney had suggested in her analysis of the "neurotic personality." On the job, neurotic drives could be compulsively contained within the rigid schedule demanded of the individual; those in managerial capacities could evidence frankly aggressive impulses under the social screen of its being necessary to do the job; those driven by ambitions with a neurotic genesis could be rewarded because they contained their ambitions within a sphere so highly approved by society. These instances show some of the channels whereby the work situation can translate neuroticism into socially constructive goals; that is, as long as the individual could function under such conditions.

Competition and the struggle for prestige, the authors found, were the most dynamic forces in the histories of some neurotic individuals. For some patients, "the struggle for achievement liberated . . . feelings of hostility which were poorly withstood." In other instances, the impossibility of achieving the wanted goals of prestige heightened already developing neurotic conflicts. This matter, by the way, is to be discussed in fuller detail in Chapter Six. Finally, among still other patients, competition for economic and prestige rewards was simply an extension of a neurotic struggle that had its genesis in childhood.

Leavy and Freedman, interestingly enough, concluded their observations on the following note: "The obligation to compete, like economic insecurity, had a double function: it was a direct threat, since failure might again endanger subsistence, and it was also more subtly involved as a social force, invoking the individual's allegiance in the pursuit of a value not open to criticism."[37]

Information about child rearing practices among the different classes might also be reiterated here as it throws light on this whole matter. The middle and upper class child, sooner and more frequently, encountered situations of psychological stress. If, for example, Green's suggestion is valid, that middle class parents threatened their children with the withdrawal of love and lower class parents punished directly and physically, it might be reasoned that middle class children learned to cope with psychological threats at a point when their personalities were still formative. This is not to suggest that it is possible to develop a kind of psychological immunity in the same fashion that one develops or can be given an immunity to smallpox, but it is known that the personality does develop typical ways of handling the environment, including psychological stress. If this were not so, then certainly one would expect a higher incidence of psychotic disorders among the upwardly mobile middle class, for mobility by its very nature demands the constant breaking of old ties with each step in the social ascent. Yet, mobility apparently has no clear relationship to the incidence of psychiatric disorders, although those who are not mobile and want to be are open to more neurotic tensions than others.

Neurosis and neurotic conflict are still the hallmarks of the middle class and perhaps the upper class as well. What these studies of mental illness have substantially proven was that such neurotic conflict does not usually become intense enough to lead to severe psychotic disorder, that the middle and upper class person somehow has learned to live with his neurosis and to mobilize it for his own purposes toward socially legitimate goals.

Class Consciousness

THE preceding sections of this chapter have considered some of the systematic consequences of class for behavior as regards mental health, fertility, and child-rearing. Along similar lines, the following chapter on social mobility will analyze other psychological consequences of class, particularly the ways in which mobility-striving can affect attitudes, prejudices, and aspirations. All of these dimensions, in effect, are threaded together by a common assumption: that class can determine, modify, or otherwise affect behavior without the individual's awareness of such force acting upon him. What is unknown to the individual, what he may not fully comprehend about his class position, for many purposes, does not alter the enormous social psychological impact. As further studies are made, it may well turn out that class has a determining influence in even more phases of behavior than are now recognized.

Yet, the matter of "class consciousness" is still important. A clear understanding of the social psychology of class obviously includes both the conscious and unconscious aspects. This goal is hindered to a large extent by the confusion that seems to be inherent in the concept of "class consciousness." In the entire battery of terminology and concepts about social stratification, except possibly for "class" itself, none is more ambiguously used than the concept of "class consciousness."

The central importance of the concept in the study of stratification is a theoretical one, although Marx gave it a central political place as well. What "class consciousness" can accomplish is to unite the generalizations about class structure with those concerning individual class behavior. This problem, of course, is a recurrent one in social science generally where generalizations and conclusions about the functioning of a social system must be translated finally into terms of human behavior. Although in some cases it may be enough to analyze the structure alone, the characteristics of a class system, its effects upon the institutions of society, or its historical dynamics, the theory is not complete unless the conclusions on the level of structure can be reinterpreted in social psychological terms as referring to individual behavior. "Class consciousness" is precisely one channel to accomplish that end.

Marx, who was the first to give class consciousness a major place in class theory, used it in just that way. It is useless at this late date to try to decipher what Marx "really meant" to accomplish by introducing the concept, but it is possible to assess the principal functions it served for his general theory.

The "class situation," which Marx had analyzed as to its genesis and its historical necessity, was the basic force, in turn, that steered and determined human behavior. "Class consciousness," thereby, became the psychological channel whereby the broader social and economic processes that Marx had described could and did enter into the range of individual action. The individual's consciousness of his class was an inevitable consequence that developed as a result of those processes. Marx recognized, of course, that what he conceived of as historical necessity in the development of a social system had to be converted somehow into human behavior and human consciousness, else he would be reduced to arguing only a metaphysical doctrine. There was thus implicit from the first, in Marx's theory, a recognition of the social psychological dimension that went along with his analysis of social and economic structure.[38]

A second related function that the concept of "class consciousness" served for Marx was to disprove the direction of argument of the earlier idealistic philosophies, which started with man's ideas as primary and drew consequences for economic and social structure from them. Marx, on the contrary, contended that the materialistic factors of production and subsistence were primary and he showed how these forces conditioned ideas, not the reverse. He had, he reasoned, turned man back on his feet where he belonged, rather than having him "stand on his head" as Marx maintained the idealists would have it.

Both purposes were intertwined in Marx's writing; the first served a theoretical purpose, while the second, perhaps, provided the motivating polemic for his argument. Furthermore, Marx was repeatedly insistent that it was the "real individual" in whom he was interested, and the social reality in which that individual lived. Marx recognized the two sides of the theory that had to be systematically joined—social structure and social person—if the theory was to have any meaning. "Class consciousness" provided the theoretical channel whereby he could tune structural necessities into the daily activities of "real" people.

> The social structure and the State are continually evolving out of the life-process of definite individuals [*sic*], but of individuals, not as they may appear in their own or other people's imaginations, but as they really are; *i.e.,* as they are effective, produce materially, and are active under definite material limits, presuppositions and conditions independent of their will.
>
> The production of ideas, of conceptions of consciousness, is at first directly interwoven with the material intercourse of men, the language of real life. . . . Men are the producers of their conceptions, ideas, etc.—real, active men, as they are conditioned by a definite development of their productive forces and of the intercourse corresponding to these, up to its furthest forms. Consciousness can never be anything else than conscious existence, and the existence of men is their actual life-process.
>
> In direct contrast to German philosophy which descends from heaven to earth, here we ascend from earth to heaven. That is to say, we do not set out from what men say, imagine, conceive, nor from men as narrated, thought of, imagined, conceived, in order to arrive at men in the flesh. We set out from real, active men, and on the basis of their real life-process we demonstrate the development of the ideological reflexes and echoes of this life-process. . . . Men, developing their material production and their material

intercourse, alter, along with this their real existence, their thinking and the products of their thinking. Life is not determined by consciousness, but consciousness by life.[39]

In addition to its theoretical importance, of course, "class consciousness" was an important device with organizational import for the political goals with which Marx was also concerned. This aspect is to be discussed in a moment, but it might be noted that the term engenders as much difficulty in its political interpretations as in its more abstract theoretical context. The judgment of when the proletariat was or was not "conscious" of its historical destiny, according to political criteria, obviously carried heavy repercussions in case of error; a theory may be wrong and can be corrected, but when political action is wrong or premature, it can be disastrous. The determination of when "true" class consciousness had been reached, then, depended upon criteria that were, at best, only implied. Lukacs, for example, interpreted Marx's political definition of the term to mean the realization by the proletariat as a class group of its "true" historical role. "Class consciousness" thereby had an organizational form based upon collective awareness and identification. "Only the consciousness of the proletariat," Lukacs stated, "can show the way out of the capitalist crisis . . . It [the proletariat] must become a class for itself led on by the necessity of the class struggle."[40] The general intent was clear here, as it was in Marx's political discourses, but the precise criteria needed to make an accurate judgment were not detailed, and probably could not be detailed in determinate political terms.

There are at least three meanings conveyed by "class consciousness" that can be distinguished. It is a potentially useful concept in the study of stratification and deserves clarification. Marx's different shades of meaning have been implied and are to be further detailed below. More importantly, however, the ambiguities unwittingly introduced by more recent users of the concept have been ever more misleading. This is more than just semantics; it leads to serious inaccuracies. In some studies the unfortunate result has been to reach conclusions about the psychological consequences of class that have made sense neither within a theory of stratification nor within a theory of human motivation.

The first meaning of the term is its most literal one. Class consciousness is the individual's awareness of his class, of his position in a class, and of his interests. The meaning appears to be fairly unequivocal, straightforward, and plain. This simplicity, however, is deceptive once the psychological process of identification is questioned and the criteria of identification are analyzed.

Can class consciousness in this meaning be determined by what individuals say about class and about themselves? Not always, for there are many instances—not at all impossible ones—when an individual's assessments are wrong; or perhaps more accurately stated, when there is no consensus given by others to the assessment or to the individual's own judgments.

In the extreme case, the opinions of a schizophrenic in a mental institution reasonably might be doubted when he answers any questions about his class position or most other matters. However, in more common situations, individuals are sometimes ignorant or vague about class and about their own class position. After all, people are differently aware of class and show different sensitivities to it. Consequently, judgments about class by one individual may be valid as far as he is concerned but not as far as anyone else is.[41] The problem here is between the subjective and objective view of the situation, a matter that has been discussed in Chapter Two in connection with the theories of stratification.

Marx's answer was to establish an independent standard against which to judge the validity of "consciousness." Unfortunately, his standard when applied raised more problems than it settled. As the quotation above from Marx implied, class consciousness could be "real" or "false." "Real" meant that the proletariat became aware of its true position under capitalism. When the proletariat attained this level of consciousness, Marx designated the situation as being a "class *in* itself"; that is, the proletariat was aware of the class situation but not yet unified as a cohesive class group, a "class *for* itself." "False" consciousness, presumably, referred to an incorrect or premature consciousness of class; when, for example, the proletariat falsely identified its interests with the bourgeoisie instead of recognizing its inherent class antagonism with them. True consciousness, then, was judged by an intuitive standard but in terms of explicit requirements. Consciousness was not a subjective and solipsistic state, but depended upon social and political judgments external to the individual.

Even though the individual may be very wide-awake about class, he may be very wrong about it. This common possibility is charmingly presented as a composite profile from Yankee City in the fictional Phillip Starr family.[42]

The Phillip Starrs were lower-uppers in Warner's terminology. They worked hard to be accepted by the upper-upper class, but their efforts were doomed from the beginning. The struggle could only be fought on the upper-upper's terms and the Starrs could not win. They were too recent, too perfect, and unbelievably gauche, according to the secure residents of the elite stratum. The Starrs tried to buy a personal history by buying antiques in wholesale lots, not realizing that the symbolic value of the antiques was lost once it was bought and sold as an ordinary commodity. They bought the most valuable ship model in Yankee City from an upper-upper family that had sold it, but the exchange made it worthless as a status object. What the Starr family illustrates in the present discussion is one way in which conflicting assessments of class position can occur, even where class consciousness is at a point of bristling sensitivity. The Starrs themselves held one view of their position and their class behavior; those below them and above them in the hierarchy held different evaluations about them. There is no "real" identification, for this is all a matter of perspective. Each interpretation carries with it its own particular justification. To those far down in the hierarchy, the Starrs might look as though they had made it to the top; the Starrs certainly showed all of the symbols of success. Viewed from the top, however, a different interpretation and a new understanding appeared. From the Starrs' own point of view, a third assessment was possible—depending on how "objective" the Starrs were ready to be about themselves

"Class-consciousness" literally can mean many different things to different people as the Phillip Starr example implies. Studies that fail to take account of such different nuances can be seriously misleading. The misinterpretation of the type just mentioned is often encountered in the survey type studies of class, not because the method is basically unreliable but because some aspects of class are still unclear—too unknown to be handled effectively by that research procedure. The objective determination of class position can be approximated by some kind of index, although as Kornhauser has pointed out in his excellent criticism, few have tried to analyze the interrelationship between the several indices and class-associated characteristics.[43] How much more the problem is complicated when subjective assessments such as "class consciousness" are included. The manner in which information on what is called "class consciousness" is obtained in the usual survey study is not only questionable, it is in many instances misleading as the researcher begins to rely too heavily on that information. The conclusion of the *Fortune* study, for example, discussed in Chapter One, was that Americans identified themselves as predominantly middle class. Centers, using different categories, concluded we were more working class in our identification. Whatever else may be involved, certainly one point is the sheer inadequacy of this kind of question to get at complex psychological identifications. In effect, the researcher allows one or two questions of the type "What class would you say you belonged to?" to serve as an index of something as complex as "class consciousness."

Criticism of this point in Centers' study, *The Psychology of Social Classes,* has been discussed at some length in earlier chapters, and need not be repeated here. Another example of the same kind that can be used for illustration here is in an otherwise capable study, *Voting,* a study of the 1948 presidential vote in Elmira, New York.[44] In one section, the authors of the study analyzed the vote along two variables: an objective measure of class and a subjective one of class identification. Socio-economic status was measured by a composite index of occupation, education, and the interviewer's rating. Generally, it was found that there was a direct relationship between status and a Republican vote; the higher the class, the greater the likelihood of a Republican vote. Class identification, meaning "consciousness" in the context of this analysis, was indexed by the class the respondent said he felt he belonged to. The percentage that voted Republican, it appeared, was also positively correlated with subjective class identification.

What is particularly relevant for the present discussion, however, was that the authors of the Elmira study went on to generalize further about class consciousness on the basis of this information. They concluded that "the development of a 'class-conscious' vote is inhibited by the status of the dominant community ideology centered in the middle class and its rural forebears [*sic*]. As a result the workers show less political solidarity and more political ambivalence."[45] The workers split their vote about fifty-fifty, but the white-collar groups went Republican by three to one. On the basis of this information, the authors went further to conclude that there was "little class-consciousness among the workers in Elmira" as expressed in the even split between Democrat and Republican, and in their responses to a number of attitude questions. For example, 13 per cent of the workers believed "it would be good for the country if labor unions had a political party of their own"; 8 per cent of the business and professional group, and 7 per cent of the white-collar group expressed the same attitude.[46] These differences, and those for similar questions, were too small, the authors concluded, to indicate that there was a class consciousness among the workers in Elmira.

Such conclusions, even though fully set forth and cautiously handled in other particulars, are misleading in that they claim more than they should. More accurately stated, what was found in Elmira was that a group of people who were categorized and who designated themselves as "working class" said that they voted for a particular party and answered several attitude questions in a particular way. Whether these several attitude questions have any relationship to one another in the minds of the people answering them (presumably they do in the minds of the people who constructed them) is an open question. The psychological dynamics connecting class identification and the answers to those attitude questions, are even more equivocal. Finally, the conclusions concerning class consciousness are equally questionable. At the very best, the analysts of the Elmira sample had to believe that the people answering their questions knew what they were talking about, and furthermore that the questions being put to the respondents produced a valid picture of what those people did believe.

This raises a further question concerning class consciousness in the meaning under discussion. Just to what degree is class consciousness a determinant, especially of political ideology and political behavior? Marx was sure that the economic and the political dimensions were closely intertwined in all particulars. Not only was the dominant economic class the ruling class, but its political needs were the ones encapsulated in the dominant political ideology.

According to the numerous studies of that relationship in the United States, there is support for Marx's argument. What they have shown has been that each class has tended to express attitudes and to vote in a manner best related to its political and economic interests. In the language of such studies, for example, the lower class favored labor unions, or voted Democratic, or was in favor of public ownership of utilities, or desired greater government intervention. The upper class expressed opinions at the opposite extreme. The pattern is tempting, not only because of what appears to be an overwhelming preponderance of evidence but also because of the plausibility of the relationship between class consciousness and behavior.

However, there are obstacles to such a ready acceptance.

For one thing, these studies have hardly made an attempt to check whether it was class consciousness or some other factor that determined the expressed attitude. "As far as the analysis goes," Kornhauser noted in writing of Centers' study, "it could be true that class consciousness is the determinant. Equally it could be that the subjective identification plays no determining role whatsoever."[47] For example, a recent study of the attitudes of a sample of automobile workers[48] found results that might have been expected on the basis of past studies. The workers voted for Stevenson and held the same kinds of opinions as most workers had expressed in earlier studies. What was surprising, however, was the high proportion of those interviewed who held highly authoritarian attitudes as well: they wanted children brought up strictly, believed the world was meant for the strong, wanted capital punishment for sex offenders, and indicated a blistering hostility toward others. On the basis of these findings, it is quite unclear whether the attitudes that they expressed were the consequence of their class consciousness or instead of their generalized social hostility. The two are not the same thing.

It is questionable, furthermore, whether these studies are indeed tapping the phenomenon of class consciousness or not. In the study of automobile workers, again, a significant proportion did not even know that they were union members even though they all were. By extension, how valid is a person's class identification? Even more at question, then, is the validity of the notion of "class consciousness"—an even more complex psychological phenomenon than is that of simple identification or labeling. "Class consciousness" in Marx's theory was the result of the individual being forced to the wall materially and psychologically; consciousness hit him hard as an emotional as well as an intellectual force. At least Marx spun an implicit psychological web around his use of the term, and therefore his conclusions concerning behavior that depended upon class consciousness were consistent within his theory. The usual survey studies of more recent years, on the other hand, have no way of knowing whether they are indeed dealing in that kind of psychological currency. At most what they seem to depend upon is a verbal response, unsupported by further questions, that probe for this dimension in a variety of unclear stabs.

Interpreting "class consciousness" in its most literal meaning, then, does not mean the idea is any better handled. The principal reason for ambiguity is that class consciousness in this sense involves a psychological dynamic that has not been fully explored. Individuals may be aware of class, but this awareness as a bald statement means but little. What is the connection between this awareness and other attitudes they express? How important is this awareness as compared with their identification with other social groupings to which they belong? Something must go on inside of individuals that functionally binds their consciousness of class to other aspects of their behavior and personality. The link may be intellectual, emotional, or mixed in tone, but there must be some kind of linkage that is reasonable from a psychodynamic point of view, otherwise the subject is an automaton, not a human being.

A second meaning of "class consciousness" has also been one that Marx delineated. By this meaning, class consciousness connoted that the class *as a group* was aware of itself. The individual, so to speak, has evolved to the point of consciousness where he has become aware of others within his class circumstances. In this phase, there was the sense of cohesiveness within the class as a social group that was absent in the first meaning, where individuals were only separately aware of their own class position. For Marx, this was a necessary sequel to the first kind of class consciousness in the evolution of the class struggle under capitalism. A class, at this point, aware of itself as a group, was capable of unified social action.

This meaning of class consciousness raises its own problems of interpretation. The outstanding one is to establish the criteria by which it is known that a class has become a cohesive group. Where the major problem in the first meaning was psychological, the problem in this second interpretation is sociological.

For Marx, it was primarily a political problem to establish

class cohesion, and one solved by political events. In other words, the level of "a class for itself" was reached when the class was able to act in a unified political fashion. That is certainly an empirically demonstrable test if one cares to wait. However, what criteria are to be used in analyzing a class situation that has not reached such a level of unified action?

Generally, class analysts have not been greatly nor directly concerned with this meaning of class. It is a difficult social phenomenon to delineate in a field sufficiently burdened with problems. It is a phenomenon in which the student of stratification has not been particularly interested. Marx had to consider this stage and dimension of consciousness because his political theory required it. Present-day analysts, on the contrary, have no such commitment.

However, this dimension of class consciousness has been implied in some of the current literature, although not very clearly. For example, the survey studies of class identification discussed above have implied that class consciousness contained an element of group character. To generalize the attitudes of, say, the "working class" as regards some set of attitudes from those of the "white-collar class" is to imply that a measure of class consensus, and thereby unity, does exist within each stratum. Centers' notion, for one, on the interest group theory of class even more clearly connoted a dimension of class unity forced upon individuals by their common circumstances. Similarly, other studies have generalized their analysis to consider the separate classes as social groups.

The interpretation of class consciousness as meaning a more or less identifiable class group has recently come into sociology from another direction that might be briefly mentioned. The growing flood of books and articles on middle class America—as suburbanites and exurbanites, as consumers, as organization men, and as the puppets of hidden persuaders—assumes somehow that we have reached a point of unified class consciousness. Middle class conformity, which most of these writings take as their main theme, is in one meaning a class grouping of the type being discussed here. The desire to identify with others, whether we are badgered into it, subtly maneuvered into it, or rationally moved into it, still means in the end a consciousness in which the class is the organizing focus. How strange that what Marx had predicted for the proletariat as a stage in their salvation has come to be reinterpreted in the analysis of the middle class as a stage in their damnation.

Aside from these relatively tangential concerns, never explicitly stated, sociologists have had little to do with this aspect of class consciousness. One notable exception was Mills's *White Collar*.[49] In the final chapter on "The Politics of the Rearguard," he explicitly analyzed the class consciousness of the middle class. In effect, he applied Marx's criteria, brought up to date to include the effect of mass media upon political ideologies. Mills concluded that the middle class was politically indifferent and would not attain to that level of consciousness needed for class unity and class action. The "white-collar workers do not have [political awareness or political organization] to any appreciable extent. . . . They will not go politically 'middle class,' if for no other reason than the absence of middle-class policy or formation, and because they will not be economically able to maintain such a status."[50]

Barriers to Class Consciousness

HAVING clarified the meanings and nuances of the concept, it is possible to go a step further and consider the factors that tend either to increase or to decrease class consciousness.

The social forces that facilitate class consciousness are essentially those that draw the individual's attention to the social scene and his place in it. Hence, as Marx noted, as the proletariat became aware of the discrepancy between what it had and what it believed it should have had, then the consciousness of class and with it the recognition of its inevitable struggle were fostered.[51] At the same time, the push toward consciousness was increased by the recognition of class differences. The proletariat, in effect, was to be forced into an awareness of the gulf separating them and their style of life from those around them. This recognition served to unite members of a class as each became aware that his fate was one also shared by others.

Class recognition was aided, Marx had noted, by the greater ease of communication brought about by the growth of cities and by the technology of mass communication under capitalism. Cities brought individuals physically closer. The mass media made communication possible and at the same time simplified rather than diversified the content of communication. In this way, the recognition of class and of the discrepancies between classes was abetted. Presumably, this physical and psychological proximity made class organizations even more necessary. Individuals could be recruited into such associations, in which their dissatisfactions were structured, stylized, and given direction.

An excellent analysis of the barriers operating against class consciousness has been set forth in an article by Rosenberg that is summarized here as a contrast to the preceding discussion.[52]

The structure of large scale industry is such, Rosenberg has argued, that the perceptions of being united with others or of being differentiated from others may not at all follow "along the lines of relationship to ownership of the means of production" as Marx had predicted. First, power and decision-making are relayed through numerous channels and cannot always be directly identified with one individual or with a small group at the top. If it can, as in the belief that "the men at the top" or the "Board of Directors" control everything, then even those policy decisions made by such individuals are transmitted through many levels before they hit the bottom of the hierarchy. Secondly, the high degree of specialization in modern industry tends to promote feelings of separation rather than of unity, even though individuals might belong to the same objective class. "For example, a machinist, a bookkeeper, and a stock clerk may actually be alike with reference to ownership of the tools of production, but perceive themselves as different from one another by virtue of the very different kinds of work they do."[53]

Finally, people from different classes may actually feel a greater affinity with one another rather than with those in the same class because they share a common working situation or because they both are associated with making the same product. Rosenberg gave the example of the barber who may feel a greater unity with his working employer than he does with other individuals of his own class who are doing different kinds of work. Identifications coming from the work situation, then, can sometimes override the recognition of an objective class situation.

The political structure, Rosenberg has argued, may be a source for class consciousness when it clearly identifies parties or political allegiances on a class basis. Such organizations become the foci for class sentiments, serving to mobilize them and direct them in a more or less structured manner. The implication in studies of voting or of candidate preferences has been that certain parties and certain candidates are symbols of that kind of class allegiance. The Democratic Party, thereby, is usually considered as the party of the lower and middle classes; the Republican, as the party of the upper privileged classes. That these characterizations are far from adequate or valid has been evident in the past few presidential elections, and even more evident in local elections. The reason they are false, as Rosenberg has noted, is that in the American political system a candidate must appeal to a heterogeneous electorate. His support comes from population segments that cut across the class structure rather than follow its boundaries. The upper class representation has been just as evident in the one political party as in the other. The $100-a-plate dinner is used by both parties. Furthermore, there is no evidence to indicate that Americans do vote or act politically along class lines. Political sentiments are stirred by a complex of factors, and class is by no means the dominant one.

A third perceptual obstacle Rosenberg has discussed was that of "multiple group memberships." Individuals in modern urban society belong to numerous social groupings and have several group allegiances that do not consistently follow class boundaries. Race, religion, and ethnicity are among the dominant affiliations competing with class, to which the individual can and does have a social reference. Class may for many persons be far down in this hierarchy of reference groupings. The lower class Negro, for example, more likely may identify himself as a Negro primarily, with his class identification as secondary, if at all. The Catholic may be a Catholic first, ethnic and class factors not considered. Doubtless, these allegiances and identifications are fluid, and the individual identifies now with one and now with another depending on the situation at hand. Social interaction moves such continuously shifting reference points. Where there is intense racial hostility, for example, individuals will identify and be forced by others to identify with the racial group rather than with any other reference group. It is clear from reports on school integration in the South, that race, not class, is the locus of social identification at the moment. The class of those involved is secondary. The motivations and the factors that determine under what conditions an individual seeks one identity in preference to another is a matter that might well be investigated in the study of class consciousness.

A fourth obstacle to class consciousness develops from the fact that consumption in the United States is not polarized into two extremes. Mass production and standardization of products have made it possible for individuals to live by almost equal standards, even though by all other criteria they are not in the same class. The absence of such differences in consumption tends to inhibit class consciousness. To be sure, this does not mean that there are no differences at all in the patterns of consumption and life styles between the classes. The very rich man can still buy and live according to a style of life that is simply not available to others. Resort areas are class defined and can be monopolized by a class. Certain items of consumption can similarly take on an exclusive class character, not through pricing alone but simply by keeping the taste patterns as a kind of secret symbol of class. A Cadillac can be bought by anyone with enough money. It can, however, be rejected as a class symbol by the upper class who instead switch their preferences to small foreign cars as a means of separating themselves from the mass. By constantly changing these taste patterns, a class can continue to set a class conscious style of consumption that is always a step or two ahead of others who try to imitate them.

The area of consumption, however, is a difficult place for maintaining class differences and creating class consciousness. The differences between the very poor and the very rich are not as neatly and as conspicuously polarized as they were in earlier generations. Furthermore, the upper class groups have become more socialized in their public behavior, and they have removed themselves in large measure from observation. The large, impressive, and well-known town house is not ostentatiously evident. Gone are the fanfares of expensive parties. Hollywood does this much better and with much more show. The city mansions of the Fricks or the Astors, say, have been reconverted into museums or public buildings. Their descendants have removed themselves to the country, or live in urban apartments that do not distinguish them as their forebearers would have liked.

A fifth obstacle to the development of class consciousness is the existence of conflicting cultural goals on the one side, and the existence of occasions when unity across class lines is demanded, on the other. As an instance of the latter, war can erase class differences temporarily in favor of a unifying feeling of national patriotism. In the case of conflicting goals, individuals may be competing with one another for the same goals, and hence enmity rather than unity is the result. Workers, for example, who come to compete for the job of foreman may recognize one another as enemies rather than as class equals.

A final obstacle is the heavy emphasis upon upward social mobility in American society which serves to keep the striving individual from identifying with his class of the moment. The self image which is held is more likely one of membership in the next higher class, and that is where his identifications point. Nor does the question of probable success need to enter the picture. Individuals may aspire, without any realistic hope of success, to emulate those in a higher social class than themselves, thereby closing off the possibilities of a "realistic" class identication. Mills, for example, in *White Collar* noted the case of saleswomen who identified with their wealthy customers rather than with the class to which they might have belonged, as white-collar workers. There are many similar instances where the individual's self-image denies "reality" and instead fastens upon some fantasy.

Class Unconsciousness

THE preceding discussion has been concerned with analyzing the nature, the obstacles, and the impelling forces toward class consciousness. There is another aspect to the matter that is of equal importance—the matter of class induced behavior of which the individual is not aware. This dimension is here labeled by the very cumbersome term, "class unconsciousness." Perhaps a better term would be the "lack of class awareness," or the more compressed German term, *"klassen unbewusstsein."*

The functioning of general social forces, and of class determinants in particular, pushes individuals into various niches in the class hierarchy. This is a result of a complex of forces: family background, occupation, socialization experiences, the values and goals that have been instilled from a variety of social sources, and basic psychological self-estimates. These, and many other factors that might be designated, force the social location of individuals in the class system, and at the same time set certain horizons and perspectives for him because of that location. This is not to say that we are in all ways tightly bound into high-walled class cells from which there is no escape and beyond which we cannot see. It does mean to imply, however, that class is still a major social category; it is a determinant in some measure of what we believe, what we strive for, and how we behave. To that extent we are prisoners of our class position whether aware of it or not. The individual may refuse to believe that his free will is so severely limited. He may refuse to believe that social inequality exists. However, the individual's assessment, even of his own personal milieu, is not always the most accurate nor the most real assessment to be made. People may love and hate for reasons that they do not even suspect, but the love and hate they hold is not the less real. The same is true for class behavior.

A dominant feature of class at this unconscious level is in the relative distances of each class from the centers of control of its environment. In several independent studies made of this general area, the outstanding conclusion has been the same: where the middle class generally participates in and strives to have some control over its social environment, the lower class does not.[54] The lower class read less, belonged to fewer organizations, had fewer friends, and was more unrealistic in understanding its environment than was the middle class. The upper class, by the way, has been almost entirely omitted from these studies; whether these people are difficult to find, hard to interview, or are not important for these matters is hard to say.

Certainly the claim can be made in the case of some of these findings that they look more important than they are; the matter of joining organizations, for example. The middle class contains a high proportion of joiners; does it then necessarily mean that they have "better control" of their environment? Control does not always mean the ability to change the world or to be in the ruling elite. Control can also mean something less universal and less spectacular. Middle class parents, for example, who belong and who are active in their local PTA chapters are able to exert some control over the way that their children are educated. At the very least, they can exert more control than if they did not belong. The same is true for many organizations to which middle class people are attracted. The organization provides them the opportunity to be heard, which is a measure of effect that the lower class apparently does not even have. There are limits, of course, to the amount of control such organizational memberships can confer. One could not thereby control the whole of his life.

The fact that middle class people read more and read serious literature, as these studies have also found, means at the very least that they have some understanding of events around them. A person whose reading, such as it is, is limited to pulp literature does not have the same exposure and hence has that much less knowledge on which to base an opinion. This is true, even if one wishes to contend that the mass circulation literature offers only canned opinions, not material upon which the intelligent person can organize a private opinion.

These activities, it is being suggested, give the middle class person a somewhat greater grasp and control over his environment. The lower class individual, on the other hand, is cut off from much of what goes on around him. He remains more or less encapsulated in his small world. He is less able to make any kind of mark on his environment, no matter how small, because he participates less in those associations that could amplify his effect. Perhaps it is no longer true, but the rank and file of the mass unions hardly took advantage of any of the educational services offered them through the union; nor usually were they concerned about any union matters except those directly bearing on working conditions. Here, in other words, was an organization that offered an opportunity and outlet for worker participation, yet without any startling success.

In the organizations to which lower class people do belong, it was also found that the leadership of those organizations was most often in the hands of middle class or upper class persons. Office-holding apparently was viewed as something too strange and too challenging for lower class individuals to assume. The total effect, thereby, is to depress even further the possible force that the lower class could exert.

The middle class, on its side, oftentimes seeks to emulate the wishes, or what appear to be the wishes, of the upper class. For example, in a study of a civil defense organization in Mobile,[55] it was found that the usual procedure for creating an organization was first to have the "real" leaders of the community decide whether the organization was necessary; secondly, for them to pick the leadership from their own businesses or from others "available" in the community; and finally, to give the organization their blessing, which, in turn, became the sign for the middle class to join and begin doing the work. In this manner, things got done in Mobile whether it was initiating civil defense, building parks, or erecting a monument. Under these circumstances, the middle class is not dictating policy according to its needs, but only following orders more or less as set by the policy makers above them.

The setting of the class situation dictates these results and others like them. The better education of the middle class, for example, endows them with a stronger willingness to believe in the need for an informed electorate in a democracy. They are motivated to take part in the activities of the community. The lower class, on the other hand, not as well educated, not attracted to intellectual values nor believing that they can do something, keeps clear of involvement in the community. These are not conscious choices, but they are class conditioned ones.

It is difficult to ascertain how conscious Americans are about class and how much difference class makes for them. The studies on class identification do not really get at the central issue. Nor are Americans, perhaps, too clear about class themselves. This does not mean, therefore, that class has no determining effect on their behavior. As this last section and as the opening sections of this chapter on class differences in behavior have indicated, class still can play a heavy role whether actual consciousness exists or not. Where the objective facts of class set the life situation for the individual, it often makes small difference for his behavior whether the awareness is there or not.

It is this latter point that some commentators have overlooked who argue that America is becoming solidly and thoroughly middle class. The basis for this belief seems to be that more and more Americans are identifying themselves with the middle class in their attitudes, in their preferences, and in their outlook. Class, as should be fairly evident by this point, is not only a matter of subjective identifications but must include the objective features of the class situation as well. That these objective features do much to establish some of the subjective conceptions of individuals should also be evident. As long as such subjective distinctions can be made, then class differences continue to exist and continue to exert some influence on behavior. Consumption standards may become undifferentiated between the classes. Voting patterns may show no discrimination by class level. Still, there remain many areas of impact where differences do exist, even in the teeth of a vehement denial of class by the many.

CHAPTER VI

Social Mobility: Patterns and Consequences

THE BELIEF IN SOCIAL MOBILITY holds a strategic place among American values. It is a hub around which much of what Americans believe revolves, whether it is shouted as a platitude or cynically rejected. The creed of egalitarianism means not only that we are social equals, though not economic equals, but even more to the point, that the class structure is open and available. The positions at the top are open to those who have the talents, aptitudes, and whatever else it takes to reach them. At the same time, of course, we must be prepared to accept the corollary: those who do not reach the top do not deserve to. Americans of all classes have held to this belief and have made it legend. The honor roll is filled with the names of heroes who give substance to the legend, and in every period there is always a fresh example of someone who has gone from rags to riches. The legend continues to remain alive and real, to the cynics as to the patriots. Horatio Alger awards, for example, are still being presented to those who most adequately personify the exploits of that hero. The award—a bronze desk plaque—was ceremoniously presented in 1958 to eight men, including a president and chairman of an investment banking firm who had been a railroad brakeman, factory laborer, and board boy in a brokerage house; a chairman of the board of a trading stamp company who had been a newsboy, Western Union messenger, errand boy, and grocery store clerk; and to the president of a coal company who had been a newsboy, barber and traveling salesman. These are the heroic achievements of social mobility and the just rewards—dramatic evidence of the verisimilitude of the Alger legend. Or so it is for some.

Those who can personify the legend successfully and give it substance are rewarded, of course, by public recognition, by bronze plaques, money or other emoluments. However, there is also a greater social impact created by such achievements than simply the rewards and bronze plaques given to individuals: such achievements serve to stimulate and keep alive the belief in the legend. In many ways it is the *belief* in social mobility that is enough to maintain the value; for it is the belief that sets the goals for individuals, that motivates them to try, and that helps keep American society on a more even keel by keeping the values realistic and consistent. Once the *belief* is shaken, once enough people begin to doubt it, then social repercussions are likely to begin. Presumably, such beliefs must be based upon social realities; that upward mobility is accomplished by enough individuals to support the belief held by many in an open class system. It is possible, however, for the belief to last longer than the reality it supposedly portrays, or for the belief to be discredited prematurely. These speculations are simply one way of noting that an analysis of social mobility is important for understanding the structure of American society.

There are more reasons, however, to commend a careful examination of social mobility. It has a place in the study of class. It is in many ways an "application" of much that has preceded this chapter, an "application," in other words, of the theories of class, in both its structural and its social psychological dimensions. In the first instance, the structural prerequisites for mobility and the changes that mobility can bring into the class system are two valuable orientations for the study of class. For social mobility introduces a dynamic feature of possible change into a class system. It can alter the structure and patterns of class relationships as the consequences of mobility introduce changes into those class relationships.

Too much mobility by too many may alert those at the top to the possible threat of making their status too accessible, hence less socially valuable. Too little mobility can bring the core values about mobility into doubt, with consequent repercussions for a wide range of the society. In addition, new channels for mobility, as they become effective, may reflect upon and modify the criteria for class. The sensational rise from small beginnings, as Schumpeter has suggested, to upper class position can be achieved by doing something novel, something not conventional.[1] The history of many class systems, including our own, has in it such instances where the extraordinary has become transformed, in time, into a regular means for mobility and then an accepted criterion of class itself.

In the social psychological dimension, also, the study of mobility has much to contribute to the study of class. An individual's behavior and his attitudes may be less a function of the class he is in at the moment, and much more a function of the class to which he aspires. Just as there is a dynamic in social structures, there is a dynamic in individual psychology. The ways in which the individual appraises his own position and estimates his class future can significantly condition his behavior. Both the point of reference and the group of reference often have to be understood, if the sense of a person's class actions are to be understood. The secure middle class person presents a different psychology than does one who has just managed a toe hold in the middle class. Each has different goals, attitudes, and self-conceptions, which can be understood only by reference to the security each feels in his class position. And both are different, again, from those who aspire to even higher class levels.

This social psychological facet has yet another feature. The general emphasis upon successful upward mobility means that individuals judge themselves and style their self-images, in part, by that standard. The "success" has personified the validity of the belief and part of his reward is the luxury of judging himself in a favorable light as he sees himself through the eyes of others. The "failure," on the other hand, judges himself negatively and critically. He has failed in the terms which others consider to be important. Many seemingly unrelated aspects of social behavior fall into pattern when considered principally as reactions, as manifestations arising from these self-judgments of success and failure. Minority group prejudice, for example, from this point of view is one outlet by which the "failures" can escape; by laying the cause of their failure on a convenient doorstep. In this way, the failure can regain some self-esteem and can push the threat away from himself by believing that others, in this case some minority, have been the cause of his failure. He can, thereby, remain as blameless to himself as he cares to believe.

Similarly, prejudice might be indulged in by the recent "success" who is still too insecure in his new position. His psychology is to hedge against the possibility of future failure by being ready to put the blame somewhere. Political attitudes—conservatism or radicalism—may be similarly traced, not so much to the person's actual class position, as to his future class position reflected in the apirations that he holds. Success and failure, similarly, enter into that equation. In short, the psychological dynamics that are set in motion and sustained by the social mobility the individual has had or wants, fan out to touch upon many aspects of his personality, his behavior, and his attitudes.

Methodological and Theoretical Cautions

THE question that occupies most of this chapter can be simply stated: Is the American class system becoming static or not? Are there fewer opportunities for getting ahead—for social mobility—today than there were before? The importance of the answer for the future structure of American society has already been suggested. The heavy commitment of American values to success, to the belief in unlimited opportunities and to the rewards of success, all distributed according to talent and ability, means that mobility striving helps make many important wheels go around. Our social equilibrium, the balance between the beliefs that individuals hold and the opportunities for realizing them, depends upon what happens to the class dynamic that is social mobility.

To ask the question is easy; to answer it, much more difficult. This difficulty arises from two general sources. First, there are substantial methodological problems that have to be settled in order to make any answer valid and intelligible. These problems, in many instances, are of the kind that arise in making social comparisons over time. The unit of measurement does not remain constant and the results produced are too variable, too ambiguous to make sense. For example, how is one to compare the dollar incomes of 1900 with those of 1950? There is no dollar-to-dollar correspondence if the dollar is supposed to index the relative worth or purchasing power of the individual. Or again, how does one compare the occupations of 1900 with those of 1950, given the astounding proliferation of new occupations and the revolution in the character of the occupational structure? There are limited solutions to these methodological problems, but each requires some adjustment or some arbitrary selection of common units which much be understood beforehand if the conclusions are to be correctly assessed.

Difficulties arise in the second instance from the arbitrary nature of the judgment to be made. Whether the American class structure is more fluid or more rigid now than it once was in the past is, from one point of view, a value judgment. It's like asking whether someone is too fat or too thin. Even though a satisfactory solution might be found for the first kind of methodological objections just indicated, it might still be impossible to decide whether there is "sufficient" mobility or not. "Sufficient," that is, for what American values say it should be. Perhaps having as much mobility today as fifty years ago is enough. Perhaps an expanding economic system such as ours requires that the opportunities for advancement must keep pace. In this sense, mobility is very much like profit; how much is enough? It is difficult to see how any judgment of the "amount" of mobility can ever avoid a dependence upon some arbitrary standard.

The unit and method of measurement are clearly so central that it is wise to begin with that. The problem here raises statements that are reminiscent of Chapter Three, where the methodologies of class were discussed. The close kinship of ideas and subject matter should be evident. The measurement of movement between classes is but an aspect of the measurement of class itself. However, the problem is confounded even further here because not only is there the basic problem of class measurement, but the added one of time changes in the units of measurement. The problem cannot be avoided, nor can it easily be answered. For most research on mobility, *social* mobility has become operationally defined as *occupational* mobility. The reasons for picking occupations as the key unit of measurement are the same as those that have made occupation so popular as a criterion of class: it is objective, available, and is related to the outstanding image of class.

There is no need to reiterate the objections to occupational measures in the study of stratification. These have been set down in Chapter Three. The gross features of some occupational categories, the arbitrary way in which the occupational continuum must be divided to yield the several classes, and the range of variation within any occupational category—all of these and other objections that have been stated before are applicable in the present context as well. *Occupational* mobility is not the same as *social* mobility, any more than occupation is exactly equal to what is meant by class.

The unit used to measure social mobility can affect the conclusions about mobility in another way. In at least one case, where education is relied upon as the unit, the measure would indicate the existence of greater mobility than would be found if almost any other index were used. The general rise of educational levels would yield the conclusion that there has been a great deal more mobility than in any previous period. This is true as far as it goes; as far, in other words, as one is willing to accept education as such an index of mobility. However, it seems equally clear that when a great many are able to rise in the class hierarchy, then some redefinition of class criteria is called for. Class membership in this sense is relative and not absolute. In an aristocracy perhaps, where membership is determined by heredity, absolute principles can operate. In the case of a class system, however, and one that is presumed to be open at that, relative judgments must be relied upon. The standard of living of the working class today, for example, is undoubtedly much higher than that of even the middle class of several decades back, but this does not mean that, therefore, everyone has suddenly become middle class or higher because of a rising standard of living available to more people. The same holds true for education. In a society where everyone is educated, then education is of less importance as a stratifying criterion.

The time perspective taken is a second factor that can condition the conclusions reached about social mobility. Economists and demographers, the specialists in trend analysis, have found that a dramatic change in the short run can be smoothed out to an almost imperceptible bump in the long run. The same problem and the same bias beset the study of social mobility. The state of the economy at the moment and at the base line period could skew the results, depending upon the particular phase of the business cycle. Prosperity, normalcy, or depression set much of the stage upon which mobility occurs, and their effects can show more, less, or no change in comparative amounts of mobility.

A third factor that can affect the conclusions about the relative extent of social mobility can be called a "standard of value." It has been alluded to above. The question here is: How much mobility is enough or "sufficient" in American society? Statistics about mobility, however measured, are necessary, but they cannot give the whole answer to the question. Is it enough to have as much opportunity and as much mobility today as in the past? Or instead, is it functionally necessary for American society to have an expanding rate of mobility that meshes with the ideology and reality of an expanding economy? That some such set of values is held by most persons who study mobility seemed to be the conclusion reached by Warner and Abegglen after their survey of the literature on the subject. "The conclusion of diminished occupational mobility," they noted, "is no doubt in part a result of a comparison of . . . present-day data with a hypothetical, 'open' past—a past which was in fact 'open' only to a limited extent."[2] The judgment of the relative "openness" of the class system is made from the data at hand, but it is not really inherent in the data. It is in the judge's point of view.

There is another aspect to this matter of judgment: Where does the mobility occur? Aside from the amount of mobility occurring, between what classes is such mobility taking place? In other words, if the total extent of social mobility consists only of movement *below* the top level, is there more or less mobility now than in the past? The elite, for example, may have effectively cut off all entry from below except for those individuals whom they wish to co-opt for whatever reason. Does this then not imply a freezing of the prime class positions making the mobility throughout the rest of the structure just so much busy work and of less consequence?[3] Fortunately, there are several studies of the business elite which illuminate this feature of mobility and its consequences. Knowing about the amount of social mobility without at the same time knowing its class range is not enough to make the kind of assessment needed about the place of mobility in American social structure.

A final consideration that enters into this judgment of how much mobility there is arises from the more or less "natural" changes that occur. Let us assume that a man in 1900 and one in 1959 had the same intensity of motivation and striving for mobility; yet one of them made the grade and the other did not, solely because the nature of the social structure that each encountered was different and thereby the final determining factor for the success of the one and the failure of the other. Obviously, something like this has occurred which greatly affects the setting for social mobility. Changes in educational standards and in scholarship aid have changed the pattern for mobility via educational channels. Wage scales, the extent of full employment, and corporation and union organizations have enormously influenced the patterns of mobility through income gains. The more numerous openings and the opportunities for higher prestige occupations in more recent years, similarly, have greatly altered the patterns of occupational mobility. The point of all of this is that these structural changes should not be confounded with other mobility elements, such as aspirations and motivations for mobility, or the relative changes in the criteria of mobility from one period to the next. To be sure, the increase in opportunities afforded by the society is part of the mobility picture, yet it is an element that should be kept separate from the other elements that compose that picture.

Along similar lines, it has been argued that during the era of heavy immigration into the United States, those who had been here longer were willy-nilly pushed up on the occupational and status hierarchies as their former lower positions were filled by the new immigrants.[4] A similar kind of process occurs when a country industrializes; the first to enter are pushed up, their place being taken by later comers.

It seems wise, therefore, to separate those factors relating to the mobility of individuals from those having to do with changes in the structure. The two sets of factors are related, of course; the growth of population, the change in living standards, and the change in fiscal policies—changes in the structure, in other words—can facilitate or hinder the opportunities for social mobility that individuals face. They make for greater ease or difficulty. However, one would still want to know something about the extent of individual effort, or even individual concern with such opportunities.

The last point needs some further amplification. There are two distinct levels of analysis: (1) the analysis essentially of individuals, of their success or failure, or of their difficulty experienced with social mobility; and (2) the analysis of class structure and its changes. The first, as Mayer has pointed out, refers to "the movement of individuals in the class hierarchy"; the second, to the "mobility of groups and entire classes" or to the "changes in the class structure itself."[5] Some measure of confusion and misinterpretation has been injected into social mobility study by the failure to clear up methodological matters, as noted earlier; some has also resulted from the failure to keep these two levels of individual and structure separate.

Four possible meanings of mobility can be discerned, two individual and two structural:

1) There is the mobility that results from cataclysmic, revolutionary, and massive changes in society. Class relationships are radically altered by a sudden change in the basis and structure of the society. This occurs, most obviously, through revolution. These are the changes that Marx, for example, had analyzed in his class study of the French Revolution and the victory of the bourgeoisie. Also to be included would be the less revolutionary, but equally significant, changes occasioned by industrialization. Under such circumstances, whole classes may rise or fall in the class structure as exemplified by the fall of the landed aristocracy and the rise of a merchant class. It is such situations that Schumpeter, for example, appeared to have in mind in his discussions of class.[6] "Every class," he wrote, "has a definite function which it must fulfill according to its whole concept and orienta-

tion. . . . Moreover, the position of each class in the total national structure, depends, on the one hand, on the significance that is attributed to that function, and, on the other hand, on the degree to which the class successfully performs the function."[7] As the structure of a society is altered, the presumed importance and functions of the several classes are reassessed, usually resulting in a class system of a different character. The individual, as a member of a class, could rise or fall in his relative prestige and power, not because of his own efforts so to speak, but because of the larger social forces around him that have altered the entire structure.

2) Consequences for mobility are also involved in those structural changes that are less dramatic and less revolutionary than in the first type, yet are just as massive in their way. Reference here is to changes in the occupational structure brought about by advanced technology, changes in income distribution brought about by unionization, or the expansion of educational opportunities by government grants or foundation scholarships. These are principally structural changes but with enormous consequences for the success of individual mobility. The very gradual development of such changes often obscures them for a time, until they have created a sufficiently great contrast with earlier periods. This kind of change is often confounded in most mobility studies with the analysis of individual social mobility. The major failure in such cases is one of concluding that the standards and criteria of class have somehow remained constant over time and all that has changed is the number of persons who have taken advantage of mobility opportunities. Education may be taken as an example. Increased support given to education and the greater prestige emphasis upon education probably have worked to make education much less important than before as a mark of class. Education has become more easily available, hence less discriminating. Simply to compare individual educational attainments between two time periods, therefore, is to overlook the shifts in opportunities for education and the shifts in the interpretations given to educational attainment.

3) One type of mobility is quite comparable to the type

just discussed. It is the study of individual changes according to some mobility criterion. A good deal of occupational mobility research would belong in this category, concerned as it is with the shifting of individuals between different occupations, or occupational shifts between generations. The conclusions about mobility, thereby, are a summation of how many occupational shifts have occurred and between what occupations those have been.

4) A final type of social mobility might be called the "individual biography." It is the climb from rags to riches according to the legend. This is the type most often taken as synonymous with "social mobility." Some of the studies of business elites or of the very rich, for example, might be placed in this category because they are studies of the mobility chances of individuals. The comparative analysis of mobility then becomes one of contrasting the relative ease or difficulty, the success or failure, of individuals to move within today's structure as compared with that of some earlier period.

The fact that a good many of the studies of social mobility have not been particularly clear about which type of social mobility they were studying has not helped matters. The suggestion here is that some of the confusion over whether the United States is becoming more rigid or not in its class system can be traced to this basic confusion. When one analyst bases his conclusions essentially on changes in individual mobility experiences, and another bases his upon shifts in the entire social structure, they are not talking about exactly the same thing.

Patterns of Mobility

Most studies of social mobility overlook or confound the separate dimensions specified above. Usually, they move at once to an analysis of essentially individual statistics of occupation, incomes, or education. To be sure, there is some justification for such an orientation: the mobility experiences of samples of individuals can be taken as indices of how much structural mobility exists. Hence, a comparison between the occupations of a sample of individuals with the occupations of their fathers reflects the extent of occupational mobility there has been during the generation and, at the same time, reflects the changes that have occurred in the occupational structure.

However, something is lost by confounding those two dimensions. The changes that have taken place in the structure obviously do not occur only because individuals want them to. Changes in the class structure, by whatever criterion they are measured, are much more subtle, much more complex than the simple addition of many individual changes would lead one to believe. The individual who raises his class position does so in part because he wants to, in part because he is able to do it, and in part because the opportunity existed.

Recognizing this separation highlights a recurrent inadequacy in the study of social mobility in particular and social stratification generally. It is the lack of concern by many analysts of stratification with matters of structure; overwhelmingly they seem to favor a concern with the individual alone. Essentially, this is but a restatement of earlier remarks concerning the emphasis given to matters of status rather than to matters of class, of emphasizing the status structures of local communities rather than power structures of a national society. All of these are part of the same complex, the same orientation. Partly, as has been suggested earlier, this orientation is a methodologically imposed one; the techniques that are available for study are not of sufficiently large scale to deal adequately with questions on the national level. However, in some measure, too, the orientation appears to be self-imposed; analysts of stratification do not seem to want to ask the larger questions, to grapple with the structural matters that almost any study of class must involve.

This omission is even more serious once it is realized that the larger questions must be answered before the smaller one; the more valid estimate of the amount of social mobility depends upon an analysis of the class structure and its direction of movement rather than upon the mobility experiences of individuals no matter how detailed these latter statistics might be. The problem almost duplicates the one phrased in Chapter Four: studies of stratification systems in local communities cannot ever fully reflect the condition of a national class system. The condition continues to apply even if it can be agreed upon that separate criteria must be employed. In other words, even if one is ready to grant that occupation, for example, legitimately indexes class, then it requires that the occupational structure of the United States be analyzed in its own right before studies of samples of that structure can have full meaning. In the case of occupation it seems clear that technology has wrought enormous changes, that economic concentration and the rise of corporations have also brought changes, and that educational requirements have occasioned even further consequences—all affecting the character of the occupational structure. What individuals have or have not been able to do occupationally is in large measure a reflection of these larger changes.

Consider, for example, the trends that are documented in the highly informative table that Mayer has described about occupational trends (Table 5).[8]

As Mayer has noted, these shifts in the class structure, here indexed by occupation and employment status, have been enormous. "In the course of a hundred years the early society of independent enterprises has virtually disappeared. . . . They have become a minority of the modern middle class where they are now greatly outnumbered by salaried employees."[9] Furthermore, the majority of the labor force is still concentrated in the wage-worker category, almost unchanged during the entire period from 1870. This is the backdrop against which studies of individual experiences with occupational mobility must be placed. It is not so much a question, then, of how *much* mobility has taken place as it is a question of what *kind* of mobility has occurred. And the time period without a doubt has had much to do with the character of that definition. The explosive increase in the proportions of salaried employees from 1870 to 1954—from 7 per cent to 31 per cent—has made this range of the labor force a terminal mobility point for many, where it once was the self-employed in earlier periods. Movement has doubtless taken place, but what are the consequences of the change in terminal points? In part, there is a continuous redefinition of class boundaries to adapt it to the current images. The middle class thereby ceases to be composed only of the self-employed, and its definition is expanded to make room for the growing proportion of salaried employees who also claim middle class status. As long as the desire for middle class position remains strong, the semantics of class redefinition can go on, as if by common consent.

Another basic economic shift is that from primary agricultural production to what Colin Clark has called "tertiary" production, trade and service industries. This movement creates and heightens the extent and the range of social mobility, as Lipset and Bendix have indicated, for it occasions the

Table 5—Distribution of the Working Population of the United States by Major Occupation Groups, 1870-1954*

OCCUPATION	PER CENT OF WORKING POPULATION 1870	1910	1950	1954
Self-Employed	*40.4*	*27.1*	*14.4*	*13.3*
Farmers	27.1	17.7	6.9	5.9
Business Enterprisers	11.4	8.3	6.4	6.0
Professionals	1.1	1.1	1.1	1.4
Salaried Employees	*6.6*	*16.1*	*29.1*	*30.8*
Professional	1.8	3.4	6.2	7.5
Technical-Managerial	1.1	2.9	4.0	3.8
Clerical	.6	4.0	12.6	13.1
Salespeople	2.5	4.6	6.3	6.4
Others	.6	1.2	—	—
Wage-Workers	*52.8*	*56.8*	*56.5*	*55.8*
Farm Laborers	13.1	7.7	5.1	4.1
Industrial Workers	28.2	37.4	51.4	51.7
Others	11.5	11.7		

* Data for 1870 and 1910 adapted from Lewis Corey, "Problems of the Peace: The Middle Class," *Antioch Review*, 5 (Spring, 1945), Table 1, p. 69; data for 1950 and 1954 adapted from *Current Population Reports*, Series P-50, No. 59 (April, 1955), Table III, p. 4.

shift of large proportions of the labor force from manual to non-manual work.[10]

Table 6—Distribution of Gainfully Occupied Population, U. S., 1850-1935*

	1850	1870	1900	1920	1935
Primary (Agriculture)	67.2%	55.6%	39.6%	28.0%	24.8%
Secondary (Manufacture and Mining)	16.2	21.9	28.1	32.7	28.1
Tertiary (Trade, Communication, Professions)	16.6	22.5	32.2	39.3	47.1
	100.0	100.0	100.0	100.0	100.0

* Adapted from Colin Clark, *The Conditions of Economic Progress*, p. 346, as reported in Lipset and Bendix, "Ideological Equalitarianism and Social Mobility in the U. S.," *Transactions of the Second World Congress of Sociology*, Vol. II, p. 39.

These are not the only major shifts that can be documented. Changes in the income structure, in educational requirements and opportunities, and in economic concentration similarly have contributed to major modifications in social structure. For example, a comparison of the character and extent of mergers and acquisitions of manufacturing concerns from 1940 to 1954 gives some evidence of an economic shift of some consequence.

The effects of having larger corporations more involved in

Table 7—Mergers and Acquisitions—Manufacturing and Mining Concerns Acquired, by Size of Assets of Acquiring Concern: 1940-1947 and 1948-1954*

	1940-1947		1948-1954	
ASSETS OF ACQUIRING CONCERN	Number Acquired	Per Cent	Number Acquired	Per Cent
Under $1,000,000	239	11.6	56	3.2
$1,000,000 to $4,999,999	365	17.7	236	13.3
$5,000,000 to $9,999,999	264	12.8	246	13.9
$10,000,000 to $49,999,999	590	28.6	640	36.1
$50,000,000 and over	604	29.3	522	29.4
Assets unknown	—	—	73	4.1
Total	2,062	100.0	1,773	100.0

* U. S. Bureau of the Census, *Statistical Abstract of the United States: 1956* (Seventy-seventh edition) (Washington, D.C., 1956), p. 488.

the mergers of the later period must mean something for the character of economic concentration in the long run. This, in turn, cannot help but affect the class structure and the opportunities and character of social mobility within that structure.

It is possible that the redefinition of changing class boundaries may, in the future, become only an empty exercise. Or, the character of the class system may become so drastically altered that an entirely new set of definitions will be required. In any case, a complete analysis of social mobility must be attuned as much as possible to the major structural shifts in the economic, power, and status systems. Although the economic dimension has been used exclusively here to exemplify the central problems, similar arguments could be made for the power and status spheres. The shift in political controls as seen in the rise of the military or in the political gains of economically privileged groups involves the same order of effects as those noted in the economic sphere. So too in the status order. The attempt by status elites to form a hereditary aristocracy, even if only a local one, and to change the criteria for membership in the aristocracy in order to traditionalize their position, is another instance of structural change.

These are not planned moves in the sense that they are deliberate. However, neither are they shifts that are totally unrelated to the basic dynamics and character of the structure. The nature of the economy, of political controls, of population growth, of an aging social structure—all of these and more have, in some sense, predetermined the general direction that the class system, in all of its facets, will move.

The studies that have been made of what are essentially individual mobility experiences are the closest available approximation that we have to the kind of answers that are wanted. This does not mean, however, that they are the best answers, but they must do for the present. Of course, such studies are related to the central question that has defined this chapter, but they are short of the information that one would prefer.

There are four areas for the study of social mobility, each one organized around a class criterion. These are occupational mobility, income mobility, educational mobility, and business elite mobility. Each of these is to be discussed with instances given of the kinds of studies made, the conclusions reached, and an evaluation of these conclusions in the light of the central question about the current state of social mobility in the United States.

Occupational Mobility

STUDIES of occupational mobility generally have been of two types: (1) inter-generational comparisons of occupations, and (2) occupational career studies of individuals. In the first type, the occupation of the individual is compared with that of his father, and in some instances, with that of his grandfather as well. In the second, the several occupations held by an individual in his work history are compared. Both types of studies rely upon occupational groupings assumed to be arranged in a hierarchy, grouped either as "manual" and "non-manual" occupations, or by census type categories as "professional," "managerial," "skilled," and so on.

Those of the first type are intended to measure and document the extent to which the father's occupation has determined the son's occupation. If the two are consistently similar throughout the sample studied, then the presumption is that little mobility has taken place. If, on the contrary, the son's occupation differs from that of his father's, mobility—upward or downward—is presumed to be evidenced.

The use of occupation as an index of social mobility, which most studies seem to assume, is more complicated than might appear at first. For one, the father's occupation can create certain expectations as regards the son's choice of an occupation. This may be the expectation that the son follow in the father's footsteps, or it may be the reverse; that the son is consistently discouraged from following the same occupational path as his father did. Even the more unconscious relationships between father and son may come into play, to the extent that the son tries to emulate the father or not. With occupation being such a major value, it is quite likely that occupation is a major frame of reference by which the son sees and judges his father. Another factor that is confounded in this father-son comparison, is the knowledge that a son receives about his father's occupation; this knowledge, in turn, can either encourage or discourage him from entering the same field. The number of sons in the family and their birth order, the stage of the business cycle when the son has to choose his occupation, and the changes in social value attached to occupations between the generations, may all contribute more or less in predetermining the occupation toward which the individual moves and is moved.

Three studies can be used to exemplify the research on occupational mobility of the first type. One of the earlier ones was that by Davidson and Anderson of a sample of some 1200 persons in San Jose, California, in 1933.[11] On the basis of plans devised by Hatt and North, the National Opinion Research Center surveyed a nation-wide cross-section of Americans in 1947 on the subject of occupations.[12] Finally, Rogoff has reported upon an inter-generational study of occupations collected from marriage license applications in Indianapolis for the periods 1905 through 1912 and from 1938 through the first half of 1941.[13]

One manner of analyzing and comparing the information from these studies is to consider what they have to say about the relative extent of occupational inheritance, that is, the freezing of the occupational structure. If sons are in the same occupations as their fathers, this indicates occupational inheritance, for whatever reason sons follow that occupation, through deliberate choice or imposed necessity. Sons may follow their father's occupation for many reasons—because they wanted to, because the occupational training and admittance to the occupation required the father's financial support and perhaps his knowing the right people, or because it was the only one they knew. Table 8 summarizes the information from these three studies, showing the percentages of sons who are in the same occupation as their fathers for each occupational category.

Table 8—A Comparison of Three Studies of Occupational Inheritance: Percentage of Sons in Same Occupation as Father

Son's and Father's Occupations are:	Rogoff 1910*	San Jose 1933†	Rogoff 1940*	NORC 1947‡
Professional and semi-professional	20.0	9.6	23.9	23.0
Proprietor and manager	36.1	73.1	32.3	31.0
Clerical and sales	15.4	7.3	21.1	15.0
Skilled	40.3	38.8	40.7	30.0
Semi-skilled	16.9	9.6	24.5	19.0
Unskilled	35.1	39.9	30.1	19.0
Service workers	6.1	—	7.6	8.0
Farmers	83.1	—	64.8	84.0

* Rogoff, *Occupational Mobility*, pp. 44-45.
† Davidson and Anderson, *Occupational Mobility in an American Community*, p. 20.
‡ National Opinion Research Center, *Jobs and Occupations*, pp. 434-435.

The characteristic immediately evident from the comparison between the studies is a clear dissimilarity. Only in the "skilled" and in the "unskilled" occupations is there any measure of agreement. In other instances, two studies agree with one another but not with the third. Both time periods of the Rogoff study and that of the NORC are generally similar for the non-manual categories, but show wider discrepancies in the manual occupations. The reverse generally holds true in the comparison between the Davidson and Anderson study with the two time periods of the Rogoff study—agreement in the manual but disagreement in the non-manual categories.

Although the Rogoff study was designed for a comparison over time, it would be unwise to attempt a time comparison between the three studies together. The methodology, the sampling, and the region of the studies vary too greatly to permit throwing them together into one analytical pot.

What the distributions in Table 8 do seem to substantiate are the following conclusions: (1) occupational inheritance is high among farmers; (2) some occupational inheritance seems to be evident in the proprietor and managerial occupations, in the skilled, and in the unskilled occupations; and (3) the professions and the white-collar occupations are among the most accessible for entrance from other occupational levels in that they indicate the least inheritance.

Mobility, then, as far as it is defined here by occupational changes between generations, does appear to be a fact. Certainly, there is no evidence at this point to indicate an extreme guild-like occupational structure. However, this is not to contend, either, that the occupations of the sons are entirely unrelated to that of their fathers, that free and open mobility exists. The more valid conclusion seems to be somewhere between those two extremes.

The methods used to organize information in order to ascertain more precisely the influence of the father's position upon his son's occupation are varied. Some are better than others, although each is an approximation. Davidson and Anderson, for example, have combined some of the occupational categories to compare the percentages of fathers on the same and "adjacent" occupational levels as that of the sons. What they found was a much closer similarity than was found by the earlier comparison. There were, for example, 80 per cent of the fathers who were on the same or adjacent levels for all sons who were professionals. The lowest percentage was found for sons in unskilled occupations, where 52 per cent of the fathers were on the same or adjacent occupational levels.[14]

Lipset and Rogoff, in another instance, have reorganized the data collected in the NORC study into three categories of "non-manual," "manual," and "farming."[15] In each case, sons more frequently were in the same occupational group as their fathers. Hence, 71 per cent of the sons in non-manual occupations had fathers who were similarly in non-manual work; 61 per cent of those in manual occupations had fathers similarly engaged; 38 per cent of sons in farming had fathers who were farmers.

These figures indicate a somewhat more restricted mobility

than was shown by the first comparison. Sons and fathers, according to these combined occupational categories, tend to be in related if not identical occupations more frequently than not. This can be translated to mean that sons are still impelled toward an occupation by the occupation that their fathers have held. Professionals may not come predominately from professional backgrounds, but they do tend more often to have fathers who are in other types of non-manual work rather than fathers employed in manual or farming occupations. Similarly, those presently in manual jobs predominately have fathers on the same level.

The mobility patterns, apparently, have not changed greatly in this century, at least according to Rogoff's study which is the only one that has been specifically concerned with this matter. The average rate of occupational mobility, she concluded, showed no significant changes between 1910 and 1940, although there have been variations in the mobility rates within each occupational category.[16] There is no need to spell out the statistical technique that Rogoff devised to measure mobility, except to say that it was a form of contingency analysis; the actual frequency of sons in the same occupation as their fathers was compared with a theoretical frequency obtained from the occupational distribution of all sons and their fathers. What was important in Rogoff's technique was that it enabled her to control for changes in the demand for certain occupations over time. The occupational distributions in each time period, then, were assumed to represent the total occupational market. Where sons were found in an occupation with a greater frequency than might have occurred by chance, then this was presumed to be the effect of the father's occupation and related effects. Where sons were found less frequently than expected, then the occupation was considered as one in which inheritance was low.

Although the average mobility rates were unchanged between the two time periods, as noted, Rogoff found that there had been changes in mobility within several categories. "The occupational move most easy to make, both in 1910 and in 1940, was from one white collar class to another.

Mobility from white collar to blue collar classes (downward mobility) was less frequent in 1940 than in 1910. Movement from a blue collar origin to a white collar destination (upward mobility) was as easy to achieve in 1940 as in 1910."[17]

What the results of these several studies show, no matter how they are organized or combined, is that the United States falls somewhere in the middle between a condition of extreme mobility and static rigidity of occupational movement. Sons generally come from occupational levels that are the same or similar to that held by their fathers. However, there are enough instances of those who have moved by broader occupational jumps so that the system cannot be considered as rigid and unyielding.[18]

What is more, those occupations that appear to be pivotal for mobility have remained fairly open and accessible. White collar work, such as clerical and sales occupations, has become one such pivot, especially for those looking to move out of the working class. This advance to a white collar job permits the individual to take a significant status step—out of the manual into a non-manual job. Apparently, the relatively low inheritance in this category, coupled with the increasing demand for such occupations, make this a real opportunity for many. Throughout most of the occupational structure, however, whatever mobility there is remains *within* the manual or non-manual occupational sets so that individuals may move into skilled jobs where their fathers held only unskilled jobs; or fathers in white collar jobs may give their sons the boost up the ladder to perhaps a higher status non-manual occupation.

Finally, what these findings substantially conclude is that the greatest amount of inheritance occurs at the top and at the bottom of the occupational structure. Rogoff's conclusions on this point deserve quotation: "Professional and semi-professional inheritance was consistently high in both 1910 and 1940. Almost as high was the immobility of sons of unskilled and service workers, especially in 1940. It seems likely that the first two classes attract their own sons because of the rewards in income and prestige that they offer. On the other hand, the immobility of the sons of unskilled and service workers is probably due to their restricted economic and educational opportunities, or to restricted ambition; the sons 'remain' in their fathers' class because they cannot leave."[19]

To complete the summary of occupational mobility, mention can be made of the second type of mobility study: the analysis of occupational careers of individuals without reference to their fathers' occupation. A major problem in the way of this kind of analysis is the inability to assess correctly the meaning of an individual's occupational history. The son of a corporation executive may go through a checkered work history, ostensibly to learn the business, whatever it is, but all the time his final success is assured. The son of an unskilled worker may go through almost the same occupational steps, yet each upward move is won by his own effort or whatever techniques he can perfect. Both occupational histories may read the same, but they certainly cannot be interpreted as the same; nor is there any objective way to take these variations into systematic account.

Furthermore, in the occupational histories of most individuals there are many jobs that were meant to be only part-time work or supplemental work to a main occupation. Summer work, seasonal work, or other intentionally temporary employment are part of many work histories, yet from the point of view of mobility are not legitimately part of the occupational history of the individual. It is difficult to set up standards which can unequivocally separate out these work experiences from the main trend of an individual's occupational history. Even with these objections, however, the analysis of career patterns can provide a dimension for analysis that is not involved in the comparisons of the occupations of fathers and sons. It affords some insight into the patterns of actual occupational mobility that the individual has experienced.

There are two studies of individual career patterns that can be specifically mentioned. One, by Form and Miller, was a study of a sample of 276 occupational histories in Ohio in 1946.[20] The second was a study by Lipset and Bendix of 935 job histories of a sample in Oakland, California.[21]

Both studies have documented a great deal of change and movement in the occupational history of the individual. In Form and Miller's terminology, the individual goes through an "initial work period," which includes part-time work until his formal education is completed; a "trial" period when he seems to be "shopping around" in different kinds of jobs; and finally a "stable work period" when he settles down more or less to what is to become his main occupation. During this occupational maturation, the individual has moved through a rather wide range of occupations. In Oakland, for example, it was found that 62 per cent of those in non-manual occupations spent some time in manual work; that 47 per cent of those now in manual jobs, spent some time in non-manual occupations.[22] This indicates, as Lipset and Bendix noted, that there is a greater tendency for those in the higher occupations to have worked some time in the lower occupations, than for those in the lower occupations to have spent any time in the so-called "higher occupations." This finding, of course, is not especially startling since it is somewhat easier to find temporary or seasonal employment in manual jobs than it is in white-collar occupations.

Both studies tend also to agree about the extent and frequency of mobility between the several occupational categories. Professionals, more than any other group, move soonest to their occupational niche with a minimum amount of time spent in any other occupation.[23] The self-employed, managers, and officials evidenced the greatest mobility of all groups during their "initial" and "trial" work periods. What is more, they also showed the most mobility measured by the occupational distance they covered, having moved to their present occupation from manual jobs.[24] Similarly, clerical and sales jobs were a major mobility destination for manual workers.[25] Among the skilled, semi-skilled and unskilled workers, there was much less mobility except for some shifting around within manual jobs.[26]

In general, these findings support the conclusions reached

by the first type of occupational comparisons. The professions at the top and the unskilled at the bottom are the most closed occupations of all—but for different reasons. The unskilled are immobile because they have no monopoly of skills and usually remain committed to the same occupational level as their fathers. The professional occupations, on the other hand, are closed to many, except to the sons of professionals, and contain individuals who most often move directly into the profession without spending time in other occupations.

Between these extremes there is still fluidity in occupational movement. Lower white collar jobs, salesmen and self-employed proprietors symbolize the major channels for upward occupational mobility for those coming from manual occupational backgrounds. Such individuals usually have moved up, not only compared to their father's occupation, but also in terms of their own work careers.

It is questionable, however, just what a move from a manual occupation to a clerical post or to a small, self-owned business really means in broader mobility terms. These may, perhaps, be considered as status moves although there is some question whether these really do still represent mobility. "It is our guess," concluded Lipset and Bendix, "that the creed of the 'individual enterpriser' has become by and large a working-class preoccupation. Though it may have animated both working class and middle class in the past, it is no longer a middle-class ideal today. Instead, people in the middle class aspire to become professionals and, as a second choice, upper-white-collar workers."[27] In other words, some of the lesser occupational moves made in the structure are more in the nature of occupational changes rather than significant class shifts.

That there is occupational mobility, there is no question. However, just what are the consequences of such mobility in class terms is much more open to question. Is the relative freezing of the "upper" occupations and the commitment forced upon those in the lowest occupations the most determining characteristic of this occupational picture? Or instead, should one look at evidences of activity in the middle section of the hierarchy created by the movement out of manual occupations into clerical and sales jobs and into self-owned businesses as the most characteristic trend? Both are factually true, but other factors have to be assessed before the significance of this movement can be properly interpreted in class and mobility terms.

Income Mobility

THE concluding impression regarding occupational mobility, of a limited degree of mobility with most opportunities concentrated toward the middle of the hierarchy, is almost duplicated in the analysis of income distributions and income mobility. Over the past quarter-century there has been a noticeable trend toward equalizing the distribution of personal income. The share accounted for by those at the top of the income hierarchy has been declining at the same time that the share taken by those at the bottom has been growing. The old maxim that the rich get richer as the poor get poorer, should be revised: the rich are getting rich less rapidly than the poor are getting less poor. This latter version is more cumbersome, but is also somewhat more accurate.

With the top coming down and the bottom moving up, there is the temptation to speak of "revolutionary trends" in income, or at least of a "steady liberalizing trend." Such statements, unfortunately, obscure rather than clarify the character of the change. What seems to be substantially true is that the median income has risen during the years and the proportionate shares of the total income going to different income groups have evened out more than in any previous period for which there is comparable information. These trends, furthermore, are real and not simply statistical anomalies shaped more by population growth or changing dollar values than by basic economic conditions.

There seems to be agreement with Kuznets' findings that the share of the upper income groups has "declined substantially" over the years; a loss that has been reflected, of course, in the gains made by the lower income groups.[28] The top one per cent income group dropped from its highest point in 1928 when it accounted for about 15 per cent of all individual income to a share of 8.5 per cent in 1948. Information on incomes reported by *Fortune* in its survey of *The Changing American Market* confirmed this general shift in another way.[29] In 1929, 2.4 per cent had cash incomes of $10,000 or more after taxes on the basis of 1953 dollars. By 1953, this figure had almost doubled to 4.3 per cent earning $10,000 or more. At the other end of the distribution, for the same period, the 16.4 per cent who received less than $1,000 in 1929 had declined to 9.6 per cent by 1953. These are indeed substantial gains, although whether they are substantial enough depends very much upon the standards one chooses to apply.

There is apparently some measure of disagreement over how well-off Americans really are, which is a reflection in part of the kind of information collected. The differences, although they can be explained by the variations in data-gathering techniques, do point up the need for some measure of caution in the interpretation of income statistics. According to the *Fortune* figures mentioned above, 25.4 per cent of "income receiving units" in 1953 received $5,000 or more.[30] The figures reported by the Department of Commerce in its *Survey of Current Business* presented a somewhat more optimistic picture of income distribution for the same year; 32.6 per cent of "families and unattached individuals" earned $5,000 or more.[31] The magazine *U.S. News and World Report* in reporting the Commerce Department's figures for 1955, indicated that the more optimistic view was still in the ascendancy; 44 per cent of American "families and unattached individuals" were then earning $5,000 or more.[32]

To insist upon making something of these percentage differences may appear to be needless quibbling, but there is apparently some difference of opinion among the experts as to what the figures really show about income distribution. The shares of upper and lower income groups have shifted and median income has risen over the past decade; that much appears to be true. But economists do not appear to be of one mind in extrapolating those statistics into generalizations concerning income equality. Margaret G. Reid, testifying in 1949 before the Subcommittee on Low-Income Families of the 81st Congress, stated: "The American economy for many decades has had a rising standard of per capita income, and no evidence exists that the distribution of income during the period was appreciably different from that which now exists."[33] Arthur F. Burns in his annual report of the National Bureau of Economic Research in 1951 stated a somewhat opposing view: "The transformation in the distribution of our national income that has occurred within the past twenty years . . . may already be counted as one of the great social revolutions in history."[34] Income or occupation, there is room for wide differences of opinion even though one would much prefer to know certainly and unequivocally about such vital matters.

For the sociologist, however, there are other elements in this analysis, for income distribution is a pivotal matter in the study of social class and mobility. Some of the questions and some of the data relating to income distribution have been presented, and the reader must come to his own conclusions. Additionally, however, there are two other matters that need to be looked into in connection with this section on income mobility: (1) how stable are these findings on income distribution, and (2) what difference does it make for social mobility? In the first case, the interest is in the factors behind the shift in income patterns and their long run consequences; in the second, in how income can affect the shift in consumer behavior that has been pointed to as the means by which Americans are gravitating into a massive middle class.

A major factor causing the redistribution of income has been the shift in the occupational structure, whereby a larger proportion of persons are employed in better paying occupations than ever before with the consequent reduction of the number in poorer paying jobs. Table 9 documents the occupational shift since 1870.

*Table 9—Distribution of the Labor Force, 1870, 1910 and 1950**

	PER CENT OF THE LABOR FORCE		
OCCUPATIONAL CATEGORY	*1870*	*1910*	*1950*
Professionals	3%	4.4%	8.5%
Proprietors, managers	30	23.0	15.9
Clerical, sales	4	10.2	18.9
Skilled	9	11.7	13.8
Semi-skilled	10	14.7	21.7
Unskilled	44	36.0	18.9
Not reported			2.3
Totals	100	100.0	100.0

* Adapted from Joseph A. Kahl, *The American Class Structure* (New York: Rinehart and Co., 1957), p. 67.

Table 9 above documents the decrease in the proportion of unskilled workers coupled with the increase in the clerical and skilled workers. The steady increase in professionals, too, has acted to raise income levels for at least portions of the labor force. In order to point up the effect of occupational change upon the distribution of income, however, Table 10 is presented below. It indicates the relative shares of income accounted for by each occupational group; the higher occupations commanding a larger proportion, the lower occupations getting a lower proportion.

Where the percentage of the income received is higher than the percentage of income recipients, then the occupation must be counted as a better paying one. Conversely, those occupations, such as laborer or service worker, that receive a lower share than their proportion of all income recipients, are the poorer paying jobs.[35]

A second factor that has affected the change in income distribution has been the increase toward full-employment and the decrease in part-time workers, thereby shifting a greater share of the income to those individuals. Since this shift to full employment affects those in the lower ranges of the occupational hierarchy, the general effect has been toward income equalization.[36] The increase in the proportion of fully employed, as Miller has pointed out, "not only narrowed the income gap within occupations, it also narrowed the gap between high-paid and low-paid occupations."[37] Thus, another factor was at work behind the shift in income distribution.

Table 10—Per Cent of Employed Persons and Income Received in 1951, by Occupational Group and by Sex*

OCCUPATIONAL GROUP	MALE Income Recipients	MALE Income Share	MALE Median Income	FEMALE Income Recipients	FEMALE Income Share	FEMALE Median Income
Professionals	7.7%	11.1%	$4250	11.6%	16.6%	$2517
Proprietors, managers	12.2	19.8	4100	5.4	6.9	2070
Clerical	6.8	6.4	3424	30.5	36.5	2165
Sales workers	5.3	6.1	3628	7.2	5.8	1281
Craftsmen, foremen	20.7	21.5	3656	1.5	1.6	—
Operatives	21.0	17.9	3108	20.4	19.6	1758
Service workers	6.1	4.3	2474	21.2	11.8	934†
Laborers	8.3	5.2	2281	.7	.5	—

* Adapted from *Current Population Reports* as reported in Herman P. Miller, *Income of the American People* (New York: John Wiley and Sons, 1955), p. 51. Percentages given as reported add to more than 100%.

† Estimated from medians given for private and service workers.

In more general terms then, the rise toward full employment, the growth of unions and their ability to withdraw a greater share of the national income for the lower paying occupations, and finally, the generally high level of prosperity in the post-war period—all of these have contributed toward the general trend of income redistribution.

However, the question, "How long will this last?" is a nagging concern. Will the shift in income distribution continue to the point where major income inequalities will be overcome? Economists are in doubt about the answer to this question as the earlier quotations by Reid and Burns have implied. The major reason for doubt appears to be the fact that the gains of the lower income groups are closely tied to the general economic prosperity of the period. What has appeared to be a steady progression in income gains over the past several decades is, upon closer inspection, a shuttling between income extremes tied to the business cycle. What is more, the groups most quickly and drastically affected by the state of the business cycle are those in the lower income brackets. For example, Table 11 presents an analysis of income shares related to the business cycle.

Table 11—Percentage Shares of Three Income Groups in Total Income During Business Cycles: Average Percentage Shares (Six Cycles, 1919-1946)*

	AVERAGE AT:		
INCOME CATEGORY	*Initial Troughs*	*Peaks*	*Terminal Troughs*
Top 1 per cent	13.0	12.4	12.4
2nd to 7th per cent	16.0	14.3	15.7
Lower 93 per cent	71.0	73.3	71.9
Total	100.0	100.0	100.0

* Presented by Geoffrey H. Moore in his foreword to Daniel Creamer, *Personal Income During Business Cycles*, National Bureau of Economic Research (Princeton: Princeton University Press, 1956), p. xxii.

The greatest fluctuation is experienced by those in the lower ninety-three per cent of the income distribution, those whose income derives from wages. The other two groups do not fluctuate to the same degree during the course of a business cycle. As Geoffrey H. Moore summarized the findings of Daniel Creamer's study of *Personal Income During Business Cycles*: "As a rule during business expansions, when employment, hours of work, wage rates, and farm prices and incomes rise, the total income of the lower income group [lower ninety-three per cent of income distribution] rises more rapidly than the total income of the whole population; during contractions the opposite situation prevails. As we go up in income scale greater stability in income appears . . . ; this leads to an inverted cyclical pattern in the shares of the income groups just below the top. But, at the very top, dividend income becomes an important source, and imparts a certain degree of instability . . . ; hence the share of the top income group is less consistently inverted."[38] What these findings suggest in the present context is the possibility that what appear now to be major and substantial shifts in income distribution patterns may only be relatively short-run effects tied to the relatively high prosperity level of the economy—an inflationary situation according to some. A major period of unemployment, major cutbacks in defense spending, or changes in union-management strength could radically alter the direction of the income trend.

Furthermore, Reid has suggested that the lessening inequality in income distributions may be tied to certain trends that will soon cease producing that same effect.[39] The reduction in the proportion of low income families, for example, reflects the reduction in the proportion of farm families in the population; a change from "receiving income in kind to receiving money income" with a consequent increase in income figures. The raising of income for aged persons by social security payments especially, also tends to show a more favorable redistribution of income for this group previously underprivileged. Relevant as these trends are for income equalization, nevertheless, they might produce a misleading statistical impression of greater income equality by the sudden shifts in income that they convey, without actually justifying a conclusion of a steady movement toward income equality in the total population.

As it seems to appear at this time, however, the conclusions about income tie in closely with those about occupational mobility. There has been evidence of relatively open mobility in both dimensions, within limits. Movement out of the bottom of either the income or the occupational hierarchy appears to be possible. In general, this movement is toward the middle ranges in both hierarchies, more than it is toward the top. Individuals can move into white collar jobs with some ease and they can raise their income above what it was before. In neither occupation nor income, however, is movement toward the very top of the hierarchy a matter of one's talents, abilities, or aspirations alone. Structural factors—redistributions of occupation and income—play the dominant role.

There is another feature to the change in income patterns

that can be mentioned. It refers to the effect of income change upon consumer behavior, for the style and manner in which the individual spends his income is a relevant factor for social mobility. Income gains can be used to live up to a newly established class position; in other words, to convert money into status.

The great advantage of using money to effect a status rise, of course, is that economic goods know only price. In the market place they are free of any other encumbrances and available to anyone who can pay the price. Most other channels by which the upwardly mobile might express their newly-won status require time, training, and such inaccessible prerequisites as a proper family background and proper tradition. There are no short-cuts by which these last mentioned class symbols can be obtained quickly. Money above all permits the individual to get his status quickly and directly, which is probably why income is so disdained by the secure upper class stratum as a measure of social position. Taste must be educated, patterns of behavior fitting to the "new" class must be learned, and the ability of knowing how to live comfortably in spite of money must be acquired slowly. It is little wonder that families that have advanced economically turn their aspirations for commensurate social advance into the only channel open to them—purchasing consumer goods that they believe can do the job for them. The major drawback in this social logic, however, is that with income levels rising for large numbers of people the relative positions between them tend to remain unchanged. Here is an instance of one of the types mentioned earlier: where whole classes can move up, then individuals within a class cannot convert such gains to their own mobility advantage because the status ante has gone up for everyone.

Unfortunately, there is no precise information on the specific points that are relevant here. A good deal has been collected about family budgets and expenditures over relatively extended time periods and by income differences. What is lacking, however, is the analysis of changes in expenditures and in budgets experienced by income gaining or income losing families and the motivations behind those changes. Complicating this picture further is the fact that general patterns of taste and consumption also change over time so that these changing social definitions become confounded with the changing income position of families.

Concerning the measurement of family budgets over time one thing is clear: there has been relatively little change in the proportions of income allotted to the various categories of expense. Table 12 below, for example, presents information on that point for the United States. The intriguing aspects of that table are developed by the few items that have changed between 1929 and 1950. Food and transportation

Table 12—Percentage of Consumption Expenditures, for the U. S., Going to Specified Products, 1929, 1939 and 1950*

	PERCENTAGE OF CONSUMPTION EXPENDITURES		
EXPENDITURES	*1929*	*1939*	*1950*
Food	24.98%	28.61%	31.58%
Clothing	13.99	12.30	11.85
Housing	14.50	13.25	10.23
Household equipment and furnishings	13.34	14.02	13.62
Transportation	9.52	9.26	11.59
Recreation	5.49	5.11	5.83
Tobacco	2.16	2.63	2.26

* Adapted from Elizabeth E. Hoyt and Others, *American Income and Its Use* (New York: Harper and Bros., 1954), p. 351.

have increased proportionately; clothing and housing have decreased. The rise in food prices brought about by the price supports for agricultural products and the added cost of packaging has been steadily increasing in the past decade. There would seem to be little choice involved here for the consumer, and the higher proportion spent in 1950 is a reflection of increased prices. The increase in transportation as well as the decrease in housing, appear to be consequences of suburbanization. The move to the suburbs has decreased the cost of housing at the same time that it has increased the cost of transportation between home and work. The smaller proportion spent for clothing most likely is a result of the increased proportion spent for other goods and services. On the whole, however, these changes have not been especially great, and American families in 1950, with larger incomes than those in 1929, are still spending their money for much the same general things.

It is known, too, that with a rise in income there are important modifications in the proportions that are allotted for various consumer purchases. Several generalizations have been reached and substantiated concerning the nature of those modifications.[40] It should be noticed, however, that these generalizations are based upon comparisons between income groups at a given time rather than upon a longitudinal analysis of changes *within* groups over a period of time as their income changes. A comparison between the expenditures of a sample of middle income families with the expenditures of a sample of all income groups points up some of the differences that can be traced to income. These have been reported by the Heller Committee in its analysis of income in the San Francisco Bay area.[41] The median income of the first group was $7,228; that of the second group, studied by the Bureau of Labor Statistics in the same area, was $5,228. The middle income group spent proportionately less on food than did the cross-section sample; a finding that matches the generalization often made that as income increases the proportion spent on food decreases. Proportions spent for housing, utilities, furnishings, and medical care were approximately the same for both groups. This, too, supports the earlier conclusions that have been reached concerning the relationship between those expenditures and income level. The middle income groups spent more proportionately for transportation, recreation, education, insurance, and gifts than did the generally lower income B.L.S. sample. A surprising difference between the two groups, however, was that the middle income sample spent less on clothing and less for personal care than did the B.L.S. sample, which is a finding counter to that usually anticipated. This finding, by the way, matches closely the differences found in Table 12 on the changing proportions of expenditures since 1929. Again, it seems to suggest that suburbanization and its accompanying life style—casual dress, need for transportation, and lower housing costs—are important elements in this change in consumer behavior.

Some analysts, such as Riesman, Whyte, and Spectorsky, are of the opinion that consumer patterns have been moving toward a more or less "standard package" of goods and services having essentially a middle class character. The broader distribution of more income to formerly low income groups, time payments, the pressure to buy, and the move to Suburbia which leaves little room between picture windows, have helped this movement of consumer equalization. Home appliances, a home, and the tools of leisure, those analysts have implied, are more within the income range and the motivational focus of more people than ever before. There has been a status leveling directly expressed in the uniformity of consumer purchases. Spectorsky has even gone so far as to hold that this trend is producing an unhealthy psychological reaction, "Destination Sickness" or the "constellation of physical and psychic disorders and discomforts which ensue on the artificial and premature attainment of deceptive and inadequate goals."[42]

These conclusions are more specific and at the same time more subtle than those reached by most consumer studies. It is, therefore, difficult to use the mass of information collected by the latter studies to test these conclusions that have been advanced. If the patterns of consumer purchasing do indeed follow along the lines suggested by Riesman and others, then it is still by no means clear what the motivations are behind those purchases. In one study, in New Orleans in 1956, of class difference in consumer behavior, the conclusion reached was as follows:[43]

> The suburban lower class sample was composed of strong appliance purchasers. More than any other group, the lower class bought television sets, washing machines, clothes driers, dish-washers—the whole array of home machinery. What was more, their urge to buy seemed to be insatiable.

On the surface the suburban middle class sample seemed to be just as much driven by the "appliance urge" as was the lower class. Upon a closer analysis of the motivations of the two samples, however, the patterns of class differentiation were found. The consumer patterns of the suburban lower class, which we believe contains the upwardly mobile individuals of the urban lower class, were direct and obvious in intent. Here were individuals who were just a step off the beat, caught in a transitional stage between the class they were moving out of and the class they had not yet moved into. The suburban lower class person is conscious enough of status to move out to the suburbs; conscious enough of status to surround himself with what were once the symbols of middle class existence. He still lacks, however, the key element which keeps him from middle class membership: the acceptance and internalization of middle class values. We also found that these heavily spending lower class people did not feel the pinch of the Protestant ethic at all in their unabating urge for the appliances. The installment plan was a way of life for them. Without hesitation, they maintained in response to our questions, that it was proper for individuals to undertake several time payment plans at once; to buy the things they "needed" and in the light of the mobility drive, to buy almost as much as they wanted.

Value conflict was much more characteristic of the suburban middle class group. In this group, people bought for use and to maintain status, perhaps, but through it all, the conflict showed between their behavior as consumers and their assessment of that behavior.

From the sum of response, it seemed clear that the suburban middle class was in conflict. Unlike the lower class that spent freely and without qualms, the middle class was in a psychic squeeze between values and behavior. The years of middle class socialization into the values of thrift, responsibility, and budgets were not easily overcome. The suburban lower class, on the other hand, was free of such conflict but remained suspended somewhere in a class limbo for the time, marginal to the class groups on either side of them.

It is information of this order that is needed to ascertain more precisely the effects of income mobility upon the consumption of goods for social effect. And tied into all of this, of course, is the whole question of the role of prosperity and economic security upon consumer behavior. The Survey Research Center's study of June, 1954, asked a sample of persons, "Do you think that something like the depression of the thirties is likely to happen again during the next five years or so?" Of those whose income was under $3000, 48 per cent said it could not happen again. Of those earning between three and five thousand dollars, 59 per cent said it could not happen. In the category of those earning $5000 or more, 71 per cent said it could not happen again.[44] These percentages indicate a generally high level of optimism. They also show that the lower the income, the less prevalent was the optimism. Certainly, such potential fears about possible future insecurity, especially among the lower income groups, means that not everybody is buying according to the status pattern hypothesized by Riesman, Whyte and others; not everybody is being hypnotized by the advertised belief in using now and paying later.

In that same study by the Survey Research Center, those with lower incomes were similarly less hopeful about buying such items as refrigerators, washing machines and TV sets in the next year.[45] Among the families with income under $3,000, only 3.9 per cent indicated there was a good chance of buying a refrigerator in the next 12 months; 7.6 per cent of those with incomes of $5000 or more indicated there was a good chance of their buying a refrigerator. Similar differences were expressed in the other items the sample was quizzed about.

In view of the tremendous expansion in the purchases of such goods as appliances, furniture, automobiles, and homes, the temptation is great to move to the generalization that income mobility has meant a necessary and concomitant increase in the social aspirations and in the consumer behavior of most Americans. What these last few points that have been mentioned have intended was to introduce a note of needed caution in such generalizations. The complex set of motives as they relate to mobility aspirations in this area of consumer behavior must be further spelled out and analyzed. It is still an area confounded by many other variables, as for example, by the fact that many families are now near the beginning of their family cycle and such heavy purchasing is a necessary, but relatively short run phenomenon. Young families with children, just beginning to set up their own housekeeping, need to buy the kinds of goods that have been so heavily sold to them. They have little other choice in view of their position. But how long this will last, and whether or not there are long-range mobility aspirations behind this behavior, are still matters that need to be more carefully analyzed.

Educational Mobility

If occupation and income are mobility roads, then the metaphor for education must be that of a modern freeway, for education has become the most frequently used means for social advancement in the class system. In many senses, education is a prerequisite to mobility via both occupation and income. Educational requirements are almost without exception the prerequisites for entry into the higher prestige occupations and into the higher income categories. The era of the self-made, self-educated success seems to be a phenomenon of the past, and the biographies of current successful men almost invariably include a college degree. This trend, of course, is enforced by the demands of a modern technology that requires adequately trained specialists. For the majority, advancement is no longer made through the ranks where experience was the hallmark, but through education where trained expertise is the quality most often needed. Both the management of men and the management of materials have become scientific, whether rightly or not, and it is only through exposure to a sequence of formal education that such information can be transmitted efficiently and rationally. One may rail against this trend as a perversion of educational goals and as an unnecessary complication of economic and social goals. However, the trend appears to be increasing in intensity rather than abating.

The social elements are many that have gradually translated the functions of the educational institutions from the "pure" pursuit of knowledge to a means for advancement and enlisted the college and university in the competitive struggle. The technical and scientific needs of American society are one major push in that transition. Another can be traced to the appearance of the second and third generation Americans for whom the next logical step in the process of assimilation to American culture has been social advancement. The spreading professionalization covering more and more occupations has meant a concomitant increase in educational requirements. And since these occupations were the ones that paid better and commanded the greater prestige, the path for mobility was clearly set. Government subsidies, as in the G. I. Bill[46] for example, opened the opportunities for education to many thousands. Industrial and government bureaucracies, more and more, have come to define job ceilings according to educational levels and only by extending his education is the individual able to raise his job ceiling, sometimes with the direct financial assistance of the organization that employs him.

One may legitimately wonder, of course, about the change in educational philosophy that has accompanied the change in function and the purpose of education. High school and college curricula have been fairly effectively culled during the past decade or so for those subjects that have no connection with the newer mobility demands. Instead, numerous courses of essentially a technical or "how-to" nature have been substituted. In this instance, however, what we see is the pressing demand of society upon the educational institutions to adjust to what are believed to be the major functions such institutions should serve. The current emphasis upon scientists and engineers, for example, stemming from a reaction to presumed Russian gains in those fields, cannot help but enlist the educational institutions into achieving new gains, whether they will or not. The inevitable result is that education, once again, becomes transformed to meet more or less immediate purposes, no matter how vital some might feel the need for scientists is for our continued survival. It is small wonder, then, that educational institutions have become so much a means to the end of social mobility, a means to learn an occupation or profession which in turn confers prestige and money often not otherwise accessible to the individual.

There are several indisputable facts about the role of education and its importance for social mobility. First, it is abundantly clear that among the rewards of higher education, gains in occupational prestige and income are fairly generally guaranteed. Table 13 below, computed from information in the 1950 census, clearly substantiates the conclusion that better jobs and better education go together.

Increased income is also a reward given to those with generally higher educational attainments. To a large extent, of course, this is a function of the occupation and the occupational ceiling for which an individual can qualify by his education. Nonetheless, it plainly appears evident from Table 14 and Table 15 below that the proportionately greater income commanded by those who are better educated soon makes up for the financial cost of the education itself.

A second apparent fact about the role of education is its relative accessibility to more people than before; presumably those who hold some aspirations for social mobility. High school enrollment has exploded since 1890 when 7 per cent of the population fourteen to seventeen years of age were in high school, to an astounding 84 per cent in 1950.[47] College enrollment has similarly increased from a mere 237,592 in 1900, to a sizeable 2,947,000 in 1956.[48] In fact there were more faculty members teaching in colleges and

Table 13—Per Cent Distribution by Major Occupation Group, for Employed Males 22 to 74 Years Old, by Years of School Completed, United States, 1950*

OCCUPATION	YEARS OF SCHOOL COMPLETED						
	ELEMENTARY		HIGH SCHOOL		COLLEGE		
	Under 5 years	*5-8 years*	*1-3 years*	*4 years*	*1-3 years*	*4 or more years*	*Median School Years Completed*
Professionals	.8	1.2	2.5	6.1	17.3	55.0	16+
Managers, proprietors	5.0	7.4	10.8	15.4	22.2	17.9	12.2
Clerical, sales	3.2	6.5	12.7	21.0	26.9	15.1	12.3
Skilled	12.6	22.1	25.2	22.3	13.1	4.5	9.5
Semi-skilled	21.3	24.5	25.3	17.3	8.3	2.3	8.8
Service workers	8.0	7.2	6.2	5.1	3.9	1.4	8.7
Unskilled	17.9	10.2	6.8	3.9	1.9	.7	8.1
Farmers	20.2	15.8	7.7	6.6	4.7	2.0	8.3
Farm laborers	9.9	4.2	2.1	1.6	.8	.4	7.6
Not reported	1.0	.9	.8	.7	.8	.7	8.9
Totals	100.0	100.0	100.0	100.0	100.0	100.0	11.2

* Adapted from Paul C. Glick, "Educational Attainment and Occupational Advancement," *Transactions, 2nd World Congress of Sociology*, Vol. II, 1954, p. 188.

universities in 1954 than there were students attending in 1900.[49] The total annual budgets of all higher educational institutions have moved up to around three millions dollars.[50]

These figures coldly document the scope that education has achieved in the United States, as well as the mobility advantages that it has come to confer in terms of better occupa-

Table 14—Average Income in 1949 for Males 22 to 74 Years Old, by Years of School Completed, United States, 1950*

Educational Level	*Average Income*
No school years completed	$1,350
Elementary School	
1 to 4 years	$1,625
5 to 7 years	2,135
8 years	2,685
High School	
1 to 3 years	$3,013
4 years	3,516
College	
1 to 3 years	$3,878
4 years or more	5,724

* Adapted from Paul C. Glick, "Educational Attainment and Occupational Advancement," *Transactions, 2nd World Congress of Sociology*, Vol. II, 1954, p. 190.

Table 15—"Life-Time" Income for U. S. Males 22 to 74 Years Old, by Educational Level, by 1949 Survival Rates and 1949 Dollars*

Educational Level	*"Life-Time" Income*
No school years completed	$58,000
Elementary School	
1 to 4 years	$72,000
5 to 7 years	93,000
8 years	116,000
High School	
1 to 3 years	$135,000
4 years	165,000
College	
1 to 3 years	$190,000
4 years or more	268,000

* Adapted from Paul C. Glick, "Educational Attainment and Occupational Advancement," *Transactions, 2nd World Congress of Sociology*, Vol. II, 1954, p. 192.

tions and increased incomes. Education may be no guarantee of higher social status, but it seems clear that for most persons no status gains could be made without it.

One final point must be assessed in connection with this discussion of education as a mobility channel: Is education equally available to all segments of the population or not? In other words, how does the condition of equality of educational opportunities compare with the opportunities found in the case of both income and occupation? The available information on this point tends to support the impressions one gains of the college population, and at the same time, comes very close to the conclusions reached about occupational and income equality. Generally, those who come from middle and upper class backgrounds will more likely attend and complete college than those who come from lower or working class origins. Opportunities for a college education are by no means totally closed to those who must start from the lower class positions, but the probability that they will have the opportunity is proportionately smaller than for those from higher status positions. Lipset and Bendix have presented the following table, which clearly illustrates this point.[51]

Those high school seniors whose fathers were professionals

Table 16—Relation of Fathers' Occupation to College Attendance, National Sample of White High School Seniors, 1947*

	FATHERS' OCCUPATION				
ATTENDANCE AT COLLEGE	Prof. and Executive	Small Business	White Collar	Service and Trade	Factory and Other
Applied for admission	73.4%	47.9%	45.3%	23.4%	20.5%
Actually admitted†	67.2	40.6	40.0	19.8	16.4
Have not applied but hope to go later	12.6	18.8	23.9	24.8	23.6
Will not go to college	12.2	30.7	28.3	48.4	53.5
Don't know	1.8	2.6	2.5	3.4	2.4
Totals	100.0	100.0	100.0	100.0	100.0

* Reported in Lipset and Bendix, "Ideological Equalitarianism and Social Mobility in the U. S.," *Transactions, 2nd World Congress of Sociology*, Vol. II, 1954, p. 43, and taken from Elmo Roper, *Factors Affecting the Admission of High School Seniors to College.*

† This line has been recalculated from data in this study; it should not be included in the total, since the figures are already represented in the line immediately above.

or executives were more likely to be admitted to college and were more definite in their intentions to attend. Those who came from working class backgrounds, on the other hand, were, if anything, more definite in their knowledge that they would not go to college.

There is no information available that would permit a comparison of these figures with those gathered at an earlier time so that something could be learned about the relative change in educational opportunities and conditions. For a valid assessment of the condition of educational equality in the United States, it would be necessary to have that kind of information; to know whether or not such opportunities are becoming scarcer or more plentiful.

In that connection there has been some speculation about the consequences of having such large numbers of students applying for college entrance. At the present time, most colleges have instituted some kind of screening process by which they are able to select only the students who are most educationally promising to fill the openings that are available. The increased birth rate of the war years is now being felt at the college level, which has meant a greatly increased demand for college entrance and, in most colleges, a demand far in excess of facilities. The alternative that is apparently being chosen by most of the better colleges and universities is not to expand their physical plant to keep pace with the demand, as many did in 1946 and later when large numbers of veterans were applying. Instead, many college administrators have decided to increase the quality of the student body by limiting enrollment and by using scores on educational achievement and intelligence tests as well as high school records to select the best qualified students.

The result of this press has been, and will continue to be, that the choice of a college education has to be made in the first year of high school or perhaps even earlier. In order to compete for the fixed number of college openings students will perforce have to become college oriented sooner. They will have to make up their minds earlier in their school experience, and what is more, will have to achieve at a high educational level for a longer period of time prior to the time they apply to a college for admission. In earlier years, the penalty for not choosing a college preparatory curriculum in high school was not too severe. Students could and did change in their last year of high school, or even were able to take entrance examinations to college to qualify without having had all of the necessary credits in high school. The present situation, however, no longer will permit such luxury and fickleness. For the majority of prospective college students, increasingly, the choice must be made earlier and must be worked at throughout high school and perhaps even through the junior high school period.

The effects of these trends, if they are realized, upon class and mobility seem clear enough. They will come to emphasize the superior position of those who come from middle and upper class backgrounds; those who by family values, economic position, and high school preparation have an enormous advantage over those from working class origins. The opportunities for a college education for superior students from the lower class groups will still be present, but to a much more restricted extent than formerly. In general those from lower and working class backgrounds will not find the support for college, the motivation for college, nor what is most important, the necessary preparation for college which is likely to become the *sine qua non* for admission. What the effect of this differential access to one of the major channels for mobility will be is hard to predict. But if one were to extend the conclusions that have been suggested, it would seem that those who lose out in this competitive race for educational mobility will find it harder to get into the better occupations and harder to command a larger share of the income distribution, insofar as income and occupation are positively related to education.

The area of education, then, is a pivotal one that would bear close watching and analysis by those interested in stratification and in matters of social equality. It might well be the case that here is a major indicator of future class trends in the United States.

Elite Mobility

THE jockeying by individuals looking to improve, raise, and better their occupation, income, and education is social mobility at the mass level. And the preceding analysis has looked at the opportunities for mobility throughout the structure as a whole. However, that is social mobility below the top. What has been described was not the situation in the upper social atmosphere. Yet, what many people really want to know, including the social analyst if he is to evaluate properly the total situation, is the relative chances for breaking into the inner circle now as compared with some earlier period. Is it becoming more difficult or not to break loose from the mundane social shuffling and to enter into the charmed upper atmosphere of wealth, position, and power? The struggles of the factory worker's son to get through college and to become an M.D. are laudable and in keeping with the ideals of equality and of social opportunity. As long as enough of that kind of mobility occurs then our ideals are real.

Beneath the consciousness of good feeling engendered by the successes of many within the limited range available to them, however, lies a more nagging question: Is the success ceiling limited? Is there, in other words, really the chance to make the grade from rags to riches as the full success story relates, or can it be at best only the shorter, less dramatic rise from rags to respectability?

Necessarily, the concern here is with the mobility of the few rather than of the many, for the elite must be small. This is an analysis, therefore, of a numerically insignificant but socially significant group of persons who have been able to reach the top of the class structure. The question to be answered is this: Do those who reach the top succeed because of family help, economic inheritance, or principally by their own efforts? If it takes family—because they own the business or have the money—then the conclusion possibly is that elite mobility is limited. If personal achievement alone is decisive, then the beliefs and sentiments about the equality of opportunity are supported in fact.

Another feature of the elite is worth mentioning. The channels by which individuals reach the inner circle may differ, but once elite membership has been achieved, the occupant usually is able to exercise power and control in a variety of ways. Some may reach it through amassing large fortunes, other by winning important political offices, still others by the natural inheritance of family fame and prestige. Once there, however, one has access to the other supports upon which the elite is secured in addition to the one by which entry itself was attained. The elite, as Mills has indicated, is an elite precisely because within itself it holds the major reins connected to the power, status and class channels of society.[52] There may be, and probably are, distinguishable cliques within the elite itself, but this seems to be due as much to the relative newness and rawness of the elite tradition as to any rational, internal elite stratification. With time, with the development of a tradition, with the creation of fixed and controlled channels for elite recruitment, the elite can come to establish itself as a more coherent and unified group. Such has been the case with all aristocracies in the past, and there is an impelling social logic that makes this development almost necessary.

Because the potential power and influence are great that can be exerted by the elite in spite of its limited size—a power that increases as the members of the elite come to recognize and legitimize each other's membership—the final test of social mobility must be made in terms of the elite. If access to elite membership remains relatively open, then their social mobility is realistically evident; if access is closed, except to the descendants of elite members or to others deliberately co-opted, then rigidity or "caste" becomes the dominating characteristic of social structure, no matter how much apparent mobility there may be at the class levels below the elite.

The elite, as it is described and analyzed here, includes principally those who, by their wealth or their position in the world of the corporation, fill what Mills has labeled the "command posts" of American society. Of course, other qualifications might have been added: those who fill major political positions, elective or appointive; those who hold high prestige positions either nationally or locally; and those in the military. These latter groups, although many might agree that they could be legitimately included, are somewhat more difficult to define and to measure than is the economic elite. Political elites, for example, could be defined, as Mills did, to include the "fifty-odd men of the executive branch of the government, [including] the President, Vice-President . . . members of the cabinet [and] the head men of major departments and bureaus."[53] For some purposes this is a reasonable definition, but it is a difficult standard to use when comparisons need to be made over time to check upon elite mobility. Elective as well as appointive political posts are sensitive to changing political values and political sentiments. Presidents and Vice-Presidents have been elected as many times for fickle and vague reasons by the electorate as they have been chosen for politically solid and sophisticated ones. It would be difficult to trace an elite tradition in the political area, then, because the vagaries of politics make it difficult to maintain that kind of tradition.

Similar objections apply to including the military as an elite group for the present analysis. The ascendancy of the military in a democracy, at the present time and throughout American history, has been integrally tied to the period. From World War I almost up to the outbreak of World War II and America's entry into it, the military establishment was treated as coldly as an unwanted child. Under those conditions, high military position meant little in social prestige terms, and meant nothing in terms of elite currency. With the military, as with the political elite, the particular social dynamics during a single period can influence the fortunes of the elite tremendously. They become too unstable a group to allow for easy analysis over a longer period of time.

The "true" upper class, in its prestige aspects, is similarly excluded from the present analysis of the elite. To the extent, of course, that economic position determines upper class membership, this group is included. However, those elements of upper class position that depend upon family, upon clique memberships, upon belonging to the proper social clubs, or upon a local acceptance of superior social status, cannot be considered in the present analysis. The principal reason for excluding this prestige elite from consideration is the lack of sufficient information about it and about the changes in its qualifications over any longer period. Indeed, of all classes in America, least is known about the characteristics and behavior of the upper class. Yet, this is a situation that is being remedied by such analyses as that of the *Philadelphia Gentlemen,*[54] of the "Metropolitan 400,"[55] and *The Proper Bostonians.*[56]

It seems most probable that the prestige features of the upper class will be included in some future trend study, which will analyze the changes in membership requirements. Information on this aspect is being collected so that a base line for comparison is now being established. More importantly, it seems clear even now that the upper class is breaking out of the local boundaries which formerly contained it and is developing into a national prestige elite. It is becoming, as both Mills and Baltzell agree, a metropolitan elite. This transformation into a national elite, which ties together the several local elites, is being accomplished, Baltzell argued,[57] for several reasons: the rise of mass communications brings them closer informationally; the rise of national corporate enterprise brings them economically closer; and the whole structure of supporting institutions socializes them to a common value standard that each member can recognize in the other, through the prep school, the Ivy League college, the club, and the church. The result of these very real social forces is to unite the upper class into a more coherent functioning social group which shares not only similar economic and political values, but also similar prestige and status goals. The currency of elite prestige has become a nationally recognized one by the members of the elite, by which the formerly separate, locally limited, prestige currencies have become converted into a single national one. Probably this trend will push the elite toward an aristocracy, in that it will be able successfully to limit the channels as well as to set the requirements for entry.

Finally, it might be emphasized that the generally high, continuous, and secure position of the economic elite—whoever they may be in any period—fits rather well with the dominating economic values of American society. It is not accidental that the economic, above all other elite bases, is the most generally recognized and accepted. In the case of the economic elite, more than for any other, power can be transferred to the other spheres that have been enumerated: into the political and the national prestige structure and the local prestige community.

As evidence of continued opportunities for amassing wealth and position, outstanding individuals in the present are constantly pointed out. Regularly, for example, the Sunday edition of the *New York Times,* in its business section, publishes the biography of a contemporary business personality. These are executives, usually, of large or sizeable corporations—men who have worked their way up from the bottom. This is not to say that they are exactly like the adventurer entrepreneurs of fifty years or so ago. On the contrary, they are usually better educated, have been trained in their company, and have acceded to executive control through the legitimate channels provided for selecting that leadership.

Others, publicly outstanding or not, are also able to amass wealth or position. One intriguing and recent case, for example, was reported in the *New York Times* on May 18, 1958. A Mr. Matthew M. Fox, president and largest stockholder of C & C Television, was able to net "substantially more" than $20,000,000 in one deal with local television stations. This was accomplished through an arrangement of bartering movie films to television stations in exchange for spot time. The film had been run and re-run so often by so many stations that it had little rental value left. What Mr. Fox arranged to do, then, was to allow the local stations to run the film at no cost in exchange for a number of spot time places—those twenty to sixty second intervals during and between programs. This was an excellent arrangement for the local stations because they had large blocks of unused time but relatively little cash to buy anything to fill them. Mr. Fox, by accumulating a number of such spot time openings with a number of television stations to give him national coverage, was able to make a package that was valuable to advertisers. The package was then sold to a company who bought the facilities for nationwide and repeated television time to advertise their product. C & C, Mr. Fox's company, sold this package to the International Latex Corporation for an absolute amount and a share of Latex' gross receipts for five years; the sale netted Mr. Fox the twenty millions mentioned before. This same C & C Corporation, it was noted in the report, had also bought control of Hazel Bishop, Inc. Future plans involve accumulating additional packages to be sold for shares of stock rather than for cash.

This is an individual success story that has undoubtedly been duplicated by others, less publicized. The major purpose of the present analysis, however, is not to list such success stories, which could never establish much more than a series of interesting sketches, but to determine the frequency of these successes and what they may have been due to.

Money, in what appears to be infinite amounts, is one sign of membership in the economic elite that most would accept readily. Not that the very wealthy are always part of an integrated elite circle, as noticed in the case of J. Paul Getty, whom *Fortune* estimated was worth between $700 million and $1 billion, and who is currently an expatriate living in Paris.[58] Nevertheless, in most instances, great wealth is the one important key to membership.

There have been wealthy men, relatively speaking, in almost every period of American history, whether such wealth was measured by land, money, or corporate ownership. The immediate question that is of concern here, however, is the general biographies of these men of wealth. Are the rich today the descendants of the rich of yesterday, or are there enough new names among the current occupants of this rare monetary stratosphere to indicate that enough new wealth is being made by enough people to mean that channels for such mobility are still relatively open?

Mills, in his study of the very rich, whom he defined as those having ever possessed $30 million or more, concluded that there was little chance to rise into the monied circles. "In none of the latest three generations has a majority of the very rich been composed of men who have risen," he has stated at one point.[59] "Wealth not only tends to perpetuate itself, but . . . tends also to monopolize new opportunities for getting 'great wealth.' Seven out of ten of the very rich among us today were born into distinctly upper-class homes, two out of ten on the level of middle-class comfort, and only one in lower-class milieu."[60] Furthermore, these proportions, Mills argued, represented a trend toward greater control by the upper class, compared with 1900 and 1925, his points of reference. In 1900, 39 per cent of the very rich came from lower-class origins, and in 1925 the proportion had decreased to 12 per cent. The upper class, on the other hand, had raised its proportion of members among the very rich from 56 per cent in 1925 to 68 per cent in 1950.[61] Or finally, "Very few of those who have risen to great wealth have spent the major portion of their working lives steadily advancing from one position to another within and between the corporate hierarchies. Such a long crawl was made by only 6 per cent of the very rich in 1900, and 14 per cent in 1950."[62] These selected sentences convey Mills's conclusions: the very rich, almost predominately, are born, not made; the channels for entry into that group are closing or, what is almost the same thing, are under the monopoly of those who already have great wealth and who thereby control the means for making more money.

Mills's conclusions are based upon extensive data ingeniously collected, about a subject where available information is scarce and often incomplete. From histories, from published tax lists, from a congressional committee's publication, and from government bureaus and agencies, Mills collected what was probably the most detailed list of those whom he defined as the very rich.

Yet, there is probably a disinclination by many to accept Mills's conclusions entirely because the belief in the idea of great wealth suddenly and dramatically made is not easily counteracted. The overnight multi-millionaire is still something of a culture hero because he is cast in gigantic proportions and because he personifies so typically the money value in American society. Even more than that, the man who becomes suddenly rich is often looked upon as someone who has managed to beat the system against tremendous odds, like a poor man winning the Irish Sweepstakes, only more so.

However, Mills's conclusions seem clear and valid, not alone on the basis of his immediate data, but additionally and in a sense more importantly, because there is a solid economic logic behind the conclusions. The only lottery-like way by which the individual today enters into the ranks of the very wealthy is by an oil discovery, and even in this case the probabilities of success are small.

In its study of the fifty-million dollar men, *Fortune*[63] identified 155 fifty-millionaires in 1954, and suggested that perhaps another hundred existed whom they did not identify. Their information, like that of Mills, indicated that the majority of the presently very rich came by their wealth through inheritance; some 55 per cent according to *Fortune's* listing. The remainder came up through their own efforts, principally through oil, and in lesser proportions through real estate, investment firms, and automobile manufacture. The fact that some 45 per cent made their way into the $50 million bracket might lead to a conclusion that the chances are really quite good for duplicating those feats. However, some 20 per cent of that group made it via the oil or auto route, a path which is no longer as open nor as likely today as it was when those men were beginning.

But for those who still insist upon the real possibilities for moving into this money elite, the lessening chances of success only mean greater difficulty but not necessarily an inevitable failure. Their point of view is aided somewhat by *Fortune's* findings that 201 individuals had incomes of a million dollars or more in 1954, a rise of 39 per cent over the preceding year. However, as *Fortune* found, there was a great deal of fluctuation around the million dollar level, dropping from a high of 219 such persons in 1950, to 145 in 1953, and then the rise to the 1954 level. Of those who were questioned in the survey, furthermore, 15 per cent thought it was impossible to start from nothing and build up to fifty million dollars today; another 40 per cent considered it improbable; and the remaining 45 per cent believed it still could be done. The path looks different, of course, when viewed from above rather than from below, but the fact that 45 per cent have made the grade in their own lifetimes, tends to lend further support to that possibility.

The evidence at hand suggests that access into the money elite is still not entirely closed. To be sure, the most frequent route is through the inheritance of wealth, but it is not the only one. Furthermore, there seems to be evidence that such success is not accomplished by the slow accumulation of wealth, but rather by a dramatic leap in economic fortunes or not at all. The Texas oil millionaires are the most frequent success men today, and they exemplify the point. Shrewdness in investments, lucky breaks, mergers, and a careful multiplication of available opportunities can contribute to raising the probabilities of success, but there are clearly no guarantees in this endeavor and all of the relevant elements must come out just right at the right time. Andrew Carnegie's advice of saving half of everything you earn may make you richer than you would otherwise be and may make you old before your time, but it is not the road to elite membership, if it ever was. Finally, the weight of the evidence is on Mills's side; in an advanced economy such as ours, the number of unexplored and untapped routes to riches is dismally small and constantly narrowing. There may be, and undoubtedly are, still new sources of wealth, such as in natural resources, which have not yet been discovered, but the chances for the newcomer finding them are small. Where the development of wealth depends more and more upon heavy initial capital investments, upon a heavily endowed and supported technical research staff, and upon access to almost unlimited amounts of credit, the probabilities for success for the person who has none of these to begin with are small, if not imperceptible.

The American Dream of Great Wealth, however, will probably not die and will be perpetually rejuvenated as, in every period, the new culture hero of success emerges and his story is told.

Elite Mobility: The American Business Elite

THE concern with social mobility and the comparative chances for successful mobility over a period of time have almost inevitably led to the study of the business elite: to those who are at the top of the business hierarchy. The advantages in specifying this group for study are evident enough. This elite can be defined with somewhat more precision than almost any other, because the variables used to measure elite status can be specified. There is enough continuous information about this group so that comparisons can be made over a period of time. Finally, the ease or difficulty of mobility into that business elite can be used as an index for the general condition of mobility even in the lower strata, as was noted earlier. If entry into the business elite becomes impossible, then the repercussions are likely to be felt throughout the social structure. As long as such entry remains relatively as open as the values of equality, hard work, and just rewards say, then that feature of social stress is not present.

A number of studies of the business elite in America are available, comprising one of the more articulated areas of knowledge in the study of social stratification.[64] In each, the central aim was very much the same: to compare the origins of the business elite in two or more time periods in order to detect changes in the amount of social mobility into the group. Even though the studies differed in the way the elite was defined and in the methods used to measure it, the common primary aim gave them an amazingly high degree of comparability.

Although the aim remained common to all these studies, the informing purpose of some of the writers did differ at times. The result was that the data each presented was often organized to express the ideology of its author. Taussig and Joselyn, for example, who undertook one of the earliest studies of the business elite, concluded in part that heredity played an important role in elite selection; elite status was, among other things, a mark of superior abilities that were transmitted from one generation to the next. Warner and Abegglen, as another example, seemed determined from the outset to prove that not only was there as much elite mobility today as there once was, but that there was perhaps even more today. Mills, on the other hand, seemed convinced from the first that there was less mobility today than before and he took this as another sign of the social rigidity into which the American class system had moved. Miller, who seemed to suspect Taussig and Joselyn's interpretations from the first, apparently undertook his study of the business elite and stimulated similar studies to find a basis for his suspicions.

These differences in orientations, which are sometimes unfairly labeled as "biases," are not necessarily undesirable, nor do they necessarily vitiate the research. As has been noted repeatedly through this book, the study of social stratification is involved with ideologies, prejudices, and for some, patriotism. In the case of these studies of the business elite, all that needs to be demanded is that the data be presented as fully as possible. The author is entitled to his conclusions and interpretations, for without a motivating purpose he would very likely not have bothered in the first place.

As Bendix and Howton have pointed out,[65] the several studies of the business elite can be classified into three general types, depending upon the definition and method of selection of the elite. In the first type, exemplified by the 1928 study by Taussig and Joselyn and the 1952 study by Warner and Abegglen, a sample of the elite at the time of study was selected, however the elite was defined. Taussig and Joselyn selected their samples from *Poor's Register of Directors,* which included directors of companies on the stock exchange doing at least $500,000 worth of business. Warner and Abegglen selected their group from among the chief executives in the largest firms in each type of industry and business. In addition to describing the characteristics of the current elite, both studies compared those characteristics with the fathers of the elite.

The second type of study, exemplified by Newcomer and Keller, sampled the elite by several independent samples drawn from selected time periods. Newcomer, for example, selected the executives of the largest corporations in railroads, public utilities, and industry, as listed in *Moody's Manuals of Investments,* for the periods 1900, 1925, and 1950. The advantage of this method, as Bendix and Howton have noted, was that the elite was independently determined in each of the time periods in contrast with the first type of procedure, in which only *one* elite was sampled and analyzed.

The third type of study, exemplified by Mills and by the Bendix and Howton research, derived its sample of the elite from biographical dictionaries, which included biographies of businessmen. In the latter study, for example, the sample consisted of every ninth businessman born between 1771 and 1920 whose biography appeared in the *National Cyclopedia of American Biography.* Other sources were also used to fill out the sample for certain years where the primary source did not produce enough names.

The studies reporting upon the character of the elite, then, depended upon a variety of sources and a variety of research procedures. They presented a rather mottled and patchy picture of the criteria for elite membership. This might perhaps have been a serious shortcoming if one were only interested in defining the elite by a single standard, with the same kind of rigor as, say, an aristocracy or a peerage might be defined. However, these studies served another purpose quite adequately: they provided the data for a comparison of elite mobility over a period of time, and it is to this question that the present section is directed.

Table 17, taken from Bendix and Howton, very clearly and cogently summarizes the information from several studies bearing directly upon the question. Although the information in that table can be read in several different ways, one of the clearest ways to interpret it is to consider the changes in percentages down any one column, cutting through all studies. Hence, Mills's data show that the percentage of the elite coming from upper class parents has increased from 1805 to 1865; where only 26 per cent of those in the elite of 1805 came from the upper class, this percentage had increased to 41 per cent by 1865. At the other extreme, Newcomer shows that the percentage coming from the poor, or lower class, has remained remarkably stable from 1849 to 1898. Although any summary table of this kind must perforce omit some information and reclassify other information from the original study, it must be said that the information presented in Table 17 excellently presents the main conclusions and the main dimensions of the several studies.

Table 17 is noteworthy, too, for the contradictory conclusions it documents. Bendix and Howton made note of that discrepancy. "Four of the studies [referring to Table 17] indicate that the proportion of business leaders who have come from families of businessmen, of businessmen and gentry farmers, or from families classified as 'wealthy' and 'middle class' has remained remarkably *stable* over time. . . . This conclusion is at variance with the one reached in Mills's study, whose major finding is the notable *instability*

Table 17—Percentage of American Business Leaders Born in Specified Eras, by Selected Occupations of Fathers, in Five Studies*

STUDY AND ESTIMATED MEDIAN YEAR OF BIRTH	FATHER'S OCCUPATION OR CLASS				NUMBER OF SUBJECTS
	Businessmen	*Wage Earners and Office Workers*			
Keller:					
1820	47	8			254
1855	50	4			168
1900	57	12			348
	Businessmen	*Gentry Farmers*	*Middle Class*	*Farmers and Manual Workers*	
Bendix-Howton:					
1785	40	25	23	12	125
1815	52	11	25	13	89
1845	66	3	19	11	360
1875	70	3	19	8	380
1905	69	5	20	7	143
	Wealthy	*Medium*	*Poor*		
Newcomer:					
1849	46	42	12		118†
1873	36	48	16		253
1898	36	52	12		342
	Upper	*Upper-Middle*	*Lower-Middle*	*Lower*	
Mills:					
1805	26	37	29	8	—‡
1835	20	37	30	13	
1865	41	29	18	11	
	Businessmen (large)	*Businessmen (medium)*	*Skilled and Unskilled Laborers*		
Warner and Taussig:					
1875	31	26	11		—§
1900	23	29	15		

* Adapted from R. Bendix and F. W. Howton, "Social Mobility and the American Business Elite—II," *British Journal of Sociology,* 9: 1-14, March, 1958, p. 6.

† The number of subjects for this table is taken from the corresponding data in Newcomer's earlier publication, *The Chief Executive in Large Business Corporations,* p. 26.

‡ No totals are given, but Mills notes that they comprise 78.8% of the 'total elite' or 1,155 out of 1,464 subjects.

§ No totals are given. The total number of cases available for comparisons between the Taussig and the Warner study is given as 7,371.

of the recruitment pattern of the American business elite during the nineteenth century."[66]

This then is one conclusion that does appear to be substantiated: except for Mills and Warner, all other studies substantiate the finding that there has been relatively little change over an extended period of time in the mobility patterns into the business elite. It is hard to establish the extent of mobility with any greater precision since the several studies differ in their definitions, procedures, and therefore their conclusions. Some seem to imply by their figures that there has been little change. Warner and Abegglen, on the other hand, are ready to conclude that, "Projecting the data to the turn of the century and including in it men born before the Civil War whose careers encompass our society's period of greatest commercial expansion, we find evidence of a long-term, continuing trend to a greater degree of vertical occupational mobility in American business."[67]

Stated in another manner, Mills alone has argued that there has been increasing rigidity in the structure of the elite because in each period *greater* proportions of the elite themselves come from elite backgrounds. Warner and Abegglen, in their conclusions summarized in the quotation above, have argued that there has been increasing fluidity to be found in elite mobility as seen by the *lessening* proportions of those coming from elite backgrounds. Most of the other studies, with slight variations, appear to conclude that the proportions drawn into the business elite from different class levels has remained relatively *stable* over the time period covered by their investigation.

The answer to the question of the present state of elite mobility compared with the past, however, lies deeper; it is necessary to get beneath the comparative percentages and question the nature of the social structure that produces and supports the elite. It is at this level that the stability or instability, fluidity or rigidity, of elite mobility should more properly be assessed.

One clear fact is that the large majority of elite members

come from elite backgrounds—from the wealthy, or from the upper-middle class, or from businessmen fathers. Newcomer, who presented an excellent summary of the "trends in the qualifications" for membership in the business elite,[68] has stated the point succinctly: "While wealth and family position have never been listed among the qualifications for top office, all the evidence points to the fact that the sons of wealthy families have a better chance of reaching the top executive position than those from poor or middle-income families."[69]

The implication of this conclusion for the question at hand would seem to be that the measure of social mobility is thereby concerned with a relatively small proportion of the population. Since fewer than 30 per cent, and sometimes as few as 4 per cent, of those in the elite come from obviously non-elite backgrounds, according to the figures in Table 17, generalizations about the relative increase or decrease in mobility depend upon a relatively few cases. From a methodological point of view, if from no other, it could be argued that the proportions are at once too small and too unstable to permit any firm interpretation.

There is even more involved, however. Most of the studies mentioned here, in one way or another, have recognized that the composition of the elite has changed markedly since the turn of the century, and almost radically if one uses an earlier time as a point of reference.[70] The composition has changed because the structure of corporate enterprise has changed from a relatively small undertaking by a single entrepreneur or a single family to a massive bureaucratic enterprise governed by several directors. "The families of the American business elite," Bendix and Howton noted,[71] "have persisted in preserving for, and in passing on to, their descendants as much of their economic success and their social status as they were able to do. But while this effort has persisted successfully, it has not been able to withstand the inroads of bureaucratization upon family influence."

Some families, of course, have successfully maintained controlling interests in their corporations and have even expanded their control to include other corporations. However, to the extent that stockholders, boards of directors, and the various regulatory governmental agencies have limited that control, individuals other than those from elite backgrounds have been able to enter the business elite. To whatever extent "business talent" has become a criterion for movement into the business elite, then to that same extent an hereditary elite has been prevented from forming. "Business talent" becomes defined as having the proper education, the proper contacts, and most importantly, sufficient business experience and expertness. Individuals coming from classes below that of the elite may possess these talents even more adequately than do the sons of the elite, and in this way they can qualify for a corporation post. This emphasis on business talent, of course, does not disqualify the heirs of the elite. They, too, have the education, contacts, and experience to make them acceptable for leadership posts in the corporation. Yet, what the changing figures in Table 17 have shown is that there is some chance for those beginning from class origins further down the scale also to qualify. The more such rational criteria are relied upon, such as those included in the definition of "business talent," the greater is the possibility for social movement into the elite from classes outside of it. However, the more the emphasis moves to such irrational criteria as family background and an Ivy League education, the smaller do those possibilities become and the greater the rigidity of the class structure.

A final observation should be made about the change in structure over the last fifty years or so which greatly affects the amount of social mobility into the business elite. The entry channels and the patterns of entry into the elite have changed. The chances have greatly decreased of someone from lower class origins starting his own enterprise. As Newcomer noted, "it takes more capital even for small enterprises, and also it is increasingly difficult for a small concern to compete with the giants already in the field."[72] The effect of this economic reality is to make the major means of entry into the business elite one that passes through the posts of a large corporation. This can be taken to mean, as Newcomer has suggested, that social mobility may have increased to the extent that entry into the elite has been shifted to include the large corporation as an elite channel, where somewhat more accessibility may be possible.

Family assistance, which could be of enormous help to the elite heirs, has decreased to a marked degree according to Newcomer's findings, but has remained somewhat stable according to Bendix and Howton,[73] although each referred to different time periods.

Table 18—Family Assistance in Business Career*

Type of Assistance	*1900*	*1925*	*1950*
First job	25.6%	16.3%	11.5%
Corporation office	8.7	19.0	14.2
Financial aid	8.4	6.5	1.9
No direct aid	57.3	58.2	72.4
Totals	100.0	100.0	100.0

* Taken from Newcomer, *The Big Business Executive*, p. 84.

From 1925 to the present, Newcomer found that each of the several types of family assistance has decreased. "For all groups of executives, family assistance increasingly takes the form of providing a college education, and perhaps, professional training at the graduate level, rather than capital or a place in the family business or the business of some friend."[74] Nevertheless, even for 1950 she found that 33 per cent of the executives in industrial corporations received direct aid from their families in getting their first job; that almost 30 per cent of these executives in corporations with assets under $100,000,000 and 18 per cent of those in corporations with assets over $500,000,000 received such aid.

From 1771 to 1920, Bendix and Howton found that the percentage of elite members receiving career assistance had remained relatively stable, varying between 55 per cent to 63 per cent. These proportions, nonetheless, like Newcomer's data are significantly large. Family assistance, therefore, makes some difference, even though it may be decreasing in relative importance. For a definitive answer, one would like to know more; for example, to what extent do the expectations for succession held by the elite family make a difference in the outlook, orientations, and the confidence of the heir that he will succeed, in one who views his succession into the elite as normal and inevitable? In contrast, the would-be aspirant to elite status from lower class origins needs an enormous self-confidence, bordering on an almost schizophrenic view of the world, to make an infinitely tougher climb than that which the heir-apparent has to travel.

In summary, then, the amount of elite mobility does not seem to have changed greatly over several decades, although the composition and the means of entry into that group have. The chances are there to make the climb from rags to riches, but they are not, nor have they been in the past fifty years or so, very great for those who must start from rags. It is now, and has been for some time, much the easier way just to inherit the riches. These conclusions, generally, check with those that have been reached about other aspects of social mobility: rigidity has not become characteristic of the American class structure, at least according to all available indices.

Whether or not this conclusion should be qualified by the phrase, "not yet," depends upon two factors: (1) one's personal ideology about class and the class system; and (2) the way one reads the current changes and developments in the current economic structure. For, it might be argued, the American economy has just recently begun to move into a relatively new phase of economic change that will greatly alter its structure and with it the character of social mobility. Just as the era of the entrepreneur has passed along with the earlier phase of the American economic structure, so, too, the executive and the type of structure he personifies may be coming more and more into focus and dominance, or perhaps already giving way to an entirely new type.

Consequences of Mobility: Social Psychological Aspects

THE opportunities and channels for social mobility that a society can provide is one consideration, one that has been the subject until now. Whether or not individuals are motivated to try to use those channels and to try to realize the opportunities is another consideration. Stated in other words, the difference is between whether individuals *can* move from one class to another, and whether they *want* to. The first is a statement about social structure, about the social setting in which mobility occurs. The second is a statement about the social psychological dimensions of mobility, about the motivations or aspirations for mobility, the intensity behind them, and the psychological feed-back upon the individual from his success or failure with mobility.

Obviously, the two facets are in reality interrelated in much the same way as the thought and deed are but different parts of a single sequence. Consider for a moment two admittedly extreme examples to point up this interrelatedness. No matter what the opportunities for social mobility are—whether many or few—they would be of little meaning unless translated into behavior by the actions of individuals to realize such opportunities. From the opposite side, no matter how intensely individuals may want to take advantage of such opportunities to change their class position, their intentions would have little significance unless the social structure provided the means for translating motivation into behavior.

The interrelationship between the structural and social psychological facets of social mobility also means that there is a continuous series of actions and reactions of one upon the other. For example, the individual who aspires to, and works for, success, but who fails in the attempt, may possibly become a threat to the society. The demagogue, in our own time, has been able to convert social discontent so created into political energy. Frustrations arising from the failure to succeed, in a setting that dwells upon success as the measure of a man, can stimulate a varied and complex set of reactions, some of which are considered later in this chapter.

There are two major considerations that need to be discussed here: (1) the values that are held concerning mobility; and (2) the consequences for human behavior of success or failure with mobility. The first is concerned with such matters as the way different classes evaluate the importance of mobility, differences in mobility aspirations, and the manner in which social reality can affect the estimate of mobility. The second category includes the after-effects of mobility striving; the effects of success or failure upon personality.

Mobility Values

THERE is the tendency, shared by professional social scientists and others, to conceive of the American value system as almost one continuous emphasis upon "success" in all of its variations. It has religious overtones derived from the Protestant ethic and the frustrating curiosity to find out if one was "chosen" or "damned." It has economic overtones of many sorts, but principally tied up with the continuous striving and searching of the entrepreneur. "Success" is part of the product sold through the mass media, just as it is part of the indoctrination conveyed through the educational system. It is a major line of the stereotype of American national character, drawn not only by others who observe them but by Americans as they observe themselves.

The question is not so much whether this conception is valid, whether the image is true or false, since that would be impossible to answer, but instead, if it is all true or not. As has been stated earlier in this book, middle class ideologies and middle class values have informed a good deal of the writing about class and related matters. for the very simple reason that most of those doing the writing are themselves middle class.

Not everyone aspires to be "successful"; nor are these aspirations, when they are held, of equal intensity or equal commitment. Certainly, "success" is differently defined, differently worshipped, and differently handled. Those at the top of the social hierarchy, by any definition, really have nowhere further to strive to go. Some, not at the top, nevertheless are as "high" as they want to go anyway, if they think about it at all. They would answer very much like the child in Colvin Hollow in the Blue Ridge Mountains of Virginia who when asked, "What do you want to be when you grow up?", answered, "I wants to be what I am."[75] Some persons hold very limited aspirations, which can be attained quickly and easily, and once they attain their goal they are content. At the other extreme, of course, are those individuals who remain perpetually dissatisfied with their accomplishments, whatever they are. Yet, such is the character of "success" that it is only finally defined and measured by the individual's own judgment of himself, of his attainments, of his aspirations and by the standard of reference he chooses to measure himself.

"Mobility values" include several distinct dimensions of beliefs and attitudes that individuals can hold. It is the sum of these, then, that can be taken as characterizing the individual's beliefs or values about mobility.

One dimension is that of "aspirations"; *i.e.*, for what goals does an individual strive, and how strongly does he strive? These questions are of a subtle psychological character. It can almost go without saying that the measurement of the psychological quantities implied by the question is difficult as well as questionable.[76] Yet, that conclusion brings us immediately to a dead-end, and misleads us by overlooking some of the information that is known and that provides some strong hunches about the character of aspirations and the individuals who hold them.

There are several independent studies, of widely different samples of individuals, that all come to a reasonably common conclusion about aspirations: the striving for "success" is strongest among those in the middle and upper class, and is lowest among those in the lower class. To be sure, the conclusion must be reached by inferences from the answers given to rather concrete questions, but the path is not a suspiciously devious one. Hyman,[77] for example, analyzed the results of several public opinion polls containing questions bearing upon aspirations. Lower class persons, and their children, anticipated relatively lower incomes for themselves than did those from the middle class. An even more startling difference was found in the answers to the question by a national sample of high school students surveyed by Roper in 1942.[78] When asked to express their preference for one of these kinds of jobs: (1) a secure job but with a low income, (2) a good paying job but with a fifty-fifty risk of losing it, and (3) a job with very high income but with great risk, the results indicated that a far greater percentage of students with executive and professional parents were willing to take the high risk job.

Class Position	*Per Cent Preferring High Income, High Risk Job*
Poor	14%
Prosperous, upper middle	29
From laboring parents	16
From executive and professional parents	31

A similar study was conducted with high school students in New Haven.[79] The students were tested for their "achievement motivation," measured by questions of a projective type. The findings showed that the higher the class of the individual, the higher was his "achievement motivation." Those in the lower class, almost predominantly, showed much lower scores according to this index.

In two studies of automobile workers, one by Chinoy[80] and the other by Guest,[81] an impression emerged that was similar to those just stated. Auto workers apparently kept their aspirations low, and kept themselves in check, so to speak, even though they may have verbalized much higher ambitions.

Guest concluded his study with the statement, "The present imperatives of security and a reasonably steady income outweigh the attractions of the job world outside."[82] And Chinoy noted too that "most workers . . . frequently try to rationalize their status as factory employees and to justify their small ambitions."[83] These are statements of limited ambitions in the lower classes.

The question that intrudes itself once this literature is read, is, "Why?" Why, in other words, is there the class difference? There are several reasons that can be given.

The first, and most obvious reason for lower aspirations among the lower and working classes is that individuals in those classes are simply being realistic. While those in the middle and upper classes may have a reasonably good chance of realizing their aspirations, within bounds, those in the lower class do not. Middle and upper class persons can afford the luxury, so to speak, of holding higher levels of aspiration for success because there is a reasonable chance that they will be able to attain them, starting from a "better" class position. Those further down the class scale, on the contrary, encounter a different social and economic reality and it is but reasonable for them to keep from over-aspiring themselves into disappointment and frustration. Hyman, for example, reported these findings from a national opinion poll by Roper in 1937; they are shown here in Table 19.[84]

Yet, the push toward success many feel is a dominating one, carried by the value system, and it may not leave the individual alone. He cannot always be content with recognizing reality and settling down to it. Some people, it is true, remain unaffected by the success striving indoctrination that the schools, the mass media, and the American legend try to instill. For others, on the contrary, there is the psychological need to achieve a balance between what they feel they have been taught to pursue and what they realistically believe they can successfully pursue.

One way to resolve the dilemma is to transfer aspirations for success onto one's children, as both Guest and Chinoy found was the case among the automobile workers.[85] Though the parents have given up, they try to assuage themselves by projecting their hopes and ambitions onto their children. The child becomes the personification and the agent of hope and realization for the things the parents did not have or could not achieve.

Another alternative is to scale down one's expectations to the point where they can be realized. This, as a matter of fact, has become a major unanticipated function of the large bureaucratic organization. The organization provides the individual with a reasonable degree of job security at the same time that it formalizes, concretizes, and minimizes the paths of advancement. The steps for advancement in the bureaucratic organization become for most people small changes, often involving a change of title or a slight change in symbols (a name on the door, a rug on the floor) in lieu of a significant salary increase or an increase in authority and responsibility. Furthermore, the way to achieve even these relatively small advancements is known to all—by seniority, by experience, by examination, or by a series of "excellent" ratings by one's immediate superior. The effect is to take the

Table 19—Beliefs in Economic Opportunity Among the Different Classes*

	AMONG EMPLOYEES WHO ARE:	
	Professional or Executives	Factory Workers
Per cent believing that years ahead hold good chance for advancement over present position	63	48
Per cent believing that following factor is important consideration in job advancement:		
quality of work	64	43
energy and willingness	56	42
getting along well with boss	12	19
friend or relative of boss	3	8
being a politician	6	4
Per cent believing that harder work would net them personally a promotion	•58	40

* Reported in Hyman, "The Value Systems of Different Classes," in *Class, Status and Power*, p. 437.

strain off of the individual. He can now strive in small doses. He can content himself that he is making some headway in this world, and through it all be secure in his job.

A realistic appraisal of one's opportunities and possibilities, however, is but one answer to the question of why class differences exist in aspirations. Although it is probably the best explanation, there are other reasons. A second, if related, explanation is that individuals are socialized into different sets of values. Not everyone, in other words, matures in the same type of environment and in the same atmosphere of stress upon success.

Hyman has reported the results of an NORC survey, in which it was found that not only the class of the individual but also the class of his parents was important in explaining his aspirations.[86] More specifically, Hyman showed that the judgments an individual made about the importance of a college education, about professional work as contrasted with skilled manual work, and his preference for a secure job over one that was congenial, were determined not only by his own class position but by that of his father as well. The conclusion makes sense. The mobility values that the parent transmits consciously or unconsciously to the child are those that the child takes over in all likelihood, even more than those transmitted by the school or by other socializing agencies. Furthermore, the atmospheres for indoctrinating such values differ widely between families from different classes. What the NORC data reflected were the differences in socialization experiences with the values of success and striving for success.

The effect of the family and its value orientation can also be seen in a concrete way, as in the emphasis upon the importance of a college education. Since education is one of the minimal requirements for rising in the class system, it should be clear that the stress put upon it by the family can make a great deal of difference not only for the chances but also for the expectations the child holds for his own success. There is clear evidence of class differences in the attitudes held toward a college education. Kahl, for example, reported some of the findings of a Harvard study of almost four thousand boys. The results clearly and consistently indicated that the higher the class of the boy's father, the greater was the expectation that he would go to college.[87] Where 80 per cent of those from "major white collar" families expected to go to college, only 12 per cent of those whose fathers were in laboring and service occupations expected to go. This difference, of course, can be interpreted as part of the reality orientation already noted above; but more than that, it can set the stage for the career and the expectations of the child.

Further support for these findings also comes from a national study reported by Hyman[88] in which the *preference,* in contrast to the expectation alone, for college was higher among those in the upper classes as compared with those in the lower classes. Hence, 91 per cent of those who were classified as "prosperous" *preferred* that their child go to college, while only 68 per cent of those classified as "poor" held the same preference.

On more intensive psychological grounds, too, there is some evidence to suggest that the family plays a pivotal role in setting aspirational levels. Douvan and Adelson, for example, in a study of a national sample of adolescent boys, found that the family provided a wide number of psychological cues and supports for individuals in regard to their aspirational levels.[89] Parents served as models to their children; they could transmit values of autonomy, could teach the child to depend upon himself and his own abilities; they could show their own ambivalence toward the value of achievement; they could be punishing or permissive toward the child. All of these elements, which are present to some degree during the socialization period, do much toward establishing the psychological dynamics, which in turn set the aspirations and ambition levels of the adult.

A final explanation as to why there are class variations in aspiration levels seemingly contradicts some of the preceding discussion. The seeming contradiction is this: individuals also hold *unreal* conceptions about their chances for success. The necessity for including this kind of explanation is that not all persons exhibit the same level of aspirations according to their class position. As even some of the preceding data have shown here, not all of those in the lower class were convinced that they could *not* succeed or could only achieve limited success. Similarly, not all of those in the middle or upper classes held levels of aspiration or expectations that were as high as those for others in the same class position.

The fantasy, like the realistic assessment, has its roots in the psychological dynamics of individual personalities and in their reactions to the world in which they live. Those who are realistic tend to scale down their expectations and to modify their ambitions so as to remain more in line with what are their reasonable chances for success. Those who prefer to daydream, to build fantasies about the future, on the other hand, use this means as a way of bridging the gap between what they feel they should do and what they believe they can do. A middle class person, for example, may keep his aspirations in check not because he realistically could not do better, but as a form of insurance against possible failure. He may not aspire high because the price of failure is therefore less severe. This reasoning is also fantasy of a sort.

Those in the lower class who still retain a belief and a faith in their own success possibilities in the face of all realistic estimates to the contrary, exhibit another type of fantasy. These were found among the automobile workers who, after years on the assembly line, still held on to the hope that someday they would be able to leave the factory and start their own business. In his study of Negro workers in two Chicago factories, Rose found that the lower the position of the worker, the more likely he was to believe that he would be out and owning his own business in ten years.[90] Where only 8 per cent of those workers whom Rose classified as "lower-middle" believed that would be their situation in ten years, 34 per cent of those classified as "lower-lower" shared the same expectations. Not only that, even their expectations as to advancement in the industry differed in the same way; 27 per cent of those in the lower-middle ranks thought that their "chances appeared to be good" for advancement, while 73 per cent of those in the lower-lower class thought so.

These are fantasies precisely because the chances of their realization are small. The individual usually had little conception of how to go about achieving such goals, but he held to them nonetheless because they provided one means of escape from a too critical self-judgment. If one is a "failure" in a society where "success" is a dominant value, then one's self-judgment tends to take on the coloration of values held by the society at large, or at any rate, believed to be held by the majority. This is psychologically a dangerous judgment to internalize. The individual can escape by several routes: by discrediting the importance of the "success" value, by emphasizing other qualities he possesses that are also valued, and by holding fantasies and daydreams by which he can achieve success in his own imagination without ever subjecting them to the test of reality.

This line of discussion brings us to another subject, closely related to what has been considered here: the consequences for the individual of his success or failure.

Consequences of Success or Failure

"FAILURE" in connection with social mobility may be of two types, although it is presumed here that the consequences produced by each are the same. There is the "failure" of not trying, for either realistic or fantastic reasons. There is also the "failure" of trying and not succeeding. In the first instance, as has been suggested above, the judgment of failure is made by the individual because he believes that he has not attained to the position or realized the potentialities which society has taught him to anticipate. In the second case, there are those who have tried for some success goal and have failed to attain it. There are also included here those who can never achieve their own definitions of success; they have internalized the social model of success to such a degree that their dissatisfaction is perpetual, their attainment always a limited one, and the plateau of success upon which they would rest, only a chimerical vision that disappears as they approach.

That such "failures" should exhibit signs of mental illness is not surprising, considering the amount of psychic energy and the extent of personality commitment that is involved in the struggle for success and its outcome. In the New Haven study by Hollingshead and Redlich, one of the most complete psychiatric inventories of a community that is available, the signs of "failure" were evident.[91] The "climbers," who "appear to move more or less successfully," exhibited reactions of "severe anxiety, depression, sometimes . . . antisocial acting out, and in some extreme cases . . . suicidal attempts which were related, in part, to blocked mobility." The "strainers," who were those who had not moved successfully but would have liked to, were defensive. They tended to be "ambitious dreamers" or "if they do not dream, they constantly plan and scheme, rush from one pursuit to another, or from one 'big deal' to the next, hoping to succeed sufficiently to climb upward in the social system, but always disappointed and frustrated, complaining and rationalizing about what they consider bad luck and failure."

The psychological consequences of failure, however, can be channelled away from the individual, projected outward psychologically so that the individual can avoid injury to his own self-conceptions and self-respect. The "fault" lies not within the control of the individual, but rather outside of him with the society or with some other group. Given certain types of personality, the individual might prefer this rationalization as a means of self-protection. The individual pours his frustration and his failure into an explanation that implicates others as the cause of it all; all of this pretense to avoid the harsher reality that would come by accepting the blame himself.

One relatively easy set of rationalizations that is available to the individual to account for his failure is in ethnic and minority group prejudices. The advantages of accepting such prejudices as one's own are clear: they keep the person free from blame, and what is equally important, they provide a ready-made set of explanations that have currency. The individual does not have to shop around for explanations; an institutionalized set of prejudices awaits his selection, which by accepting he can join with others. Two independent studies have given a good deal of empirical substantiation to the relationship between mobility and prejudice. Although the two studies differ somewhat in their conclusions about which group is the most prejudiced, they both substantially found that mobility experience can support prejudice. The earlier study, by Bettelheim and Janowitz,[92] of one hundred fifty Chicago veterans of World War II, found that the greatest prejudice toward Negroes and Jews was exhibited by those who had experienced sudden downward shifts in occupational status. The Negro and the Jew became the "causes" of failure in the individual's mind, and at the same time the focus of his hostility and animosity engendered by that failure.

In a study in Elmira, New York, in 1948, Greenblum and Pearlin[93] also found a relationship to exist between mobility and prejudice. However, the most prejudiced group they found consisted of those who had shown no social mobility, either up or down. This finding was contrary to the conclusions of Bettelheim and Janowitz who had found that the downwardly mobile were the most prejudiced. Much more study would be needed as well as the use of more intensive techniques for measuring prejudice in order to determine which of the two groups really tends to be the most prejudiced. However, the point that should not be overlooked is that both found a definite relationship between prejudice and mobility; that there were psychological consequences of mobility striving.

The general importance placed upon "success" and the indications of several studies as to some of the consequences that develop from failure are grounds for believing that there probably are many other possible reactions. Hostility engendered by failure need not only become translated into feelings of prejudice. Such feelings in turn could become structured into an entire political orientation by which one's politics and political views have been formed not by good and sound assessments but by the need to lay the blame on others. Incorporating such attitudes into a "political philosophy" has the advantage of further socializing the basic hostility of the individual by dressing it up into a coherent and formal thing seemingly far removed from the causes which gave it birth.

In a similar manner, major facets of the personality could become affected. Attitudes towards others, towards authority, towards democracy, towards children, or towards foreign countries could be determined and set by what at the root has been the failure to succeed or the fear of failure to try. This is not to say that the experience with success is at the root of all human behavior and all human ideas, but it does imply that such experiences can play a determining role. Attitudes, as social psychologists have long known, are not just a façade that is slapped on and maintained, but rather a deeply ingrained set of beliefs that the personality is forced to maintain for its own self-respect and well-being.

Success, like failure, can also take its toll. For successful social mobility necessarily entails a readjustment, often a major one, by the individual. He must reject the way of life of the group he has just left and assume the new way of life of the group he has just entered. It is a process of class "acculturation" as Blau has suggested in his analysis.[94] Depending upon how great the change required, the reorientation of the individual can be massive. Depending upon the recency of the change, the reorientation can involve a great deal of insecurity.

For successful mobility places the individual, for some period of time, in a marginal social position. The individual's former friends and associates may find him threatening; his success is a mark of their failure.[95] His newly-created friends and associates, produced by his successful move, may find him too "different," too "raw," and too recent to be accepted as a *bona fide* member. The individual thus finds himself suspended in a "success limbo," socially unattached for the moment to any group. The insecurity he feels in this situation can produce a prejudice and hostility similar in focus and in intensity to that of his counterpart, the "failure." For as long as that insecurity lasts, the reactions, in fact, may be the same as those exhibited by the failures.

Some of the consequences of success at the executive levels in the corporation are almost nakedly documented by Whyte in the study by *Fortune* in 1951.[96] Successful promotion up the ranks of the corporation means moving to a better home, joining the proper country club, trading in the car for a new one of the proper make and style, and enrolling children in new schools. The consequences of such successful promotion are directly felt in interpersonal relations. The friends one had before must be exchanged for a new set in keeping with one's newly-gained position. The old friends obviously were those at the same level and now, being a level or so below the successful one, no longer share a common basis for friendship, nor would they even feel comfortable with the personification of success were he to remain in their midst. Some corporations, Whyte found, suggested that under some circumstances the individual drop his wife in the same manner and for the same reasons that he must drop his former friends. The wife who cannot adjust to success, who cannot take over the corporation attitudes and guide her life by them as her husband does, could be a liability to the continued success of the husband. If she complained that she "liked" their former friends and did not want to drop them, then this attitude produced a source of conflict and dissatisfaction in the husband's life that impaired his efficiency and utility to the corporation. Not the individual alone, in other words, but his whole family must perforce become implicated in his success, just as they do in his failures.

Success, then, very much like failure, has its psychological costs depending upon the personality of the individual that must assimilate such changes. Nor need success produce at least a somewhat more comfortable material position, for as one moves upward in class position his standard of living usually must keep pace. The effect may be to place the individual in a worse financial position than he was in before the supposedly successful move took place. Yet, it seems unlikely that all individuals will forego success and be content with staying where they are as a means of avoiding the psychological, social and economic costs of success. In large measure, individuals will probably react as products of their training, their orientation, and the values that have been instilled in them by a variety of social agents. Unfortunately, however, in either the case of success or failure, many psychological pitfalls may await them that can be handled only by mature, well-adjusted personalities.

In a very suggestive, and at times brilliant article, Tumin has set down some of the consequences for society of this emphasis upon social mobility, upon seeking and achieving success.[97] One result he noted, is the "diffusion of insecurity," as more and more people become involved with trying to get ahead rather than developing any lasting and sure sense of the group and its needs. The traditional beliefs and standards of the society thereby become threatened as behavior is more and more oriented toward "status-acceptance and prestige-ranking."

Perhaps an even more important consequence of such mobility is the "denial of work." In other words, the very goals which American success values were supposed to stimulate in individuals have become transmogrified. "The emphasis has shifted from the importance of work and striving to the urgency of appearing to be successful. . . . the social productivity of one's occupation, the social value of products which one distributes, and the skill required to produce these items are [in some circles] ignored. Instead, almost exclusive preference is given to the open portrayal of *being* successful, as measured by the power and property which one openly consumes."[98]

Other effects that Tumin noted were almost equally damaging to the social structure. A "severe imbalance" of social institutions can ensue as a result of rapid mobility among large numbers of the population as religion, education, and the family become tied to the struggle for economic success. "Fragmentation of the social order" may also develop as more and more individuals become rivalrous with each other; competition does not always lead to the greatest good for the greatest number. Finally "rapid social mobility generates in the older portions of the population a cranky and bitter conservatism and worship of the past; and in the new mobile segments a vituperative contempt for traditions."[99]

The advantages of mobility, therefore, are not an unmixed social blessing, even if one is ready to accept the significant role which competition, and rivalry so induced, has played in American society. Perhaps we have reached a point of saturation in this area, just as limits have been imposed in the economic sphere upon unlimited and unfettered competition. In the latter case, it has been found that beyond a certain point in economic development, the axioms of the classical economists do not hold. So too, perhaps, in terms of human personalities and human happiness, we have reached the apogee of social gain by motivating individuals to strive for success. Beyond that point the toll in social conflicts, insecurities, and damage to personality is too great to justify the relatively smaller gains that accrue from the success of the few.

CHAPTER VII

Continuity and Change

IN HIS ESSAY ON THE SOCIOLOGY OF the intelligentsia, Mannheim[1] made a disturbing observation. He contended that Marx tailored a "conceptual apparatus" to fit the needs of one social stratum, creating thereby a "proletarian" or a "class" sociology. The effect of that orientation, Mannheim went on to argue, was to establish a theoretical framework so narrow that social phenomena were immediately polarized into the two alternatives of being either "class" or "non-class." Any phenomenon, any occurrence, that was non-class was summarily dismissed as socially and theoretically irrelevant. Mannheim went on to compare this kind of gross analysis with that of making a woman see herself only as a housewife or a harlot; the narrow alternatives made it impossible for her to "associate herself with any of the additional roles which the emancipation movement made possible."

The disturbing feature of Mannheim's observation was not the designation of Marx as an intellectual champion of the proletariat; that characterization was valid enough. Tawney, in *Religion and the Rise of Capitalism,* argued the same point with telling effect: as Calvin served as a spokesman for the rising middle class, so too Marx served as the intellectual spokesman for the proletariat. Rather, what was disturbing in Mannheim's remarks was the implication that a great deal was omitted by a theory and an orientation that followed only the two alternatives that Marx bequeathed—as much as would be lost by the view of woman as housewife or harlot.

There is no need to argue the validity of the point. It is fairly accurate. It has, in fact, been considered in detail in Chapter Two. Weber's theory of class, it was noted there, can be considered as a systematic attempt to escape the conceptual encirclement of Marxian theory by opening up categories other than "class" as Marx had defined it. Mannheim, too, sought to avoid the same kind of encirclement; his statement above is an example, and others are found throughout much of his writing.

Neither is there any special point in entering into a discussion of sociological theory and the logic of theoretical models. It is enough to point out that any theory must depend upon certain categories, whether they are "class" and "non-class" or something else. For in the very character of theory, *some* set of categories must be used. Furthermore, it follows that each set of categories shares the common disadvantages of putting all other possible categories into conceptual darkness where they are irrelevant or unimportant in terms of the particular categories the individual has decided to use as his vantage point. Marx's use of "class" is no more "unnatural" in this context than the theologian's use of "good" and "evil" or the logician's preference for "a" and "non-a." Each proves its utility by the purposes at hand, and each shares the common characteristic of making all else irrelevant.[2]

What Mannheim's observation is taken to suggest here is

the need for some balance in the analysis of class. Although Mannheim goes on to develop the point in his own way for the study of the intelligentsia, it is not too far amiss to use his observation as an exegetical point in a somewhat different context here.

The emphasis on balance means only that some attention must be paid to the socially unifying features of the class system. The major part of this book can be considered, from one point of view, as a detailed elaboration of the divisive features of class; from its initial effect of dividing society into separate, partly antagonistic, social worlds through to its final effect of engendering, nurturing, and sometimes magnifying social differences between those class strata. By far the greater interest in class has been in the latter contexts; the point of study has almost always been to find differences between classes and to elucidate upon the consequences those differences can have for society.

To play up only that dimension of conflict, important as it is, and to overlook how class can function to unify, is to see the class system in an unbalanced and incomplete manner. Given the fact that all human societies are stratified, it would be false to conclude that stratification can only function to divide a society, without at the same time having any unifying functions. The structural-functionalist view, although it does overstress the unity rather than the conflict of class, still has a point here. There must be some element of unity created by the class system and by class relationships, otherwise there could be no basis for explaining why it is present in so many different societies and why it exists for so long a time. Marx, it is true, stressed the conflict and inherent disunity created by the class system, but primarily because of his ideological commitment.

Interestingly enough, Marx also implied that there was a cohesive force exerted by class. "Class consciousness," for example, can be viewed as the progressive development of cohesiveness within a class. It was to be fashioned by the productive forces of society that finally created a common awareness and established a common identification among all those in the same class circumstances. The bourgeoisie, like the proletariat, reached a stage of class unity; class peers came to be recognized and the individual realized ultimately that his destiny was as one with the destinies of all others of his class. Even more importantly for Marx, of course, the triumph of the proletariat was the triumph of the ultimate in class unity. At that final stage, when the basic class antagonism had been laid bare, the unity of the proletariat became a social fact. From the divisiveness and conflict which class had created in society, there emerged the final unity of mankind.

That ideology, insightful as it was for developing a theory of class conflict, was not enough to serve also as a view of class cohesion. An explanation of cohesion is, instead, implied by functional theory. There is no intention here of following that theory completely, but as might be expected from the basic orientation of functionalism, social cohesion is emphasized where Marx did not see it so. A principal assumption in the following discussion is that the cohesive functions of a class system are to be found in what the functionalists have referred to as the "core value system": that package of social beliefs and values that each society considers to be its basic ethos, its unique rationale, and the primary basis behind its own organization. As the functionalists have indicated, the manner in which the class system is "explained"—its character, its goals and the social relationships it induces—stems directly from a society's "core value system."

These explanations, in effect, account for the existence of social divisions. To be sure, each society establishes its own particular "explanation" because its values are more or less distinctive. Just as the character of the class system is likely to vary from one society to another, so too, the character of the explanation and the values it depends upon are also likely to vary. Yet, the final purpose of all such explanations is the same: to create unity in the face of divisiveness; to institutionalize and to regularize social relationships which might otherwise be antagonistic.

One point in this needs to be kept clearly in mind. The

fact that classes are "explained" does not mean that the social conflict and disunity that they can create is necessarily dissipated. The functionalist, for one, strongly implies that such class conflict is somehow unintentional and that given enough time the society will achieve a social equilibrium by which the conflict is reduced and contained. Marx and Weber, on the contrary, did not share that point of view. There was for them no stage of unity and cohesiveness to which class systems tended for theoretical or practical reasons, except for the proletariat triumph visualized by Marx.

The major focus at the moment, however, is on the social explanations that can justify the existence of classes as normal and expected, thereby attaining some measure of unity in the face of the disunity that class divisions ordinarily imply. The many variations in explanations can be reduced essentially to three types. Each of these fits in with a different system of "core values," for each presents a somewhat different "explanation" of why social divisions exist at all. There is no question of a "choice"; societies do not rationally choose one or the other of these explanations. Rather, these beliefs tend to develop like other values in the society out of the force of necessity, tradition, and even culture exigencies of the moment. Yet, there is a rationality behind the explanations, in the functionalist's meaning of the term, that makes them mesh somewhat coherently with those values that are held to be most important. To repeat: if no unifying explanations were present, woven into the beliefs and values that individuals are taught to consider as sacred, then no social arrangement could long endure in the face of the conflict, disunity, and antagonisms that are so much a feature of any system of class divisions.

Type One: Class as a Natural Order

THE "simplest" kind of explanation that societies can offer for the existence of classes is one of a "natural order." Classes exist, in other words, because they have been ordained or because thev are the natural consequences of social forces beyond the control of man. Designating the class system as a natural event, then, has the social effect of removing it from the arena of human concern. One does not try to "do" anything about nature; nature is accepted and man adjusts to it.

The effect of this explanation in removing class from the bundle of concerns that humans might try to improve or want to think about, is to establish the class system on a most stable social basis. Classes in this type of value setting are thought of as inevitable social arrangements that individuals simply must accept, and almost without question. As long as this belief is dominant, classes remain immutable. They remain as integral parts of the social scenery, not to be tampered with either in thought or action.

Social stability is further achieved by this "natural" explanation because class divisions come to be accepted as primary social categories. A person's class, in other words, is the central social feature that in a real sense predetermines all else that he is and does. It sets his occupation, whom he marries, how he behaves and what he thinks. It goes even further to predetermine a vast range of minor actions that he performs: what he can wear, what he can eat, whom he can talk to, what he can touch, and at times, where he can walk. The primacy of class as a social category means all of these things. Class sets the social range and pre-selects the duties and the rights that comprise the social life of the individual.

The values by which this type of class system can be made socially legitimate vary, but they are usually religious, biological, or social in tone. "Caste" is an example of a system of social division heavily dependent upon a religious rationale. Even though caste is economically important, as in determining occupation, its primary strength is derived from a religious tradition that strikes deep to the emotions and moral beliefs of men. Each caste is specified, and its social obligations and responsibilities are established. This includes, in theory, the whole spectrum of social interaction, and all social relationships between castes are fully incorporated into the caste mold. In practice, of course, such rigidity may be loosened. Yet the caste order is pushed by a social momentum that moves it to include as wide a scope of social activity as possible in order to insure its continuance and stability. By encompassing all human activity—or as much of it as possible—within the structure of a caste system, few areas of social life are left to chance or to the vagaries of spontaneous human reactions. Change is thereby combatted most effectively.

Biological explanations have also been used as a justification for a "natural" class order, notably in the case of an aristocracy. In this instance, social divisions are "natural" because they are considered to be somehow the consequences of human genetics. The belief that socially important and socially favored qualities are genetically transmitted becomes an institutionalized belief, not a scientifically hedged generalization. The aristocracy holds its position of social superiority because they alone are believed to monopolize such traits, and therefore they alone are able to transmit them. The breeding of aristocrats, therefore, is carefully controlled and socially enforced especially through strict endogamy, else the entire belief structure is subject to possible question. There is no room for the commoner here.

The biological principle is somewhat less stable than the religious. Science, after all, can point up the fallacy and thereby constitutes a steady threat to this kind of aristocratic biology, even though many individuals may prefer to believe the opposite. Religious explanations, however, are beyond the range of scientific attack. They are deeply ingrained. Social superiority based on a biological rationale can be and has been questioned. Superiority that is religiously defended, however, brooks no such argument for it manages to make the individual feel guilty for even questioning the point.

A final ground upon which the "naturalness" of the class order can be based can be called the "social," for want of a better term. The example here would be that of "station."

One has a certain "station" in life that is the result of a complexity of social forces. To be sure, one is born into the station of one's parents and this does make a difference, but it need not be a lifetime commitment. It is possible, although by no means required, that an individual change his station.

The supporting values do not force the individual into a competitive struggle to better his position. On the contrary, they strongly support the calm acceptance of it, and even lend a certain dignity to every station. Hence, the social differences between high and low stations are accepted as part of the "natural" order, and each can retain its own measure of dignity. There is also a measure of obligation in living up to one's station or position as in a caste or aristocracy. It is upon such obligations, indeed, that the system is maintained in an orderly fashion.

Each of these variations—religious, biological, or social—share in common the belief in a natural social order. Furthermore, they each produce a society of relatively great stability, and what is also important, of relatively great unity and integration in spite of the severest kinds of social divisions. The fact that such divisions are accepted as natural indicates the way that social unity can be achieved in the face of classes separated from one another in a most extreme form. Stratification functions as a pivotal point for that unity.

Type Two: Class as a Reward System

EXPLANATIONS of this second type recognize the existence of classes, much as did the first type, but they justify classes on different value grounds. Class differences are recognized but they are not explained away as natural phenomena. Missing, too, in these explanations is the implication of a biological superiority reflected in class position. Instead, the class system is seen as a system of differential rewards distributed according to the contributions that persons are believed to have made to society. The "rewards" and the "contributions" are interpreted in terms of the values held by the society. It is what the society values, in other words, that counts. The rewards may be materialistic such as money or a higher living standard. They may also be honorific, such as in terms of recognition or prestige. In any case, that they are valued and are considered to be rewards commensurate with one's contribution, is the important element of this type of social explanation.

In theory, perhaps, this reward system operates efficiently and rationally. The type and amount of rewards tend to be set by a standard of achievement which is accepted as satisfactory, just, and desirable. Each person is supposed to accept his class as a just recompense for the level to which his achievement has moved him. In this manner, ideally, there should be few frustrations and little conflict produced as a result of the class system and the social differences it creates.

In practice, however, such problems seldom operate so perfectly; at any rate, not in large societies such as our own. The imperfections occur at many points. There is seldom consensus that the reward system is really as efficient, as rational, or as perfect as it may seem in theory. After all, many people get the rewards even though they don't follow the accepted standards. Indeed, some of them get where they are because others are put at a disadvantage by playing the rules of the game.

In practice, too, frustration and discontent arising from class differences are not so easily dispelled. As was indicated in the last chapter, where class is considered as a reward system there are always bound to be some persons who feel that they have not been justly rewarded. These are the Willie Lomans who have gone through all of the necessary steps and played the game by the rules, but who are never successful. They are the miscalculations, the errors of the system, doomed to frustration because they don't know what went wrong. Similarly, a reward system such as this might function in a runaway manner. It can motivate some individuals so strongly that they are never fully satisfied; the rewards never seem to be enough, and individuals strive ever harder for a goal they can never attain, for it is always out of reach. Human frustration and discontent again are the result.

This type of social explanation, then, is not as stable as is the first type. There are too many possibilities for malfunctioning and for imperfections; the reward system does not always work the way it is supposed to, or there is no consensus upon the standards to be followed. Nevertheless, this does not mean that this type of explanation is only conflictful. For a time, a class order based on this type of reward system can achieve a measure of social unity—as long as individuals are collectively convinced that it is fair.

There are dissatisfactions, to be sure, but the majority has achieved what it believes are commensurate rewards. Upward mobility has given the individual a better standard of living, greater prestige and responsibility, and more income than before. There have been, undoubtedly, some disappointments here, but those have been more the exception than the rule. For the most part, too, opportunities have been available for such achievement. The notion of a reward system, in other words, is not entirely a fantasy or a mechanism that produces only frustration.

What is significant for the present discussion, however, is that though great class disparities have been created by this type of social explanation, they have seldom been used as a focus for mobilizing psychological dissatisfactions. If individuals find fault with those class differences or with their position, they have seldom "blamed" the class system, but rather have come to blame themselves or other groups. Even in our own society, individuals have been culturally indoctrinated to accept those differences as just and reasonable. Even though the idea of equality has been held high, the rationale to explain inequality has been readily available. This does not imply that everyone likes it; but it does mean that, for the majority, a cultural explanation has been provided to account for what happens—those who work more, deserve more.

The basic source of instability in this type of explanation is that it rests so heavily upon consensus; an agreement that the reward system is just and that equality of opportunity really exists. The inequality of rewards is accepted as the necessary outcome of differences with success, but the opportunities for success are thought to be equally open to all. We start out the same. Hence, the importance of inheritance, of family background, and of one's beginnings are underemphasized by this explanation. The important thing, as far as the explanation goes, is how much the individual himself has achieved by his own efforts.

Type Three: Class as Non-existent

BY FAR the most curious of the three types of social explanations, because it is so illogical, is that of class as non-existent. It is an explanation that is apparently inconsistent, yet as a belief can function to unite a society in spite of existing class divisions and class differences. What is strange about this type of explanation is that it denies the existence of classes at the same time that classes obviously do exist. Although there are variations in the way this explanation functions, all variations share one common feature: the strong ideological need to deny the existence of classes at the same time that classes emerge as necessary social consequences.

That ideological component is not to be summarily discredited as unimportant. Quite the contrary, it is usually the major value around which the society is organized and upon which it depends. The Soviet Union and Israel[3] can be thought of as two examples that fit this type. Each has its own variation; yet, in both cases, there is present a strong equilitarian ideology. The ideology is one of the major reasons for the society's existence; the principal way in which the society explains itself. Yet, in both instances, classes have developed as responses to the social conditions under which each society functions.

As might be expected, however, this kind of explanation depends upon strange anomalies and ambiguities. The fact that classes exist cannot be denied. Their existence, however, comes to be justified in terms of the equality values; *i.e.,* those who achieve a higher class position are those who somehow are working hardest for the equality of all. The statement is illogical but not socially inconsistent. The ruling elite in the Soviet Union, for example, came to justify their better standard of living and the special privileges they have on the ground that they are most responsible for the well-being of the nation. Or so the explanation would go. It is not so much that they are rewarded for past achievements—the past in this sense has little existence in Soviet ideology—but rather that they must be in a proper position to advance the aims of society as a whole. In many ways, it is reasoning analogous to that given for the fact that union leaders sometimes earn more and usually live better than the members whom they represent. Such men need these advantages, the argument goes, if they are to be in a position to do the most for the rank and file union member.

The conflict between ideology and class reality may also be accounted for in another way. Some persons in the group must assume certain responsibilities that cannot be shared. They must make decisions and be held accountable for those decisions that affect the group as a whole. The Israeli *kibbutz,* for example, depends for its successful operation upon the few who have the ability, experience, and judgment to manage the collective. The managers, by that very dependence upon them, came to hold a higher status than other *kibbutz* members.[4] Given this "necessary" differential in power and status, stratification is the inevitable result. But it is stratification based on the belief of the greatest good since power is given to those who are presumably best equipped to make the correct decisions for the majority.

The common thread that runs throughout these several alternatives is that classes are not recognized as such nor socially seen, even though they show all the characteristic differences of any class system. The reason they cannot be "seen" is that the guiding ideology of the society does not permit their recognition. Whether this is enforced by a set of explanations that tend to underplay class distinctions, or whether it is enforced by police action, the social consequences tend to be the same: equality continues to hold as the dominant symbol.

Because of the strong ideological need to preach equality —much more so than even in the United States—there are limits to the actions of those who fill the elite positions in such a society. They cannot be conspicuous in what is a superior class position. It is a "quiet" elitism in this sense and such persons cannot live the life of the aristocrat or even be as conspicuous as the upper classes in the Type Two society. On the contrary, the more obvious class differences must be kept constantly in check: the clothing that is worn should be subdued, differences in the standard of living should be inconspicuous, and material privileges must be secretly consumed. Under these requirements, the individual must be on guard not to magnify nor to display his superior position, except where necessary when it is in keeping with the ideal that he is doing something for the benefit of all.

This type of class explanation is the most unstable of all, because it cannot traditionalize class differences nor systematically incorporate them into a cultural heritage. The social requirement of denying the existence and open recognition of classes means that whatever class advantages the individual attains are his alone and are only conditional. He does not become heir to them. Indeed, an attempt to regularize and to institutionalize the power and prestige of his class position can be the cause of his downfall. Each individual, each generation, must in a sense fight for his own class niche and in the peculiarly unique currency that the situation requires. The process becomes a giant façade with the ideal world and all of its values loudly proclaimed, but with the real world going on behind. Yet, in spite of this instability, of this essential inconsistency, a measure of unity is still attained because everyone accepts the same myth; equality is supposedly triumphant, and class divisions developed out of personal design or social necessity are explained away.

Change and the Future of Class

A CLASS system is not static. As a society is in constant process of change, so too its class system must also change in response. It could not be otherwise. The point arises then: Is there a pattern to this change and if so, what is it?

There can, unfortunately, be no firm description of patterns of change in class systems. Too much is unknown about the history of class systems and about the way they respond to different social changes to provide the necessary basis for such a theory. However, what is suggested here in briefest outline is a speculative theory about the pattern of change in class systems.[5] It is by no means a theory that is proven either by its own fully internal consistency nor by the needed empirical materials. Yet, it is not entirely without logic, and it does tend to account for such widely different changes as those found in fully industrialized societies and those in societies that are much less industrialized.

There is little need to reiterate the major points that have been made before, although it should be evident that much of what is stated here draws upon the theories and the studies of class that have been discussed. Instead the purpose here is to outline a "theory" about the development of class systems, and to indicate some of the reasons why the development follows the pattern it does. In many ways the proof for some of these ideas is to be found in the developments of underdeveloped countries, which in their current class history are repeating much of our own past history.

Because it is necessary to begin somewhere, let us start with an aristocratic type of class order, similar to that described as Type One above. The relevant feature of this kind of order is that all principal class elements are concentrated in a relatively small aristocratic elite. That is, the economic, political and status dimensions of class are concentrated in the hands of a few. They hold the power in all three spheres. Furthermore, much of this power stems from a superior economic position, usually one based upon extensive, monopolistic, and hereditary land holdings. These were the great estates of the landed aristocracy in England and the Continent, and these are the *latifundios* of the aristocracies in many Latin American countries today.

By their superior position, such aristocratic elites are able to dominate not only the economy but obviously the political and social life of the society as well. Where the majority of the population is contained in a rural peasantry, with perhaps a small urban proletariat, the problem of control by the elite is not a great one. They can justify their position on hereditary, traditional, and rational economic grounds, and from that post can organize an effective system of control over all major features of social organization.

The class system, for most purposes, is divided in two: this elite and the peasantry. In the middle there are a few positions such as those held by the clergy, the military, land and labor force supervisors, and government officials. But power ultimately resides with the elite, and it is their stamp that characterizes the class system of the society.

This sort of elitism has disappeared from many sections of the world, and is in the process of disappearing from those areas now being swept by the ideology of nationalism and the movement toward industrialization.

Industrialization, in a word, is the force that breaks the hold of the aristocracy and that introduces sudden and dramatic changes into formerly stable class relationships. One major effect is that industrialization introduces a new basis for wealth, for status, and for political power. In place of land, which is limited and thereby amenable to monopolization, industrialization brings a money economy and, more importantly, the means whereby wealth can be created in greater variety and profusion than landed wealth would allow.

Concurrently with this trend, industrialization also brings urban growth in the very nature of its operation. The population is moved away from the land and away from the culture of an agricultural society.[6] The tight social controls that were exerted within a small rural society are broken by the exodus of population to larger urban centers, where different values prevail and a different tradition is established.

Another outstanding effect of this industrial movement, as far as class is concerned, is to open up the ranks of the middle class as a new status for a significant segment of the population. At first, of course, this is a class that is small, attracting the "malcontents" of the earlier aristocratic order. It draws those who believe they have the most to win by successful industrialization. With the hold of the elite broken, with the class alternatives expanded, the educated middle class sees its future, rightly, in successful industrial development of the country. A political way to achieve that goal is through nationalism.

As the history being written now by underdeveloped countries clearly shows, the major proponents and leaders of the newer nationalism are those of this "new" middle class, not the aristocracy or the peasantry. Having broken out of the constricting village ties of an earlier period, the middle class becomes cosmopolitan and worldly. The village is no longer the real social horizon as it is and was for those bound to the land and village life. On the contrary, as urban citizens, the middle class sees the nation on an international scale. The need for a nationalistic philosophy and ideology then is to preserve the unity and the integrity of the nation at that international level, at the same time that it is the ideological means to mobilize a total effort for social and economic development.

As Silvert has noted specifically for Guatemala and by implication for other underdeveloped countries as well: "Nationalism is being adopted . . . as the value which will serve to gain that social cohesion at home which will also allow the government to operate externally as a more powerful unit than before."[7]

The middle classes, in this early industrial era, are the

better educated, the most committed and therefore the more vocal. Their education equips them to lead what is a major social revolution. And, importantly, they fight on two fronts. First, they must fight on an internal battlefield, the aristocratic elite with its socially ingrained traditions that seeks to hold on to the old way of life upon which their power depends. Secondly, they fight on an external front for national autonomy against encroachment by other more powerful nations that threaten them and the gamble they have taken. For of all groups involved in the tremendous social upheaval created by industrialization, the middle classes probably have the most to lose and the most to gain. To lose means to return to a society in which they could not function effectively; to win, means to gain new status and a larger share in the power mechanisms and institutions of society.

In Western civilization, this process was the history of the rise of the bourgeoisie. Today, it is the current history in almost every underdeveloped nation with aspirations—in Latin America, Egypt, India, and some sections of Africa. In each of these countries, the carriers of the nationalistic ideology and the major spokesmen are almost undeniably from the middle classes or, at the least, spokesmen and men of power who derive their power from the middle classes.

"The middle class, whose identity is tied to the success of the industrial urban pattern, finds in nationalism the means to hold its position, with an ideology that bestows its efforts with a blessing of working for the 'common good' at the same time that it rewards the effort by achieving political autonomy for the nation. This may be a hard posture to hold, given the economic dependence of underdeveloped countries upon others who hold the key to power and economic survival. However, the alternatives of either colonial domination, or continuance of a rural agricultural pattern are even more deadly to the middle class."[8]

In time the revolution subsides, for it would be impossible to continue indefinitely. The middle class achieves its success, both in breaking the monopolistic power of the landed aristocracy and its tradition, and in establishing the nation. To be sure, the economic and political difficulties facing countries going through that process today, are infinitely greater than they were two centuries ago when the older industrial nations underwent the same process. The international market, for one, is no longer the same today as it was in an earlier period. The problems of successful economic competition, of control, of trying to enter a world market so much dominated by great industrial nations, are much more complex today. This is a large subject in its own right that cannot be explored here. However, it should be pointed out that much of the nationalism of underdeveloped countries today is the result of the attempt to gain some measure of control in an international sphere that is economically, politically, and militarily dominated by the older and more powerful industrial nations. It is not a situation of competition among equals, but rather a situation calling for a more subtle foreign policy of trying to parlay one's political weakness and economic inadequacy into the best possible gain in a world power struggle going on between giants.

As industrialism matures, it divides the several aspects of class into its separate components. Economic, political and status dimensions, in other words, come to reside in as many different groups, rather than being concentrated in an elite. Hence, in our own history, those with economic power did not always hold commensurate political power. Similarly, men who held political power were not always those who held great economic power. And over all of this, status or prestige could reside in still other groups and strata of society.

To be sure, those of great wealth tended to be the status leaders of the society in terms of etiquette, in the setting of taste patterns and in consumption styles. However, they could not monopolize such status power and status advantage. The celebrity and the idol could almost as easily gain similar command. The movie actress, the matinee idol, the adventurer, and the artistic prodigy could all, by their achievements, exert a tremendous influence upon large sections of the population in what they would buy, what they would think, or how they would behave. Of course, in the very nature of fame so attained, there was the ever present danger of change, of the fickleness of public adoration. Idols frequently were displaced. Those of wealth, on the other hand, could look forward to a somewhat longer life expectancy as style setters.

The characteristic mark in this earlier phase of industrialization was the separation of class powers. Characteristic, too, was the rise and expansion of the middle class. Expanded industrial development brought with it a growing dependence upon the white-collar clerk, the professional, the bureaucrat, and the salesman. These became the typical channels for attaining middle class status. As the Type Two explanation above indicated, the class system operated on a reward basis. Industrial society depended upon skills, and in exchange, a higher standard of living and increased status became the rewards offered to those who successfully achieved those needed skills.

However, in time, and as the period of later industrialization is reached, the next development of the class system begins to occur. It is a process of the reconvergence of the separate dimensions of class power into the hands of an elite. This is generally the kind of process that Mills has described in *The Power Elite*. The causes behind this process are different than those that enabled an aristocracy to hold a monopoly of power; the people are different, the setting is different, and so is the time, but the results are surprisingly repetitious.

The economic and political power dimensions converge in the era of late industrialization because they become functionally interdependent. The men of political power, more and more, come to depend upon the men of economic power in order to attain their position and to secure it. This occurs not only because of the greater amount of money needed today to run for election and to achieve political successes, but also because of the dependence upon the men of economic power for their skills and resources in the conduct of politics in a period of advanced industrialization. These men, or their appointees, fill important and pivotal political offices, as Mills has pointed out. The dependence arises, too, because the conduct of international politics more and more must mesh with economic decisions and economic policy.

From their side, the men of economic power have become increasingly dependent upon those with political power. In later industrialization, governmental regulation and supervision is practiced to a great degree. There are few instances of what were formerly "purely" economic decisions. Increasingly, such decisions involve political overtones and political consequences. The investigations by the Congress into unions, corporations, and business leaders have shown the extent to which economic affairs are considered as falling within the legitimate range of government scrutiny. The steady stream of former political officials into economic bureaucracies is a further indication of the close nexus between politics and economics. Where a knowledge of governmental policy and governmental procedure become essential to the successful conduct of business enterprise, it is only to be expected that corporations will co-opt talent away from the government wherever they can.

The elements of status and prestige also tend to become concentrated in those who already hold economic and political power. They are in the position to maximize their prestige potentials, and by their very position, are accorded high prestige and status. Furthermore, there is a tendency to traditionalize such prestige power wherever possible. As Weber pointed out in commenting upon the change of class systems, there is a desire by those who hold elite status to establish their power more lastingly and more securely by tying their position into a traditional basis, as in Type One societies.

The typical direction that this desire takes, and the means by which it is socially implemented, is to construct irrational barriers against unrestricted entry by others into the elite. The reward system of Type Two societies is essentially a rational procedure; those who can attain the preferred goals are eligible for elite membership as part of their reward for achievement. The major disadvantage of this practice, as far as those in the elite are concerned, is that it does not permit the exercise of full control and selection by the elite. What is more, it does not insure to the elite that its heirs will be automatically guaranteed the family's status. The attempt is made, therefore, by the elite to traditionalize elite status and to exercise monopolistic control over the selection process.

One means by which these objectives can be achieved is by establishing the elite upon an aristocratic basis as in a former period. Family background, endogamy, the protracted inculcating of elite patterns and preferences, and even some recourse to the former biological notions of Type One societies are utilized for the effort. Entry into the elite, thereby, becomes not simply an unequivocally given reward readily available to all who qualify, but rather a privilege that is specially conferred and needing a history of elite parentage and proper background to attain. Money, the rational symbol, becomes displaced by "background," the irrational and vaguely defined symbol. The individual has it or not; he cannot simply achieve it. Essentially, these kinds of qualifications differ not at all from those established by former aristocracies to insure their dominance.

All of these trends in the political, economic, and status spheres converge on the same point: toward the creation of a small elite in whom the principal class powers are concentrated. And the development of the class system has come through full circle: from aristocracy to aristocracy, from elite to elite.

As pointed out above, these are speculations about the way that the class system has seemed to develop as one tries to generalize from a segment of the most recent human history. Whether or not this last stage is an inevitable one for the United States, for example, is still an open question. Many indications seem to point in that direction as suggested in the preceding chapter. Mobility to the top, for example, seems to have been choked off, even though remaining open at the middle levels.

As was pointed out in Chapter Four, the argument that America is moving toward a stage of more or less wholesale middle class dominance through middle class conformity does not seem to be substantiated either by the facts or by the logic of these speculations. The numerical growth of the middle class should not be confused with middle class domination. More people, perhaps, are middle class today by almost any criterion that one chooses to use. More people are buying, thinking, and aspiring towards the goals that have characterized the middle class until recently. This is conformity, but it is not dominance. The sources of power, if the analysis offered here has any valid basis, are being shifted and located in an elite group that is far outside of the range of middle class standards even though historically it emerged from the middle class. The elite sets its own standards that others may attempt to follow.

The argument for conformity has been, unfortunately, most misleading. What it has done in effect is to turn attention to the obvious and apparent similarities in certain aspects of class behavior. The consumption patterns, for example, of the American public probably have evidenced a good deal of similarity, regardless of class. However, this is as much due to the standardization of consumer products by industry as it is to the standardization of tastes by the consumer. There are a finite number of variations in most appliances, automobiles, and even items of apparel. There is even a ceiling to the price for such items. Under conditions of relatively full prosperity, many individuals may be able to buy those goods. Given the limitations of price and variety, it seems wholly possible that what looks like outward conformity by the many is simply due to the limited number of alternatives available. The same is true for suburban conformity and for so-called "organizational conformity."

The emphasis upon conformity is misleading, too, because it overlooks and thereby understresses the differences that still exist between classes. As was noted in Chapter Four, the differences in aspirations and goals between the middle and the working classes are still important enough to determine many other differences about them. Their attitudes differ, as do their prejudices, aspirations and images of the "good life."

The prophets of conformity, in other words, have allowed themselves to be misled into a generalization by two related developments in American society: the expansion of the middle class and the condition of relatively high economic prosperity. These developments, major though they are, are not themselves the final indices of what is happening to the class system. It is not accidental, for example, that those who argue conformity take their stand on psychological grounds almost exclusively, and if they do make their contention on behavioral grounds, it is in such relatively unimportant areas as consumer practices and behavior. The matter of power in its economic, political, and prestige forms is by far the more crucial variable confronting one who is interested in class and its trends. The arguments and comparisons with alternative views have already been fully stated in Chapter Four, and they apply here as well.

This is not to say that a firm prediction can be made about the future of class or the class structure in the United States. The conclusions that have been stated here are admittedly tentative, but they are based upon a reasonable assessment of trends now emerging. In a real sense, much of the future existence and character of American society, indeed the world, depends upon an understanding of what these trends are and towards what future state of affairs we have already begun to move.

Appendix

Alphabetical Listing of Occupations and Prestige Scores

Based on North-Hatt scale of occupations. Those not listed in the original scale were obtained by interpolation using similarities of job describtions to establish a prestige score for a new occupation between known prestige scores for occupations above and below it in standing.

OCCUPATION	SCORE
Accountant	81
Actor	83
Architect	86
Artist	83
Attendant—filling station and parking lot	52
Author	80
Auto repairman	63
Baggageman	52
Baker	54
Banker	88
Barber	59
Bartender	44
Biologist	81
Blacksmith	63
Board member—large corporation	86

OCCUPATION	SCORE
Boilermaker	63
Bookkeeper	68
Brakeman—railroad	58
Bricklayer	65
Building contractor	79
Butcher	54
Cabinet maker and pattern maker	73
Carpenter	65
Cashier in a bank	66
Chemist and metallurgist	86
Chiropractor	75
Civil engineer	84
Clergyman	87
Clerk—in a store	58
College professor and instructor	89
Compositor and typesetter	67
Conductors—bus and street car	58
Conductors—railroad	67
Contractor—building	79
Cook	54
County agricultural agent	77
Credit manager	70
Dancer and showman	52
Dentist	86
Designer and draftsman	70
Editor	71
Electrical engineer	84
Electrician	73
Elevator operator	47
Farm owner and manager	76
Farmer (no other designation)	50
Fireman—fire department	67
Fisherman	58
Foreman—manufacturing	67

OCCUPATION	SCORE
Garage mechanic	62
Garbage collector	35
Government worker (no other designation)	70
Guard	49
Insurance and real estate agent	68
Janitor and porter	44
Laborers—manufacturing	48
Laundry operative	46
Lawyer and judge	86
Lineman and serviceman	48
Linotype operator	68
Locomotive engineer	77
Longshoreman	47
Lumberman	53
Machinist	73
Mail carrier	66
Manager—small store in city	69
Motorman—streetcar and bus	58
Musician	81
Night watchman	47
Operative—manufacturing	60
Optometrist	75
Optician	81
Osteopath	79
Painter—building trades	65
Pharmacist	79
Photographer	73
Physician and surgeon	93
Plasterer	65
Plumber	63
Policeman	67
Policeman—supervisory capacity	69
Proprietor—mining, construction, manufacturing	82

OCCUPATION	SCORE
Proprietor—eating and drinking place	62
Proprietor—retail trade	69
Proprietor—printing shop	74
Purchasing agent	68
Psychologist	85
Radio announcer	75
Reporter	71
Roofer and sheet metal worker	64
Routeman or deliveryman	54
Scientist	89
Salesman (exc. clerks and agents)	68
Sharecropper	40
Shoemaker	59
Shoe-shiner	33
Social and welfare worker	73
Soda clerk	45
Stationary engineer	78
Street sweeper	34
Surveyor	70
Switchman—railroad	58
Tailor	62
Taxi-driver	49
Teacher—public school	79
Technical engineer	84
Tenant farmer	68
Timekeeper	65
Truck driver and deliveryman	54
Undertaker	72
Union official and representative	75
Veterinarian	86
Waiter	48
Welder	58

Notes

CHAPTER I

Perspectives

1. W. Lloyd Warner and Paul S. Lunt, *The Social Life of a Modern Community* (New Haven: Yale University Press, 1941). Succeeding volumes were: *The Status System of a Modern Community* (1942); Warner and Leo Srole, *The Social Systems of American Ethnic Groups* (1945); Warner and J. O. Low, *The Social System of the Modern Factory* (1947). Walter Goldschmidt has made a telling observation concerning the social scientists' practice of giving fictitious names to the communities they study. Ostensibly the purpose is to protect the identity of the community in keeping with the ethical codes of confidentiality and anonymity. A latent aim behind that code, Goldschmidt suggests, is the desire to claim that the community studied is typical—a feeling that can be more easily promoted when the real identity is camouflaged. At times it is clear that the community is not at all typical, at least by any acceptable statistical norms or determinate standards. "Social Class in America—A Critical Review," *American Anthropologist,* LII (October-December, 1950), 483-98.

2. Lewis Corey, "The Middle Class," *The Antioch Review,* Spring, 1945; C. Wright Mills, *White Collar* (New York: Oxford University Press, 1951).

3. *Cf.* C. Wright Mills's review of Warner's first volume of the "Yankee City" study, *American Sociological Review,* VII (1942), 263-71. Also, Joel B. Montague, Jr., "Class or Status Society," *Sociology and Social Research,* XL (May-June, 1956), 333-38.

4. Quoted by Genevieve Knupfer in "Portrait of the Underdog," *Public Opinion Quarterly,* Spring, 1947, p. 105.

5. Richard Centers, *The Psychology of Social Classes* (Princeton: Princeton University Press, 1949), p. 77.

6. The aspirations of automobile workers according to one study were found to be much more realistically based than they had been in the past. This emerged in the workers' recognition that their chances were not very good for leaving the factory to open up their own business or otherwise taking advantage of some "opportunity." This realism replaced a previously hopeful set of aspirations that apparently had little chance of realization. There was, in other words, an acceptance of the working class position without the aspirations that turned the individual's attention to "higher" class levels. *Cf.* Eli Chinoy, *Automobile Workers and the American Dream* (New York: Doubleday and Co., 1955). Also, Chapter VI of the present book.

7. There is some criticism of the frontier thesis advanced by Frederick Jackson Turner among historians. Some maintain that the undue attention paid to the social force of the frontier underplayed such equally important facts as the rural-urban movement, the generation of democratic ideas in the Eastern states and Western civilization generally, and the oppression and conflicts in American society not alleviated by the "safety valve" operation of the frontier. These criticisms are of a different order from the reference to Turner's thesis in the present context. Even if the frontier failed to provide all of the social force that Turner attributed to it, it cannot be doubted that it did exist and produced an effect of importance in the ideology of American society. *Cf.* Richard Hofstadter, "Turner and the Frontier Myth," *American Scholar,* XVIII (October, 1949), 433-43.

8. Talcott Parsons (trans.), Max Weber's *The Protestant Ethic and the Spirit of Capitalism* (London: George Allen and Unwin, Ltd., 1930); R. H. Tawney, *Religion and the Rise of Capitalism* (England: Penguin Books, Ltd., 1926). A valuable addition to these classics, especially as the ethic is applied in the United States, is Irvin G. Wyllie, *The Self Made Man in America* (New Brunswick, N. J.: Rutgers University Press, 1954).

The summary of the personality type ideally described by the Protestant ethic is taken from the latter book.

9. Wyllie, *op. cit.,* pp. 40-54.

10. *Ibid.,* p. 54.

11. Philip Taft, *Economics and Problems of Labor* (Harrisburg: Stackpole and Sons, 1942), p. 519. Historical information was also taken from this source, pp. 518-520.

12. *Ibid.,* p. 338.

13. This is the central thesis, and one well-documented, of Selig Perlman, *A Theory of the Labor Movement* (New York: The Macmillan Co., 1928).

14. Exurbia, the land beyond the suburbs, appears to be even more socially homogeneous. The impressionistic description of three exurbs around New York by A. C. Spectorsky in *The Exurbanites* (Philadelphia: J. B. Lippincott Co., 1955), conveys not only the sense of difference in tone and feel between them, but also the remarkable similarity of life within any one exurb.

15. Daniel Bell (ed.), *The New American Right* (New York: Criterion Books, 1955).

16. Richard Hofstadter, "The Pseudo-Conservative Revolt," in *The New American Right,* p. 43.

CHAPTER II

Theories of Class

1. W. Lloyd Warner, *Structure of American Life* (Edinburgh: The University Press, 1952), p. 1.

2. The need for clarifying the concepts used in the study of class has been stressed by several writers. Somewhat in opposition to this view is one that holds such clarification should come about through more detailed empirical descriptions, through the greater specification of concepts as more and more is learned about the nature of class. It is pointless to dictate one or the other approach. The reason for the confusion in definitions is due to the confusion in the theories used, as suggested in this discussion. The difficulty is not simply a mechanical one of agreeing upon a single set of definitions, but an organic one tightly related to difficulties of a more thorough

sort. Furthermore, as suggested here, the concepts that are selected and used force a commitment about the nature of class that is too frequently overlooked. Perhaps this aspect, in the spirit of a sociology of knowledge, is worthy of detailed investigation in its own right. Part of this latter purpose is accomplished in Charles Page, *Class and American Sociology* (New York: The Dial Press, 1940). For discussions of concepts see Llewellyn Gross, "The Use of Class Concepts in Sociological Research," *American Journal of Sociology,* LIV (March, 1949), 409-421; Milton M. Gordon, "Social Class in American Sociology," *American Journal of Sociology,* LV (November, 1949), 262-268. A more detailed attempt at conceptual reorganization is presented by Gordon in "A System of Social Class Analysis," *The Drew University Bulletin,* August, 1951, and in his *Social Class in American Sociology* (Durham: Duke University Press, 1958).

3. Goldschmidt, in one of the very few published recognitions of this matter of moral commitment in the study of class, suggests a point of view quite similar to that mentioned here. He has made an effort at a "taxonomy of moral positions with respect to social classes" that categorizes the following views: "(1) Status differential is an inherent element in society and serves the virtues of selecting an elite to provide leadership and maintain the social order," where the elite can be considered as "(a) a special body in a quasi-racial sense . . . (b) [as] persons of special endowments needed by society . . . (c) [as those who] earned their position through sacrifice, hard work and the like. . . . (2) Status differentiation is a weakness characterizing [mass] societies, and the evils inherent in it should be ameliorated by social action. . . . (3) Status differentiation and classes are a moral fault . . . and should be eliminated from any healthy society."

This is a good beginning that needs further analysis, especially as to the consequences of these stances for the theory that is constructed. See, Nelson N. Foote, Walter R. Goldschmidt, Richard T. Morris, Melvin Seeman, and Joseph Shister, "Alternative Assumptions in Stratification Research," in *Transactions of the Second World Congress of Sociology* (London: International Sociological Association, 1954), II, 378-390. The quotation above appears on p. 384.

4. This discussion of the theoretical problems faced in class analysis draws heavily upon an article by Paul K. Hatt, "Strati-

fication in the Mass Society," *American Sociological Review,* XV (April, 1950), 216-222. Further relevant considerations are mentioned in Foote, *et al, op. cit.*

5. Guy Rocher in a book review of *Les Classes sociales aux Etats-Unis* by F. Bouriez-Gregg, in *The Canadian Journal of Economics and Political Science,* XXII (August, 1956), 405-407, esp. p. 406.

6. Data supporting this conclusion can be found in C. Wright Mills, *The Power Elite* (New York: Oxford University Press, 1956), Chapters VIII and IX. Also Leonard Reissman, "Life Careers, Power, and the Professions," *American Sociological Review,* XXI (April, 1956), 216-221.

7. *The Manifesto of the Communist Party* (New York: International Publishers, 1932), p. 9.

8. *Ibid.*

9. This summarization was taken from M. M. Bober, *Karl Marx's Interpretation of History* (Cambridge: Harvard University Press, 1948), especially Chapter V, "The Class and Class Struggle." This work is a skilled and careful presentation of Marx's theory organized around a number of salient subjects for social scientists. Another source worth the attention of sociologists is Rudolf Schlesinger, *Marx: His Time and Ours* (London: Routledge and Kegan Paul, Ltd., 1950).

10. Marx's theory of surplus value clearly enters at this point. It was omitted from the main presentation because it was not essential for understanding his theory of class. Briefly, the theory of surplus value held that labor increased the value of a commodity beyond the wage the employer-owner had to pay to the laborer. In that fashion the laborer received a share of the profit only sufficient to maintain himself. The difference between his share and what the employer obtained from the sale of the commodity constituted a "surplus" gain in which labor had no share. Hence, Marx charged that labor was exploited and was denied its just share of a value that labor alone had created. Probably no other facet of Marx's argument is as weak as this one. Why Marx, who was clear and incisive in other aspects of his analysis, should have failed to see that "value" is a social quantity and an expression of complex market-forces is not fully understandable. All that might be said, and it is no explanation, is that Marx at this point did not avoid the overwhelming impact of classical economics as well as he did in other respects.

11. *The Class Struggles in France, 1848-1850.*
12. *Communist Manifesto,* p. 20.
13. *Ibid.,* pp. 12-14.
14. *Ibid.,* pp. 11-12.
15. Karl Marx and Frederick Engels, *The German Ideology* (New York: International Publishers, 1947).
16. *Ibid.,* p. 18.
17. *Ibid.,* p. 19.
18. In H. H. Gerth and C. W. Mills (eds. & trans.), *From Max Weber: Essays in Sociology* (New York: Oxford University Press, 1946), Chapter VII. This volume contains an excellent introduction written by the editors, especially Part III, "Intellectual Orientations," on the comparison between Marx and Weber.
19. *Ibid.,* p. 47. See also the comments of Karl Lowith, "Marxismus und Geschichte," *Neue Deutsche Hefte,* XLII (January, 1958), 876-888, pp. 882-883.
20. *Ibid.,* pp. 68-69.
21. For comparisons between Marx and Weber, especially in terms of their approaches to the phenomenon of capitalism, see N. Birnbaum, "Conflicting Interpretations of the Rise of Capitalism: Marx and Weber," *British Journal of Sociology,* IV (June, 1953), 125-141. Also, Karl Lowith, "Max Weber und Karl Marx," *Archiv fur Sozialwissenschaft und Sozialpolitik,* LXVII (March and April, 1932).
22. Gerth and Mills, *op. cit.,* p. 180.
23. A. M. Henderson and Talcott Parsons (trans.), *Max Weber: The Theory of Social and Economic Organization* (New York: Oxford University Press, 1947), Part IV, "Social Stratification and Class Structure."
24. *Ibid.,* p. 434.
25. Gerth and Mills, *op. cit.,* pp. 184-185.
26. *Ibid.,* p. 187.
27. Henderson and Parsons, *op. cit.,* p. 428.
28. Weber has been criticized on this point, but not conclusively, by Oliver C. Cox, "Max Weber on Social Stratification: A Critique," *American Sociological Review,* XV (April, 1950), 223-227; also his *Caste, Class and Race* (New York: Doubleday, 1948).
29. Gerth and Mills, *op. cit.,* p. 193.
30. *Ibid.,* p. 194.
31. *Ibid.,* p. 194.

32. C. Wright Mills, *The Power Elite* (New York: Oxford University Press, 1956).

33. James S. Martin, *All Honorable Men* (Boston: Little, Brown, and Co., 1950).

34. The functional theory of stratification has been best presented in two basic essays, upon which the present discussion is based. The first is that by Talcott Parsons, "A Revised Analytical Approach to the Theory of Social Stratification," in R. Bendix and S. M. Lipset (eds.), *Class, Status and Power* (Glencoe: The Free Press, 1953), pp. 92-128. The second essay is by Kingsley Davis and Wilbert E. Moore, "Some Principles of Stratification," and originally appeared in the *American Sociological Review*, April, 1945, pp. 242-249. It has been reprinted in L. Wilson and W. L. Kolb (eds.), *Sociological Analysis* (New York: Harcourt, Brace and Co., 1949). Page references to the Davis and Moore paper are to the last reference.

35. See for example, Bronislaw Malinowski, *A Scientific Theory of Culture* (Chapel Hill: University of North Carolina Press, 1944), or "The Group and the Individual in Functional Analysis," in L. Wilson and W. L. Kolb, *op. cit.*, pp. 168-173.

36. Parsons, *op. cit.*, p. 93.

37. *Ibid.*, p. 94.

38. The possession of an original masterpiece appears to have become a prestige item among the very rich in America at the turn of the century. Not only was the price of these art treasures sufficiently great to limit them to the upper classes, but buying them became a means of emulating European aristocratic traditions in a shorter space of time. It is still the practice to make note in reproductions of great paintings of the person who owns the original. Endowing a whole museum, of course, leaves no question about the prestige of the giver, if indeed there was any doubt before. J. Pierpont Morgan was one of these. In an article by Aline B. Saarinen in the *New York Times Magazine*, December 16, 1956, the scale of Morgan's operations was recounted. These operations can only leave the ordinary citizen reeling. It was reported that in two months Morgan spent $770,627 in the art market. "He would buy a Louis XVI gold box for $21,845 as casually as a commuter picks up a morning paper." When he died, his art collection was valued at $60,000,000. All of this was accomplished in less than twenty years. Morgan, and others like him, it seemed, were just in too much

of a hurry for whatever it was they were trying to get to quibble over prices.

39. Parsons, *op. cit.*, p. 97.
40. *Ibid.*, p. 100.
41. Davis and Moore, *op. cit.*, p. 435.
42. *Ibid.*, p. 435.
43. *Ibid.*, p. 436n.
44. *Ibid.*, p. 437.
45. *Ibid.*, p. 437.
46. *Ibid.*, p. 439.
47. Melvin M. Tumin, "Some Principles of Stratification: A Critical Analysis," and the rejoinder by Davis and Moore, *American Sociological Review*, XVIII (August, 1953), 387-397.
48. *Ibid.*, pp. 392-393.
49. Nelson N. Foote and Paul K. Hatt, "Social Mobility and Economic Advancement," *American Economic Review*, XLIII (May, 1953), 364-378.
50. *Ibid.*, p. 367.
51. Warner's research and writing on the subject of class is best contained in the following references: Warner and Lunt, *The Social Life of a Modern Community;* Warner and Associates, *Democracy in Jonesville* (New York: Harper and Bros., 1949); Warner, Marcia Meeker and Kenneth Eels, *Social Class in America* (Chicago: Science Research Associates, 1949); Warner, Robert J. Havighurst and Martin Loeb, *Who Shall Be Educated?* (New York: Harper and Bros., 1944); Warner, *American Life* (Chicago: University of Chicago Press, 1953); Warner and James Abegglen, *Big Business Leaders in America* (New York: Harper and Bros., 1955).
52. Warner and Lunt, *The Social Life of a Modern Community*, p. 110.
53. *Ibid.*, p. 81.
54. *Ibid.*, p. 82.
55. One of the best critical discussions of Warner is by Harold W. Pfautz and Otis D. Duncan, "A Critical Evaluation of Warner's Work in Community Stratification," *American Sociological Review*, XV (April, 1950), 205-215. In their criticism, Pfautz and Duncan have discussed the errors that Warner reported in the use of his class measures. They noted that while Warner gave favorable attention to his overall error of only 16 per cent in predicting social class by the EP measure *from* the ISC scores, it was a misleading calculation. That average error, they found,

ranged from an 18 per cent error in predicting upper class membership, 22 per cent in upper-middle and 32 per cent in upper-lower. They concluded that "the over-all error of prediction would, therefore, be substantially greater than the reported 16 per cent, if the total population were considered rather than the sample alone" (p. 209). Another excellent essay that has reviewed Warner's work and summarized the criticisms was one by Ruth R. Kornhauser, "The Warner Approach to Social Stratification," in R. Bendix and S. M. Lipset, *Class, Status, and Power.*

56. These characteristics are summarized in Kornhauser, *op. cit.*, pp. 230-231.

57. Warner and Lunt, *The Social Life of a Modern Community,* pp. 141 ff.

58. Quoted in Kornhauser, *op. cit.*, p. 231.

59. Once again, these features are excellently summarized in Kornhauser's essay, *op. cit.*, pp. 233-236.

60. An excellent review of Warner's first study takes him seriously and justifiably to task for the "sponginess" of his class concept. C. Wright Mills, review of *The Social Life of a Modern Community, American Sociological Review,* VII (1942), 264-265.

61. Pfautz and Duncan, *op. cit.*, pp. 214-216.

62. Warner and Abegglen, *op. cit.*

CHAPTER III

The Methodology of Class

1. F. Stuart Chapin, *Contemporary American Institutions* (New York: Harper and Bros., 1935), Chapter XIX, "A Measurement of Social Status." Another more elaborate study of the use of living-room possessions as a measure of social status has been done in Liverpool. *Cf.* Dennis Chapman, *The Home and Social Status* (London: Routledge and Kegan Paul, 1955).

2. Chapin, *op. cit.*, p. 374.

3. *Ibid.*, p. 375.

4. Louis Guttman, "A Revision of Chapin's Social Status Scale, *American Sociological Review,* VII (June, 1942), 362-369.

5. William H. Sewell, *The Construction and Standardization*

of a Scale for the Measurement of the Socio-Economic Status of Oklahoma Farm Families (Stillwater, Oklahoma: Oklahoma A. & M. Agricultural Experiment Station), Technical Bulletin No. 9, April, 1940. Also by the same author, "A Short Form of the Farm Family Socio-Economic Status Scale," *Rural Sociology,* VIII (June, 1943), 161-170.

6. Louis Wirth, "Social Stratification and Social Mobility in the United States," *Current Sociology,* II, 4 (1953-54), p. 293.

7. *Ibid.*

8. David Riesman and Howard Roseborough, "Careers and Consumer Behavior," in Lincoln H. Clark (ed.), *Consumer Behavior,* Vol. II, "The Life Cycle and Consumer Behavior" (New York: New York University Press, 1955), pp. 1-18.

9. *The Changing American Market* (Garden City, New York: Hanover House, 1955), pp. 122-123.

10. Harold Kaufman, *Prestige Classes in a New York Rural Community* (Cornell University Experiment Station, March, 1944), Memoir 260. Reprinted in part in Bendix and Lipset, *Class, Status, and Power,* pp. 190-203. References are to the latter reprinting.

11. *Ibid.,* p. 203. Kaufman, by the way, has recognized some of the limitations inherent in the method. "Members of a Rural Community as Judges of Prestige Rank," *Sociometry,* IX (1946), 71-85.

12. W. Lloyd Warner, M. Meeker, and K. Eels, *Social Class in America: A Manual for Procedure for the Measurement of Social Status* (Chicago: Science Research Associates, 1949), p. 35.

13. Harold W. Pfautz and Otis D. Duncan, *op. cit.,* p. 209.

14. Richard Centers, *The Psychology of Social Classes: A Study of Class Consciousness* (Princeton: Princeton University Press, 1949); Hadley Cantril, "Identification With Social and Economic Class," *Journal of Abnormal and Social Psychology,* XXXVIII (1943), 74-80; Arthur W. Kornhauser, "Analysis of 'Class' Structure in Contemporary American Society—Psychological Bases of Class Divisions," in G. W. Hartmann and T. Newcomb (eds.), *Industrial Conflict: A Psychological Interpretation* (New York: Cordon, 1939).

15. Kornhauser, *op. cit.,* p. 200. Italics in the original.

16. Centers, *op. cit.*

17. Arthur W. Kornhauser, "Public Opinion and Social Class," *American Journal of Sociology,* LV (January, 1950), 333-345.

18. Centers, *op. cit.,* p. 27.

19. *Ibid.,* p. 27.
20. *Ibid.,* p. 27. Italicized in the original.
21. *Ibid.,* pp. 28-29. Italicized in the original.
22. *Ibid.,* p. 78. Italicized in the original.
23. *Ibid.,* p. 210.
24. *Ibid.,* p. 76.
25. *Ibid.,* p. 114. Table 34.
26. *Ibid.,* p. 161. Table 67.
27. *Ibid.,* pp. 94-100. Tables 24-27.
28. *Ibid.,* p. 216.
29. *Ibid.,* p. 215.
30. *Ibid.,* p. 219.
31. Kornhauser, "Public Opinion and Social Class."
32. Centers, *op. cit.,* pp. 82-83. Figures 7-8.
33. Alba E. Edwards, *Comparative Occupational Statistics for the United States,* 16th Census, 1940 (Washington: U. S. Government Printing Office, 1943).
34. Paul K. Hatt, "Stratification in the Mass Society," *American Sociological Review,* XV (April, 1950), 219.
35. Quoted in Theodore Caplow, *The Sociology of Work* (Minneapolis: University of Minnesota Press, 1954), pp. 33-34. Caplow presents an excellent analysis of the assumptions underlying occupational classifications of this type, pp. 42-48.
36. Robert S. and Helen M. Lynd, *Middletown* (New York: Harcourt, Brace and Co., 1929), p. 22.
37. Centers, *op. cit.,* p. 49.
38. *Ibid.,* p. 48.
39. Warner *et al., op. cit.,* pp. 140-141.
40. George S. Counts, "The Social Status of Occupations: A Problem in Vocational Guidance," *School Review,* XXXIII (January, 1925), 16-27. Other studies of the same type include: W. A. Anderson, "The Occupational Attitudes of College Men," *Journal of Social Psychology,* V (1934), 435-466; M. E. Deeg and D. G. Patterson, "Changes in Social Status of Occupations," *Occupations,* XXV (January, 1947), 205-208; H. C. Lehman and P. A. Witty, "Further Study of the Social Status of Occupations," *Journal of Educational Sociology,* V (1931), 101-112; Mapheus Smith, "An Empirical Scale of the Prestige Status of Occupations," *American Sociological Review,* VIII (April, 1943), 185-192; M. K. Welch, "The Ranking of Occupations on the Basis of Social Status," *Occupations,* XXVI (January, 1949), 237-241.

41. National Opinion Research Center, "Jobs and Occupations: A Popular Evaluation," *Public Opinion News,* IX (1947), 3-13. Also reprinted in L. Wilson and W. L. Kolb (eds.), *Sociological Analysis,* pp. 464-474, and in Bendix and Lipset, *Class, Status and Power.*

42. Paul K. Hatt, "The Prestige Continuum," in R. W. O'Brien and others (eds.), *Readings in General Sociology* (New York: Houghton Mifflin Co., 1951), p. 305. See Appendix A for an expanded occupational listing using Hatt's suggestion of interpolation.

43. "Jobs and Occupations" in Wilson and Kolb, *op. cit.,* pp. 467 ff.

44. *Ibid.*

45. Hatt, "The Prestige Continuum," in O'Brien and others, *op. cit.,* p. 305.

46. *Ibid.,* p. 308.

47. George Simpson (trans.), Emile Durkheim's *The Division of Labor in Society* (Glencoe: The Free Press, 1947), p. 182.

48. In addition to the explicit treatment of this point in Chapter II, it can be noted that Weber has dealt with the social function and importance of occupations in his theory of social organization. He has tied the study of the occupational structure to the study of the system of social stratification. *Cf. The Theory of Social and Economic Organization,* translated by Henderson and Parsons, pp. 250-254, "The Concept of Occupation and Types of Occupational Structure."

49. F. W. Taussig and C. S. Joslyn, *American Business Leaders* (New York: The Macmillan Co., 1932); Percy E. Davidson and H. Dewey Anderson, *Occupational Mobility in an American Community* (Stanford: Stanford University Press, 1937); Natalie Rogoff, *Recent Trends in Occupational Mobility* (Glencoe: The Free Press, 1953).

50. Alex Inkeles and P. H. Rossi, "National Comparisons of Occupational Prestige," *American Journal of Sociology,* LXI (January, 1956), 329-339.

51. Kornhauser, "Public Opinion and Social Class," p. 339.

CHAPTER IV

Class and Social Structure

1. Robin M. Williams, Jr., *American Society* (New York: Alfred A. Knopf, 1952), p. 30.

2. The implication of this orientation is discussed below.

3. Kroeber, *Anthropology* (New York, Harcourt, Brace and Co., 1948), pp. 274-276.

4. This list could be dreadfully long. However, a few selected examples should be enough to give the idea. J. Useem, P. Tangent, and R. Useem, "Stratification in a Prairie Town," *American Sociological Review,* VII (1942), 331-342; James West, *Plainville, U. S. A.* (New York: Columbia University Press, 1945); Warner and Lunt, *The Social Life of a Modern Community* and *The Status System of a Modern Community;* August B. Hollingshead, *Elmtown's Youth* (New York: John Wiley and Sons, 1949); Allison Davis, B. and M. Gardner, *Deep South* (Chicago: University of Chicago Press, 1941), and, of course, the "classic" of community studies, Robert and Helen M. Lynd, *Middletown.*

5. Floyd Hunter, *Community Power Structure* (Chapel Hill: University of North Carolina Press, 1953). Hunter's second study very closely follows the outline, methods and conclusions of the first and need not be separately considered. *Community Organization: Action and Inaction* (Chapel Hill: University of North Carolina Press, 1957).

6. For David Riesman's view, his *Lonely Crowd* (New Haven: Yale University Press, 1950) can be taken as the primary source. William H. Whyte, Jr., has expressed his views in *The Organization Man* (New York: Simon & Schuster, 1956). C. Wright Mills has really been arguing from the same post in all of his books, but most relevantly in *The Power Elite* (New York: Oxford University Press, 1956). Floyd Hunter's views are detailed in the two volumes noted above.

7. Riesman, *op. cit.,* p. 260.

8. *Ibid.,* p. 153.

9. Whyte, *op. cit.,* p. 312.

10. Mills, *op. cit.,* p. 28.

11. *Ibid.*, pp. 28-29.
12. *Ibid.*, p. 29.
13. Hunter, *op. cit.*, p. 246.
14. Whyte, *op. cit.*, p. 324.
15. *Ibid.*, p. 404.
16. Riesman, *op. cit.*, p. 368.
17. *Ibid.*, pp. 371-372.
18. Mills, *op. cit.*, p. 361.
19. Robert S. Lynd, "Power in American Society as Resource and Problem," in Arthur Kornhauser (ed.), *Problems of Power in American Democracy* (Detroit: Wayne University Press, 1957), p. 24.
20. *Ibid.*, p. 25.
21. *Cf.* Chapter II.
22. A whole area for investigation that would be most valuable could be centered around this point. To what extent do individuals use or fail to use the institutional power of their position? Further, what are the structural and psychological correlates of that behavior?
23. Hunter, *Community Power Structure.*
24. Mills, *The Power Elite,* pp. 375-380.
25. F. W. Taussig and C. S. Joslyn, *American Business Leaders* (New York: Macmillan, 1932); Mabel Newcomer, *The Big Business Executive* (New York: Columbia University Press, 1955); Suzanne I. Keller, "Social Origins and Career Lines of Three Generations of American Business Leaders" (Ph.D. thesis, Columbia University, 1954). See also Chapter VI.
26. Referred to in Mills, *op. cit.*, pp. 383-384.
27. *Concentration in American Industry,* Report of the Subcommittee on Antitrust and Monopoly to the Committee on the Judiciary, Eighty-fifth Congress, First Session (Washington: U. S. Government Printing Office, 1957).
28. *Ibid.*, p. 11.
29. The points here are all taken from Arthus Feiler, "Democracy by Class and Occupational Representation," in Max Ascoli and F. Lehmann (eds.), *Political and Economic Democracy* (New York: W. W. Norton, 1937).
30. *Ibid.*, p. 178. This point was also raised by Marx, in a slightly different context, as one of the prerequisites for effective class-consciousness.
31. It is recognized, of course, that prestige can be converted into a power potential insofar as those according prestige are

willing to grant authority and decision-making prerogatives to the prestige holder. *Cf.* Robert Bierstadt, "An Analysis of Social Power," *American Sociological Review,* XV (December, 1950), 730-738.

32. This idea has been indirectly suggested by Reinhard Bendix's analysis of the "entrepreneur" and "manager" in *Work and Authority in Industry* (New York: John Wiley and Sons, 1956).

33. Sigmund Diamond, *The Reputation of the American Businessman* (Cambridge: Harvard University Press, 1955), p. 178.

34. *Ibid.*

35. (Garden City, New York: Doubleday and Co., 1956).

36. *Ibid.*, p. 10.

37. Russell Lynes, "Visit to the World of Expense Accounts," *New York Times Magazine,* February 24, 1957.

38. *The Wall Street Journal,* Oct. 29, 1957, article on "Status Symbols."

39. *Ibid.*

40. *Ibid.*

41. John B. Knox has called this type the "relationship specialist" and correctly recognizes this as a new role created by the new demands of management. *The Sociology of Industrial Relations* (New York: Random House, 1955), pp. 78 ff.

42. *Op. cit.,* p. 179.

43. Francis X. Sutton, Seymour E. Harris, Carl Kaysen and James Tobin, *The American Business Creed* (Cambridge: Harvard University Press, 1956).

44. Reinhard Bendix, "Social Stratification and Political Power," in Bendix and Lipset, *Class, Status and Power,* p. 596.

45. Bell, *The New American Right.* Also, Ascoli and Lehmann, *op. cit.*

46. Richard Hofstadter, "The Pseudo-Conservative Revolt," in *The New American Right.*

47. Hans Kohn, *Nationalism* (New York: D. Van Nostrand, 1955).

48. K. H. Silvert *A Study in Government: Guatemala* (New Orleans: Middle American Research Institute, 1954), pp. 92-94. See also Chapter VII.

CHAPTER V

The Social Psychology of Class

1. These quotations about Piaget's ideas taken from Theodore M. Newcomb, *Social Psychology* (New York: The Dryden Press, 1950), p. 305.

2. Martha C. Ericson, "Social Status and Child-Rearing Practises," in T. M. Newcomb and E. L. Hartley (eds.), *Readings in Social Psychology* (New York: Henry Holt and Co., 1947); A. Davis and R. J. Havighurst, "Social Class and Color Differences in Child-Rearing," *American Sociological Review,* XI (December, 1946), 698-710; R. J. Havighurst and A. Davis, "A Comparison of the Chicago and Harvard Studies in Social Class Differences in Child Rearing," *American Sociological Review,* XX (August, 1955), 438-442; Eleanor C. Maccoby and Patricia K. Gibbs, and the Staff of the Laboratory of Human Development, Harvard University, "Methods of Child Rearing in Two Social Classes," in W. E. Martin and C. Stendler (eds.), *Readings in Child Development* (New York: Harcourt, Brace and Co., 1954); Richard A. Littman, R. C. A. Moore, and John Pierce-Jones, "Social Class Differences in Child Rearing: A Third Community for Comparison with Chicago and Newton," American Sociological Review, XXII (December, 1957), 694-704; Martha S. White, "Social Class, Child Rearing Practices, and Child Behavior," *American Sociological Review,* XXII (December, 1957), 704-712.

3. Erickson, *op. cit.,* p. 464.

4. *Ibid.,* p. 501.

5. Havighurst and Davis, "A Comparison of the Chicago and Harvard Studies," *op. cit.,* p. 442.

6. Littman, Moore, and Pierce-Jones, *op. cit.,* pp. 701-702.

7. *Ibid.,* p. 702.

8. This summary is taken from their article. *Op. cit.,* pp. 702-704.

9. Arnold W. Green, "The Middle-Class Male Child and Neurosis," in *Class, Status and Power,* pp. 292-300.

10. *Ibid.,* p. 293.

11. *Ibid.,* p. 294.

12. William H. Sewell and A. O. Haller, "Social Status and the Personality Adjustment of the Child," *Sociometry,* IX (June, 1956), 114-125. Includes bibliography.

13. Celia B. Stendler, *Children of Brasstown* (Urbana: University of Illinois, Bureau of Research and Service of the College of Education, 1949).

14. *Ibid.,* p. 91.

15. *Ibid.,* p. 89.

16. Frank W. Notestein, "Class Differences in Fertility," in Bendix and Lipset, *Class, Status and Power,* p. 272.

17. *Ibid.,* p. 280.

18. Rudolf Heberle, "Social Factors in Birth Control," *American Sociological Review,* VI (December, 1941), 794-805.

19. K. A. Edin and E. P. Hutchinson, *Studies of Differential Fertility in Sweden* (London: P. S. King and Son, 1935).

20. Heberle, *op. cit.,* p. 801.

21. See, for example, Evelyn M. Kitagawa, "Differential Fertility in Chicago, 1920-1940," *American Journal of Sociology,* LVIII (March, 1953), 481-492.

22. Clyde V. Kiser and P. K. Whelpton, "Social and Psychological Factors Affecting Fertility: IX. Fertility Planning and Fertility Rates by Socio-Economic Status," *Milbank Memorial Fund Quarterly,* XXVII (April, 1949), 188-244.

23. Kiser and Whelpton, "XI. The Interrelationship of Fertility, Fertility Planning and Feeling of Economic Security," *Milbank Memorial Fund Quarterly,* XXIX (January, 1951), 467-548.

24. Jurgen Ruesch, "Social Technique, Social Status, and Social Change in Illness," in C. Kluckhohn and H. A. Murray (eds.), *Personality in Nature, Society and Culture* (New York: A. Knopf, 1950).

25. *Ibid.,* p. 124.

26. *Ibid.,* p. 124.

27. *Ibid.,* pp. 124-125.

28. Robert E. L. Faris and H. Warren Dunham, *Mental Disorders in Urban Areas* (Chicago: University of Chicago Press, 1939); Robert E. Clark, "The Relationship of Schizophrenia to Occupational Income and Occupational Prestige," *American Sociological Review,* XIII (June, 1948), 325-330; August B. Hollingshead and Frederick R. Redlich, "Social Stratification and Psychiatric Disorders," *American Sociological Review,* XVIII (April, 1953), 163-169; Hollingshead and Redlich, "Social Strati-

fication and Schizophrenia," *American Sociological Review,* XIX (June, 1954), 302-306; Jerome K. Myers and Leslie Schaffer, "Social Stratification and Psychiatric Practise: A Study of an Out-Patient Clinic," *American Sociological Review,* XIX (June, 1954), 307-310; Mary H. Lystad, "Social Mobility Among Schizophrenic Patients," *American Sociological Review,* XXII (June, 1957), 288-292; Rema Lapouse, M. Monk, and M. Terris, "The Drift Hypothesis and Socioeconomic Differentials in Schizophrenia," *American Journal of Public Health,* XLVI (August, 1956), 978-986; August B. Hollingshead and Frederick C. Redlich, *Social Class and Mental Illness* (New York: John Wiley and Sons, 1958), have brought together many of the separate articles reporting on the New Haven study.

29. Robert C. Clark, "Psychoses, Income, and Occupational Prestige," *American Journal of Sociology,* LIV (March, 1949), 433-440; Clark, "The Relationship of Alcoholic Commitment Rates to Occupational Income and Occupational Prestige," *American Sociological Review,* XIV (August, 1949), 539-543.

30. Hollingshead and Redlich, "Social Stratification and Psychiatric Disorders," p. 167.

31. Faris and Dunham, *op. cit.,* p. 172.

32. *Op. cit.,* p. 309.

33. Stanley A. Leavy and L. Z. Freedman, "Psychoneurosis and Economic Life," *Social Problems,* IV (July, 1956), 55-67.

34. *Ibid.,* p. 56.

35. *Ibid.,* p. 59.

36. *Ibid.*

37. *Ibid.,* p. 67.

38. For a collation and analysis of these social psychological views in Marx's writing, see Vernon Venable, *Human Nature: The Marxian View* (New York: A. Knopf, 1946).

39. Marx and Engels, *The German Ideology,* pp. 13-15.

40. Georg Lukacs, *Geschichte und Klassenbewusstsein* (Berlin: Der Malik Verlag, 1923), esp. pp. 67-93.

41. *Cf.* Bernard Barber, *Social Stratification* (New York: Harcourt, Brace and Co., 1957), pp. 190-197. On the functions and dysfunctions of ignorance, see Wilbert C. Moore and Melvin M. Tumin, "Some Social Functions of Ignorance," *American Sociological Review,* XIV (December, 1949), 787-795.

42. W. Lloyd Warner and Paul S. Lunt, *The Social Life of a Modern Community,* Chapter VII.

43. Arthur Kornhauser, "Public Opinion and Social Class,"

American Journal of Sociology, LV (January, 1950), p. 339.

44. Bernard R. Berelson, Paul F. Lazarsfeld, and William N. McPhee, *Voting* (Chicago: University of Chicago Press, 1954), esp. pp. 56-59.

45. *Ibid.,* p. 57.

46. *Ibid.,* p. 58.

47. Kornhauser, *op. cit.,* p. 339n.

48. A. J. Kornhauser, A. J. Mayer, and H. L. Sheppard, *When Labor Votes* (New York: University Books, 1956).

49. C. Wright Mills, *White Collar* (New York: Oxford, 1951).

50. *Ibid.,* p. 353.

51. These factors have been well summarized in R. Bendix and S. M. Lipset, "Karl Marx's Theory of Social Classes," in the authors' volume, *Class, Status, and Power,* p. 30.

52. Morris Rosenberg, "Perceptual Obstacles to Class Consciousness," *Social Forces,* XXXII (October, 1953), 22-27.

53. *Ibid.,* p. 24.

54. Floyd Dotson, "Patterns of Voluntary Association Among Urban Working Class Families," *American Sociological Review,* XVI (1951), 687-693; Genevieve Knupfer, "Portrait of the Underdog," *Public Opinion Quarterly,* XI (Spring, 1947), 103-114; Mirra Komarovsky, "The Voluntary Associations of Urban Dwellers," *American Sociological Review,* XI (1946), 686-698; William G. Mather, "Income, and Participation," *American Sociological Review,* VI (1941), 380-383; Leonard Reissman, "Class, Leisure and Social Participation," *American Sociological Review,* XIX (1954), 76-84.

55. T. Ktsanes, F. E. LaViolette, and J. H. Rohrer, *Community Structure, Organizational Structure and Citizen Participation in Community-Wide Activities* (New Orleans: Urban Life Research Institute, 1955).

CHAPTER VI

Social Mobility: Patterns and Consequences

1. Joseph Schumpeter, *Imperialism and Social Classes* (New York: Meridian Books, 1955), p. 133.

2. W. Lloyd Warner and James C. Abegglen, *Occupational Mobility in American Business and Industry* (Minneapolis: University of Minnesota Press, 1955), p. 17.

3. This point seems to be similarly the intent of Tumin and Feldman's argument that "wide divergence between fathers' and sons' occupational distributions may occur without significant change in the distribution of prestige, power, or property." Melvin M. Tumin and Arnold S. Feldman, "Theory and Measurement of Occupational Mobility," *American Sociological Review,* XXII (June, 1957), p. 283. See also Nelson H. Foote and Paul K. Hatt, "Social Mobility and Economic Advancement," *American Economic Review,* XLIII (May, 1953), 364-378.

4. Elbridge Sibley, "Some Demographic Clues to Stratification," *American Sociological Review,* VII (June, 1942), 322-330.

5. Kurt Mayer, "Recent Changes in the Class Structure of the United States," *Transactions of the Third World Congress of Sociology* (London: International Sociological Association, 1956), pp. 66-67.

6. Schumpeter, *op. cit.*

7. *Ibid.,* p. 137.

8. Mayer, *op. cit.,* p. 70.

9. *Ibid.,* p. 71.

10. Seymour M. Lipset and Reinhard Bendix, "Ideological Equalitarianism and Social Mobility in the United States," *Transactions of the Second World Congress of Sociology* (International Sociological Association, 1954), Vol. II, pp. 34-54.

11. Percy E. Davidson and H. Dewey Anderson, *Occupational Mobility in an American Community* (Stanford, California: Stanford University Press, 1937).

12. National Opinion Research Center, "Jobs and Occupations," in *Class, Status and Power,* pp. 411-426.

13. Natalie Rogoff, *Recent Trends in Occupational Mobility.*

14. Davidson and Anderson, *op. cit.,* p. 26.

15. S. M. Lipset and N. Rogoff, "Class and Opportunity in Europe and the U.S.," *Commentary,* December, 1954.

16. Rogoff, *op. cit.,* p. 62.

17. *Ibid.,* p. 63.

18. Herman P. Miller, in his monograph, *Income of the American People* (New York: John Wiley and Sons, 1955), has summarized some of the conclusions of the study of *Labor Mobility in Six Cities* by Gladys L. Palmer. "About one-third of the sons of men who were professional workers, craftsmen, and operatives," he wrote, "were employed in the same occupational groups as their fathers. . . . The data clearly suggest that men in such well-paid jobs as professional and managerial workers

are more likely than are other workers to have their sons employed in these two high-paid occupation groups. . . . However, a rather large proportion of the sons of men employed in several other occupations also became professional or managerial workers . . . about 37 per cent of the sons of sales workers were professional or managerial workers, as were 27 per cent of the clerical workers and 22 per cent of the craftsmen and service workers" (p. 33).

19. Rogoff, *op. cit.*, p. 58.

20. William H. Form and Delbert C. Miller, "Occupational Career Pattern as a Sociological Instrument," *American Journal of Sociology,* LIV (January, 1949), 317-329.

21. S. M. Lipset and R. Bendix, "Social Mobility and Occupational Career Patterns, II: Social Mobility," in *Class, Status, and Power,* pp. 454-464.

22. *Ibid.*, p. 456.

23. Form and Miller, *op. cit.*, p. 322; Lipset and Bendix, *op. cit.*, p. 457.

24. *Ibid.*

25. *Ibid.*

26. Form and Miller, *op. cit.*, pp. 322-326; Lipset and Bendix, *op. cit.*, p. 456.

27. Lipset and Bendix, *op. cit.*, p. 462.

28. Simon Kuznets, *Shares of Upper Income Groups in Income and Savings* (National Bureau of Economic Research, Inc., 1950), Occasional Paper 35. Also reported in *Statistical Abstract of the United States: 1956* (77th ed.; U.S. Bureau of the Census [Washington, D. C., 1956]), p. 304.

29. Reported by Kurt Mayer, *op. cit.*, p. 72.

30. *Ibid.*

31. Reported in *Statistical Abstract of the United States: 1956,* p. 308, Table 370.

32. July 20, 1956, p. 37.

33. Quoted in Miller, *Income of the American People,* p. 97.

34. *Ibid.*

35. Miller, *op. cit.*, p. 114.

36. *Ibid.*

37. Miller, *op. cit.*, p. 117.

38. Geoffrey H. Moore in his Foreword to Daniel Craemer, *Personal Income During Business Cycles,* National Bureau of Economic Research (Princeton: Princeton University Press, 1956), pp. xxi-xxii.

39. Margaret G. Reid, "Changing Income Patterns," in Elizabeth E. Hoyt and Others, *American Income and Its Use* (New York: Harper and Bros., 1954), pp. 130-131.

40. Emily H. Huntington, *Spending of Middle Income Families* (Berkeley: University of California Press, 1957), pp. 23-24.

41. *Ibid.*, p. 22.

42. A. C. Spectorsky, "Destination Sickness," *What's New*, No. 204 (1953), pp. 6-9.

43. Thomas Ktsanes and Leonard Reissman, "Suburbia—New Homes for Old Values" (Mimeographed, Tulane University, Department of Sociology, 1956).

44. George Katona and Eva Mueller, *Consumer Expectations, 1953-1956* (Survey Research Center, University of Michigan), p. 29.

45. *Ibid.*, pp. 74-75.

46. Warren Breed, "The G. I. Bill and Class Mobility" (Mimeographed, Tulane University, Department of Sociology). Breed obtained figures from the Veterans' Administration that showed the following: By March 31, 1952, 7,791,000 veterans of World War II had taken training under the Bill—about half of all veterans. Average duration of courses was 17 months. The cost to the government exclusive of administration, was $12,347,-162,546 to the end of July, 1951.

47. Quoted in William Petersen, "Is America Still the Land of Opportunity?" *Commentary*, November, 1953, p. 482.

48. *Statistical Abstract of the United States: 1957* (78th ed., U.S. Bureau of the Census [Washington, D. C., 1957]), Tables 149 and 152.

49. *Ibid.*, Table 151.

50. *Ibid.*

51. S. M. Lipset and R. Bendix, "Ideological Equalitarianism and Social Mobility in the United States," p. 43.

52. C. Wright Mills, *The Power Elite*.

53. *Ibid.*, p. 231.

54. E. Digby Baltzell, *Philadelphia Gentlemen* (Glencoe: The Free Press, 1958).

55. In Mills, *The Power Elite*.

56. Cleveland Amory, *The Proper Bostonians* (New York: E. P. Dutton and Co., 1947).

57. Baltzell, *op. cit.*, pp. 389-396.

58. Richard Austin Smith, "The Fifty-Million Dollar Men," *Fortune*, November, 1957.

59. Mills, *op. cit.*, p. 104.
60. *Ibid.*, p. 105.
61. *Ibid.*, p. 105.
62. *Ibid.*, p. 113.
63. *Op. cit.*, November, 1957.
64. Reinhard Bendix and Frank W. Howton, "Social Mobility and the American Business Elite," *British Journal of Sociology*, VIII (December, 1957), 357-369, and IX (March, 1958), 1-14; Suzanne Keller, "The Social Origins and Career Lines of Three Generations of American Business Leaders" (Ph.D. dissertation, Columbia University, 1953); William Miller, "The Recruitment of the American Business Elite," *Quarterly Journal of Economics*, LXIV (1950), 242-253; C. Wright Mills, *The Power Elite* (New York: Oxford University Press, 1956), Chapters 6 and 7; Mabel Newcomer, *The Big Business Executive* (New York: Columbia University Press, 1955); F. W. Taussig and C. S. Joslyn, *American Business Leaders* (New York: Macmillan, 1932); W. Lloyd Warner and James C. Abegglen, *Occupational Mobility* (Minneapolis: University of Minnesota Press, 1955); Warner and Abegglen, *Big Business Leaders in America* (New York: Harper and Bros., 1955). A more limited study, in scope and in time, is that by Gordon F. Lewis and C. Arnold Anderson, "Social Origins and Social Mobility of Businessmen in an American City," *Transactions of the Third World Congress of Sociology*, Vol. III, 253-266.
65. *Op. cit.*
66. Bendix and Howton, *op. cit.*, p. 7.
67. *Occupational Mobility*, p. 67.
68. Newcomer, *op. cit.*, pp. 144-148.
69. *Ibid.*, p. 144.
70. This matter is discussed by Newcomer, *op. cit.*, p. 145, and Bendix and Howton, *op. cit.*, p. 12.
71. *Op. cit.*, p. 12.
72. Newcomer, *op. cit.*, p. 146.
73. Newcomer, *op. cit.*, pp. 83-86; Bendix and Howton, *op. cit.*, p. 10.
74. Newcomer, *op. cit.*, p. 85.
75. Quoted in Sherif and Sherif, *An Outline of Social Psychology* (New York: Harper and Bros., 1956), p. 703.
76. *Cf.* Leonard Reissman, "Levels of Aspiration and Social Class," *American Sociological Review*, XVIII (June, 1953), 233-242.

77. Herbert H. Hyman, "The Value Systems of Different Classes: A Social Psychological Contribution to the Analysis of Stratification," in *Class, Status and Power,* pp. 426-442.

78. Reported in Hyman, *op. cit.,* pp. 433-434.

79. Bernard C. Rosen, "The Achievement Syndrome: A Psychocultural Dimension of Social Stratification," *American Sociological Review,* XXI (April, 1956), 203-211.

80. Eli Chinoy, *Automobile Workers and the American Dream.*

81. Robert H. Guest, "Work Careers and Aspirations of Automobile Workers," in H. D. Stein and R. A. Cloward (eds.), *Social Perspectives on Behavior* (Glencoe: The Free Press, 1958).

82. Guest, *op. cit.,* p. 220.

83. Chinoy, *op. cit.,* p. 124.

84. Hyman, *op. cit.,* p. 437.

85. Chinoy, *op. cit.,* p. 124; Guest, *op. cit.,* p. 220.

86. Hyman, *op. cit.,* p. 441.

87. Joseph A. Kahl, "Educational and Occupational Aspirations of 'Common Man' Boys," *Harvard Educational Review,* XXIII (Summer, 1953), 186-203.

88. Hyman, *op. cit.,* pp. 430-431.

89. Elizabeth Douvan and Joseph Adelson, "The Psychodynamics of Social Mobility" (mimeographed paper, June, 1957).

90. Alvin W. Rose, "A Socio-Psychological Analysis of the Ambition Patterns of a Sample of Industrial Workers" (Ph.D. dissertation, University of Chicago, 1946), p. 54.

91. August B. Hollingshead and Frederick C. Redlich, *Social Class and Mental Illness,* pp. 367-370.

92. Bruno Bettleheim and Morris Janowitz, *The Dynamics of Prejudice* (New York: Harper and Bros., 1950).

93. Joseph Greenblum and Leonard I. Pearlin, "Vertical Mobility and Prejudice," in *Class, Status and Power,* pp. 480-491.

94. Peter M. Blau, "Social Mobility and Interpersonal Relations," in Stein and Cloward, *op. cit.,* pp. 470-475.

95. Blau, *op. cit.,* p. 475.

96. "The Wives of Management," *Fortune,* October, 1951, and "The Corporation and the Wife," *Fortune,* November, 1951.

97. Melvin M. Tumin, "Some Unapplauded Consequences of Social Mobility in a Mass Society," *Social Forces,* XXXVI (October, 1957), 32-37.

98. *Ibid.,* p. 34.

99. *Ibid.,* p. 36.

CHAPTER VII

Continuity and Change

1. Karl Mannheim, *Essays on the Sociology of Culture* (London: Routledge and Kegan Paul, Ltd., 1956), pp. 103 ff.

2. These conclusions about the nature of theory, of course, do not say anything about why some categories are selected rather than others. It is at this point of selection, as sociologists of knowledge have pointed out, that the orientation of the scientist makes a difference. For an interesting discussion of this matter, especially as applied to structural-functional theory, see, Ralf Dahrendorf, "Out of Utopia: Toward a Reorientation of Sociological Analysis," *American Journal of Sociology,* LXIV (September, 1958), 115-127.

3. For the Soviet Union, see for example, Alex Inkeles, "Social Stratification and Mobility in the Soviet Union," *American Sociological Review,* XV (August, 1950), 465-479. For Israel, see Eva Rosenfeld, "Social Stratification in a 'Classless' Society," *American Sociological Review,* XVI (December, 1951), 766-774.

4. Rosenfeld, *op. cit.*

5. This has been previously indicated in Leonard Reissman, "La Ciudad: Un Problema de Metodologia," in *Seminario de Integración Social Guatemalteca,* Publicación No. 3 (1956), pp. 71-91.

6. For some of the differences this movement can make and what is involved, see Clark Kerr and others, "The Labour Problem in Economic Development," *International Labour Review,* Vol. LXXI (March, 1955). Also, Wilbert E. Moore, *Industrialization and Labor* (Ithaca: Cornell University Press, 1950).

7. K. H. Silvert, *A Study of Government: Guatemala* (New Orleans: Middle American Research Institute, Tulane University, 1954), p. 93.

8. Reissman, "La Ciudad," *op. cit.*

Index